THE MUSICAL LIFE OF
JOSEPH MARTIN KRAUS

Joseph Kraus

THE MUSICAL LIFE OF
Joseph Martin Kraus

Letters of an Eighteenth-Century
Swedish Composer

BERTIL H. VAN BOER

INDIANA UNIVERSITY PRESS   *Bloomington & Indianapolis*

This book is a publication of

INDIANA UNIVERSITY PRESS
Office of Scholarly Publishing
Herman B Wells Library 350
1320 East 10th Street
Bloomington, Indiana 47405 USA

iupress.indiana.edu

Telephone orders 800-842-6796
Fax orders 812-855-7931

© 2014 by Bertil van Boer

♾ The paper used in this publication meets the minimum requirements of the American National Standard for Information Sciences–Permanence of Paper for Printed Library Materials, ANSI Z39.48–1992.

*Manufactured in the
United States of America*

*Library of Congress
Cataloging-in-Publication Data*

Kraus, Joseph Martin, 1756-1792, author.
  [Correspondence. Selections. English]
  The musical life of Joseph Martin Kraus : letters of an eighteenth-century Swedish composer / Bertil H. van Boer.
    pages cm
  Includes bibliographical references and index.
  ISBN 978-0-253-01274-6 (cloth : alkaline paper) – ISBN 978-0-253-01277-7 (ebook) 1. Kraus, Joseph Martin, 1756-1792 – Correspondence. 2. Composers – Sweden – Correspondence. I. Van Boer, Bertil H., editor. II. Title.
  ML410.K736A413 2014
  780.92 – dc23
                                    2013046359
  1 2 3 4 5   19 18 17 16 15 14

For Margaret

Hat einer gesagt, wenn ein Mensch Leidenschaft
hat, so hat er vermuthlich Gefühl.

(It has been said that if a human being has
passion, he probably also has feelings.)

JOSEPH MARTIN KRAUS,
Etwas von und über Music, 1778

Contents

Preface

This edition of the letters of Joseph Martin Kraus is the result of many years' work that started some thirty years ago. At that time, the first of a series of symposia on the life and works of Kraus was initiated by the Royal Swedish Academy of Music and the newly established Joseph Martin Kraus Gesellschaft headquartered in Buchen, West Germany. The local Bezirksmuseum, or regional museum to use the English, was the repository of the Kraus family effects, including personal items such as the composer's court uniform (indicating, by the way, that he stood about five feet, five inches in height) and his much-pawned and always redeemed pocket watch. While ambitious, the biennial symposia, alternating between Buchen and Stockholm, pointed out the fact that there was a considerable gap in knowledge about Kraus's life and times, and that research was an absolute necessity in order to place him within an historical context and not just as "the Swedish Mozart," as many were wont to do. Early biographers such as Fredrik Samuel Silverstolpe and Karl Friedrich Schreiber, the latter a descendant of Kraus's brother Alois, had begun the work and written small monographs, based mostly upon the surviving letters that the composer sent his family over his short lifetime. Schreiber had even published in 1925 a list of musical works, based upon what he had been able to discover on a trip to Sweden. Although he was not a musician, he had many copied, and donated his collection to the Bayerische Staatsbibliothek. Over the course of the years, sporadic attempts were made to "resurrect" Kraus from oblivion, notably by Joseph St. Winter, who perished in the Second World War before finishing his dissertation; Walther Liebermann, who began publishing a series of compositions with Breitkopf in the 1950s; and Adolf Hoffmann, who published a number of string quartets in the following decade with Möseler Verlag of Wolfenbüttel. There was a revival in research prior to the first Kraus Symposium in 1978, but these were mostly genre studies, such as Volker Bungardt's dissertation on the songs. Swedish scholarship had been active since the 1920s thanks to the work of Birger Anrep-Nordin, Albert Mayer-Reinach, Hans Eppstein, and Richard Engländer, though much of the work was in the local language and mostly inaccessible to the mainstream. But the pioneering work of Irmgard Leux-Henschen began to change the atmosphere with a series of articles, still somewhat controversial, outlining Kraus's participation in an important aesthetical debate in the Stockholm newspapers of the eighteenth century and culminating in 1978 with her pioneering edition of Kraus's letters. Published in Sweden, these served as the impetus for a new wave of research, which has resulted in several popular biographies by Friedrich Riedel (in German) and Hans Åstrand (in Swedish), as well as the present author's thematic catalogue (published in German in 1989 and in a second edition in English by Pendragon Press in 1998). Further, attention by international scholars such as A. Peter Brown, Martin Stahelin, and others has led to a veritable Kraus revival, which is particularly evident in an ever-expanding discography. At the present time, he is no longer to be considered an obscure composer languishing on the periphery of the European continent, but rather as one of the major musical figures of the time, whose reputation for his innovative and powerful compositions was recognized by the most important composers of that period.

The purpose of this book is to expand upon this background by providing an English edition of Kraus's letters, within which one may find material that gives a good portrait of the man, as well as important observations on many varied facets of eighteenth-century life, not just music. This could not have been done without the support and encouragement of many. For their pioneering work, I am indebted to the foundational work by Anrep-Nordin, Silverstolpe, Schreiber, and Leux-Henschen. The generosity and perceptive encouragement of the late Helmut Brosch of Buchen must be acknowledged; few people were more familiar with the letters and other documents of the Kraus legacy than he, and his publication of the composer's various literary works and biographical documents paved the way for this book. I would also like to thank Hans Åstrand for his friendship and advice over the years; his counsel has been a godsend beginning all the way back when I was a graduate student, with of course acknowledgment of his edition of the letters and his biography of the composer, all, alas, in Swedish. The president of the Joseph Martin Kraus Gesellschaft, Gerhard Darmstadt, is owed thanks for his encouragement to publish an edition in English to stimulate scholarship outside Germany and Sweden, thus broadening the numbers delving into Kraus and his music. For their permission to use the few illustrations included here, I would like to thank Gerlinde Trunk of the Bezirksmuseum in Buchen, the Department of Manuscripts of the University of Uppsala Library, and the Royal Academy of Music in Stockholm. Finally, my deepest appreciation goes to my editors, Raina Polivka and Jenna Whittaker, for their help in editing an often long and tortuous manuscript with patience and enthusiasm, as well as to the readers who provided many useful and critically astute comments and observations.

Bertil van Boer
Bellingham, Washington, April 2013

THE MUSICAL LIFE OF
JOSEPH MARTIN KRAUS

Facsimile of the letter from Kraus to his parents dated 3 April 1778 (Bezirksmuseum Buchen, Kraus-Sammlung, Signatur Kr 14).

Portrait of Joseph Martin Kraus in Erfurt, 1775, by an unknown artist (Original, private collection).

Kraus's silhouette (Bezirksmuseum Buchen, Krasus-Sammlug, Inv. Nr. 851).

Joseph Martin Kraus as a Correspondent

THE SURVIVING CORRESPONDENCE OF GERMAN-SWEDISH composer Joseph Martin Kraus (1756–1792) is a microcosm of both the life of an active, gregarious musical figure and the world in which he lived and worked. Sometimes referred to as "the Swedish Mozart" (due to similarities in lifespan and output), Kraus demonstrated talents as a composer at a young age and went on to lead an illustrious, if brief, career as an acclaimed classical composer. At the age of twenty-six, he embarked on a four-year grand tour, receiving accolades from some of the most important musical luminaries of the period (Joseph Haydn, Christoph Willibald von Gluck, Antonio Salieri, Johann Georg Albrechtsberger, Johann Friedrich Reichardt, and others) as well as achieving a reputation, reported by C. F. Cramer in the 1786 *Magazin der Musik,* as one of the top six most important active composers of his age (the others being Haydn, Mozart (here one presumes Wolfgang Amadeus and not Leopold), Antonio Rosetti, Ignaz Pleyel, and Reichardt). A literate man, he was also an author, pedagogue, and poet, whose nonmusical works include numerous published poems, a philosophical treatise, and a tragedy.

Over the course of the past two decades Kraus has begun to be restored to the important position in eighteenth-century music he had attained during his lifetime. Like Mozart, he was a prolific correspondent, whose many observations include musings on the music and musicians of his time. His intimate letters to family also give an unusual picture of the private man, showing a slice of domestic life in the eighteenth century among the emerging middle class. His letters include one of the few descriptions of the great Handel Centenary Festival from an out-sider, critiques of the operas by Niccolò Piccinni performed in Paris, the first mention in history of Mozart's *Le Nozze di Figaro,* and descriptions of the art and archeology of Pompeii. As such they are invaluable documents that are crucial to the understanding of not only Kraus's life and works, but also of the eighteenth-century life of an important composer and his milieu.

Kraus's letters were the main means of communication with friends, relatives, other musicians, clients, and business partners during this period. Much of what was written, however, was subject to the various issues and protocols that affected everyday life, and as a result, the tone of each letter had to be tailored not only to the position and status of the recipient; they also had to pass through several layers of inspection, from censors to ordinary people who were entrusted to transport or deliver them. In a time where the literacy rate was variable and the delivery of mail equally so, such letters were of necessity meant to be documents that not only were personal connections between the correspondents, but also at times had to include copious amounts of information. As a result, they became quite descriptive generally whenever longer distances were involved, but often short and perfunctory if, as happened in a number of courts and cities, mail was be delivered quickly and efficiently several times each day, either by officials or couriers, or by way of mutual friends or acquaintances. As informational documents, letters were of considerable value, both for what they said and for what they did not say, or for what could be read "between the lines" if both writer and recipient were aware of any particularly sensitive matter and expected the letters to be read, as often occurred, by state censors. As such, Kraus's correspondence is also of immense historical value, whether or not the information contained therein was factual or merely a personal opinion.

The composer's letters not only present an erudite, highly educated view on eighteenth-century life, they are a window through which his own personality, and along with it his thoughts, foibles, and personal habits, can be discerned. At times admonitory, sarcastic, opinionated, critical (especially with an eye toward music and his colleagues), highly emotional, and even caustic, his voice reflects a keen observation of his own position (or occasionally lack thereof), his relationship with his loved ones and friends, and the world that surrounded him. Through it one can also glimpse personal attitudes, likes, and dislikes. In short, Kraus was a thoroughly human character, but he was also one whose tone and manner reflected a highly eclectic and perceptive intelligence. Thus one can find a treasure trove of items that transcend his personal life to include intelligently formulated and often precisely detailed commentary on the world around him. Not surprisingly these include descriptions of art and artists, the literature of the period, architecture, archeology (with the newly discovered Pompeii at the forefront), religion, theology, as well as even a comment about eighteenth-century aeronautics. Of course, there is also music. His life experiences as expressed in these letters (and in the reminiscences of those who knew him best) are therefore global in content and contain materials that are multifaceted and speak to a wide variety of subjects beyond his profession.

There are currently a fair number of collected correspondences that contribute to biographical information on particular eighteenth-century composers. First and foremost are the letters of Wolfgang Amadeus Mozart, who was a prolific writer throughout his life and whose letters have been thoroughly researched.[1] Less extensive are those written by Ludwig van Beethoven, English versions of which were produced in three volumes by Emily Anderson in 1961.[2] These multiple-volume compilations, however, are not entirely the norm, for most other composers have had their correspondence confined to a single monograph. For as important a composer as Joseph Haydn, for instance, the standard compilation remains H. C. Robbins Landon's work from 1956,[3] and in 1962 Hedwig and E. H. Müller von Asow finally published their volume of the collected correspondence of Christoph Willibald von Gluck.[4] The comparative amount of correspondence is thus quite variable, ranging from exhaustive collections, thanks to the archival disposition of the originals, to fragments that have somehow survived the vicissitudes of history. Given the amount of archival research that is necessary for many important figures, the task has sometimes been both monumental and tortuous. For Gluck, Kraus's idol and mentor, his own papers were destroyed in a fire, and the few surviving letters he wrote were assiduously gathered by the Asows over a period of fifty years, from 1913 to 1962, when they were finally published in London in English, rather than the original languages. For most other composers of the period, the publication of a collected correspondence languishes, although individual letters are often published in articles or monographs as documentary evidence of some aspect of their life and music. In rare instances, such as with C. P. E. Bach, the original languages have been supplemented by an edition, mostly of selected letters, in another language – in Bach's case in English – thus allowing for a broader dissemination.[5] There are some exceptions to this general state of affairs, such as a recent supplement to the *Denkmäler der Tonkunst in Österreich* for Carl Ditters von Dittersdorf,[6] and, of course, the letters of Kraus, which have been published only in their original languages, in the latter's case German and Swedish, with translations into both as necessary.[7] This edition is intended to complement these editions, as in the case of Bach, by providing a complete text in English, making the letters more accessible to a broader audience.

BIOGRAPHY

In order to place Kraus within a historical context, it is first necessary to provide a brief biographical framework. While the correspondence itself is kaleidoscopic in breadth, it would be difficult to know just how the narrative unfolds without some information regarding his life and career, thus setting a context for their contents.

Joseph Martin Kraus was born in the small town of Miltenberg am Main on 20 June 1756. His father, Joseph Bernhard Kraus (1724–1810) was a town official in the nearby town of Amorbach, the site of a large Benedictine monastery.[8] His mother, Anna Dorothea née Schmidt (1733–1804), was the daughter of a local merchant, and the birth took place in the home of her parents, as was a common practice of the time. In 1759 the entire family moved south to the town of Osterburken, which had been an important trading center since Roman times. In 1761 his father was appointed *Amtskeller* in the nearby larger town of Buchen.[9] It was there that Kraus attended the local school, whose rector, Georg Pfister (1730–1807), and cantor, Bernhard Franz Wendler (1708–1782), provided him with his earliest education. This included initial study in both Latin and music, at which the young child excelled to such a degree that he was accepted at the age of ten as a scholar at the Jesuit Gymnasium und

Musik Seminar in Mannheim, once his primary education had been completed.

In the fall of 1768 he began his studies there, being instructed in literature, both Latin and German, by Pater Anton Klein (1746–1810) and in music by Pater Alexander Keck (1724–1804). He also studied violin and probably basic musical composition under several teachers from the famed Mannheim orchestra. Both Klein and Keck reminisced about Kraus as a student, describing him as extremely gifted, both as a musician and in literature.[10] The former noted that he felt a particular kinship with Kraus, in whom he instilled a sense of critical thought and creativity. Klein specifically mentioned that his young pupil was drawn toward German literature, writing poetry of "considerable length," as he puts it.[11] Keck also described him as one of the "best and most talented of the students that I ever had."[12] Indeed, his earliest compositions appear to date from this age, and Pfister noted that he was considered a *discipulus ultra Magistrum,* or a disciple who excelled beyond his teachers, being able to perform "the most difficult concertos [on the violin] of various authors, such as Ignaz Fränzl, Christian Cannabich, Wilhelm Cramer, and others."[13] Pfister also hints that his teachers included other members of the *Kapelle,* almost certainly including Franz Xaver Richter, who taught general bass to the students at the Gymnasium.[14] As a proficient and talented scholar, he was allowed on occasion to sit in as a supernumerary in the second violin section of the orchestra, as well. In short, in Mannheim Kraus was trained as both a composer and a violinist, achieving according to the brief documentary evidence considerable accolades for his ability.

In 1773 Kraus matriculated at the University of Mainz, where he continued his education in philosophy. Nothing is known about his brief and possibly abortive career as a student there, other than he was able to publish a book of poetry, organize a student society, and write a scathing diatribe against the pedantic academicians he encountered.[15] The following year Joseph Bernhard Kraus moved his son to the University of Erfurt, a more prestigious institution under the control of the Electorate of Mainz that specialized in the study of jurisprudence. Here he was to be trained as a state bureaucrat like his father in a broad liberal arts curriculum that would enable him to obtain an official post, possibly even as his father's successor. During the year he spent there, he also studied music, almost certainly under Georg Peter Weimar (1734–1800), but also possibly under Johann Christian Kittel (1732–1809), a student of Johann Sebastian Bach. Through these teachers, he became acquainted with the music of the Bach family, mainly Carl Philipp Emanuel and his father, remarking to Pfister a year later that in Erfurt he had finally learned what real composition meant.[16]

After only a year in Erfurt Kraus was forced to return to Buchen when his father was accused of misuse of office by a zealous official in the electoral court and suspended from duty.[17] This meant that his family no longer had the means to support his studies, and for over a year he was confined at home, where he wrote music for the local musical ensemble and petitions to the court on behalf of his father. He also published a play, *Tolon,* which exposed in dramatic form issues of social tyranny.[18] Although Joseph Bernhard Kraus was eventually found guilty and his family underwent considerable familial stress throughout the judicial process,[19] by the fall of 1776 the situation had been ameliorated enough so that his son could return to university. This time, it was to the University of Göttingen, which specialized in a thorough curriculum that would allow for the completion of a law degree within an accelerated time span. While there, he became friendly with literary figures, such as Friedrich Hahn (1750–1779) and Johann Heinrich Voss (1751–1826), who had formed the Sturm und Drang literary circle, the Göttinger Hainbund, in 1772. Although this group had disbanded, through Hahn and other professors of literature, Kraus also met Matthias Claudius (1740–1815) and Friedrich Gottlieb Klopstock (1724–1803), some of the foremost literary figures of the day. At the same time, he began to dedicate most of his energy and time toward music, composing a large number of mainly instrumental works and writing a treatise, *Etwas von und über Musik fürs Jahr 1777,* which he published in Frankfurt the following year.[20] It was at this stage, with the resolution of his father's indictment still pending, that Kraus decided to seek his fortune elsewhere as a musician, no doubt encouraged by a fellow student from Sweden, Carl Stridsberg (1755–1819), who was on the lookout for talented artists with potential to contribute to the cultural establishment of King Gustav III.

Toward the end of April, 1778 Kraus departed Göttingen, traveling by way of Hamburg and Lübeck to Copenhagen, from which he traveled north to Stockholm, arriving on 3 June. It is uncertain what he expected to find there, since his friend Stridsberg had preceded him, traveling onward to his home in Härnösand several hundred kilometers north of the Swedish capital, but it is certain that the position with the state-subsidized Royal Spectacles that he expected did not materialize immediately.[21] He nonetheless decided to remain, hoping to break into the musical establishment, but in an effort to precipitate the matter, he and Stridsberg wrote a Swedish opera, *Azire,* that was not accepted by the arbitrator of the Royal Opera, the Royal Academy of Music. Although he wrote continually of his becoming deeper in debt for living expenses, it is clear from other documentary evidence that his abilities were slowly being recognized, as works were performed in the public concert series, the *Riddarhuskonserter,* as well as in private households.[22] Kraus was approached by Adolf Fredrik friherr von Barnekow (1744–1787), the director of the Royal Theaters, who offered him a trial piece, but Kraus, apparently finding the substance lacking, rejected it, thereby making Barnekow a powerful enemy.[23] When the administrator was deposed in favor of Carl Reinhold von Fersen (1716–1786) in 1780, Kraus's fortunes changed, and he was finally given an official commission for an opera after being admitted as a member of the Royal Academy of Music. This work, *Proserpin,* was successfully performed before Gustav III in June of 1781, whereupon he was immediately awarded the post of *Vize-Kapellmästare.*

One of the provisions of his position was that the King was to give Kraus a stipend to travel throughout Europe to observe the latest trends in opera and theater, as well as possibly recruiting additional musicians for the Stockholm Hovkapell. Before this, however, he was commissioned to compose the inaugural opera for the new theater, a work outlined by Gustav III himself and versified by Johan Henrik Kellgren (1751–1795), the librettist of *Proserpin.* In the spring of 1782, however, this opera was put on hold by the flight of the lead soprano, Caroline Müller (1755–1826), and her husband, violinist Christian Friedrich Müller (1752–1827), to avoid debtor's prison, leaving the composer with permission to embark upon his journey. The work, *Æneas i Cartago,* was only partially complete. In November of 1782 he traveled south to Germany, stopping at Wismar in Swedish Pomerania, Berlin, Dresden, Leipzig, Jena, and Erfurt before arriving at the end of December on Christmas Eve at his parents' home in Königstein an der Taunus, just north of Frankfurt am Main.[24] After only about a week, he made a small excursion to Frankfurt, Mainz, and Mannheim, where he observed the various musical stages and ensembles, even though the bulk of the main orchestra in the last-named city had already moved to Munich with the electoral court in 1778. Returning briefly to his parents' new house in Amorbach, to which they had moved in the intervening time, he came into contact with Pater Roman Hoffstetter (1746–1815), a Benedictine monk at the monastery there with whom he established a strong friendship.[25]

In the middle of March he continued his journey to Regensburg, where he observed the famed Thurn und Taxis Kapelle, and by the first of April he arrived in Vienna, where he took up lodging on the Kohlmarkt around the corner from Wolfgang Amadeus Mozart. Although evidence of any meeting of these two composers of equal age remains largely circumstantial, it is known that Kraus was both introduced at court and met other musical luminaries of the time, including Antonio Salieri, Joseph Haydn, Christoph Willibald von Gluck, Johann Georg Albrechtsberger, and Johann Baptist Vanhal.[26] Here he also formed a close friendship with a Hungarian merchant, Johann Samuel Liedemann, as well as being inducted into a Masonic lodge. He also apparently instructed some pupils, including Paul Wrantizky (1756–1808), who thereafter promoted himself as a student of "le compositeur Suèdois, J. K.," as well as arranging for the distribution of his music with music seller Johann Traeg.[27]

In October, he left for Italy to join up with the retinue of Gustav III, traveling by way of Esterháza, Graz, Slovenia, and Trieste to Venice. After visiting the famed Padre Martini in Bologna, he made his way to Rome by way of Florence, eventually joining the entourage of Gustav III and being introduced to Pope Pius VI. A brief artistic and diplomatic visit to Naples was followed by a longer sojourn in Livorno before Kraus took a ship to Marseilles in France. By June of 1784 he had arrived in Paris, where he was to spend the next two years. All along the way he wrote copiously about the various arts he encountered, and it is clear that he was expected to make a name for himself as a composer in the French capital prior to returning home to Stockholm. In Paris he wrote a lengthy critique of the opera *Didone* by Niccolò Piccinni (1728–1800), which was published in Mannheim that year. Kraus also made a brief side trip to London, where he experienced the Handel Centenary Festival in 1785. Although he had intended to return that year to Sweden, his detractors in Stockholm had succeeded in undermining his position to the extent of hiring Abbé Vogler to replace him, and while the various intrigues and issues were worked out, Kraus had to remain in Paris, where, like Mozart, local success eluded him.[28] Finally, when the lackadaisical and inattentive administrator of the Royal Theaters, Cristoffer Bogislaus Zibet (1740–1809), was replaced by one of Kraus's friends and supporters, Abraham Niklas Clewberg-Edelcrantz (1744–1821), the situation was resolved and the composer allowed to return home. In August of 1786 he once more briefly visited his family in Amorbach, and by the end of December he had arrived back in Stockholm.

Upon his return, Kraus was appointed as curriculum director of the Royal Academy of Music, and in 1788, upon the retirement of *Kapellmästare* Francesco Antonio Baldassare Uttini (1723–1795), he was named as his permanent replacement.[29] The next several years were spent in an active musical life as principal conductor of the Hovkapell, occasional conductor at the public concerts, composer and arranger of all opera productions at the Royal Opera and the Royal Dramatic Theater, court composer, and administrator at the Royal Academy of Music. His Turkish *drama med sång* (drama with music) *Soliman II* won high praise, as did his ballet collaboration with Antoine Bournonville (1760–1848) entitled *Fiskarena*. He introduced the works of Mozart to Stockholm audiences, beginning with a symphony in 1789, and he was an enthusiastic participant in the literary-artistic circle led by Gustava Palmstedt, wife of Gustav III's chief architect. The political situation, mainly the war between Sweden and Russia, prevented the intended premiere of *Æneas* in 1790, but his reputation was further enhanced by short operatic works and incidental music for the Royal Dramatic Theater and the privately run Swedish Comedy led by singer Carl Stenborg (1752–1814). He was also a welcomed and congenial guest at virtually all houses and gatherings in the Swedish capital. In March of 1792, his patron, Gustav III, was attacked by an assassin, Jakob Anckarström, and he succumbed to his wounds several weeks later. While his death might have foreshadowed serious consequences for Gustavian artists such as Kraus, the prince regent, Gustav's brother Carl, took on the reigns of the government on behalf of the late king's son, and there was only minimal disruption of the pace of artistic life in the Swedish capital.

Kraus himself was affected deeply by the loss of his king, however, writing a moving *Funeral Music* that demonstrated this close connection with his employer. Nonetheless, by the fall of 1792 it appeared that he had also established a good relationship with the prince regent, composing in October of that year a one-act comic opera, *Marknaden* (The Marketplace). At this point, Kraus's own health deteriorated somewhat rapidly. He had never sufficiently recovered from a virulent respiratory illness in 1791, and during the summer of 1792 he had a serious bout of hemorrhoids. When added to an unusually damp and cold early winter, his otherwise comfortable life was made difficult from the standpoint of his health. In early December it worsened, and Kraus passed away at the age of thirty-six on 15 December 1792.[30] He was buried on a peninsula on the shores of Brunnsvik Lake outside Stockholm at Bergshamra in a highly romantic scene where his casket was carried across the frozen lake by torchlight.

KRAUS AS CORRESPONDENT: AN INTRODUCTION TO THE LETTERS

There are many reasons why Kraus's letters ought to be regarded as important eighteenth-century documents, not only for their subject matter, but because they are interesting and engaging as an insight into eighteenth-century life. Far from being, as the Germans were wont to categorize all but the very few "great masters," a nondescript and ordinary *Kleinmeister,* Kraus was in fact a professional, highly regarded, and successful composer during his lifetime. Moreover, he not only received a thorough advanced university education, he was both aware of and participated in the various intellectual cultural and artistic discussions of his time. As a student, he was trained in German literature by one of its leading proponents, Pater Klein, expanding beyond this to becoming a published author of poetry and drama. As a theorist and aesthetician, he wrote one of the few treatises on music that reflects the literary Sturm und Drang philosophy, and further he participated enthusiastically and actively in the polemical debates in Stockholm on the efficacy of opera and drama. He was also a perceptive critic, whose review of Piccinni's opera *Didone* was expansive and detailed, being published separately as part of a growing trend of music criticism during the time. As a composer, he was trained in numerous styles of music, from the Italianate Mannheim School to the north German style of C. P. E. Bach. He was well aware of the strict conventional species counterpoint, probably from his work with Franz Xaver Richter, but he also became familiar with the contrapuntal intricacies of Johann Sebastian Bach through his teachers in Erfurt. During his grand tour, he absorbed many of the latest musical idioms in Vienna, Regensburg, Italy, and France, not to mention coming into contact with the music of George Frédéric Handel in London. When one adds to this his own adulation of Gluck and André-Ernest-Modest Grétry, in addition to a talent for colorful orchestration, a good sense of varied rhythm, and the lyrical melodic line, there is little room for doubt that his music achieved a certain stylistic uniqueness, even as it displayed many similar elements found in that of his contemporaries. Finally, he held a position of importance for much of his productive life, albeit somewhat on the periphery of mainstream Europe. Gustav's artistic vision was well-known and admired, though it involved principally a homegrown audience in Sweden, and Kraus was an important person in his official posts, enough so that he attained a high social status, the equivalent of colleagues (and friends) Haydn, Salieri, or Reichardt. He was not, in eighteenth-century eyes, a minor musician with a variable career, a forgotten figure languishing on the periphery of Europe, but rather a person of note, a Kapellmeister in the loftiest sense of that term.

This stature is reflected in contemporaneous comments by these colleagues, some made during Kraus's lifetime and others solicited ex post facto. For the former, for example, there is a reference in *Dilettanterien,* a contemporary commentary on music in which Christian Gottlieb Neefe (1748–1798) lauded the music of Joseph Haydn, further noting: "Mozart, Kozeluch, Kraus, Pleyel, Reicha, and Rosetti all stand beside him or follow in his worthy footsteps."[31] Two years later, Carl Friedrich Cramer, visiting Italy, stated: "Among the various musicians who have been here for a time, both Herr Kraus from Stockholm and [Herr] Pleyel from Vienna have been well-liked and favored everywhere, both for their beautiful playing and their compositions, and for their excellent proper behavior."[32] In 1792, Johann Friedrich Reichardt, whom Kraus befriended in Vienna almost a decade earlier, commented in his *Musikalische Monatsschrift* regarding Kraus's music to *Æneas* and *Amphitryon* that "throughout the both works Herr G. M. Kraus displays quite different characters, as a thinking artist who has studied thoroughly and diligently to practice his art; everywhere the contemplative artist, who understands how to create and execute engaging effects and entertaining nuances, shines forth."[33] Finally, in the memorial address given in 1798, Kraus's friend Stridsberg noted: "A Haydn, a Salieri, an Albrechtsberger cannot today speak of him without words of praise and with the greatest expression of the loss to themselves and the world of the artist." The information from the Viennese composers were, of course, solicited by Silverstolpe during his several years in Vienna as Swedish chargé d'affaires at the end of the eighteenth century, during which time he gathered materials for the first Kraus biography, but they nonetheless indicated that the composer was considered an important colleague by his peers, themselves famous musicians.[34] For instance, the diplomat met with Antonio Salieri, who remembered being present when Kraus met Gluck and who heard the older composer exclaim: "This man has a great style, the like of which I have not seen in anyone else."[35] He also noted that librettist Abbé Giovanni Battista Casti (1724–1803) called Kraus "a man of genius and the creator of a new taste in his science."[36] The most important reminiscence, however, was that by Joseph Haydn, who not only linked Kraus to Mozart in his own mind, but also commented to Silverstolpe that he was "the first man of genius that I have known," lamenting his death as "an irreplaceable loss for our art."[37]

Finally, in his gathering of information Silverstolpe noted that Kraus in Vienna was not just known as a composer, but rather he achieved a considerable reputation as an intellectual: "Here in this place the artist is equally famed and esteemed, recognized by the intelligentsia thanks to his other multifaceted and extensive knowledge."[38] In short, Kraus must be seen in eighteenth-century eyes as a mature, curious intellectual whose education, manners, and deportment were indicative of his important position in that society, and by analogy his own letters ought to contain many important insights in that they reflect this stature. It also seems logical to presume that they would go beyond the bounds of familial intimacy or rote official notes, petitions, and the like, providing a wealth of observations that were focused upon not just music, but other aspects of life and society as well. Finally, given that he was heavily involved in literary efforts, one might expect a writer's tone to his observations, a critical eye couched in voluble language.

Kraus was, by any measure, a prolific and effusive correspondent. He wrote often to a large number of people, from official letters to his superiors in the Swedish court to missives in aid of his father during the latter's trials, from intimate notes to his family and friends all the way to more descriptive and perceptive commentary to all and sundry. Unfortunately, as with many other composers of the period, the bulk of this correspondence either has vanished or remains undiscovered. Indeed, there is some evidence of deliberate destruction on the part of early biographers, notably Silverstolpe himself, as will be noted. There is some documentary evidence of this lost correspondence. For example, on the inside cover of his travel diary, meant most likely as a device to jog his own memory for the required reports back to Stockholm during his grand tour, Kraus jotted down a list of people. These comprise names, places, and three enigmatic symbols: a circle, a circle crossed through, and a check mark.[39] The rubric of this list reads "*Brf:*," that is to say, "letters" either in German, his native language (*Briefe*) or in Swedish, his adopted language that he spoke with native fluency (*Bref* or, in modern Swedish, *brev*). Thereupon follow a list of cities: Stockholm, Berlin, Wismar, Erfurt, Mainz, Frankfurt, Mannheim, Amorbach, and Regensburg. Underneath these can be found a list of as few as one and as many as ten names, with an equally variable number of the symbols following them. The symbols themselves are not further identified, but the manner in which they are used allows for a reasonable suggestion to be made. Circles are letters that Kraus wrote, and when an answer was received, the circle was crossed through; a check mark may indicate the receipt of an unsolicited letter that did not require a response. This, of course, is only a suggestion, and other possibilities could be postulated.

Not surprisingly, the name with the most symbols following it is Cristoffer Zibet, his main contact with the Swedish court and no doubt the administrator to whom he was to submit reports. Unfortunately, save for several short fragments sketched into the diary itself, these letters have not survived in either the official archives or the court ledgers now in the Riksarkiv in Stockholm. The other names are familiar ones to those who are aware of Kraus's friends and colleagues throughout his lifetime: his librettist Johan Henrik Kellgren, his friend from university Carl Stridsberg, a poet well known in Stockholm for his parodies, Carl Israel Hallman (1732–1800), his composition pupil and friend Johan Wikmanson (1753–1800), his colleague woodwind player Johann Friedrich Grenser (1758–1795), a member of the exchequer and amateur musician Gabriel Kling (1719–1797), Petter Schiernell, a linen merchant and Kraus's landlord, professor of Latin Karl Kellman (1721–1807), and Johan Stolpe (1757–1798), a poet and amateur musician. There is no doubt that some of these, apart from Zibet, were requests or responses of a more official nature. For example, in Dresden in December Kraus hand-delivered a letter from Grenser to his father, famed Dresden woodwind instrument maker Carl Augustin Grenser.[40] The exchanges in Berlin were with Burchard Hummel (1748–1797), the brother of Johann Julius Hummel, both of whom ran one of the largest and most prestigious publishing firms during the period. Kraus was publishing a set of six string quartets (Op. 1) with them, and no doubt these letters were written to that end.[41] His Wismar correspondents, however, were more personal: his friend Johann Friedrich Hallardt (1727–1794), the postmaster in Stralsund, and Caspar Gabriel Gröning (1752–1799), a lawyer for whom Kraus had written a birthday cantata for Gustav III during his brief visit. His letters to Erfurt most likely involved his early teachers (or putative teachers): Georg Peter Weimar and Johann Georg Arnold (ca. 1740–1801), the latter the organist at St. Severi Church in the city.[42] The letters under Mainz included bassoonist Franz Anton Pfeiffer (1754–1792) and an unidentified man named Scheber.[43] In Mannheim he renewed contact with his old teacher, Pater Klein, and in Frankfurt wrote to a relative, painter Johann Georg Schütz (1755–1813), who was to paint the composer's portrait.[44] The last remaining name is that of Swedish ambassador to the Thurn und Taxis court in Regensburg, Magnus Olof Björnstjerna (1738–1785), who was a gracious host during Kraus's visit and who became a close friend. All of these letters, save for drafts to Zibet, Kellgren, and Björnstjerna contained within the diary itself, have been lost.

Silverstolpe himself collected no fewer than 131 other letters, but chose to incorporate only 50 into his 1833 biography.[45] Some, principally those from Johann Traeg in Vienna, Kraus's music distributor, were tacitly ignored by the biographer, while others to his close friend, Liedemann, were purposely suppressed and destroyed. The reasons for this have never been entirely clear, though the tone of several were overtly emotional. Silverstolpe explained his censorship in these blunt terms: "Everything that contained only unique situations, confidences, or similar subjects have been destroyed."[46] Leux-Henschen believed that this destruction was based upon the need to avoid slandering those who intrigued against the composer and whose relatives were still living, while the letters to Liedemann may have been considered too explicit in terms of their language, so that the possibility of a close, perhaps even intimate, relationship could have been construed.[47] More recently, however, Ingrid Fuchs has recovered other letters from Liedemann, at least, in which Kraus is mentioned frequently but without the sort of effusive and sensitive language one might expect of someone who was more than just a close friend.[48] There is no doubt that Kraus's sense of language could sound strange to twentieth-century, let alone nineteenth-century, ears, in that it is often absurdly intimate, but given that he was a child of the linguistic peculiarities of the wildly emotional Sturm und Drang, it would be a mistake to read too much of a relationship or sexual orientation into them. Thus, as much as he assiduously collected and documented Kraus's life, Silverstolpe may have compromised his intended portrayal of Kraus through his own interpretation of the tone and substance of the letters he destroyed, censored, or omitted.

As for the letters themselves, it is important to note what they do and do not show. As mentioned earlier, they currently form the core of any biographical study of Kraus and his music, with their content being either taken at face value or interpreted in the light of whatever information might have been extant or come to light. Silverstolpe is entirely dependent upon them for his discussion of Kraus's life, with comments regarding his reputation and music coming largely from ancillary, often anecdotal sources. That is not to say that his biography is entirely subjective or filled with errors, but the dependence upon the letters casts a certain light on the events that may have different causes or interpretations. For example, as noted above the entire Liedemann friendship is presented in a highly truncated, censored form, so that future biographers have found it difficult to separate poetic hyperbole from descriptive fact. In 1783 Kraus writes to Liedemann from Florence with a detailed view of his travels to Italy, including his activities as a cultural tourist in Venice and Bologna – a picture by Paul Veronese is described precisely – as well as musical events, such as the feast of St. Anthony in the Bolognese church of San Giovanni in Monte. This is the letter such as an interested party who is also a close friend might expect to receive. It is objective but not particularly intimate. In March 1785, however, Kraus writes a more emotional letter to Liedemann that is effusive and personal, concluding with the reassurance that Kraus has "only one friend."[49] A little over a year later, in June 1786, an even more emotional letter was written to Liedemann, in which Kraus is completely enthralled by his feelings. He concludes, almost in a Wertherian manner, with a wish: "May heaven ordain that we shall wander calmly hand in hand into another better world!"[50] What is one to make of this clear "development" of the correspondence relationship, that goes from a curious intellectual of the Enlightenment writing to an interested friend to something that is fraught with wild emotions and seemingly clear erotic overtones? The answer is: not much. The final letter is only an excerpt of something much longer without context, the second contains answers to questions that Liedemann has apparently posed on a cerebral philosophical level, and only the first seems to indicate something that could be considered a normal objective correspondence. According to Silverstolpe's catalogue, three other letters to Liedemann from Paris from July 1784 to February 1785 once existed but were destroyed, as were five more letters between July 1785 and February 1786. What they contained is anyone's guess, though Leux-Henschen suggested that these were suppressed because they cast a dim light on the professional cabals that attempted to keep the composer from returning to Stockholm.[51] This cannot be substantiated, however, and although the increasing emotional state of Kraus due to his own concerns about his future is evident in this sequence, it is completely without situational context. Moreover, reading between the lines is impossible in terms of objective information in the two last surviving letters, given their fragmentary state. What can be said is that Kraus and Liedemann were close friends who hit it off in Vienna, but there is no evidence of any other sort of more private relationship in either the newly discovered letters of the merchant wherein Kraus is mentioned nor in fact that he willingly turned over to Silverstolpe the originals of all of the correspondence he still had in his possession at the beginning of the nineteenth century. Therefore, one can note that the first letter brings a critical eye to art and music of the period in two Italian cities, but all one can say about the fragmentary other letters is that one ought to read them without implying anything else, biographical or factual. Any conclusion that these could represent some sort of social impropriety is no more true than suggesting Mozart's often explicit letters to his cousin represent an erotic, perhaps even indecent, attachment.[52]

The bulk of the surviving letters are, of course, written by the composer to his parents. It is interesting to note that these have been cited as late as the revised Schreiber, Riedel, and Åstrand biographies as support for the course of his life.[53] Leux-Henschen, on the other hand, cautions the reader of her German edition that "he clearly let his imagination run amok and reported things that did not quite correspond with reality."[54] Reading them one finds the usual allusions to personal familial situations and friends, off-the-cuff expostulations, and responses to obvious concerns. Given that the last were probably frequent, it is clear that Kraus was torn between assuaging his parents' concerns on one hand and not imparting too much worrisome information on his true state of affairs on the other. Thus he self-censored much of his written personal interactions with them. Such lacunae are obvious in both the tone and substance of these letters, and moreover they caused him to become quite defensive at times. For example, his conscious decision to abandon the trajectory of his life as his father's successor in the state bureaucracy for the more uncertain employment prospects in music caused them no end of regret and concern. His parents supported him to the best of their ability during hard times, but it is plain from the inferences and answers in the letters that they were continually importuning him about his decision. It is also clear that they were immensely proud of him and his position, a social status that they themselves could never attain. A different tone can be found in his letters to his siblings, first his brother Franz, who died prematurely in 1790, and then his sister Marianne. In them he relished the role of eldest brother, encouraging the exploration of their artistic talents and attempting to mentor them as much as was possible from a distance. The letters also show a devotion to his other brother and sisters, with indications he was continually supplying them with small tokens of his affection. He is also quite free with his advice on their lives and careers, especially in the case of his sister Marianne. Kraus, however, rarely describes his own profession, and he is far more anecdotal than objective in the various missives. This in turn leads one to suspect that such superficial information was deliberate, with the writing angled to correspond with whatever needed to be said or divulged at any given time. During the early Stockholm years, he describes himself repeatedly as a human being in dire economic straits, begging his parents for any sum of money they can afford to keep him alive. In one letter he is on the verge of arrest and incarceration in debtor's prison, and in another he bemoans the fact that his underclothes are nothing but rags and that he cannot last the winter without proper clothing. One could conclude from this that his entire plan for employment as a composer in Sweden was a pipe dream, a fantasy for which his parents bore the financial brunt. Yet, during the early years he made a number of trips to the north of Sweden, probably Härnösand and elsewhere, all of which he apparently had money for, and it would seem that his progress at obtaining an official position proceeded on course, with his becoming well known as a composer and even participating in the polemical debates of the time. This evidence collides with the portrait of desperation that he described to his parents in his letters, demonstrating that one must reconcile two very different documentary issues. In another example, he reassures his mother that, as a Catholic in Lutheran Stockholm, he was able to practice his faith in three locations, but he fails to mention his close contacts with members of the Protestant churches in the city, such as Pastor Magnus Lehnberg (1758–1808), for whom he was to write music for celebratory functions. During his last year, he states that, at thirty-six, he is not yet married, excusing it by saying that he cannot afford a *Kapellmeisterin* on his salary, and yet the inventory of household goods at his death in

1792 are those of a wealthy and important upper-class citizen. Indeed, a recently rediscovered portrait of the new *Vize-Kapellmästare* painted in 1783 by a relative in Frankfurt shows him to be a prosperous individual of rank, as does the better-known picture painted in Stockholm by Per Krafft Sr. (1724–1793) about 1788, none of which can be reconciled to the self-described anxiety, poverty, and precarious state of his employment he frequently describes in his letters to his parents. In short, he consciously slanted his writings home, playing with the language and adapting it to whatever sort of mood or purpose he felt necessary, either to mollify or to deflect the anxieties and inquiries of his parents. As biographical material, the letters may give a glimpse into his own character, but as objective outlines of his life they must be taken with a great deal of caution in terms of the overall picture, and certainly not as entirely absolutely accurate biographical documentation, no matter what or who is named within.

The more objective letters are those where Kraus felt himself moved as an observer to comment on life and the arts. Most of these were written to friends, such as the Benedictine monk Pater Roman Hoffstetter in Amorbach or Pater Anton Klein in Mannheim. He often describes performances, art, architecture, and other items that would interest these men on a more intellectual level. When he visited the recently uncovered ruins of Pompeii, he told not only what he saw, but also how the ruins and other attractions of Naples Bay were to be visited. In Bologna, he describes the precise contents of a special concert at the church of San Giovanni in Monte, critiquing them according to his own musical aesthetic. When in London, he gives a complete catalogue of the Handel works he encountered, and when he writes officially to his administrative contacts in Stockholm, he is often quite descriptive and factual. Even as a student, his somewhat voluble missives often contain precise detail, such as the curriculum at Göttingen University. There is also an underlying sense of humor and self-parody at times, such as equating the lectures of his professors with the braying of donkeys while at the same time clearly implying that he intends to join in that chorus. He is not in awe of colleagues, even those better known than himself (as he sees it), but notes how he interacts with them. He observes Haydn's character, describing what he sees as shortcomings but not diminishing his own respect, and although he revered Gluck as the ultimate model, his meeting was more between equals than a disciple with a master. He could be quite diplomatic, especially concerning the political situation, giving just enough information to substantiate what his parents and others were reading in their local papers about the political state of his adopted country, but not mentioning his interaction with officialdom. He shows remarkable acuity in his understanding of economics, literature, art, and handicrafts. He also mentions music, but the comments are almost always contained within some other context. Knowing this in the letters in turn helps one understand his life from his point of view: not a biography but biographical on several different levels.

There is not much to be said about Kraus as a person that is clear and unambiguous in the letters, apart from the sort of friendly interactions noted by other contemporaries and his own rather substantial personal reputation. From these, however, it is known that he was quite gregarious, favored a somewhat sybaritic lifestyle, and had a love of good spirits and tobacco. As a youth, he described local German wines, and as an adult he remarked upon good English porter, for instance. He suffered fools badly, and could be both direct and cantankerous if the mood struck him. He was fond of dogs and hunted enthusiastically, as well as taking long walks in the countryside, enjoying and observing nature. He liked to travel and was quite fastidious in his personal habits. Kraus was an avid reader, an important prerequisite for someone who also had a talent for languages; Kraus spoke German, Swedish, French, and Italian fluently, as well as reading Latin and Greek. He also may have learned some English, and was competent enough in Dutch and Danish to set songs idiomatically to texts in those languages. He was well-read in terms of literature of the time, including Goethe and Richardson, and he wrote (and published) poetry himself. In other words, as a human being, he was a polymath with a wide range of interests and abilities, all of which coalesced into his everyday actions and writing.

Kraus was also fortunate to have found a champion in the person of Swedish diplomat Fredrik Samuel Silverstolpe (1769–1851), who, as already noted, published the first biography of the composer. In preparation for this, he contacted Kraus's family, friends, and relatives for information, much of which was freely and willingly given. Kraus's father and his brother Alois solicited information from his early teachers, Rector Pfister and Paters Klein and Keck, while Silverstolpe himself corresponded with Kraus's sister Marianne, now married to state councilor Paul Lämmerhirt, as well as Hoffstetter, whom Kraus had befriended during his grand tour. Finally, Silverstolpe posed a series of questions that Kraus's sister and her husband answered in writing, thus providing a good secondary documentary foundation for his biography. This was the source of much supplementary material, albeit much of it anecdotal, and it makes an interesting comparison to note what the composer wrote in his own correspondence and what the reminiscences of his teachers and family were over a decade after his death.

THE EDITION OF THE LETTERS

Finally, a word must be said about this edition and translation. The present author has used Kraus's own autograph letters whenever possible; the appendix likewise uses the original letters from friends and family where these exist. As noted earlier, Kraus was a prolific correspondent with a wide variety of people, but the majority of the letters that have been preserved were written to his family. These are currently to be found in the Kraus Sammlung at the Bezirksmuseum in Buchen, Germany, where they were donated by Kraus's heirs over a century after his death. The advantage is clearly one of conservation, but during the intervening years a number of the letters have been lost. Fortunately, Silverstolpe made copies of the majority in preparation for his biography, though not all of them were copied out whole for the reasons already noted. As a result, some of the now lost original letters exist only in fragmentary form in these copies; such have been included from this source with the caveat that they represent only a portion of the original. Silverstolpe's copies of the correspondence, along with the autograph travel diary, are preserved in the library of the University of Uppsala in Sweden (Folio X270a). Although the Swedish diplomat kept a detailed inventory list of this correspondence,[55] he was not able to or chose not to use all the available letters from Kraus's family, no doubt for the same reasons that he did not include letters from Liedemann or Traeg. Many of the first group were subsequently incorporated into German editions of the letters by Leux-Henschen and the Swedish edition by Hans Åstrand.[56] These editions, along with a series of Kraus letters from Göttingen in a new German transliteration by Martin Stahelin, have been consulted and compared for this edition. In addition, a Kraus letter to Hoffstetter was published by Friedrich Noack in 1953.[57] While this source was unavailable in autograph form, Noack's careful diplomatic transcription appears complete in all details and was used here. The only other published source was a lengthy letter written to Pater Klein from Paris in 1785, which the Mannheim author and Kraus's former teacher had printed that year in the Pfälzische Museum verbatim. The Swedish sources include draft copies to Zibet and Björnstjerna found in Kraus's travel diary, several to Abraham Niklas Clewberg-Edelcrantz from Paris and later Stockholm from the Royal Library (Kungliga Biblioteket) in Stockholm (Clewberg-Edelcrantz Correspondence), and a testimonial for publisher and composer Olof Åhlström along with Kraus's last will and testament in the Royal Archives (Riksarkiv). These sources have been used and compared with both Leux-Henschen and Åstrand. Unfortunately, the bulk of the letters to Sweden seem not to have survived, or have resisted rediscovery; a careful perusal of the official theater correspondence has not revealed any of these. Finally, the letters from Kraus's family and friends that form the appendix of this edition were all translated from their autograph originals in the Silverstolpe collection in Uppsala (Folio X270f), where they were donated following the diplomat's death. These, as well as the travel diary, have also been published in diplomatic editions, which have been consulted and compared by the present author.[58] It should be noted, however, that this edition probably represents only a fraction of the number of letters that Kraus actually wrote during his short lifetime, and therefore it is likely that others will resurface over time to complement this compendium.

As a writer, Kraus often wrote idiomatically and without regard to orthographic standards (such as existed during that time among university-trained people), punctuation, or grammar. He freely inserted Greek and Latin epigrams into his letters, used loan words from other languages frequently, and was conversant in the various proverbs and sayings of the time, some of which not only defy exact translation but were inserted to make specific points. There are also allusions to local stories and inside jokes that cannot be clarified at present, since the subjects have left little or no trace of the matter at hand. Clearly, a literal translation would not come close to reproducing the tone and gist of his often conversational tone or language, and in some cases there is obviously something contextual that is missing. Such is the difficulty in any translation, but here the present author has attempted to come as close to the original substance, tone, and language of the letters as possible, retaining the colloquialisms or providing as close an equivalent as possible for some of the irregularities. Finally, a word needs to be said about both spelling and italics. The former is particularly inconsistent with regard to proper names and places, as was common for the period. For example, the last name of his executor and friend, Henrik Engmark, was often spelled with an additional letter, i.e., Engmarck, and one of his mentors, Axel Gabriel Lejonhuvud, could appear also as Löwenhaupt or Lejonhufwud, all of which can be considered correct. In such cases, I have chosen to regularize these for consistency. In the case of italics, Kraus uses them mainly for specific emphases. These may appear for any word sometimes to make a particular point and others to indicate some sort of subtext. Often these are people and places, but at times it is difficult to discern exactly why he italicized something. In the interest of keeping his own points consistent, these have been retained in the translation, even though they might not correspond to a more traditional modern usage.

It is hoped that this will allow for Kraus's voice to emerge intact, not as an absolute literal translation, but rather to reflect his own mannerisms of writing and, one might hope, speaking. To facilitate this further, an extensive commentary has been provided for virtually all of the letters, setting the context, clarifying the original terms or statements for a modern reader, as well as documenting the various references made therein, where possible. In addition, a brief transitional narrative (entitled in Krausian fashion *Interludium*) links the gaps in the correspondence. Finally, some extra autograph documentary material has been added. Internally, this consists of his fragmentary travel diary, an official (and tortuously wordy) recommendation, and his last will and testament.

There are, of course, numerous references that are of a distinctly eighteenth-century sort, some of which might seem odd to today's readers. For example, the political situation was somewhat fluid. Kraus was formally a citizen of the town or region within which he was born in central Germany, more specifically, the Electorate of Mainz. Given that close associations existed between Mainz and the Palatinate, his education in Mannheim was a natural consideration for a talented youth. The universities in Mainz, Erfurt, and Göttingen were all associated with the electorate from a sociopolitical standpoint, although the last was also closely linked to the Electorate of Hannover. While Kraus was able to travel rather freely between these principalities or states as a subject of the Holy Roman Empire, when he embarked for Sweden from Lübeck in 1778, he was required to have a local notary issue him a passport, the content of which caused some degree of awkwardness when he arrived in Sweden, as he himself noted in his letter dated 12 June 1778.[59] Later, he had little difficulty negotiating the various states during his travels, due primarily to his official position as Kapellmästare to the Swedish court and as a member of Gustav III's official entourage. As such he was considered a Swedish citizen and, moreover, could move about as any diplomat throughout Europe with little more than a letter of introduction to the various Swedish embassies.

Another of these references is in regard to the currencies mentioned in his letters. There were a wide variety of currencies in circulation, all of which had extremely variable rates of exchange. Moreover, in order to circumvent the continual problems that would be encountered, letters of credit were often circulated in lieu of coinage. Kraus would automatically have known how each currency he encountered would have functioned on a local basis, but converting them to modern equivalents to understand his own economy is both tortuous and notoriously awkward. The situation becomes all the more difficult when one realizes that specie currency and purchasing power may be two very different things during the period. This is not unknown even today: for example, the purchasing power of the American dollar is quite different in the United States, Panama, and Ecuador, all of which use it as the national currency. The rate equivalency remains constant, but there is a fundamental disconnect between purchasing power and specie currency among these countries. So too was it among the much more varied currencies extant even in the Holy Roman Empire. Fortunately, there was a stable currency that could be found, and, because records of equivalencies have been kept up to the present day, a relative modern comparison with the money mentioned by Kraus can be established: this was the British pound. There do exist a number of online conversion applications that allow for an approximate or reasonable equivalence to be established, using the pound as a median currency baseline.[60] The present author has made use of these to show Kraus's expenditures at several junctures, always with the caveat that the modern conversions are indeed approximate, not absolute.

All of this is intended to provide both the primary documentation that consists of the letters themselves and supporting commentary, resulting in not only Kraus's own voice, but also information that will help to define the life and times of one of the more intriguing and intellectually capable composers of the Classical era.

NOTES

1. The standard early attempt was Emily Anderson, *Letters of Mozart and His Family* (London: Macmillan, 1938), with further editions, popularized versions, selected editions in 1956 (edited and with a preface by Eric Blom [Harmondsworth, Middelsex, England: Pelican Books]), 1961, 1966, 1989 (New York: Norton), and 1990 (Boston: Bullfinch Press). Anderson's English translations were presented in eloquent and proper English. German originals were published as *Mozart: Briefe und Aufzeichnungen*, 7 vols. (Kassel: Bärenreiter, 1962–1975), edited by Wilhelm Bauer, Otto Erich Deutsch, and Joseph Eibl, with supplementary documentation in Cliff Eisen, *New Mozart Documents: A Supplement to O. E. Deutsch's Documentary Biography* (Stanford, Calif.: Stanford University Press, 1991). The French translation is Geneviève Geffray, *W. A. Mozart: Correspondance*, 7 vols. (Paris: Harmoniques, Flammarion, 1986–1999). Other partial works include Joseph Eibl and Walter Senn, *Mozarts Bäsle Briefe*, 4th ed. Munich: DTV, 1991; and Robert Spaethling, *Mozart's Letters, Mozart's Life* (New York: W. W. Norton, 2000). Earlier editions were by Ludwig Nohl in 1865 and Hans Mersmann in 1928.

2. Emily Anderson, trans., *The Letters of Ludwig van Beethoven,* 3 vols. (London: Macmillan, 1961). A *Gesamtausgabe* in the original German is presumably being created by the Beethoven Haus in Bonn as part of the complete works edition. As an important complementary source that includes correspondence to Beethoven, see Theodore Albrecht, ed., *Letters to Beethoven and Other Correspondence* (Lincoln: University of Nebraska Press, 1996). Another composer whose complete correspondence has been published in a multivolume set is Carl Philipp Emanuel Bach; see Ernst

Suchalla, ed., *Carl Philipp Emanuel Bach Briefe und Dokumente: kritische Gesamtausgabe,* 2 vols. (Göttingen: Vandenhoeck und Ruprecht, 1994).

3. H. C. Robbins Landon, *The Collected Correspondence and London Notebooks of Joseph Haydn* (New York: Essential Books, 1959). Rather than provide a second edition, Landon subsumed other documents and letters into his monumental *Joseph Haydn: Chronicle and Works* (Bloomington: Indiana University Press, 1976–1980). Like the Beethoven edition, it is assumed that the *Joseph Haydn Werke,* now well advanced, will eventually include a critical edition of the documenta and letters.

4. See Hedwig Müller von Asow and E. H. Müller von Asow, eds., *The Collected Correspondence and Papers of Christoph Willibald Gluck,* trans. Stewart Thomson (London: Barrie and Rockliff, 1962). In the preface, both editors acknowledge that the project would have come to naught without the intervention of H. C. Robbins Landon.

5. See Stephen Clark, *Carl Philipp Emanuel Bach Letters* (Oxford: Oxford University Press, 1997).

6. See Hubert Unverricht, *Carl Ditters von Dittersdorf: Briefe, ausgewählte Urkunden und Akten,* Studien zur Musikwissenschaft 54 (Tutzing: Hans Schneider, 2008).

7. There are two editions of Kraus's letters. The standard edition is Irmgard Leux-Henschen, *Joseph Martin Kraus in seinen Briefen* (Stockholm: Edition Reimers, 1978), hereafter LH-JMK, and Hans Åstrand, *Joseph Martin Kraus Brev 1776–1792* (Stockholm: Gidlunds förlag, 2006), hereafter HÅ-JMKB.

8. Biographies of Kraus include Fredrik Silverstolpe, *Biografi af Kraus* (Stockholm: J. Hörberg, 1833), hereafter Si-JMK; Karl Friedrich Schreiber, *Biographie über den Odenwälder Komponisten Joseph Martin Kraus* (Buchen: Bezirksmuseum, 1928; rev. and expanded ed., ed. Helmut Brosch, Gerhardt Darmstadt, and Rainer Trunk, Buchen: Bezirksmuseum, 2006), hereafter Sch-JMK; Friedrich W. Riedel, *Das Himmlische lebt in seinen Tönen* (Mannheim: J und J Verlag, 1992), hereafter FR-JMK; and Hans Åstrand, *Joseph Martin Kraus: Den mest betydande gustavianska musikpersonligheten* (Stockholm: Gidlunds förlag, 2011), hereafter HÅ-JMK. There are to date no biographies in English. Joseph Bernhard Kraus's official title was *Stadtschreiber,* or town registrar. As a state official, he had been trained in law at Mainz University in 1751.

9. The position of *Amtskeller* was an important one, for Joseph Bernhard Kraus became the local representative of the elector-archbishop of Mainz, in whose territory Buchen was located; today it is on the northern fringes of Bavaria. His duties included collecting rent and taxes, adjudicating issues, and providing administrative oversight for his ruler.

10. The letters from both of his teachers are translated in Appendix B.

11. Klein writes: "Er hatte eine große Fertigkein in lateinischen Versen und verfaßte einige Gedichte von ziemlichem Umfange." (He had great competence in Latin verse and authored several poems of considerable scope.) The priest also noted that Kraus received first prize among the students in literature in an annual competition at the age of thirteen or fourteen. See Appendix B.

12. Ibid., Appendix B. The original reads "eines meiner besten und

geschicktesten Eleven, die ich jemalen hatte."

13. See Appendix B, where the entire letter is quoted in English translation. The reference here is to members of the Mannheim orchestra, Ignaz Fränzl (1736–1811), the violinist for whom Mozart had greatest respect and even began composing a double concerto for violin and fortepiano KV 315f, Christian Cannabich (1731–1798), and Wilhelm Cramer (1745–1799), all of whom wrote technically demanding solo concertos for the instrument.

14. His other teachers from *Kapelle* are not identified, though both Cannabich and Fränzl were active as teachers on the violin. Keck and his relatives later stated that Kraus studied with "the world-famous" Abbé Georg Joseph Vogler, but given that Vogler had little or no experience as a teacher at the time – his position was court almoner – and, moreover, was only a few years older than Kraus, such a connection is unlikely. Vogler came to Elector Carl Theodor's attention only in 1768, when he performed a pianoforte solo in Würzburg, and by early 1769 the young man embarked upon a grand tour to Italy to study music with Padre Giovanni Battista Martini. At the most, contact between Kraus and Vogler would have been casual and sporadic; further evidence against this is the later strained relationship between the two men as they became rivals in Stockholm. Most likely, the distance of several decades caused the confusion between Vogler, who was well known at the beginning of the nineteenth century, and Richter, who was known to devote considerable time and energy to talented students at the Music Seminar.

15. The poetry book is *Versuch von Schäfersgedichte* (Mainz: n.p., 1773) and an unpublished essay entitled "Wie in den letzten Zügen liegenden sogenannten Mainzer Universität noch aufzuhelfen sei und wie?" (How the so-called Mainz University lying in its death throes should still be aided and why?) The book has not survived.

16. According to Kraus's relatives' descriptions, he may have traveled to Hamburg to meet C. P. E. Bach, and possibly to Magdeburg as well, though there he would have met with Johann Heinrich Rolle (1718–1785) rather than any of the other sons of Johann Sebastian Bach, as the statement indicates. Such a journey cannot be substantiated, however. See Appendix A. That his relationship with C. P. E. Bach was equivocal, however, may be determined by the critical review of Bach in Kraus's 1778 treatise (see note 20) as well as the fact that when Bach solicited subscriptions for a set of keyboard sonatas in 1787, Kraus's name was among the subscribers.

17. The "crime" was the acceptance by the elder Kraus of "tokens of esteem" from petitioners, a common practice of the time. It was not a matter of bribery, but rather favoritism that the officials felt compromised the authority of the state bureaucracy and its representatives.

18. *Tolon* (Frankfurt am Main: Kessler, 1776). The work was published anonymously. The play was savagely reviewed in both the *Nürnbergischen gelehrten Zeitung* and the *Kritischen Archiv* in 1777, with the first equally anonymous critic remarking: "If the art of an author of tragedy depends upon slaughtering every one of his characters without mercy, then the author of *Tolon*

is indisputably a greater master than Shakespeare or Goethe [Wenn die Kunst eines Trauerspieldichters darinnen besteht, seine Personen samt und sonders – ohne Erbarmen niederzuwürgen, so ist der Verf. des Tolons unstreitig ein größerer Meister als Shakespeare und Goethe]."

19. See note 18. The verdict also recognized that this was a common custom, and the elder Kraus was pardoned and reinstated, though this required a move to the city of Königstein an der Taunus, north of Frankfurt am Main.

20. *Etwas von und über Musik fürs Jahr 1777* (Frankfurt am Main: Eichenbergischen Erben, 1778; fac. ed., ed. Friedrich W. Reidel, Salzburg and Munich: Emil Katzbichler, 1977). This too was published anonymously.

21. Indeed, as Stridsberg later reported in a memorial address in 1798: "He would certainly have become known and recognized as a composer here much more quickly had he been able or moved to employ certain not unusual means, but Kraus hated the least appearance of being a charlatan, and decisiveness was a main component of his noble character, and thus a considerable time passed before anyone even knew that he was a musician; he was long held to be only a musical amateur." His documentation did not help in this regard; in Lübeck he was given a passport that called his profession a "student of law." This, however, may have been Stridsberg's own excuse for his not following through with his own recruitment promises.

22. Indeed, Stridsberg's reminiscences aside (see note 16), his friend Carl Kämpe wrote to Cristoffer Gjörwell on 25 February 1779 that, in contrast to the reticent Stridsberg, the gregarious Kraus, called specifically a "Musicus," was particularly popular among women he met, and his music was performed beginning in 1779 with some frequency in public as his circle of friends grew.

23. This work is unknown. LH-JMK (43–44) noted that the work may have been a Nordic Singspiel entitled *Yngve,* which was to be based upon a draft by Gustav III himself. There is no evidence of this, however, and the actual work remains unidentified.

24. His father had been given the post of assessor in Königstein in 1779, but by the end of 1782 he was already being reassigned as assessor in Amorbach, to which the family moved in January of the new year. During his journey, Kraus kept a travel diary, probably for his own recollection as part of the conditions of support; this is translated herein as no. 45.

25. This is described both in letters written to Hoffstetter by Kraus and in the biographical information contained in letters written by the Benedictine to Silverstolpe in the first years of the nineteenth century. These are reproduced in Appendix C. The originals have been published in Hubert Unverricht, *Die beiden Hoffstetter* (Mainz: Schott, 1968).

26. Conditions for a putative meeting with Mozart are contained in the present author's "The Case of the Circumstantial Meeting: Wolfgang Amadeus Mozart and Joseph Martin Kraus," *Eighteenth-Century Music* 1 (2004): 85–90. Although there may be evidence that Kraus may have obtained a march from *Idomeneo* that he later paraphrased for the Riksdagsmusik of 1789 from miscellaneous pirated copies available in Vienna at the time, the fact that both visited the same Masonic lodge, they lived in close

proximity, and they had mutual friends or acquaintances makes it impossible for them not to have met. Moreover, Kraus was aware of Mozart's composition of *Le nozze di Figaro* four months before the first official notice that the opera was being written. See HÅ-JMK, 94–95.

27. Åstrand (HÅ-JMK, 95) mistakes Paul for his brother Anton as the alleged student of Kraus.

28. It appears that several symphonies were composed there with the hopes of having them presented at the Concerts spirituels. Unfortunately, these works were eventually published under the names of other composers, and his abortive attempt at an opera, *Oedip*, came to naught after he learned that Antonio Sacchini was writing a work to the same text under the patronage of Queen Marie Antoinette.

29. Vogler, who had no doubt expected to supersede Kraus for this post, was given an "alternative," being named director of music (a nonexistent position) and tutor to the crown prince. It took very little time for him to fall into disfavor, and although relations with Kraus were collegial, they remained cool and distant.

30. The cause of Kraus's death remains unclear. His friends Johann Friedrich Hallardt (1724–1794) and Henrik Engmark stated in their letters to the composer's parents that it was tuberculosis, and biographers have all accepted this diagnosis, several basing it on an early episode of spitting up blood that occurred during Kraus's student years in Göttingen. Because consumption was a conventional cause of death, the actual examination of the symptoms overlooks the fact that only in the last stages of the disease does one cough up blood, and so this symptomatic explanation is unclear. A more reasonable cause may be some sort of pneumonia or bronchial infection, for which there was neither diagnosis nor remedy at the time, and which could under dire circumstances mimic the symptoms of tuberculosis.

31. See HÅ-JMK, 95.

32. Ibid. See also Carl Friedrich Cramer, *Magazin der Musik,* Hamburg, July 26, 1787, 1378. Cramer goes on to state: "They have entry to the most respected houses, where they are always gladly seen. It is not easy to see such virtuosos as these two excellent men depart so reluctantly."

33. *Musikalische Monatsschrift* (Berlin, 1792); see HÅ-JMK, 96. Reichardt also met Kraus in Vienna, where both men sought out Gluck. See his *Autobiographische Schriften* (Halle: MDV Verlag, 2002), 165.

34. Much of this documentation is either in the Silverstolpe family archives, now held by Riksarkivet in Stockholm, or at the University of Uppsala library (Folio X270a and f).

35. Si-JMK, 132.

36. Letter to his father dated Vienna, 9 November 1796: "Er ... hat Kraus als einen homme de génie und den Schöpfer eines neuen Geschmacks in seiner Wissenschaft gekannt." See C. G. Stellan Mörner, *Johan Wikmanson und die Brüder Silverstolpe* (Stockholm: Ivar Hæggströms boktryckeriet, 1952), 310. Casti was a rival to Lorenzo da Ponte and author of librettos for Antonio Salieri, among others, including *Prima la musica e poi le parole.*

37. See LH-JMK, 110–111. In his book *Några Återblickar* Silverstolpe noted: "Welcher Verlust ist nicht diesen Mannes Tod! Ich besitze von ihm eine

Sinfonie, die ich zur Erinnerung an eines der grössten Genies, die ich je gekannt habe, aufbewahre!" (What a loss is not the death of this man! I possess a symphony by him that I preserve in memory of one of the greatest geniuses that I ever knew.)

38. See the letter of 20 June 1798: "An diesem Ort ist dieser Künstler sowohl berühmt als auch estimiert und dank seinen übrigen vielfältigen und gründlichen Kenntnissen auch von den Gelehrten geachtet." See Mörner, *Brüder Silverstolpe*, 332.

39. Reproduced in the present author's article "The Travel Diary of Joseph Martin Kraus: Translation and Commentary," *Journal of Musicology* 8 (1990): 274.

40. He may also have been passing on an official commission for the elder Grenser to supply woodwind instruments to the Stockholm orchestra on behalf of his son.

41. He may also have been passing on correspondence from one of his friends, soprano Franziska Stading, the godchild of both Hummel brothers.

42. See Wolfgang Sawodny, "Einige Bemerkungen zur musikalischen Vorbilduing von Joseph Martin Kraus," in *Joseph Martin Kraus in seiner Zeit*, ed. Friedrich Riedel (Munich and Salzburg: Emil Katzbichler, 1982), 32. The relationship with Arnold is unclear, although it is likely that Kraus intended to use this connection for future commissions, having composed a Miserere for the church in 1775. This commission was to include a Requiem for the death of Joseph II (now lost) that was performed in 1791.

43. The name reads "A. Scheber," possibly Anton, and the most likely conclusion is that he was a musician whom Kraus had met during his travels, possibly related to the bassoonist in Stockholm, Christian Gottlieb Scherber (ca. 1750–1831).

44. This was rediscovered in the city archives in Frankfurt by Gerhard Kölsch and is reprinted in HÅ-JMK, plate 7.

45. The list of these letters, inventoried by Silverstolpe himself, can be found in the present author's *Joseph Martin Kraus (1756–1792): A Systematic-Thematic Catalogue of His Musical Works and Source Study* (Stuyvesant, N.Y.: Pendragon Press, 1998), 331–332, along with a more thorough discussion of the various marks, etc.

46. Handwritten note appended to his catalogue, now Uppsala, University Library, X270a, 50–51. The original reads: "allt hvad som endast innefattat enskilda förhållanden, förtroenden, eller likgiltiga ämnen, har blifvit förstördt." In his biography in a footnote he elucidated on this subject with regard to one letter in highly excerpted form: "Though the reader cannot obtain from this letter a clear understanding of its reason, which probably would not lead to any reality, for it leaves behind it no known trace, nonetheless the letter has a singular interest for our day by presenting the author's degree of education and emotions, his sharp judgmental ability, and its special character. One reads through it without discovering correctly its purpose, nor without clearly seeing the person who speaks. Likewise, the letter that follows next is founded on a rumor, completely without solution, but within which the character speaking is also lying open and will be most satisfactory to the reader." See the present author's *Thematic Catalogue*, 331, and HÅ-JMK, 97.

47. LH-JMK, 113–114.

48. See HÅ-JMK, 96. These letters from Liedemann are at present unpublished.

49. See LH-JMK, 305.

50. LH-JMK, 317.

51. LH-JMK, 305, footnote (unnumbered).

52. The letters by Wolfgang Amadeus Mozart were written to his cousin Maria Anna Thekla Mozart in Augsburg. Much of the "humor" consists of descriptions of bodily functions, as well as "declarations" of love, but it is clear from the context that they have much the same sort of interpersonal connection. For example, writing to her from Mannheim on 13 November 1777, he states: "Do go on loving me as I love you, then we'll never stop loving each other." If taken out of context this could be said to be an ardent confession, but in context – the sentence prior he speaks of defecating – one simply cannot take it seriously. See Spaethling, *Mozart's Letters*, 93.

53. Leux-Henschen (LH-JMK, 12) also notes that "Kraus's surviving letters depict his personal experiences during a short two decades of the waning eighteenth century [Kraus' erhaltene Briefe schildern seine persönlichen Erlebnisse während knap zwei Jahrzehnten des ausgehenden 18. Jahrhunderts]." This undermines her caution.

54. LH-JMK, 13. The complete original sentence reads: "Ausser diesem bewussten Verschweigen wichtiger Umstände und Namen kann man in Kraus' Briefen gelegentlich auf Angaben stossen, bei denen] er offenbar seiner Phantasie recht weiten Spielraum gelassen und Dinge berichtet hat, die mit der Wirklichkeit nicht recht übereinstimmen." The truncation of this sentence by the present author does not change the point made.

55. See the present author's *Thematic Catalogue*, 331–332. This list prefaces the collection in Uppsala and contains various annotation symbols. Silverstolpe wrote an explanation: "The letters that have this marking, -o-, have been used in the biography, either in their entirety or as excerpts [De bref som hafva detta märke, -o-, äro till biographien bilagde, antingen hela, eller i utdrag]." The list has been expanded by the present author to include those that Silverstolpe did not have in his possession, drawn from the Buchen archives and LH-JMK.

56. These are, as noted, LH-JMK and HÅ-JMKB.

57. See Friedrich Noack, "Eine Briefsammlung aus der ersten Hälfte des 19. Jh.," *Archiv für Musikwissenschaft* 10 (1953): 324. The letter was once in the possession of Johann Christian Heinrich Rinck (1770–1846), though how it got there cannot be determined.

58. These are found in the periodical *Mitteilungen der Internationalen Joseph Martin Kraus Gesellschaft* 4 (1985): 21–30 (letters from Kraus's teachers), 5/6 (1986): 1–35 (letters from Kraus's family), and 9/10 (1989): 8–21 (travel diary). The letters from Hoffstetter to Silverstolpe were published in diplomatic transcriptions in Unverricht, *Die beiden Hoffstetter*, which have also been compared with their originals in Uppsala for this book.

59. See LH-JMK, 209. The passport, now preserved in the Bezirksmuseum, Buchen, lists Kraus as *juris licentiat*, or someone having a diploma in jurisprudence. It is certain that this was the result of the composer not having the documentation required to establish credentials as a musician. Carl Stridsberg later noted in his 1798 *Åminnelsetal* that for a period of time this was considered

his "profession" among official acquaintances in Stockholm, and therefore he was seen only as a musical dilettante.

60. The currency issue has been broached by numerous studies, most recently by Christoph Wolff in *Mozart at the Gateway to His Fortune* (New York: Norton, 2012, 197–198), in which he uses a "rough estimate," provided with the help of the Mozart Institute of the Mozarteum Foundation, that 1 Florin Viennese currency is the equivalent to 65–85 United States dollars (or 45–60 Euros) in "comparative purchasing power." It is useful to compare the monetary units versus the list of prices and incomes; using the figures presented, a loaf of bread would be the equivalent cost of ten dollars, which of course, is far too high relative to the normal economy, even for the inflated prices of that time. It does, however, underscore the difficulty in such direct currency conversions and comparisons.

PART TWO

The Letters

1. Letter to his parents dated Göttingen, "the third of the Christ Month" [3 December] 1776

Dearest Parents!

That it is no fun to write letters is certainly true. Did I not have to pay five good pennies[1] for two small uncanceled letters, one to you and one to Herr Kessler[2] in Frankfurt? Moreover, after my own investigation and in my opinion, Göttingen is a wretched hovel. It is a region that doesn't yield to the Odenwald[3] in terms of unfriendliness – very wild all about the place. The size is similar to Aschaffenburg,[4] and in terms of grossness, the inhabitants here have no equal. It seems by my honor that I need to appear so damned Spanish, that I have to organize myself like a Philistine. I had to obtain coffee [or] tea mugs – a half-dozen cups – and even napkins. It was proclaimed *solemnly* by my landlord[5] that: *primo,* I had to pay the quarterly rent promptly upon receipt of the bill, and the lady who attends all five of us for laundry, breakfast, and maid services;[6] *secondo,* he would not stand for any trouble from me; *tertio,* he did not want to get mixed up in my business, so that a simple "Good Morning" or "Good Day" whenever we might meet would suffice. Quite logical conditions. The exchange rate is very high here. The Louis d'or is accepted at 5 Thalers only for food and lodging, but for exchange purposes and other special considerations brings only 4 Thalers 16 Groschen[7] – and in the first instance the Sir Philistines know how to equip themselves so that nothing is lost through it. Ducats[8] too are at 2 Thalers 16 Groschen. To clean shoes and boots one must give the man one Gulden every month, and baths and haircuts, everything down to the last little notion, are excruciatingly expensive. Now something about the professors, as well. As an aside, I have to tell you that it is the fashion here to visit the *Herrn* professors on Sunday morning. The most famous are, in religion: *Walch, Leß, Miller,* in jurisprudence: *Meister, Pütter, Beckmann, von Selchow, Claproth.* In medicine: *Baldinger, Murray, Richter, Gmelin, Blumenbach.* In philosophy: *Michaelis, Kästner, Gatterer, Heyne, Feder, Slözer, Alb. Lud. Frid. Meister, Erxleben, Meiners.* In language arts: *Gall, Martelleur, Ressegaire, Pomais, Gerard, von Colom, Calvi.*[9] With the exception of three or at the most four, all of the others are the most insufferable pedants.

The number of guys[10] has risen now to 900 at the most, and in vain I have guessed at the chaps from home and hoped to meet Herr v[on] Dalberg[11] here. I have already said in my first missive that unfortunately I arrived much too late for this half-year *term.*[12] You can recognize this yourself from the enclosed list of lectures, which already began on the 14th of October[13] – thus I have to study the bulk of things alone for this half year. As a result, I have therefore chosen jurisprudence for myself, and I think I shall be, insofar as possible, satisfied and will satisfy others. In one year alone? I'll tell you, and then you can judge for yourself. In the coming summer *term* I will take *Roman Law* with Meister – the *Canonicum*[14] with Böhmer (who I notice I've forgotten in my previous list of the professors), *Criminal Law* likewise with Meister, *Trial Law* with Beckmann, *Medical Law* or *Natural History,* however it is done, with [either] Wrisberg or Blumenbach,[15] and *Natural Law* with Feder. This being said, all of the professors change about lecturing in every term. The following winter term I will subsequently take *Economics*[16] with Beckmann, *Universal History* with Gatterer, *German Imperial History* with Herr von Selchow, [and] the *General Encyclopedia of the Arts* with Dieze.[17] [Then] all that will be left will be Feudal Law, the *Private Rights of Princes, German Private Rights,* and the divisions of Greek, Hebrew, French, Italian, and English among these, as well as three other courses* – in short, I need two full years. But there you can determine what you will.

*and what is most necessary is the *Practicum*

1a. Continuation of the letter, 6 December 1776

I have awaited letters – in vain – but I would like to receive news of a fortunate change in our fate soon!

Half my baggage has been soaked by the unusually rainy weather, and what infuriates me the most is the abominable thing that the yellow vest and pants[18] are done for – four or five shirts have been colored, and one cannot eradicate the stains through any artifice, and now on to other items. The condition of my own person is not the best. The water here – the air – the most impertinent expenses on God's green earth – everything afflicts me.[19] With regards to all this – I've begun to take medicine and that each day.

COMMENTARY

Original Buchen, Bezirksmuseum. The conclusion of the letter is missing. What survives seems to have been written over the course of several days, with the first two paragraphs separated by some hours only; the reason may be given in the first lines, i.e., the cost of postage. This earliest surviving letter by Kraus is meant to give his parents an idea of both his living circumstances and his intended curriculum. It is also principally an excuse as to why he could not begin his studies even though he has matriculated.

1. Orig. *Groschen,* here translated as "pennies." While this may be an appropriate linguistic translation, the equivalent cost was larger than this implies. The currency in the area near Hannover/ Braunschweig was the Reichsthaler, divided 1 Reichsthaler = 36 Mariengroschen = 8 Pfennige. An equivalent of the period in English currency for the postage thus would be 8 d., or the modern equivalent of US$1.75 (see the Introduction regarding historical exchange rates).

2. Johann Joachim Kessler was the publisher of Kraus's anonymously published drama, *Tolon.*

3. Orig. *Rau,* which according to LH-JMK (185) and HÅ-JMK (14) is a pun on the geographical name of the hills surrounding Göttingen, the Rau-Gebirge, or Wild Mountains.

4. According to city census records of the period, Aschaffenburg had a population in 1750 of about 6,000.

5. Orig. *Hauspatron;* this was cabinetmaker Johann Nikolaus Münder, according to Martin Stahelin, St.-Göttingen, 201. He lived at No. 66 in the Weender Straße.

6. Orig. *Bettmachen,* the equivalent to maid service that extended to cleaning the room.

7. Kraus's further grousing about the various exchange rates is a good example of the difficulties involved in multiple and not mutually inclusive currencies in circulation at that time. Thus the dual rate – 1 Louis d'or = 5 Reichthalers for "necessities," but otherwise 4 Reichthalers 16 Groschen – reflects a substantial

discount. Using a conversion calculator, the former would be equal to £1. 2s. 6d., which would be the approximate equivalent of US$75–150; the second rate would make 1 Louis d'or = £1, a more even rate of exchange.

8. Orig. *Die Herr Philister,* probably refers mainly to Münder and the various Göttingen merchants (see no. 5 of this commentary).

9. The professors are (in order) Johann Georg Walch (1693–1775), Gottfried Leß (1736–1797), Johann Peter Miller (1725–1789), Albrecht Ludwig Friedrich Meister (1724–1788), Johann Stephan Pütter (1725–1807), Johann Beckmann (1739–1811), Johann Heinrich Christian von Selchow (1732–1795), Julius Claproth (1728–1805), Ernst Gottfried Baldinger (1738–1804), Johann Andres Murray (1740–1791), August Gottlieb Richter (1742–1812), Johann Friedrich Gmelin (1748–1800), Johann Friedrich Blumenbach (1752–1840), Johann David Michaelis (1717–1791), Abraham Gotthelf Kästner (1719–1800), Johann Christoph Gatterer (1727–1799), Christian Gottlob Heyne (1729–1812), Johann Georg Heinrich Feder (1740–1821), August Ludwig Schlözer (1735–1809), Johann Polycarp Erxleben (1744–1777), Christoph Meiners (1747–1810), Frances Martelleur (1734–1788), Bernhard Ressegaire (1743–1793), Franciscus Pomais, Alexander Gérard (1728–1795), Isaac von Colom DuClos (1708–1795), and Johann Baptista Calvi (1721–1807). Pomais probably refers to François Pomey, the namesake of a famous theologian and philologist from half a century earlier, but Gall is unidentified. Kraus's original orthography is insecure; for instance, he misspells "Leder" for "Feder," and he seems unaware that Walch had in fact died the year prior to his arrival.

10. Orig. *Purschen* (e.g., *Burschen*), meaning male students. Martin Stahelin estimates the number at about 773; see "Joseph Martin Kraus in Göttingen," *Göttinger Jahrbuch* (1992) [hereafter St-Göttingen]: 202.

11. The reference is to Johann Friedrich Hugo Freiherr von Dalberg (1760–1811), later governor of Erfurt, who arrived only in the spring of 1777 to attend the university. His brother, Carl Theodor Freiherr von Dalberg (1744–1817) was shortly to become elector-archbishop of Mainz.

12. Kraus actually matriculated on 26 November 1776 as "Josephus Krautse, Moguntius." See Gotz von Selle, *Die Matrikel der Georg-August-Universität zu Göttingen* (Hildesheim, Leipzig: A. Lax, 1937), 226, No. 10666. The list of classes or lectures has not survived, nor has his first letter referred to here.

13. Orig. *Weinmonate.*

14. Orig. *Pandenken. Canonicum* refers to *Jus canonicum,* or the canon law of the Roman Catholic Church. The professor is Georg Ludwig Böhmer (1715–1797).

15. The professor is Heinrich August Wrisberg (1739–1808).

16. Orig. *Camerale,* or business and finances of a state treasury.

17. The professor is Johann Andreas Dieze (1729–1785), who was also omitted from Kraus's earlier list.

18. The clothing described by Kraus seems to be of a type that was faddish among young men in Germany following the publication of Johann Wolfgang von Goethe's *Die Leiden des jungen Werthers* in 1774.

19. The "medicine" and his state of health are probably signs of hypochondria, as can be inferred by the jocular tone of the letter.

2. Letter presumably to his parents dated
Göttingen, 20 January 1777

Now I must let you know that in my boring world I play the role of polymath. How is that going? Quite naturally. There are many people here who through their self-informed comings and goings made my head spin so much that I truly thought myself an idiot. Perhaps I was right. Then I came, took off my domino mask, and looked upon the contentious triflers *in natura*.[1] When I say that the matter pleased the *Spektatoribus*,[2] as well as the respective *Auditoribus,* I began to demonstrate the truth of the law with geography, argued philosophy with music, interpreted the German with the Italian, and thought myself ever so grand. *Note bene,* it is the fashion here.

COMMENTARY

Original lost; published in Swedish translation as No. 1 in Si-JMK, 38. The lack of salutation and conclusion denotes that it is perhaps a very small excerpt from a much longer letter. Silverstolpe's copy of the German original (Folio X270f) is cursory, and therefore the exact context of this rather vague letter is lacking. It is possible, however, that Kraus was commenting upon either his social networking or some of the specific seminars he attended.

1. *In natura* = as they really are.

2. *Spektoribus* = spectators or observers; *Auditoribus* = listeners or audience.

3. Letter to his parents dated Göttingen, "one week, 4 days, 9 hours before Easter" [i.e., either 8 April or 18 March] 1777[A]

Dearest Parents!

I have received your last two letters at the same time. I thank you a thousand times for all your great care and love, for all of the good memories. What else can I do but to wish that I can make myself worthy of all

A. These dates would depend upon which calendar Kraus was using; according to the Julian calendar still in use in parts of Germany, the date would be 4 April 1777, but if the Gregorian, 18 March. Kraus himself is imprecise, noting with excruciatingly lacunar detail "Eine Woche, 4 Tage, 9 Stunden vor Ostern."

this over time. May my dear father's days be happy – he should think no more of the distress and for the rest – may it not last long! Driven away as the result of the blessing of the Almighty! So, Herr Lorkandt[1] is beginning again to add more to our misfortune?

> Oh, it will certainly happen one day –
> Where deceitfulness, misanthropy, and evil ripen –
> Oh, his lot will be the certain plague –
> When his heart becomes hell to him![2]

We ought to think well of him, as it says in our moral code. But those who laugh cannot also turn aside from their torment, if the overt and covert afflictions affect others.

My dear mother wants to know about the story of *Tolon*? It is inconsequential. Some of the gentlemen critics had at me – I played my trump – there was dirty laundry, and whoever had to dry it was a native master. *À propos*[3] – the *Nürnberger gelehrte Zeitung* and *Das erste Stück des kritischen Archivs* have had a relatively good laugh at my expense. I could also have done the same – *Tolon* is *Tolon* and remains thus – it has its mistakes – fine – but these mistakes too have their reasons. Nothing has become of my operetta project, for the Herrn Östreicher[4] only wanted good phlegmatic prose – *proficiat!*[5]

Perhaps I should have been more concerned over this matter, were I not working on a *review of modern music*.[6] God knows when the thing will be finished. What people, large and small, young and old, will say about this, I'll learn eventually.

I did not receive the letter from Herr Chamberlain von Bentzel[7] from Herr Kessler but rather in a letter from you, [that is,] if what you mean is whatever this gentleman sent to you on the 5th of January.

Now, to come to something real. There was nothing that could be done about the cloth, for nothing is *contraband* merchandise here, but rather much, indeed most has an *impertinent excise* tax imposed, by my soul. To avoid these *formaliter et cathegorice*[8] is a matter of conscience to me. The merchant or middleman ought not to write on it *ex[empli] gr[atia]:*[9] *Cloth* or *Merchandise,* but rather only *Violins and Music,* etc. Then all will go well. I shall remain at my lodgings for the summer, for my gross Philistine and I are now bosom buddies. I am an American – he an Englishman. Damn, we often arrange *colloquia* that could not be more scholarly. For example, he begins: "If I were King of England, that is, my most merciful King and Lord, . . ."

> *Exceptio:* "It would surely not be possible to drum up the three million immediately."

> *Replica:* "That would be a miracle. Here *in loco* are alone eight or nine thousand souls, so *per grudas* multiplied from one *locus* to the next I would certainly *exfluirt* as many troops as I wanted."

> *Duplica:* "But what it if the Americans also did this?"

> *Sententia definit:* "One must *strictissime* forbid them!"

and rightly so.[10]

Who would not like this guy for his philosophy?

Herr Franz has heavenly Rhine wine[11] – it tastes wonderful! Give my heartfelt greetings to everyone, sisters and brothers. In my and your names I shall send in my next [letter] to you a petition to H[is] E[lectoral] G[race] and a letter to Herr v[on] Straus,[12] covered so that you can forward it to the right place.

Is this not an abominable scribble? No I shall read through the letter once more, and, as briefly as I can, keep silent about another honorable man.

> *Hee Haw! – Doctorum, magistorum et supradoctorum*
> *Manus vident ex, ut palpæ asinorum –*[13]

If I am not reckoned among one of the three categories, at least I too shall end up in [-]*orum.*

Send money soon

Your

Good Joseph

[P.S.]I shall remain owing Herr Knörzer[14] an answer until after Easter.

COMMENTARY

Original Buchen, Bezirksmuseum. This letter is the first written intimation of Kraus's involvement in his father's three-year suspension for financial irregularities, which themselves inspired the composer to write and publish the tragedy *Tolon*.[B] It is clear from the content and veiled allusions that he is both hard at work on the issue, hoping to contribute to the favorable resolution of the difficulties, and still contemptuous of the university and its values.

1. Franz Joseph Lorkant, who according to Helmut Brosch was the temporary occupant of Bernhard Kraus's position and the instigator of the allegations that led to the criminal proceedings against the elder Kraus. The latter was eventually exonerated (though found guilty) and reinstated with a figurative slap on the wrist, though the process was to take several years and cause much anxiety for the family, as can be read already in this letter.

2. Orig. *O! deß wart gewiß an einem Tage/wo Arglist, Menschenhaß und Bösheit reift/O Seiner ward die sichre Plage/Wenn ihm sein Herz zur Hölle wird!* It is unknown from which play this obvious quote was taken. It does not, however, appear to have originated in Kraus's own *Tolon*.

3. Orig. *a propus,* in this case meaning "such as"; the reviews were published in the *Nürnbergischen Gelehrte Zeitung,* third issue, dated 11 January 1777, as well as in the *Allgemeines kritisches Archiv* (Frankfurt am Main: Eichenbergische Erben, 1777), 1:90–92. Both reviewers were anonymous. It is curious matter that the second review appeared with the same publisher that Kraus himself was to use later for his own "review of modern music." (See comment 6 below).

4. The "Operette" project was apparently, from the context, one for which Kraus was exploring the writing of a libretto. The two "Herrn Östreicher" are not identifiable.

5. *Proficiat* = original Latin something like "Thus I have stated," but used here as a typical Kraus expression to mean "So there!" Modern German and Dutch use the term to mean "Congratulations" for a propitious event, which does not fit Kraus's usage.

6. The "review of modern music" refers to *Etwas von und über Musik fürs Jahre 1777* (Frankfurt am Main: Eichenbergische Erben, 1778; fac. ed., ed. Friedrich W. Reidel, Munich and Salzburg: Emil Katzbichler, 1977), as will become clear in subsequent letters.

7. Orig. *H. Hk. Von Benzel,* meaning Anselm Franz Freiherr von Bentzel-Sternau (1738–1786), chamberlain of the Electorate of Mainz and one of those to whom Kraus appealed on his father's behalf. Kessler refers to the publisher of *Tolon.*

8. *Formaliter et cathegorice* = officially and categorically.

9. *Exempli gratia,* or free samples, which were subject to an excise customs tax as salable merchandise; Kraus is attempting to avoid paying duty.

10. This is a satirical example of a scholarly rhetorical debate, no doubt mirroring his jurisprudential training. The allusion is to the American War for Independence, which was reaching its culmination at the time and which

B. See Helmut Brosch, "Die Jugendjahre des Joseph Martin Kraus in Buchen," K II, 16–25. This article contains a complete description of the official events surrounding the allegations and punishment directed at Bernhard Joseph Kraus (1724–1804).

was the subject of newsworthy interest throughout Europe.

11. "Herr Franz" is probably a reference to a local barkeep, and one might suggest that the "Rheinwein" was a Riesling Sylvaner.

12. The reference is to Gottlieb August Maximilian von Strauß (1738–1796), the *Staats- und Konferenzminister* for the Electorate of Mainz.

13. An oblique reference to the subject of Kraus's scorn. The doggerel, which begins with a written-out cry (*I-nu*),[C] is a clever Latin pun, which translates as: "The hooves of doctors, masters, and super-doctors are like the jaws of a donkey." His comment that follows shows that he expected at some point to become one of this distinguished crowd, leaving unsaid but clearly intended to be read between the lines: "if I continue to write along these lines."

14. "Herr Knörzer" is unidentified, but if it does not refer to a real person, it may well represent a nickname derived from *Knorzer,* meaning a knot in wood, or, in colloquial terms, "knothead." If so, then it may be suggested that this was a member of his family or a close friend, possibly even his brother Franz Anton Leonhard Kraus (1760–1791).

4. Letter to his brother Franz dated Göttingen, "such and such – it was before Easter" 1777

My brother!

In the name lies everything that I feel when a pure, righteous love takes an interest in me and my destiny. I love you with all my heart, and even more I am happy that you love me too. Would that finally your terrible circumstances[1] disappear completely!

Because I have begged you for the *oratorio,*[2] can you surmise the wretched state of music here? This conclusion was, strictly speaking, not entirely logical: but you have hit it on the head. Consider that there are between 800 and 900 fellows – 300 of which are certainly music lovers, for there is no dearth of good and bad pieces – and therefore do not wonder about a concert that in its fashion could not have been more miserable! Why? Among these 300 music lovers are not to be found three knowledgeable. Such a confusion of dabblers – bunglers – [and] self-proclaimed virtuosi I have not seen in one spot in all my days as here. By my poor soul! Anything that looks like a note eludes them. That

C. As Martin Stahelin notes (St-Göttingen, 216), this was probably an attempt to imitate the cry of an ass, which in modern German is "*I-A.*" The translation follows the English equivalent.

notwithstanding, I have already composed two large symphonies, one large vocal motet with two recitatives and two arias, and one sinfonia concertante with four solo parts, i.e., violin, viola, flute, and cello, with eight ripieno parts.[3] You will have them eventually. You should have seen the nonsense! I brought the first symphony to a private concert that takes place every Monday and Thursday at the house of *Professor Pütter*.[4] *Pütter* himself conducted. *Holla* – how the bows struck! Begun! Within twenty bars it was already *formal* chaos. Now the violins hunted the bass, the bass the viola, and the viola the seconds – the oboes quacked a bit alongside, and horns very wisely shut up. Thus it went! The most splendid thing about it was this, that all of the gentlemen imagined that they had done it wonderfully well. Now the second symphony went up. Shot to hell![5] Oh, my poor symphony! If the first was broken asunder, then the second was burned alive without mercy, and that in due course.

You are right – the desk is more valuable if I were to obtain it from England myself.[6] When will that occur? That will have to be figured out at home!

I wish my sisters happiness *solemniter*[7] with hat in hand and freshly washed stockings, as well as Mademoiselle Barbé[8] ten times over for her nameday now three months past, and I appoint you with full authority as proxy to bestow upon the three aforementioned maidens all *beneficia juris inclusive* in Rastad measure.[9] *To bestow*? Is that right? That is a little term for you!

In Buchen they lie horribly – you say? They do that here too – *me Hercle!*[10] If one takes all of the Americans together that have been shot dead, stabbed, hacked down, clobbered, knocked about, drowned, etc., you could pave all nine of the Electorates with them.

How high was Mt. *Sinai*? Here's a *polemic – critic – historico – dogmatic – biblioco – philosophico – mosaic – logico – Theologico quaestio*[11] – in short – a fundamental question for you.

Therefore – How tall was Mt. *Sinai*?

"Herr Pastor! This tall!"

"No!"

"This tall – this tall, Herr Pastor."

"No, my children – you have not guessed it."

"Then tell us, Herr Pastor!"

"Quite so, my children, you are all curious, and that is a *virtus optima.*

"Therefore, I repeat my question. How high really was Mt. *Sinai?*

The answer: On really can't say. Ay! Ay! Ay!

τοῦτο γαρ ἐτιν, ὁ ἀει προχειται τῳ χαλῳ χαι ἀγαθῳ. q[uod] e[rat] d[emonstrandum][12]

My Herr Colleague, the Herr Composer Pfister greets me *ex officio collegiali*[13] with the postscript that I must this very hour construct something on his excellent letter on the com- and addposition, as well as the musical blending of the Mass. For his edification I shall send him a nonauthorized recipe for an Easter Mass or (because doubtless I will be too late) for a Mass for Pentacost.

Recipe.

Κυριε Coegel Op. 1 No. 3[14]

Φουγα *Schmidtiana tota*

Γλορια It is finished! – *ad libitum*[15]

Laudamus – old is not new – $\frac{2}{3}$ IV[16]

Cum Sancto – Three penitents have escaped through the gate – Adieu!$\frac{2}{3}$[17]

Credo – this depends upon what he believes in most.[18]

Incarnatus. He needs to sing this solo "woo-hoo" in falsetto.

The Herr *Cantor Senior accompanies* on the organ

principaliter after the composition *in die tam clara.*[19]

Crucifixus – this is not needed, because the above will already sound miserable enough.[20]

Et resurrexit – ave maria – ipse fecit.[21]

Sanctus – for a greater sound the congregation can sing along. O! O! O![22]

Pleni – let Schmidt rest in his grave in peace!

Hosanna – we'll give him this one this time.[23]

Benedictus. My brother Franz will sing this with marvelous woodenness

after the composition

of the *Gloria* with the violin solo from Vogler's *Miserere,* which the Herr Com- and Addpositor should play himself with the proviso, that he not

stick a

Sardine on his fiddle, so that it is not too soft.[24]

Agnus dei – the march – Tum Tum-te-rum – *ipse fecit*.[25]
Dona nobis pacem – yes, sir – only with the town council! according to the composition rēmdĕdĕdēm. The last *dem* must be repeated, if one wishes to exit with a correct hexameter.[26]

Nonauthorized is how I want to give it to the Herr Composer, just in case a performance of the Mass should go like that recently with the *symphony* that Herr *Greich*[27] wrote me about, and in order to settle his peptic stomach caused by his full-on rage, a good glass of schnapps is to be recommended, *probatum est.*

Just so you don't think that your brother has suddenly gone weak in the head, here you have a *frustum* of my travelogue *en miniature* – I don't have the rest right at hand. Even if you can't read everything, it is all the same. There, where one first looks upon *Kassel*,[28] my beloved brother, I had one small glass of wine too much for my head. I wasn't drunk – Pfui! – who would think of something so obscene? To this I remain

Your brother Joseph

COMMENTARY

Original, Buuchen, Bezirksmuseum. This playful and satirical letter was prompted both by Kraus's disgust at the musical environment at Göttingen and also by the failings of a former teacher in Buchen, who had evidently sent him a "revision" of one of his oratorios into a Mass.[D] The "recipe" contains a compendium of the sort of musical hodgepodge he considered reprehensible and later castigated severely in both his letters and his treatise *Etwas von und über Musik*, the "review of modern music" noted earlier.

1. Orig. *böser Zustand*. His brother had been assaulted by bullies, who in the course of their beating had given him a severe concussion, which in turn had caused extensive nerve damage that prevented him from continuing his studies or embarking upon a career.

2. The *Oratorium* refers to one of the two he composed for Buchen the previous year, either *Die Geburt Jesu* (VB 17) or *Der Tod Jesu* (VB 18)

3. See the letter of 28 December 1777 for a complete list of works composed to that time and since arriving in Göttingen.

4. Professor Johann Stephan Pütter was also an amateur musician who apparently conducted an equally amateur

D. This has been proven to be the Mass in E minor (VB A/1), which is mentioned in the letter from Kraus's sister Marianne to Silverstolpe dated May 28, 1801.

orchestra twice weekly during portions of the school year. The two symphonies by Kraus that were performed probably belong to a set of six works for two oboes, two horns, and strings that he composed during the first months in Göttingen; see the letter of 28 December.

5. Orig. *Frisch in die Hände gespukt,* or literally "freshly spit into the hands." An equivalent colloquial meaning has been used, though others, such as "blown out of the water," would also work in a generic sense.

6. Kraus has obviously requested a writing desk of some sort, with the inference that it is of English manufacture.

7. *Solenniter* = solemnly.

8. *Mademoiselle Barbé* probably refers to his deaf sister, Anna Barbara (1755–1807).

9. *Beneficia juris inclusive* = all of the lawful benefits; a "Rastatt measure (*Rastadter Maas*)" is a pun on a village outside the town of Rastatt, Maas, which was known for the fertility of the soil; the real meaning would translate to "in abundance."

10. *Me Hercle* = "By Hercules." The allusion to the "Americans" that follows reflects his interest in the American War for Independence and its causes, which as noted earlier were topical conversations among intellectuals of the time; today, his would be considered a progressive point of view; cf. the previous letter.

11. The anecdote is clearly a paraphrase of a pompous schoolmaster giving an incomprehensible parable to the students, described here as a "polemical, critical, historical, dogmatic, biblical, philosophical, Mosaic, logical, theological" issue. The students obviously take it literally, but the teacher obfuscates, probably itself a reference to the convoluted logic of the entire legal complaint against his father.

12. Recte τοῦτο γάρ ἐδτιν ὃ προκεῖται τῷ καὶ ἀγαθῷ or "This is what always awaits the person who is good and noble," along with a common Latin epitaph "Thus is it demonstrated."[E]

13. The reference is to Rector Georg Pfister (1730–1807), schoolmaster in Buchen and one of Kraus's earliest teachers, and possibly the butt of the parable just noted. The "recipe" refers to a Mass that Pfister concocted from Kraus's oratorio *Die Geburt Jesu,* as his sister makes clear in a letter to Silverstolpe dated 28 May 1801 (in appendix B). This is the so-called Mass in E minor (VB A/1), which she also sent to the diplomat. This "recipe" is replete with Greek, Latin, and German puns, not to mention "normal" movements spelled in the Greek alphabet. This is no doubt in response to the now-lost letter from Pfister to Kraus, informing him of his reworking of the oratorio and asking his opinion. In calling him *ex officio collegiali,* or a composer/addposer, he turns back the salutation with a sarcastic mild insult.

14. For the *Kyrie* (written in Greek), Kraus recommends the third piece in a set of trite keyboard sonatas published in 1746 as the *Obiectum pinnarum tactilium* by Pater Peregrinus Pögl (1711–1788), which were used to teach school children

E. I would like to thank my colleagues Diane Johnson and Eileen Osterhaus for their help in finding the proverb, correcting Kraus's Greek, and making an accurate translation.

throughout the Holy Roman Empire (here misspelled deliberately as "Coegel"); alongside this he states that one should "fugue [Latin, written in the Greek alphabet] Schmidt to death," a probable reference to Ferdinand Schmid (1694–1756), a Viennese composer of quirky and extremely rigid contrapuntal works that were likewise performed widely much in the manner of those by Pögl.

15. *Gloria* (written in Greek letters); the orig. statement, *Nun ist geschehn*, to be performed in whatever manner the performers desire (*ad libitum*) is a gloss on one of the last words of Christ on the cross, but with the implication "Now you've done it!"

16. Orig. *Alt ist nicht neu*, the meaning of which is unclear, but may advise Pfister to plagiarize a piece from some older work and alter its meter or rhythm to fit the fraction.

17. This is a pun on the folk song "Es ritten drei Ritter zum Tore hinaus! Adieu!" Kraus replaces the term "Knight" (*Ritter*) with the synonym "Penitent" (*Reuter*), subsequently completely altering the meaning.

18. That is, the movement must be taken with a grain of salt to be believed.

19. Orig. *Das singt Er* [presumably Pfister] *Solo Hu He durch die Fistel*. Herr Cantor Senior refers to Bernhard Franz Wendler (1702–1782), another of Kraus's early teachers in Buchen. The admonition is to use only the highest stops on the organ "in order to make it sound clear" (or *in die tam clara* = as if on a clear day).

20. The implication is that the music itself has already been crucified.

21. The *Ave Maria* is a pun with the context of the modern expostulation "Oh Lord!" One can almost imagine

Kraus's eyes rolling, with the colophon *ipse fecit*, or "he did that all by himself."

22. Kraus means that the small Buchen church choir can be augmented (badly) with congregational singing.

23. The *pleni sunt coeli* of the arrangement seems to have been also set as a fugue, which explains the admonition to leave Schmid's remains be after "fugueing" him to death in the *Kyrie*; magnanimously, Kraus lets Pfister have the *Osanna in excelsis*.

24. This description of the *Benedictus* is riddled with puns. His brother is asked to perform "without pay" (*unentgeldlich*, a likely pun on *unentbehrlich*, or "indispensably") with "marvelous woodenness" (*wunderbarer Holzseeligkeit*, a play on *wunderbarer Holdseeligkeit*, or "magnificent sweetness"), accompanied by Pfister on his violin (*Geige*, here in this context a folk fiddle), upon which he is to place a "sardine" (*Sardine*, a pun on *Sordine*, or mute). The composition referred to is Abbé Georg Joseph Vogler's Miserere in E-flat major composed about 1775, one of that musician's first compositions to gain recognition outside of Mannheim.

25. Orig. *Tum Tumterum*, or a stereotypical march rhythm of dotted-half-quarter-eighth-quarter; the *ipse fecit* implies that all of the music is entirely to be by Pfister.

26. This entire reference pokes fun at the insertion of nonsense syllables in order to shoehorn the extant music into the text; the example, of course, is poetic pentameter, not hexameter, but the implication is that Pfister won't know the difference.

27. The identity of "Herr Greich" is not known. It may well be an epithet referring to Pfister, who informed him

of the performance of one of his Buchen symphonies, done in a manner apparently identical to the Göttingen performance described earlier.

28. Orig. *Dort wo Kassel steht oben an,* or the place where one first sights the city of Kassel. Kraus evidently made a brief trip there, though his travelogue has not survived. The *frustum* (summary or excerpt) is likewise lost.

5. Letter to his parents dated Göttingen, 20 April 1777

Much beloved parents!

I received the letter along with the money on the 18th of this month. To be sure, I would have wished that I had received them earlier and together, but it was not to be, and I still hope to receive the remainder before the beginning of the last quarter. The cloth pouch with the violin has not yet arrived. There must have been an error – or did the procurer think that there would yet be time enough. It pleases me no end that you are as well as I could wish, and I desire that this will also be the same for me. The holidays were the most unpleasant that I could ever have experienced for myself. All of my good projects were ruined by a twofold attack of spitting up blood, and along with that came a persistent cough that was not at all welcome to me.[1] Fun? Healthy boys have sailed away with all the fun, and unfortunately I had no desire [to join them]. By my poor soul! It was a miserable[2] period for me – the best invitation was a canceled trip to Erfurt – to an extraordinarily good glass of Rhine wine in the north, everything, everything answered itself with a no. Now things are going well again, and I also now think that I have become used to fare which on God's green earth one cannot find worse. *Ex[empli] gratia.* Today I had soup – green pea with a slice of sausage – beef with horseradish that is properly prepared quite appetizingly with small and large raisins, and a bratwurst in a *Soce pyderiable.*[3] That was a feast! Ah well, one doesn't have anything else, for the poor nuns at Poor Clara[4] in Mainz have to eat vegetables sautéed in oil, and in my soup there were nineteen blobs of fat.[5] *Proficiat!*

Just now I've stood up from the table – six courses including bread and water. Blessed supper! – Thanks very much. – It tasted delicious.

Herr von Dalberg was here with three of his herd, the first of which was his tutor *Pfeiffer* who has the title of state councilor; the second his servant, and the third *Schmidt,* who is a student at Mainz.[6] Dalberg is polite – friendly – in short, a much beloved male doll. He laughs quite politely – can play the keyboard very prettily – draws with a red pencil – wears quite a fine waistcoat, and is above all else a man from *Mainz*[7] – May the D[evil] take them all! For I am so grieved to the heart by the entire *nation* that I would not want to be reconciled to them even on my deathbed.

The 26th.[8]

Today the chest finally arrived. I give you my unbounded thanks once more for everything. I am enclosing the petition[9] – I hope it helps! I've forgotten again to put the address on the outside, but you can do this yourselves.

My brother with all my sisters and good friends I give a thousand greetings

I am your obedient son, Joseph.

[P.S.] Think also of me, that I need the remaining money before the end of *June*. Perhaps I'll see a little something before the year is out. If God wills it! It should be as I would wish it.

I don't know any more the title on the memorandum and to the state councilor, [but] my sister can write it on it.

Arrange it so that the second portion of the money is here by *Johannis*.[10]

COMMENTARY

Original Buchen, Bezirksmuseum. This is the first "official" letter to his parents following the satirical one to his brother Franz. This one clearly was written following the usual university break that occurred around Easter time. He paints a different picture for them, his financial supporters, than for his brother, particularly with regard to his travels. Instead, he notes his culinary feast as a diversion.

1. It seems clear that Kraus reports his illness during the break (though see the previous letter), but the *Anfall von Blutspeien* was probably not, as earlier scholars have indicated, an indication of tuberculosis, even with a cough, for this symptom generally occurs only during the last stages of this disease.

2. Orig. *hundsfütisch,* or like a son of a bitch.

3. *Soce pyrderiable* = perpetual sauce, or an herbed gravy.

4. The Poor Clara Cloister (*Armerklarakloster*) refers to the Mainz nunnery where his sister Katharina Josepha (1758–1781) lived.

5. Orig. *Fettaugen,* or eyes of fat.

6. Dalberg (see letter of 3 December 1776) was later canon of Worms, Trier,

and Speyer. He was an amateur composer and poet. *Pfeiffer* is probably Johan
Friedrich von Pfeiffer (1717–1787), the
state councilor for several small German
states. *Schmidt* is Peter Heinz Schmidt, a
student from Erfurt who matriculated at
the university there on 11 April 1777.

    7. Orig. *ein Mainzer.*

    8. The letter was clearly concluded
on 26 April.

    9. The petition refers to an inter-
cession to the state minister Count
Friedrich Wilhelm von Sickingen on
behalf of his father.

    10. *Johannis* = the saint's name day, or
14 June.

6. Letter to his mother dated Göttingen, 20 May 1777

My dear Frau Mother!

    I will take care of everything that you have written me concerning the petition. Now two prospects have opened up for me all at once. One [is] in Copenhagen[1] and the other in Zweibrücken. The former is employment in music, and the latter a sort of confidential and dictation-taking secretary. Of course, the first appealed to me best,[2] but the conditions about it were somewhat difficult, which was not according to my taste. And with the last, I do not know the gentleman yet, nor the situation. I have decided to make a trip to Zweibrücken and look around. If this is satisfactory, please be good and send me my money so that I have it in time, for I need to take with me as much travel funds as I need. The costs will be nothing more than traveling money, for court councilor *Hahn*[3] in Zweibrücken has offered that I can stay and board with him as long as I am there, and I have accepted that something may come of the trip. My beloved F[rau] Mother, good-bye and think about it.

    Your obedient [son]

    Joseph

    Greetings to my sisters.

P.S. If you agree to my trip, I would ask that you don't tell anyone about it in advance.

COMMENTARY

Original Buchen, Bezirksmuseum. The letter is addressed: *à Madame/Madame Krausz née Schmidt/pst./à Maience.* This short confidential missive is unusually directed solely to his mother, with the postscript implying that he was hoping that his father would not be party to it. This in turn implies that he expected that his mother would fund the travel through her household allowance rather than from his own quarterly school funds. The formal and awkward salutation and address of the envelope is unusual and contrived.

1. Nothing is known about any musical position in Copenhagen, since that seems not to have been a vacancy at that time. The "difficult" conditions probably alluded to this; see the next letter.

2. Orig. *Natürell,* or natural disposition, i.e., was appealing to Kraus, as translated here.

3. Hofrat Hahn is Johann Christoph Hahn (1721–1781), the father of Kraus's close Göttingen friend Johann Friedrich Hahn (1753–1779), who probably arranged for the offer of employment for a French gentleman (see next letter).

7. Letter to his parents dated Göttingen, 11 June 1777

Dearest Parents!

Nothing has come of my project in Zweibrücken. The conditions were more than bad, and the most wretched thing of all was to acknowledge as my lord a Frenchman, who wants to keep a German for the fun of it. I am happy that the ending was just like the beginning. Immediately after my arrival, I was with the [friends from] Zweibrücken, through whom I had the acquaintance of H[err] von Commin,[1] who had just returned from Leipzig where he wanted to learn German. He was going from here to Paris via Zweibrücken, where he acquired an *appetite* for a German fool – I cannot put it better. In the beginning the thing appealed to me by reason of which I would have had the opportunity in the easiest manner to become fluent in his language and in this fashion make my way through France, for my dear Herr von Commin had his home in Marseilles. But, everything vanished. He wrote me from Strasbourg (and I shall give you a portion of his letter [which I have] translated into German):

> "I shall expect you as early as possible in Zweibrücken, where I will surely arrive next month. The conditions will please you without doubt, for they are easy and certainly very respectable. What does this mean? Each day you will speak and read German with me for three hours. You will have board and room free, and a stipend that is *bon*.[2] If within a half a year you no longer have any German in you, then I shall modify them. I hope to get everything from you and more than the ten German beasts that I had in my service in Leipzig, Berlin, etc."

Ha! The fellow! To treat Germans like this – he has had *ten* already that didn't want him to make a fool of them and then he came to me!

I said good-bye to the fool and he to me, so everything was fine. I am deeply indebted to Councilor Hahn, whose son studies here, for his hospitality.

In Denmark[3] – who gave you that ridiculous description? Had I gone to Hamburg with *Claudius*,[4] who passed through here on his way from Darmstadt to Hamburg and made me an offer, I subsequently would have been able to travel across comfortably with Count von Stollberg,[5] who departed a few weeks ago – it doesn't concern me. A knowledge of music and the stage was required, and for that I felt myself well-endowed. But – to obtain a position that is now occupied but not maintained by *Baumgarten*[6] – my pride will not allow. Pride? Truly, it is nothing that is good for anything nowadays. But – God knows – it is in my nature, not *affectation,* be it a foible or human nature. I would rather creep about and lick the feet of despots for my sustenance; I would rather be uncouth, if I could not make my life bearable through my own strength. Our Elector bears witness daily in Erfurt and now in Heiligenstadt how popular and human he is – or has become. There are often times when I want to go over there and tell him myself what we desire. But – then I think about what he has done – reflect upon our misfortune that was done at his hands. Ha! My heart and courage rise when I think – Look at the chap! That man that you praised – you have twisted yourself like a worm in front of that man. When I think of this, it fills me with loathing.[7] I am in agreement with myself – it will cost hungry days and years – I am not obligated to be grateful to my fatherland. *Patriotism* is idiocy,[8] and the last spark has long been extinguished. On foreign shores my happiness awaits me. And if I don't find it, what does it matter? Does not the number of those who have lived in unhappiness and died outweigh those that are forever happy? Is it not a true blessing to strive against the storms of one's own fate and be as patient as a wanderer?

I know nothing new about the Mainz neighbors and Herr v[on] Dalberg is just like all the other people from Mainz. God! When I think of Reider,[9] my teeth gnash! But –

Today I am writing to Kessler about a manuscript.[10] For all I care, he either accepts it or not – if the latter, off it goes to Leipzig. It is about music. Ha! One has to take the idols by their heads, shake them by their rear ends, and mock them!

I thank you most obediently for the money, as I shall also the secretary of the post in F[rank]furt for the aggravation.

H[err] Knörzer I wish all the best in his position – my mentor of everything good.

My sisters – my brother – you know what you can demand of my heart.

Good friends – those you do not have – and therefore commend me to good acquaintances.

Your Joseph

[P.S.] Why hasn't *Benzel* answered me? Is he also a *man of Mainz*?

COMMENTARY

Original Buchen, Bezirksmuseum. The letter contains the address: *Monsieur/ Monsieur Krausz Baili/d[e] S[on] A[ltesse] E[lectorale] de Maience/à Buchen/p Miltenberg.* It is clear that the travel funding asked for in such an awkward manner in the previous letter was forthcoming. The frustration with the officials of the electorate and his family's situation is apparent throughout.

1. Exact identity unknown but most likely a member of the noble Commin de Comminge family from Provence.

2. It is obvious that the *bon* (good) stipend was unsuitable to Kraus, though apparently not to his putative employer. Kraus strives to maintain the insulting tone of Commin's letter to him.

3. This refers to an unknown travelogue about Denmark that must have been fictitious but that his parents read with considerable trepidation, considering the offhand remark about a "situation" in Copenhagen in the previous letter.

4. Matthias Claudius (1740–1815), one of the leading poets of the time, a mentor of the Göttinger Hainbund literary group, and a favorite poet of Kraus,

whose verses he often set later. The intimation is that Kraus became enough of an adherent of the group for the poet to deal with him.

5. Friedrich Leopold Graf von Stolberg (1750–1819), also a member of the circle and a poet in his own right.

6. Most likely Karl Friedrich Baumgarten (ca. 1740–1824), a composer resident in Lübeck. He did not actually retain an absentee post in Copenhagen, nor did he compose for the stage.

7. Orig. *Spei ichs mir ins Gesicht* ("I spit into my own face"), a colloquialism from the time that is akin to the modern *Es ist mir alles zum speien* ("Everything is spit to me"). The translation as "fills me with loathing" reflects the euphemism, though it is not entirely literal.

8. Orig. *Patriotismus ist Torheit,* reflecting a very Leisewitzian political philosophy.

9. Bernhard Gottfried von Reider, confidential secretary and director of the electoral internal affairs office, which was responsible for prosecuting Kraus's father.

10. The manuscript is *Etwas von und über Musik.*

8. Letter to his parents dated Göttingen, 20 September 1777

Dearest Parents!

I have not yet received the letter containing your permission for my continued stay here. The last one did have the particulars, for which I render a thousand thanks. But, my dears, 8 Louis d'ors?[1] Consider wood, university fees, etc., must all be paid, as must the money for lodging – how can I make it through? – impossible! I ask on everything sacred that you arrange it so that I receive another 12 pieces in a couple of weeks. I have been invited to Klopstock's place in Hamburg[2] over the holidays – but with a small purse – oh well, it doesn't have to happen – and it is my own fault. *Bok* in Hamburg[3] offered me respectable money for six quartets, but I was too obstinate and wanted first to wait upon the fellow from F[rank]furt, but look, the jackass[4] sent back my manuscript to me with a thousand excuses: for example, *Deinet* in F[rankfurt] also had misfortune on account of the Mannheim opera *Günter von Schwarzburg*,[5] for the Elector demanded an apology and had [him] retract it, [because] the gentlemen hit a little too close to home, and even more such things. He can lick my ass[6] – it will be published at some point, even if there is only one press in all of Germany. It only angers me that it has taken so long. Patience – it has to be cast about a bit, and it will happen.

Enclosed herewith letters to the fat cousin and my sister.[7] The nun would earn my most sincere gratitude if she would make me a hat band; write her that. The situation in *The Hague*[8] is nothing but hot air, but on the other hand I have one in *Uppsala* in Sweden. I would like it to happen, and therefore I am learning Swedish like hell – if I don't want to go there, then at least I still get to set a Swedish opera to music.

It is correct regarding the *keyboard*,[9] but for all that, *Bauer* is a complete jerk. Just allow my little Marianne to continue to play – it would be better on a good than on a bad *keyboard*. So, everyone is shaking their head that I don't wish to seek some position in Mainz? Hmm! – I would shake my head so that people want to shake theirs. Answer me soon.

Here is my silhouette.[10]

Your most obedient

Joseph

COMMENTARY

Original Buchen, Bezirksmuseum. Kraus is responding to the receipt of funds to continue his studies, as well as possibly answering an inquiry about his future career plans. It is clear that he has now focused his attention on the field of music.

1. The "particulars" refer to funds: 8 Louis d'ors = £8 or about US$450 in present-day currency.

2. Friedrich Gottlieb Klopstock (1724–1803), author of *Messias* and another mentor of the Göttingen Hainbund poets. Leux-Henschen (LH-JMK, 196) states that there is no evidence of a meeting between Kraus and Klopstock, although this invitation would appear to suggest otherwise. Alternatively, it is possible that this was arranged through intermediaries, such as Matthias Claudius, whom Kraus did meet and befriend.

3. Michael Christian Bock, a music publisher; Kraus originally states *Quadros,* but these are likely the six string quartets that he lists among his "completed compositions" in Letter 11. This set (VB 173–177) has been lost.

4. Orig. *Schlingel,* or "rascal" if one is being polite about the epithet; Kraus is not. This refers most likely (St-Göttingen, 222) to Kessler, his former publisher, and suggests that the mention of the man from Frankfurt (*Ffurter*) refers to the royalties owed him by Kessler for his play *Tolon,* even though the context refers to a person, not a place. Moreover, Kraus has conflated the offer from Hamburg as a composer with his work for Frankfurt as a playwright, and it is not

clear why he has rejected a "respectable" sum if he was in need of money, as the beginning of the letter implies. *Deinet* refers to Frankfurt publisher Johann Conrad Deinet (1735–1797).

5. The reference is to the opera in three acts by Ignaz Holzbauer (1711–1783) to a text by Kraus's erstwhile teacher Anton Klein, which premiered on 5 January 1777 to great acclaim. It was published the same year by Götz in full score with a dedication to Elector Carl Theodor. Kraus's comments reflect the rumors circulating during the year that the text, based upon a fictional account of the Wittelsbach dynasty of the Palatinate, was considered invidious. Indeed, author Christoph Martin Wieland, writing in *Der teutsche Merkur,* noted: "In Mannheim, I hear, there is a great row about the ex-Jesuit Klein's so-called opera. . . . The thing is so monstrous that I fear the Mannheimers will accuse me of envy or ill will if it is reviewed in the *Merkur* as planned." Saxon diplomat Andras von Riaucour also noted that the work was mercilessly pilloried in the Frankfurt papers, causing the reaction by the elector to which Kraus alludes. Ironically, the same day as this letter was written, Mozart and his mother arrived in Mannheim, taking in the opera the next night and reporting favorably on the work.[F]

6. Orig. *muscheln,* or the act of wiping one's bottom.

7. The "fat cousin" and sister are unidentified, although the latter may

---

F. See Daniel Heartz, *Music in European Capitals: The Galant Style 1720–1780* (New York: W. W. Norton, 2003), 578–594, and references contained therein.

be Maria Anna Walburga (1765–1838), whom Kraus refers to earlier (see Letter 5). The "nun" refers to his elder sister Katharina Josepha; see the previous letter.

8. Nothing is known about the *Vokation* in The Hague, but it was clearly not anything that interested Kraus. The Swedish *Vokation,* on the other hand, is the first reference to the eventually successful efforts by his friend and fellow student Carl Stridsberg (1755–1819) to lure him to Sweden.

9. The term used, *Klavier,* is generic, but probably refers to either a small spinet or a clavichord. Kraus is clearly responding to a question about the instrument and music obtained for it. Bauer is unidentified, but may refer to minor composer G. C. Bauer, who published a collection of songs in 1785, or may indicate a local builder of keyboards of questionable quality.

10. The silhouette is now in Buchen, Bezirksmuseum, Kraus-Sammlung Inv. Nr. 851. See illustration 2.

9. Letter to his parents dated Göttingen, 14 October 1777

My dearest parents!

I received your letter together with the 12 *Louis d'ors*[1] and thank you from the bottom of my heart for it. But, my God! What will finally become of our fate? If these are not enemies, who have throughout always had a hand in the play, then it is inexplicable to me. But – I know with certainty that they've torn the roof off of you once. If one is thereafter able to calm down, then one ought to forgive. He who has found himself in the same boat knows how huge that is. Well and good, has not all mankind been created to be wholeheartedly forced to serve those vile persons with plays – or small diversions? Small comfort for the honest man who still possesses a pair of fists. In everything, my dear ones, I foresee few prospects for myself in my fatherland. What good does it do if I also obtain an appointment through doing what I am able? It proceeds through the hands of a man who has shown me the grace of giving me the appearance of being a friend in the moment, but to whom I would remain a dedicated snake hereafter throughout my entire life. H[err] von B[enzel][2] has on the basis of experience, which I regard myself as far too dangerous, given me the advice to take the cloth. Is it better in any of the rubbish bins of one of our secular princes? The entire fortune of a man who has served is ready to be whipped away at the death of his patron, and only then does he recognize that this world is a chimera – in short, a true lie that one can wade in sincerity through manure that is deeper than he himself is tall. The little honor that allows jackasses to have to be able to doff their hats to a titled brow is, by my soul, not in the position to mix in honesty – if he is disappointed, he is an ass, great as he is up to the point where he sees that jerks are jerks, as soon as Herr Councilor is given his dismissal with all politeness. What does all of his damaging experience mean to him then? Nothing. It is regrettable, nothing more, and not a *sou* will help the fellow.[3] And *gentlemen*? From the beginning I could portray them so well, so politely, so that I could hardly be able to expect the moment when a gracious lord or noble *Excellency* would have such a high regard for me as to accept me to his *Scripsit*,[4] and then drag me or I him through the world. Now I have what I so long desired – I opened the little box – looked upon their majesties in the light that I was able to see them in – curiosities, hmmm, as good as anything carried about by a Savoyard[5] and found, if I consider it quite correctly, that everything was hot air – nothing but hot air. I have now met several more than I thought a year ago I had to meet in order to become more of a fortunate man than I had dreamed, but now I see that there is hardly one in a thousand who would be good enough to tolerate. Therefore – my dear parents! Therefore – where to from here? In half a year my academic studies will cease – I've had about enough of them and now I think that it is truly the time to think about my own situation. I have it.

I have already written to you once about my Swedish project, and now you will see it explained more clearly and in detail. The entire *situation* involves music and moreover in *Stockholm*.[6] Several have been approached, I among them, and of course by a Swede that I met about three-quarters of a year ago and who is now back in his fatherland. I made a small practice piece. It was approved and the offer was tendered.

1) If I am able to come to an agreement to come to Sweden, each and every one of my conditions would be fulfilled; these being

2) If [I] would deliver at the first opportunity a work for the stage, for which I could hope for the most handsome present from the King.

3) If I would be able to venture to conduct the entire opera orchestra, I would be free to take over either the French or Swedish, to which *Johnsen*[7] the vice-Kapellmeister has pledged, for he has

responsibility for both and would like to hand over one or the other to me.

4) I would be able to choose and receive a permanent position either in Stockholm or in Uppsala.

5) My entire engagement would last on my part only for a year, and if at that time I should not be pleased with it, [I] would be delivered free of charge back to Hamburg. For this reason, a specific *Solarium*[8] cannot be given to me to date until I have made the pledge after my arrival to remain for either one or several years.

My acquaintance wrote to me about this that even if after a year things did not please me, I would still have the very splendid opportunity to undertake a profitable journey. He is the chamberlain for the Count *Löwenhaupt*[9] in Uppsala. Counting from Easter onward for a year his young heir will attend German *universities* and prior to this he will undertake a journey through England, France, and Italy, and because he is a lover of music, he wants to take along with him a secretary who is a musician. If this *station* is acceptable to me, I can thereupon embark upon the most magnificent journey without cost and come away from it with the *Manier*.[10]

Well, what do you have to say to this? I have thought through everything thoroughly and decided to accept this *station,* for in all probability I can foresee that this is my fortune. Of what use would it be for me to sit an entire year in a rubbish bin, only at the end to be reduced to begging for money, when one can do either a lot or little and be happy. Now everything rests on your consent. You should see the difficulty in being able to consider the thing properly. With respect to religion you need have no worries, for in Stockholm there are more than 10,000 Catholics and two churches.[11] But what is the most critical circumstance concerns the costs that have to be made due to the journey and provisions. My thoughts are these. The costs of the journey I have to bear myself and have something that is intelligently suited to my appointment. I have done the calculations and found that I need 200 Ducats.[12] Certainly, if I prefer, I can soon earn the sum through my craft.[13] But the question is whether it will be possible for you to procure it for me before Easter in the circumstances that we now find ourselves in. If it is impossible or too difficult, I shall sacrifice all of my fortune gladly. Consider the matter seriously – it concerns my fortune – all of this for which you have endured so often so many cares when you entrusted me to foreign hands. If you agree with my thoughts, please keep the thing secret so that our enemies do not learn of it before I have reached my final goal. Because it is now my most important occupation to work on this last point, I have not participated in any juristic *Kollegia*[14] up until now; rather I practice at home with a good friend. My main emphasis is now Swedish and Italian and French therewith, and then music.

COMMENTARY

Original Buchen, Bezirksmuseum. The letter is lacking the last several lines in the autograph, no doubt from a separate, now-lost sheet. Some of the additional ones have been added from the copy taken by Silverstolpe from his collection (Folio X270a). Kraus both has received the funds he asked for in the previous letter and has learned that his parents were advised that he seek an official state clerical position, something he seems unlikely to have accepted.

1. 12 Louis d'ors = £12 or about US$675.

2. See Letter 3.

3. Orig. *Nüzt dem Kerl keinen Pfiferling,* or no small mushroom is of use to a fellow; the modern German saying would be *keine Pfefferling wert,* or [one] doesn't give a rap, modified to the circumstances here.

4. *Scripsit* = literally, "employment."

5. Savoyard = eighteenth-century water carriers who were highly esteemed for their wares and abilities. The "little box" (*Kästchen*) refers to a peep show, a carnival curiosity presenting tableaux through a type of camera obscura.

6. It is noteworthy that in the previous letter the city mentioned was Uppsala, a university town, but now it is Stockholm, the capital. Leux-Henschen (LH-JMK, 32) assumes that the "Swede" is Stridsberg, but this is still open to debate, given that Stridsberg was still a resident in Göttingen at the time of the letter. He was to leave only after receiving his magister degree in April 1778, and, moreover, he would hardly have been in the position of tendering Kraus a formal offer of any sort.

7. Hinrich Philip Johnsen (1717–1779). Kraus refers to the peculiar situation in Stockholm whereby the Hovkapell, ostensibly unified in 1772 under the direction of Kapellmästare Francesco Baldassare Uttini (1723–1795) as the primary orchestra of the Royal Spectacles (including the Royal Opera) was still officially divided into two separate ensembles for administrative purposes. These were the Kungliga, or court orchestra, that had arrived as the personal ensemble of the late King Adolph Fredrik, and the Statliga, the official state orchestra that had existed prior to the former's arrival in 1743. Johnsen, who was also organist at the Clara Church, was the leader of the Kungliga, although he officially held the position

of "Directeur de Musique" rather than Vize-Kapellmästare. While he did occasionally conduct the combined group, he had no position or power to appoint anyone, let alone an unknown student from Göttingen, to any musical post. Moreover, Kraus errs in his mention of the French opera troupe, since Gustav III had dismissed it in 1772 and another, led by the famed actor Monvel, was not to arrive before 1781. Therefore, one ought to conclude either that Kraus misunderstood both the situation and the details or that he is deliberately building a castle in the air for his worried parents.

8. *Solarium*, meaning actual contractual dates for the year.

9. Axel Gabriel Lejonhuvud, also spelled Leijonhuvud or Lejonhufwud (1717–1787). His Swedish name has been translated by Kraus into German. The "chamberlain" is probably Erik Stridsberg (1755–1805), Carl's cousin, who was associated with the noble household in Uppsala.

10. *Manier* = class advancement. *Station* is used later in the same sense as situation or position.

11. Kraus overstates the actual number of Catholics in Stockholm. While Sweden did allow a certain freedom of religion, only the chaplains at the embassies of the Holy Roman Empire, Spain, and France were allowed to minister to Catholics at the legations. The number was actually closer to 300 worshipers.[G]

12. 200 Ducats on exchange in Hamburg would be approximately £200 or a bit over US$1,000.

13. Orig. *Handwerk*, meaning his music.

14. *Kollegia* = tutorials.

10. Letter to his parents dated Göttingen, [December 1777]

Dearest Parents!

You have misunderstood my intentions and thus me and my heart. My heart is proud – yes, it is proud, and if it were not I would take it between my knees and squash it to bits – it is proud and will remain so – no misfortune will alter it. But – no, it is not arrogant. I know what I naturally have to expect concerning my fate; I know it and to order it about is as little my thing as to crawl – and if I know it, why do you remind me of it? I believe now firmly that my fortune awaits me under foreign skies, toward which I did not run in vain. Why do you call me back into the bondage that I am beholden to you and my siblings? Can I fulfill this honorably until I achieve happiness? Is not everything I have unified? Religion? Dearest parents, religion is no matter of upbringing alone; it is feeling – inner feeling of the veritable truth of those things

G. See Arne Palmqvist, *Die Römisch-Katholische Kirche in Schweden nach 1781* (Uppsala: Almqvist och Wiksell, 1954), 1:125.

that are presented with it. "Faith, it is said, is a *gift of God and Light*," not the product of education invented through systematic tables. I thank religion for a support that I cannot do without and that you have given me, and for that what do you have to fear? If I were no true Catholic in my heart, what would it matter if I returned to my fatherland as well? – So that you will certainly be able to be convinced that I have accepted so warmly the religion that I have become accustomed to from my childhood as you have, what would it matter if I went to *California*?[1]

Or – do you find yourselves only now moved to direct more precisely my strengths toward a profession?

From the bottom of my heart to the top, quite warmly, I thank you for everything that I may not express and consider myself obligated for in all eternity. Was this, however, not in accord with the fact that I desired coincidentally to go to a foreign place, to get a break without costing me anything, incidentally, and thus to make a profit in language and other small matters? Is it arrogance to want to be yoked and work like a young ox for practically nothing? Is it arrogance that to save you and my siblings much cost I would sweat so horribly, incidentally, until the merciful God would bestow upon me something better? And that is what I wanted – and you make it out to be a misdeed? My God, how can you so misjudge me?

Music! – For [the] first [thing], if it is easier to be a musician than a lawyer, if so much [more] power and omnipotence is laid upon the knowledge of the law than it is in music, then if there are better men, then I shall curse music that it never more lure me into a better situation, but not now. Of course, I know that I am a poor devil and that all about me can be found thousands upon thousands of poor devils who are content and love to have their necks put into a noose, even if they have a hundred times the strength of the mighty. – Unfortunately, I know it all and because I am so certain it can be said of me that I take my ego by its head often during the days and even more often during the quiet hours of the night and shout to it: "*Fool!*[2] Here in the Holy Roman Empire we are all at once conditioned either to have to choose a patron from among the four faculties or must surrender to a craft with devilish power. *Fool!* Become a theologian, lawyer, doctor, philosopher, philologist, if you have enough of a mind – for this [is] entirely the *recipe for the study of earning one's bread*[3] in our country and for that you are obligated by the Lord – but God preserve you from that company." It is obvious that I go along with the *Sacratissimi Principis*[4] of Roman law, just like the predecessor Hirsch did with his Braunen.[5] But, my beloved parents! You have never demanded anything from me, and it would be insulting for [both] you and me if you demanded that I should keep a secret from you. You know me and know that I feel needs that not everyone recognizes, that you perhaps wish to drag me along on a parallel with a straight arm. You know that I have much fire. Why then do you wish me most forcefully to wander along the regular path?

Along with law I want to learn languages, want to gather material for my own satisfaction, and – you calculate the expenses in a tone that depresses me.[6] Yes, I am obligated for everything to you and my siblings, and I will repay you again at such time as God blesses it and when I have to repay it. You know my heart – why do you deal with me so harshly? I sit here in a place where I have no pleasant hours and do what I think is useful, and yet you make up the most ill-conceived notions about me! – and tell me that I have given you cause?

I shall help myself out of this through what I have learned and what good nature has given me – not through anything else. I find it necessary to remain here yet another winter. I know that this will be received by you as a blow. Listen to my explanation. My portion of that which I once hoped for from you as a blessing of God I've long since studied away. I have never made any claim upon it, but I have perhaps slighted my siblings also. God knows, I love you all as myself, and I believe it is superfluous if I were to promise you most dearly that I would sometime divide with you my last little piece of bread, and rather than that perhaps I have the powers that are able to provide for my sustenance. Let me [remain] here this winter and vouchsafe me the expenses. It is a request that I do not make gladly, if it were possible! If you support it, then – how could I express my gratitude? If you reject it, then I also have to be content.

Oh, that the day was over, eternally over, so that I would have no other needs but my own, so that I am taught that, whether small or nothing, I should be content with the simplest efforts of everyone. Where a word of praise of a teacher innocently was so interesting to me, for now my life is not! God! What is a human being if he does not begin to feel his surroundings and sees his limits that may not be exceeded and never leapt over?

H[err] von Benzel has not yet written to me – I don't wonder about it at all. Why? –Ha! [if] a human being opens his heart and reads – a language that no mortal, that the Creator alone understands – read it, you poor worms!

Should I go to Heiligenstadt? – I can bow and scrape, I can – but not forced to do so through misfortune, not crawling, but rather as I determine it. I have long since sent the petition to H[err] Count von Sickingen, but to go to him myself is once and for all nothing I wish to do! A week ago the *man from Mainz*[7] was at his home here – a man who has enough money and only wished to take the *cure* with him through obligatory homage. The conversation was –

"Does *he* study at Göttingen?"

"Obediently in attendance, Your Excellency."

It may be that *you, he, thou, him,* etc., etc., is all the same when a great man says it, but to me it is bullshit[8] that I can take only once each year. What am I to hope for from him? – Miracles? – or nothing more than I have been able to say to myself that I have had the high grace to be obediently in attendance, Your Excellency? Probably.

H[err] von Reider? –Ha! He was not able to insult me in Mundau[9]? – but he wanted to. Is it as easy to swallow as to ask for a beating? A beating by the jailer? The vile soul. Ha, he should first rectify the harm that he has done to you – but he can never do it. Unfortunately, Reider does not have to be Reider all the time, but he will remain so in all eternity and should, for it is the only punishment that God can give him, if it is made known to him how it was. I have become zealous, if you forgive me, for the fire of youth burns within me and for which I thank my Creator with all my heart.

I thank my sister for her good missive.

Oh, continue, always continue to love

Your

Joseph

[P.S.]I wrote the letter the moment I received yours and read it; perhaps many expressions are too heated in it, and for that forgive me!

COMMENTARY

Original Buchen, Bezirksmuseum. The letter is obviously a vituperative response to a letter from his parents (now lost) expressing their concern in strong and forceful language. One may assume reading between the lines that they did not believe either his outline of employment possibilities or his description of the ability to practice Catholicism in Lutheran Sweden. Too, the clear indication of abandoning a career as his father's successor for music resulted in both remonstrations and Kraus's emotionally charged response. These whining and half-defensive excuses give an insight into Kraus's rather impetuous Sturm und Drang personality. The letter is undated, but given the October date of the previous, as well as the indications that they have taken considerable time to formulate their response to it, it was likely written either at the end of November or beginning of December 1777.

1. The reference to *Kalifornien* is meant to denote figuratively "the ends of the earth," for it was known in Catholic European circles that this was a new frontier just being opened for settlement at the time. The great curiosity, however,

is that Kraus refers directly to this new Spanish colony that consisted largely only of mission outposts.

2. Orig. *Lips,* which can mean either fool or idiot.

3. Orig. *Recepta Brodtstudia.*

4. *Sacritissimi principis* = most sacred principles.

5. The reference to Hirsch and Braunen is unclear, but probably indicates a German equivalent to the Johnson-Boswell relationship in England about this time.

6. It seems clear that Kraus's parents have sent him a detailed accounting of how much his education had cost them to this point, along with indications that they were no longer willing to foot the expenses for his lifestyle or dreams.

7. The *Mainzer* refers to Count von Sickingen, as the allusions illustrate.

8. Orig. *Rhabarber,* or rhubarb, but colloquial for a stronger term than simply "rubbish."

9. Reider, Kraus's father's antagonist, had apparently attempted to slander the composer in the town of Mundau, where many of the composer's relatives lived, including Häussler, his godfather.

11. Letter to his parents dated Göttingen, 28 December 1777

Dearest Parents,

I have received *Günter*[1] along with the enclosure in your letter delivered on the last post day, for which I say a thousand thanks to you. But the letter that you mention in writing as having been sent by way of someone from Buchen to H[err] Seiler[2] in Frankfurt has not yet arrived. Where must it have gone?

You now hope for an end to the miserable *affair* – if only you could soon give me news, and the most joyous and best of it, no less. [May] God grant it! You place so much confidence in the choice of my own circumstances that I cannot thank you enough. I now work toward my goals, doing as much work in order not to disappoint either myself or others in this matter. But – my dearest and best parents – is it not a principal necessity to have a specific sum once and for all for my fate that I wish to embark upon? Is it not possible to have no less than 200 Ducats? – You will easily perceive that I cannot lack the smallest portion of the requested sum. My departure is scheduled before Easter, because I will thus be able to have the company of a Swede from *Lübeck* onward[3] – that I will be able to make this possible depends entirely upon whether it is doable to have the money three weeks prior to Easter. It would be best if you could arrange for me to have 100 Ducats *specie* and a[nother] 100 in a letter of credit sent from Frankfurt to Hamburg. But, all of this depends upon your circumstances and your generosity, all of which I leave to you.

If you can send me the remaining quarterly allowance, pack it just like you did previously in music paper – in this way it will cost less postage and is secure enough. I require, moreover, quite urgently some very good and strong *Subregal,*[4] the best of which can be procured from F[rankfurt]. NB: Not with staves but rather completely white, about 6 reams. Both – money and paper, I need soon. – You would thus show much love for me to expedite it. For the New Year and all previous and subsequent namedays and birthdays, etc., etc., I wish only good wishes for all and sundry who want them.

My completed works[5] are:

6. *Quartets for 2 Violins, Viola, and Violoncello*
6. *Symphonies for 2 Violins, Viola, and Basso, 2 Oboes and Horns*
1 *Sinfonia concertante for Violin, Flute, Viola, and Violoncello solos*
And 2 Violins, Viola, and Basso with 2 Oboes and horns
1 *Concerto for Violin solo and other instruments*
1 *Concerto for Flute solo [and other instruments]*
1 *Concerto for Violin and Viola solos with other instruments*
1 *Trio for 2 Violins and Violoncello*

[A] *Cantata for Soprano and the other instruments*
1 *Duet for Violin and Viola*
1 *Duet for Harpsichord and Violin*

Any of these that my brother has an interest in I will have copied for him, but if he will only wait, surely a majority of them will appear in print. P.S. I don't go to Nörten's place[6] anymore, because I don't have time. I am, however, often with the H[errn] von Dalbergs.

Write soon
Your most obedient son
Joseph
[P.P.S.] Greet everyone.

COMMENTARY

Original Buchen, Bezirksmuseum. The address on the outer fold is *Monsieur/Monsieur Krausz Baili pour/S[on] Alt[esse] Electoralede Maience/p[ar] Cassel … à/Frankfurt et … Buchen/ Miltenberg.* This letter is one of the few instances when Kraus actually mentions the compositions he has written. The implication of requesting more blank paper is that this sort of clearly frenetic musical activity will continue, and the predominance of instrumental works, particularly concertos involving four particular instruments (violin, viola, flute, and violoncello) may indicate his focus at this point. It was also probably written to prove to his still skeptical parents that he was indeed actively pursuing a musical career. The context is also that they have relented and consented to Kraus's choice, albeit reluctantly.

1. The reference is to the printed libretto for *Günther von Schwarzburg,* the opera noted earlier.

2. Herr Seiler is unidentified, but clearly a family friend or relative.

3. See Letter 14 for the exact route Kraus takes. The *Swede* is most likely Stridsberg, who intended to be finished by the spring term.

4. Subregal is a type of thick cotton paper suitable for music manuscripts, and six reams indicates that Kraus has considerable work in progress. Staves were generally added by means of a rastral, one of the tools in the kit of most composers of the period.

5. These compositions are, respectively, VB 172–177, 132–137, 153, 151, 150, 164, 43, 156, and 157. Here Kraus uses the term *Quadros* explicitly to mean string quartet, and there is a long empty underline following the title for the flute concerto, clearly meaning ditto from the previous line, e.g., *Stromenti altri.* The only works that have survived are the violin concerto, the cantata (entitled *La Scusa*), and the "duetto" for harpsichord (here clearly called *Clavicembalo* by Kraus) and violin, which is actually a violin sonata with continuo figuration. These were later given by Kraus to the Viennese

publisher Johann Traeg in 1783 to be sold in manuscript copy. While it remains a remote possibility that some form of the quartets may survive in those that are extant, there is no evidence to support this fact, whatever "stylistic" interpretations have been offered to the contrary.[H] For the other instrumental works, Kraus specifically mentions an orchestra consisting of pairs of oboes and horns, plus strings and *Fondamento,* which is generically rendered as "Basso" here. This implies the use of a continuo, but could just as well mean only violoncello and contrabass without keyboard. In the violin concerto and cantata the oboes have been replaced by flutes, and therefore it is logical to assume that the definition of *stromenti altri* can be expanded to include this interchangeable combination.

6. The identity of Nörten is unknown, but the context suggests a community gathering place, perhaps even a public house.

12. Letter to his parents dated Göttingen, 2 February 1778

Dearest Parents!

Yesterday I received the manuscript paper together with the funds – today the second letter. I have thus an almost complete answer to my last missive that you will have received during this time as well. The news that you have already come up against the final verdict was unforeseen, for the judgment itself went its merry way from word to word. That was tragic enough! Of what use is it? Fortune has always smiled upon it. But for what kind of *university* was the thing fabricated, God only knows. As much as it is possible, at the majority of them [i.e., the universities] such things have always been spoken about thusly. The *professor of law*[1] cannot do otherwise than to judge according to the acts that have been laid before him, and – what sorts of acts are these? Of what use is it to make insinuations against them? – and to come out simultaneously with null and void is not always advisable and betrays for the most part a half or complete conspirator and, according to our circumstances (precisely those in which we find ourselves), an idiot. If the person who is making the *Responsum*[2] comes across the questions in the proceedings: "Have you given the official a consideration?" and the answer to it is the bucolic: "Yes," then it is impossible for him to conclude that between the question and the answer an approximate agreement with this or another could

H. See Sonja Gerlach, Foreword, in *Joseph Martin Kraus: Kammermusik I* (Stuttgart: Carus Verlag, 2006), xvi. Gerlach's discussion is, of course, highly problematic.

have happened, etc. It may well be that the *Commissarius*[3] has slipped up, as a lawyer could see a hundred times. Of course, there remains only a single way – to beg and see whatever one can always arrange for money. But – because I really want to begin the *pro memoria,*[4] it occurs to me that I no longer have either the address or titles for either Count Sickingen or the Elector. It is naturally and better that I write it myself. – You must send me the stuff with the next post. It should be powerful enough, if anything can be of use.

Now for myself. I thank you a thousand times that you wish me so much happiness. Regarding money, it would depend upon whether I knew or could foresee how much and for what I needed for everything. My recommendation would be this – to send me 50 Ducats *specie* and obtain a letter of credit in F[rank]furt for exchange in *Stockholm* of 100 – both of which I must have in the most urgent way before the first of *April.* The remaining 50 could then be sent to me in the manner in which you would consider best.[5] It is impossible for me to make do with only a hundred.

May I now also renew my request regarding the watch[6] – you will have read a more complete supplication in my last letter.

I have to hurry, because the post departs right now – if my letter only doesn't come too late, otherwise I'll have to let it lie until Sunday.

Greet everyone.

Your most obedient S[on]

Joseph

COMMENTARY

Original Buchen, Bezirksmuseum. The original date is "2nd Hornung." The rather oblique opening indicates that Kraus's father has received the final verdict on his indictment, but Kraus, with his training in law, finds it completely baffling and convoluted, which indeed it is. The upshot is that Bernhard Kraus was found culpable, but his "punishment" was to be reinstated in his old position in another town. Kraus is clearly appalled by this twisted logic, but he is unsure how to write a response to the rulers of the electorate.

1. Orig. *Fakultist,* or faculty member in law.

2. *Responsum* = response.

3. *Commissarius* = person investigating the indictment.

4. *Pro memoria* = memorandum or petition in reply to the verdict.

5. Kraus has clearly received a counteroffer to his request for 200 Ducats for half the sum. His compromise is that his original sum is to be divided into yet another scheme whereby he receives three-fourths of the amount and the final installment at an unspecified date. The funds would be dispersed as coin (*specie*) and a redeemable letter of credit, similar to a bearer bond or today's travelers check.

6. The watch is currently on display in Buchen, Bezirksmuseum, having been returned to the Kraus family in 1792 as part of the composer's personal effects. The "supplication" probably refers to a now lost letter that was sent in between this one and the last.

13. Letter to his parents dated Göttingen, 3 April 1778

Dearest Parents:

This is without doubt the last letter that I shall write in Germany. For me, the thought has much that is solemn, cheerful, and depressing. To be sundered from all that is most precious and dear to me, and to be distanced afar from those who are dearest to my heart – If one thinks about such things, then the journey is soured for one. But to excuse it all – here, now externally, here in the breast the thought smolders and becomes ripe for decision. It has not been given to me to find rest close about me – not given to me to seek it, and not once to expect it. Rest I call here that point about which I want to live and weave. Many found it before me – perhaps in a place above which my glance easily passed. Good – must the *melon* please Peter just because it pleases Hans?[1]

> "In a single minute your possible happiness – and along with it your best intentions – can be annihilated, of what use is foolishness – of what use is it to have noble reasons for departing? – and into the danger that you now put yourself, etc."[2]

To this and all other sorts of objections the only [response]: Not even a louse walks about without the permission that I rely upon, neither in my own nor your head – even less are you or I entwined, dear mortals, with earth and water without His word. And His word – His voice – resounds even so strongly over a step as over a thousand miles above or beneath our earth. Comfort enough for you – enough for me!

In my fatherland and in the entire circle in which I wandered since I began to think for myself, I have found apart from you, my loved ones, a single individual that I wanted to be loved by you as much as I was loved – the sure sign of friendship, which is rare. It is the young *Hahn* of Zweibrücken – the only one that I have met who is like me through and through – completely to the core – that I have studied down to the last fiber and remained as he once was and lost nothing in the analysis because he completely – Ha! The picture – it is imbued so completely, so deeply within me and I cannot express what I gladly would. And he – he has taken me from the same page, and I from him in *everything*. God! I thank you – it is much – I repeat – it is much, very much to find in one's life a single friend, for among a thousand, 800 do not know the definition and in the remaining 190 are deceived, and only a single one – perhaps not even this one, can be found that one can retain. I therefore have less to regard as true to my heart – you – my siblings and my only friend – and for all of you – this is nothing more than a further distancing. My pre-sentiment – and it is a presentiment of my good spirit – tells me that I shall see all of you again – a happy reunion, as you will all [see] me. Per-haps – if He, the Almighty, has prepared my tomb in the place where I seek solace – Enough! That is my destiny! Those that have courage will go against it, [but] the cowardly shake, trembling in the face of their fate, but their pilgrimage is not delayed a minute longer than the former because of it. Dearest ones! Pray for me – Think well of me – Oh, it is an eternal web and sympathy for those whose fates are intertwined.[3] – God blesses it and whatever is in His hands is solid. I thank Him that I have calmed myself – the cost was considerable. The thought was terrible, extremely terrible: "You have embraced your loved ones for the last time about a year ago – and leave those you know, your fatherland!" – "For-ever!" – God! This raged around inside of me until I wept it away. God knows that it was not easy – No – with the violence for which all of nature should forgive in me. I have to suppress the picture that is ever present and powerful, and that indeed, if it rises in me a thousandfold, shall re-main so powerful, and for this I have prayed to Him and He will never refuse me.

I have received everything by your generosity, money, letters of credit – everything. Rightly, can I now thank you more inwardly – most inwardly?

Everything is prepared – small debts I still have, but I have taken them on myself to absolve after a year's respite if my circumstances allow it.

I embrace you, my loved ones, with the warmest love that can be given – embrace my dear sister and my dear brother – all my siblings, whose debtor I am, with a farewell that will forever tremble warm on my lips. Farewell, dearest ones! Farewell – parents and siblings!

Forever well!

Joseph

COMMENTARY

Original Buchen, Bezirksmuseum. Apparently, despite their concern, his parents have given in and sent him the funds he requested. While it is wildly emotional, the undercurrent is that Kraus seems both happy to pursue his dream and suddenly brought up short that his plans have come to fruition.

1. A German proverb, *Muß Petern die Melone just behagen, weil sie Hansen behagt?* means that not everyone needs to be satisfied with the same thing.

2. Clearly a quote from a letter to him from his parents questioning his decision.

3. A reference to his close friendship with Hahn, replete in the language of male bonding of the time.

Interludium

It is clear from the final letter that Kraus wrote from Göttingen that he intended to leave imminently; the sensitivity seems genuine, although this is tempered by the simple expression of gratitude for the funds that his parents had obviously sent. In reality, the journey was delayed for a further three weeks, during which the specifics about his life are unclear, apart from later hints of restless anticipation. Indeed, his own life is rather obscure during the last four or five months prior as preparations were being made and final details resolved. The question of what he actually did during the time is largely unanswerable. It is, however, not beyond the bounds of reason to suggest that he occasionally attended lectures at the university, though he never did complete the necessary steps to be awarded a diploma or degree in law. He also probably visited friends, such as the Dalbergs and his hapless "bosom" friend Hahn, and, if his list of works presented in Letter 11 is any indication, continued to compose music at a rapid pace, possibly for future use in Sweden.[1] As will become clear in the next section of letters, written during his first years in Sweden, he was also putting the finishing touches on his treatise *Etwas von und über Musik,* finding another publisher after Kessler rejected it.

As for the journey itself, it was to take him a bit over five weeks, thanks to a detour to Copenhagen, Denmark. It is clear from the chatty tone of his description of the trip that he was less anxious to arrive in Sweden for his proposed "situation" that one might have expected, given the effusive statements from Göttingen. He was also incautious about reporting political events in the Danish capital, which could have caused him (or his family, just coming out of a long period of politically in-duced tribulation) considerable difficulty had they been discovered. Nonetheless, the route of travel is clearly delineated, although details of his actual experiences on the last leg in Sweden are purposefully left rather vague.

14. Letter to his parents dated Stockholm, 12 June 1778

My departure, as well as my journey, was delayed longer than I had thought at the outset. Instead of the first of April, it was the 26th, and with everything going on in my farewell [it] was so chaotic that it all became rather a trial for me.[1] I still had various small debts – at least nothing so overwhelming that I found it impossible to repay. You would have at least thought it remiss of me if I had broken my obligatory con-fidence to you in the manner through an inconsiderate silence. Dearest ones! Consider my situation. The first step in the initial important period of my destiny – and thus [to] be so confounded, always thus plagued by small affairs of the heart[2] (and you know that I have had many such) – would not I be able to be excused? I have promised my creditors satis-

I. Such works may include further string quartets, such as those in F minor and C minor (VB 178–179), the Sonata for flute and viola (VB 158), and quite probably the recently rediscovered viola concertos as well as the double concerto for viola, violoncello, and orchestra (VB 153a–c). The handwriting style of the autograph of the Concerto in E-flat major, now in Berlin (Deutsche Staatsbibliothek, Mus. Ms. autogr. Hoffstetter N 1) and once attributed to Pater Roman Hoffstetter, shows that it may belong to this period, when he maintained an interest in these instruments.

faction in a year, if it were possible on my account. Should it be so difficult for them to wait for so long when I am utterly convinced that they have completely taken advantage of me? Has this not been the fate of all and sundry from the beginning? If you count Göttingen in this, it was there that the first serious thoughts of the future matured – the rest have been said in secret only to our beloved God. Restless I left Göttingen and wobbled off on a post coach to Hamburg. Here I met up with my traveling companions.[3] In the beginning we wanted to travel through the countryside of Holstein up to Kiel and from there to Copenhagen. But our purses gave us other advice, for the journey by sea would be remarkably cheaper without it. Therefore, we went to Lübeck. Here we had to hang about for eight days due to the wind. It is 100 miles[4] by sea from the Lübeck harbor in *Travemünde* (one mile from Lübeck) to Stockholm. But I and my traveling companions were of a mind to see over Copenhagen and the southern provinces of Sweden, for we calculated that we could do the trip with minimal cost. We therefore left Travemünde on a Danish freighter with moderate wind. From there to Copenhagen is 36 miles. The Baltic, however, made the passage very dangerous. It was a completely new experience for me when I first looked out upon the sea. No other sight has made such an extraordinary impression upon me as the sunset of the first evening and sunrise the following day. About five o'clock in the evening on the first day there occurred a complete calm that lasted until about ten o'clock the day after. This was inconvenient for the journey, for we didn't move from the spot, but it made the spectacle all the more attractive for the eyes. That which one often fears will occur did. Toward evening of the second day the sea rose and made us rather afraid. My other traveling companions were all confined to their bunks (small bed-nooks) with seasickness. In order to alleviate this discomfort completely I took myself up to the foredeck and was so thoroughly soaked by the spray of the waves that I did not have a dry thread on me. If one includes the severe cold that is always found at sea at night during this time, then I became rather exhausted. Toward morning we found ourselves thrown back to Stralsund, almost 30 miles. Everyone, including the captain of the ship and passengers, marveled that I alone among my traveling companions, all of whom had already made several voyages by sea, was the only one who was not seasick. My cure for this was tobacco and brandy and deliberate movement that I made myself do with handiwork[5] on the foredeck. We approached the island of *Moen* on the fourth day, where we lay for an entire day and night until we once more got a favorable wind, and thus we came to Copenhagen only after eight days – something that one reckons at 36 miles from Travemünde to there can be done with a quite good wind in 20–24 hours. Our ship was dual-masted and carried 183,600 pounds in the cabins – apart from the great cabin with four bunks, there were three quite comfortable rooms. We remained in Copenhagen for six days. The business affairs of my traveling companions and the extraordinary kindness of the Count von Schulenburg, who was on board the ship with us – everything coalesced. Here I saw for the first time ever the largest of all warships that traverses the sea. I met various acquaintances here that I had known earlier at the academy. The theater is small – the orchestra mediocre – and the actors extremely wretched, although this may have been because I understood very little Danish. The city is quite large, somewhat more spread out than Mainz and decorated with many beautiful buildings. Count *Schulenburg* showed me the prison where *Struensee* and *Brandt*[6] were both executed. Both previously lived in the palace. From here our journey took us to Helsingör, three miles from Copenhagen, where we had to cross the *sound*. This is a narrow passage from the Baltic to the North Sea. The most beautiful thing I could imagine was – over 300 ships lay at anchor here awaiting the wind. The first ground upon which one sets foot on landing is Swedish, namely *Helsingborg,* the foremost city in *Skåne* (as the province is called). From here we traveled through *Landskrona* to *Lund.* There is a university here – an archbishopric and a cathedral. I was introduced around by my traveling companion here, and we remained for four days. We continued our journey through *Kristianstad, Växsjö, Eksjö, Linköping, Norrköping,* [*Söder*]*tälje,* and thus we arrived in *Stockholm* on the third. The city is very large, 2½ strong German hours long. What I didn't expect was that the King had been at his summer residence since the 20th of May in Uppland[7] and consequently would not return before the military review in Skåne has occurred, which is to happen in three months at the earliest. Thus, the theater is closed for this length of time. Fortunately, the birthday of the King took place, and to honor him an opera was given at the behest of the Queen. I was extraordinarily curious. The music was by *Naumann*[8] from Dresden, who has been here since the previous summer. He conducted the opera himself and only departed on the 11th. But, my God! It would have been impossible to imagine it more wretchedly. The orchestra was better than in Copenhagen, but the singers and actors even worse. The patriotism of the King shines forth in everything, for no cost was spared, and Naumann himself had 24,000 Dalers Kppm [Kopparmynt] along with free lodging and necessities[9] for eleven months (as long as he was here) – that is, he received about 700 Ducats in our money. Now, no opera is anticipated before the winter – and thus I also cannot expect to receive a secure commission. One has to learn to wait upon great lords, and even *Naumann* had to wait eleven months. Now, my dear ones, I am here and hope with time to improve my lot with God's help – there will be no lack of effort and industry on my part. The other thing that doesn't help my lyre is that I have found myself rather short in my calculations. Because it was impossible for me to be here before the 28th of May, when the letter of credit was to expire, I had no other option but to redeem it in Hamburg, and therefore I lost 9 Ducats in the process.[10] How did this happen? – First, the exact coinage in Ducats was not specified, or so 10 or 12 independent merchants told me, so that I was already conned out of 25 Gulden, and because the Dutch exchange rate was not higher at the moment, I was forced to give up my dear 9 pieces of gold for free. Moreover, our calculations were off, because the journey with all of its incidentals all at once became so high. I am otherwise no great spendthrift, but I learned that one cannot find eight or nine places in the approximately 70 Swedish or 96 German miles (which is the distance between Helsingborg and Stockholm) where one can eat one's fill. Further, it is far more expensive here than one can conceive. Of course, I hoped for reimbursement, but I must wait. I save as much as I can. I have not once even attempted to clothe myself in the costume of the place, for I worry about how much it will cost and how I am better able to use it. I eat once each day – once coffee and thus drink more beer, which is good and cheap here. But regardless, I fear that I must have help until the fall, or I shall become as naked as a baby at his mother's breast. I place my hopes on your generosity and great love for me so that I shall not be left in the lurch, for I still retain the view that I shall be able with time to earn it back and reimburse it, and perhaps at that time you too will be in a better position. Do not abandon me. You know that my heart feels when something good is done to it and suffers much when it is not in the position to recognize it enough. I will owe everything to you, such as it is. God! If only I could in happier circumstances sometime throw myself into your arms and say – it means everything, your work – your love for me, that I have done everything for it. Would you be so kind and begin to think already about the gift that I hope for this coming fall – so that I am not totally abandoned? – Following your orders I have enclosed the letter to *Keßler*,[11] for I do not know your situation at present. Write to me soon. Oh, my brothers and sisters! I am obliged to you all – would that the minute would be closer when I would be able to absolve a portion of my debts! I love you all so much, so much – the tears that I weep many a night when I think of being parted, you from me and I from you, so distantly parted, tells you that I love you deeply! And the friends – everything – everything! A farewell to you all! The directions of the post office makes it possible so that you don't need to set anything more as an address than Krause, the jurisprudence candidate – but NB – in French, otherwise the Herr Postmaster here won't understand. And nothing more than *Stockholm*.

Krause? Why not Kraus? The notary in Lübeck who made up my passport[12] is at fault. If you would have so much love for me that you would make me happy in the fall with a letter of credit; it doesn't matter [how much] (even if it is 20 Ducats more or 50 strong), then your Herr Son will issue a very pretty letter of thanksgiving. E[xempli] G[ratia]: a pair of shoes costs 3 fl. 8 to 9 [kr].

COMMENATARY

Original Buchen, Bezirksmuseum. The cover sheet–envelope, which no doubt contained both the address, opening salutation, and final words or signature, is missing. In the margins can be found a note, probably by Kraus's father: "The answer to this letter was sent off on 9 July." There is no mention of whether or not they included the requested letter of credit, but they could not have been happy about the somewhat frivolous manner in which Kraus undertook the journey, nor the implication that there were further and more extensive debts from Göttingen that had not been settled. Kraus's explanation that the opera would not be anticipated before winter ought to be revised to read "new opera," which was generally commissioned for a premiere on 28 January, Gustav III's birthday.

1. Orig. *daß er mir ordentlich sauer wird,* or that it made me become quite sour, but translated more idiomatically.

2. Orig. *von kleinen Herzensangelegenheiten.* According to Leux-Henschen (LH-JMK, 37), these were unidentified interactions with "the fairer sex," something about which he does not confide in his parents. This stands in contrast to the rather effusive language regarding his male friends, which must be seen as part of the male bonding cult of the time, but not necessarily evidence of anything more intimate.

3. The traveling companions are not identified, although one of them was certainly Carl Stridsberg, who introduced Kraus to his relatives in Lund. It would seem that some of them left the party in Copenhagen, as implied by the reduction of the identification to the singular.

4. Here and elsewhere Kraus uses a distance measurement in *Deutsche Meilen* (German miles), the exact distance of which varied from state to state during the period. His mention, however, of it being one mile between Lübeck and Travemünde allows for an estimation of his measurement to be made. It is 22 kilometers or 14 modern miles in between these two places, which then allows for a calculation of his 100-mile distance from the last to Copenhagen to be estimated at 225 kilometers or 140 miles, which is not far off of the actual sea distance of 233 kilometers or 145 miles. A "strong German hour" (*deutsche starke Stunden*) is the distance it takes for one to walk briskly for an hour; roughly 6 kilometers or 4 miles.

5. Kraus fails to mention what the handiwork (*Handarbeit*) was, though previously it referred to music composition.

6. The reference is to the notorious Streuensee affair involving the Danish court physician Count Johann Friedrich von Streuensee (1737–1772) and Enevold Brandt (1738–1772). Streuensee embarked upon a liaison with Queen Carolina Matilda, which resulted in an illegitimate daughter and the usurpation of the Danish government. Streuensee's rule was crushed in late 1771 by a revolt, both Streuensee and his henchman Brandt were executed, and the queen was sent into permanent internal exile. Which of the counts von Schulenburg Kraus befriended is not identified.

7. The summer residence was Ulriksdal, where Kraus was later to have his opera *Proserpin* performed.

8. The reference is to the opera *Amphion* by Johann Gottlieb Naumann (1741–1801), which was first performed on the king's birthday, 26 January 1778. The Royal Spectacles was normally closed during the summer, for no other reason than many of the audiences were at their country estates or attending outdoor performances of the Swedish Comedy at the park theater in Humlegård.[J] Kraus attended one of the last performances of the season, which took place on 1 June, two days after his arrival.

J. See the present author's "Gustavian Opera: An Overview" in *Gustavian Opera: Opera, Theatre and Dance 1771–1809,* ed. Inger Mattson (Stockholm: Kungliga Musikaliska Akademien, 1991).

9. Orig. *Notwendigkeiten,* meaning in-kind payment. The 24,000 Kopparmynt is the equivalent in Ducat exchange rate to about US$6,000 for Stockholm (according to the Swedish Riksbank historical exchange information), but Naumann would also have received the proceeds from several performances. See Letter 43.

10. This entire passage is indicative of the difficulties with the various rates of exchange during the period, which varied from person to person, city to city. The *Leier* is one of Kraus's expressions that means his travel purse.

11. From the context, it is probably a different Kessler than Kraus's erstwhile publisher.

12. The passport (Buchen, Bezirksmuseum) reads "Joseph Krause, *juris licentiate,*" or "Joseph Krause, the Law Student."

15. Letter to his parents dated Stockholm, 20 August 1778

Much Beloved Parents!

I received your second letter of the 28th of July on the 18th [of August] and only just today your first one.[1] Your love for me – I would not have earned it due to little trust, had not other circumstances mitigated my errors. I should have disclosed my situation at my departure from Göttingen more honestly, you say. Right! I am guilty. But, all the more honest. Because I thought the improvement of my situation was close, certainly imminent – [and] saw few or no difficulties at all before me, in short, that I would be able to relieve all of my debts myself before I had to place the burden upon you – truly, that makes me less guilty. I left it to my friends, the business of satisfying my creditors with this assurance, but as I now see, this was followed through poorly. Today I am writing [them] myself. The majority have been too anxious about me – it is my fate and, unfortunately, often my own fault. But I nonetheless thank God that this happened more on account of my heart that through carelessness. However much I desire, I am not now in a position to prohibit the croaking of the frogs without your help. I ask you sincerely and for what? The eternal request – I would rather slap myself upside the head if it would resolve them. As I live and breathe,[2] I am a living mortgage, but it is only that men are not served by it. I appeal to your love to satisfy the following small obligations as soon as possible. *1.* 18 Reichsth [Reichsthalers] to the merchant *Wiese; 2.* 5 Rcht [Reichsthalers] to the porter *Frike; 3.* Around 6 Louis d'ors to the Madame Doctor *Sothen; 4.*

6 Louis d'ors to the medical doctor *Jaeger*. If you send them the money, do not write on the letter anything more than: "for *Joseph Kraus*." Don't sign your name. You also don't need a receipt for this, for I already have it. 5. My *landlord* 5 Louis d'ors; 6. 9 Rt [Reichsthalers] 27 Mg [Mariengroschen] for the notary *Müller* for a bill of a tailor whose children he is the guardian. The Louis d'or is fully equal to 5 Rth [Reichsthalers]. The other creditors that I have put off until next Easter are: 1. *The Jew Gumbrecht,* 82 Thl [Thalers], but not only for one watch; 2. *Neuburg* 10 Th [Thalers]; 3. *Berkenbuch* 10 [Thalers]; 4. The laundress and tailor about 6 Thl [Thalers]; 5. *Sothen* the remaining 3½ Louis d'ors and 30 Gr [Groschen].[3] Damn! My debts have run a lot higher than I thought myself – that I have been such an idiot! But – the beginning of my recovery is already made.[4] Since I left Göttingen I have not tasted a drop of wine; *proficiat*! –I don't fear the lawsuits of my creditors, even if they will not wait – for in the end not even half of it belongs to them. But rather – God knows if I had such a great reason to hang my head, I would not let my serious melancholic thoughts take over, for I see my dear father once more in harness. Of course, one would rather be in such a harness than calmly singing in misery in Buchen. Oh, dear ones, if only I could see my hopes fulfilled – and then be able to return home to your bosom with my fortune – that would be a feast for me! The time will come – hopefully, if it is not absent. Outlook – this has always been good for me – but not fulfillment. The conceited asses[5] then gave me a libretto – that Herr *Klein* in Mannheim would have been ashamed of, and then – it must have been really bad, by my poor soul, and it really was – Our King has the weakness to be gladly praised. Enough!

It is going quite well with the language. I already speak like a native Swede. Congratulations on my sister's wedding,[6] and in order to make it really nice, no one but I was missing; and one who shouldn't have been there was; Reider, whose enemy I am on my honor forever as long as I breathe. God forgive me this sin! I have often inflicted violence on myself[7] and wished good upon him – an imminent little mortal sin wished upon him in all piety, as I also wish the rogues of Ingolstadt to have dust brooms for the bad and for the good, bad wives.[8] This [it is] ever with mankind. One must be a plague to another, whenever one ought to be able to contribute to another's happiness. In Sweden it is very cheap to travel. Two Swedish miles is equal to 3 German. In only costs 12 Stüber[9] per mile for a horse – as much as 11 Kreutzer, and the roads are extraordinarily good. A month ago I undertook a brief journey to Lapland[10] – in company – 140 Swedish or 210 German miles for 1 Louis d'or. You must understand that it was all free except for tips. In Lapland they don't have bread – they use dried fish instead. The countryside is quite rough, but nonetheless pleasant, and the people extraordinarily good. On the entire route I took the people had never seen a German, nor had they heard the name of the place. Oh, thus the sheep are strewn about!

Now, back to Germany. I am most curious about the *Pfälzische Musiklehrbuch*.[11] Can you please give it to me as a favor? A really huge one? It must be well-packed and delivered either through the normal address or sent by way of Lübeck, so that I can receive it by ship. For more clarity you should put the following address on it:

> To M[on]s[ieu]r.
> Krause
> To be left with the Herr Merchant Schiernell, living on Götegatan in
> House No. 130[12] in Stockholm.

Normal letters don't need it. Oh! Do not forget me in the fall! My dear sister – my brothers, all of my siblings I greet most fondly. Thank you! And wish Herr Knörzer luck. A letter from Hamburg here costs 24 Stüver – 22 Kreutzer.

> *Your*
> *Eternally obedient son*
> *Joseph*

[P.S.] The money for Herr Frik and the 6 Louis d'ors for Mdme [Madame] Sothin can be enclosed in the [letter to] Herr Wiese.

COMMENTARY

Original Buchen, Bezirksmuseum. Apparently, Kraus's Göttingen creditors had contacted his parents for restitution, resulting in the rather detailed list of debts incurred. Hidden within this missive is an indication that the initial offer of an opera commission was in fact tendered, but that Kraus rejected it as unsuitable, thus placing him in an untenable position with respect to future employment that would have made his career.

1. The first letter was no doubt the answer to Kraus's previous one of 12

June, which his parents had sent off on 9 July.

2. Orig. *wie ich stehe und gehe* = as I stand and walk. The colloquial epithet is equivalent to the one used here.

3. The total sum is about 231 Reichthalers or around US$3,000–10,000 today. It is not possible to identify these creditors more precisely, though the landlord was certainly Münder (see Letter 1).

4. Orig. *Der Anfang meine Besserung ist schon gemacht,* indicating most likely that he has begun working at his profession.

5. Orig. *Die Geken.* The identity of these people is unknown, but Leux-Henschen (LH-JMK, 43) postulates that it may have been the administration of the Royal Spectacles, led by Adolf Fredrik friherr von Barnekow (1744–1787), basing her assumption on a letter by Naumann from 18 August 1777 in which he describes Barnekow as a "ramrod in portfolio." The text too is unknown, but both the epithet and the final comment concerning the vanity of Gustav III indicate that he had finally been given an honorific commission as a test piece, the first step in the process of official employment. "Klein" is Pater Anton Klein, his early teacher and librettist of *Günther von Schwarzurg.*

6. Orig. *Schwester Hochzeit,* referring to the final vows of his sister Katharina Josepha at the cloister in Mainz.

7. Orig. *Hab ich mir doch oft Gewalt angethan.* The statement is sarcastic and contrarian.

8. The reference is to a folk tale wherein the men of Ingolstadt, a town in Bavaria, were given brooms to chastise wives who were considered disobedient, but in their zealousness they also swept away those who were virtuous as well, claiming that they were only preventing sin.

9. *Stüber* or *Stüver,* a coin worth 4 Pfennige or 2 *deute,* another small coin in circulation. The approximate value today would be about US$0.25. The Kreutzer (exchanged at a rate of 12/11) was yet another small coin used in northern Westphalia.

10. The distance Kraus mentions to "Lapland" places it no further north than the Swedish town of Härnösand, about 435 Km or 270 miles north of Stockholm. The actual Lapland is appreciably further north. That the journey cost so little can be explained by the fact that his friend, Carl Stridsberg, was a teacher at the local school in the town. The comment that the people use dried fish instead of bread is, of course, nonsense; most likely, this refers to dried cod on *knäcke,* a type of Scandinavian hardtack made from rye and a principal source of food in the northern reaches of Sweden during the eighteenth century, according to the records in the Folk Museum, Stockholm.

11. This refers to *Tonwissenschaft und Tonsetzkunst* by Abbé Georg Joseph Vogler, published in Mannheim in 1776.

12. Orig. in Swedish: *"Till Msr/Msr. Krause/aflämnas hos Herr Handelsmannen Schiernell, boendes på Götegatan i Huset No 130 i Stokholm."* Archival research by Gunnar Larsson has revealed that this address, in Stockholm's Gamla Stan (Old Town), is now on the corner of Götgatan and Svartansgatan, No. 25. The building, the home of a linen merchant named Petter Schiernell, was torn down in 1850. Schiernell, Kraus's landlord and later close friend, was subsequently instrumental in resolving some of the debts that Kraus incurred in Stockholm.

16. Letter to his parents dated Stockholm, 10 September 1778

Dearest Parents!

Everything here is brilliant and merry, because the Swedes have the hope of obtaining a Prince. There are so many preparations that one cannot anticipate an end to the festivities: and I move about with my hypochondria that gets worse day by day. It really doesn't mean a lot, for it is more a consequence of my temperament than the frailty of my body; the rotten mood robs me of the desire to work for many hours and many days and what is more annoying, the desire to work for my own satisfaction. It often prevails and that is enough! Last week I received a blow that put me off my composure. I made a contract with a Dutch sea captain for a specific sum of money for some music. On Monday I played them for him in the company of a Russian, who was his passenger. They pleased him, but we were not yet in agreement. On Tuesday morning he retrieved six pieces, promising me the agreed-upon sum that I was to collect on his shop the following day. I came and the son of a bitch[1] had sailed off the previous night. To my misfortune, the copy and original were one and the same. Good luck on your journey! Now I'm consoled; I'll now fabricate others. I see now that I myself am the cause of burying my tranquility often without reason, and then blaming the discomfort on something else – if I only could! I want to laugh in the face of those who would convince me that one is one's own master. If it is capricious: yes, yes. If it is passion, then debate helps about as much as dogs barking. If all at once one has a paroxysm of courage, hah! Then it is easy every 3–4 months to bundle up everything that one can encounter with a little string of independence – [but] let three circumstances that one has not foreseen appear, then the fellow stands there without a clue. If thereafter an itinerant preacher comes and remonstrates that now and again one has to have many difficulties, then I do what Götz von Berlichingen did to the Imperial commander: "Lick my a[ss],"[2] and close my window. It is miserable enough that one leaves behind composure just when one is in need of it the most. God knows, that I do myself a disservice sometimes in order not to be able to complain that I have consciously thrown a rock into the path of my fortune. –But anyone who can leave things alone if a privileged moron with a judgmental demeanor messes around with his art – is either greater than I, which I gladly acknowledge, or a parasite and a sh[it]head.[3]

In my last letter I asked you about the *Pfälzische Musikalische Lehrbuch,* [and] now I repeat my request. It was only this week first announced in the Swedish newspapers, and the learned mouse-trappers expressed their mockery with it. "First rate," it says therein, "it would be funny if farmers, city prostitutes, and fauns in Germany all were able to whistle, play the organ and fiddle; as well as sing, or, when the voice fails, croak." I was so annoyed by this that I would have liked to have punched out the fellow, whom I know quite well[4] – but for the sake of good will it had to be suppressed this time.

Otherwise, what else is new? Although, what do I care about news if it doesn't concern you or friends – and how few of these do we have? How is my dear godfather in Mundau? I send effusive greetings to him and his entire family. And the man that I treasure so very much, love so very much – my confirmation sponsor – tell him that I think of him quite often with affection – I know that he loves me. Fall is here – my purse, everyone knows all about it.[5] Please think about me! I faint when I think about it. One cannot live here in the winter without a coat. Of course, such a thing doesn't cost much, only money. And I must also have clothing. Dear God, how is it with human beings; a poor little creature, who, if he sticks his head in the door, doesn't have the strength to dance over the threshold. Think of me now that I am in desperate need – the more, the better. Hopefully, this will be the last time that I have to beg, if God will preserve me my good mood to flog my ill fortune. I am already so indebted to you and my siblings and am not yet in a position of paying back something! When I wander back and forth during the evening on the seashore, left alone to myself and my melancholy – and compare this place with my fatherland – all of my days that have passed idle and in misery for the most part – and my loved ones, to whom I belong with all my heart, all of this appears magically in front of me, and the pictures hover like ghosts, and – I weep! – Hah! Do you not see still all of the tears that an undivided heart weeps, you who are sundered from me across the sea! I know that you know me – but not the source, my only one which is a sorrow, my own heart. Have I not often grumbled about my irresponsibility – it has often been a source of dismay to both you

and me – but if I did not have it, the little pity that holds me up when
sometimes the dismal black passion wells up in me – I am convinced that
I would have been torn to pieces long ago. Continue to keep me warm
in your hearts – Would that it would show that I deserve it truly only by
saying it! An affectionate greeting to my siblings

    Your most obedient son
    Joseph

COMMENTARY

Original Buchen, Bezirksmuseum. Despite the obvious purpose of the letter eliciting further funds to support the composer's existence in Stockholm, Kraus's effusive and sometimes halting emotional language betrays an insight into both his personal circumstances and his somewhat melancholic character. While it may be tempting to interpret this only on the basis of an attempt to obtain sympathy for his plight, the description of his moods and character are corroborated in characterizations of him left by a Swedish official, C. G. Gjörwell. One of these was done at the request of Stridsberg and composer Pehr Frigel (1750–1842), a student of Kraus, for the memorial festival held in March of 1798: "He had a face that was full of emotional sweetness, but along with that [he] possessed a strongly-marked somber expression. He had his own dark brown hair, [and] in both dress and manner [was] without pretense, inwardly and outwardly. He did not have precise mannerisms; [but] on the other hand, true friendship brought his complete honor."[K]

1. Orig. *Hundsfut*. The identity of these six works (*Sechs Stücke*) is unknown, although Karl Schreiber opined (Sch-JMK, 56) that they were "probably piano sonatas." His suggestion no doubt comes from the comment that Kraus played them on the fortepiano, but there is no documentation that actually supports such a claim.

2. The quote is from a play of the same name as the character written in 1773 by Johann Wolfgang von Goethe.

3. Orig. *Schmarozer und ein Sch . . . kerl.*

4. The identity of the critic in unknown, but he was certainly among Kraus's circle of new Swedish friends. Leux-Henschen believed that it may have been Johan Henrik Kellgren (1751–1795), later the composer's librettist, as she noted in a series of articles on the polemic debates on music that occurred about this time in Stockholm. This remains uncertain, however.

5. Orig. *Der Herbst ist da – mein Beutel, alles spürt's.*

K. This manuscript description can be found in Stockholm, Kungliga Biblioteket, autograf-samling; translation by the present author.

17. Letter to his parents dated Stockholm, 3 November 1778

Dearest Parents!

The fall has passed and I have been forgotten. If you really could have been put in my place, I am certain that you would not have forgotten me. Not counting the fact that I am really lacking money, for the past four weeks I have been lying ill with a cold fever[1] – the most horrible dissatisfaction with myself was the impossibility of removing the terrible emptiness from my throat and – not to have the desire to do anything, neither to work nor to take it easy, all of it far more annoying that simply not having any money, not even enough to procure a poor coat for the winter. My dear ones! I know that it is my own fault that I've deserved to be loved with less warmth than previously, but I am equally certain that if you have decided to leave your poor Joseph in the lurch, that I would love you with as much affection, ever so much affection as before. I have not once been in the position of sprinkling my observations with the pleasures that are now in full bloom here on the account of my infirmity and the nasty weather, for we have had snow for weeks already. Last Sunday morning the Swedes were given a young prince[2] – fireworks, operas, balls,[3] etc., bear witness daily to the utmost joy of the inhabitants for an heir to their good and great King. But I am too thick in the head, for I doubt that the greatest happiness is able to illuminate me. Comfort

Your

Ill Joseph

COMMENTARY

Original Buchen, Bezirksmuseum. As a side note to this short letter filled with self-pity, no doubt caused by some sickness, it may be said that Kraus was perhaps fortunate that he did not participate in the festivities he describes. During the initial celebrations there was, according to the local newspapers, an outbreak of measles or chicken pox (*Wattenkoppor*), and soldiers roamed about among the celebrants to quarantine those affected; Kraus's symptoms, however, indicate probably a severe cold or flu. When the full celebrations resumed on 30 December, the citizens of Stockholm erected a huge tent at Normalmstorg and invited the entire town to celebrate with free spirits and music. When the gates were opened, more than 64 people were trampled to death in the rush to get in, their bodies remaining for several hours on the ground as the people danced around and on top of them. The drunken mayhem was only curtailed when the king ordered the tent cleared by the military so that the corpses could be taken to a makeshift morgue and those wounded in the melee could be treated at a local hospital.

1. Orig. *kalten Fieber krank,* probably indicating cold sweats. See the commentary.

2. The new prince was Gustav Adolf, later Gustav IV Adolf (1778–1837), who was born on 1 November.

3. The newspaper *Stockholms Posten* announced on 2 November that Queen Sophia Magdalena was delivered of a baby boy at 6:45 AM, immediately following which a salute of 256 rounds was fired by the palace guards to alert the populace to the event. These continued throughout the day during the celebratory church service that followed. The new prince received his name only on 10 November during his baptism, and fireworks continued throughout the night of 12 November, whereupon a parade of the nobility was organized and prisoners given general amnesty by Gustav III.

18. Letter to his parents dated Stockholm, 6 December 1778

Dearest Parents!

I have received neither letter nor book. I expected support from you for my distressing situation, and that already in the fall. Now several months have passed – which I have lived through most wretchedly, for I lacked everything and I received not once an answer to my three letters. I now see that you have thought of me, but how little has that helped me? I don't know anything about *Cämerer,*[1] hardly even knowing what I am to do about the name, and concerning the rest of the things, Imperial ambassadors, high officials, etc., one is as good as the other to me. You would have been able to save me if you had supported me in October, for I would not have needed to endure what I endured. If you *now* still want to do me a favor, it is this; that I shall be able to forget my rotten time, but you are not allowed to delay. God knows! that I am now a poor rascal, for I see that hundreds are satisfied with me, only not I alone. To be short and sweet – I am now making a little opera,[2] not gladly, as the Saints know. Why? I can't write about it – I'd like to tell, but of course this is not possible the way things stand. It is a hard thing to have to work in order to be able to pay off China and herring! It's all the same! I'm going to let our most wonderful Father deal with it, for He will make good with me, make good with those who have demands upon my limbs. Send me something – previously I asked for it, and now I must beg. It is certainly not a shame if I beg from my dear father and dear mother. – If it were a shame, I would rather starve. Thus can one be such a fool with his honor.

I would gladly write my sister the nun, but what? If it is good for me, it is even better for her; but what sort of letter? Oh beloved, beloved, do not forget me in such a state that I have never before seen myself – I don't want to pass on to you the rotten hours that I have actually painted for you. Give the poor wretch alms of 100 Ducats, and I will gladly pay you back with a small opera. Greet all of the other people – I am half crazed.[3]

Your

most obedient

Joseph

COMMENTARY

Original Buchen, Bezirksmuseum. The subtext of this half-pleading, half-sarcastic letter is that his parents have written him news of home, but sent along no funds. They have obviously recommended him to someone who might be able to help him out in the circumstances, but did not enclose a subvention. He does imply, however, that he has begun to make inroads into the Stockholm musical establishment, primarily on his own (and not official) terms.

1. Cämerer (most likely Kämmerer. Kraus's spelling of the name is quite variable and inconsistent, calling him Kämmerer, Kämerer, Cämerer, and Cämmerer; this translation uses Kämmerer hereafter for the sake of consistency) cannot be identified, although Schreiber (Sch-JMK, 57,60) believed that he was a member of the staff of Holy Roman ambassador Count Friedrich von Kageneck. Apparently, he was known to Kraus's father from his official Mainz contacts.

2. This is the first intimation that he was at work on his first opera, *Azire*. Given that he had turned down an official commission (see Letter 15), he no doubt thought it imprudent to say much more about it, given that it was probably being done on speculation. His next thought seems to indicate that he was hard at work to survive, implying that he was still composing music. The reference to China and herring (*China und Häringe*) can be translated figuratively as "board and bread," though the original expression is far more colorful.

3. Orig. *ich bin halb toll im Kopfe,* or I am half mad in the head.

19. Letter to his parents dated Stockholm, 5 January 1779

Dearest Parents!

Don't think badly of me that I have not answered you of late. I really have already begun letters three times, and three times torn them up again. It is not my usual way, but this time there were reasons. I now know *Kämmerer* as a very good man, but by far not so close [an acquaintance] that I would like to be indebted to him for money. I cannot tell you more how much I am grateful to you for the letter of credit you sent, other than to admit honestly that I don't have a single red penny in my purse.[1] There was thus a little reason why the second letter of credit was not there along with it. H[err] *Kämmerer* then helped me out of this difficulty, so that he has earned a bowing and scraping from me; as soon as I go out, he shall have it. It is not very strange that I have not seen him in three weeks. He has much to do, and the road long, about half a German hour,[2] and the weather extraordinarily cold, something that one can expect in the north at this time; as a result we see each other seldom and concerning the recommendations!!![3] – I don't want any. I want once and for all my fortune and misfortune to be thanks to myself alone; – it is always surprising to me that among so many others who wander before me, behind me, and everyone about me has given me such a varied nature, I alone know how I am and how I am not able to be otherwise.

Now to my situation. All of my projects regarding travels and sustenance have marched forward in crab fashion.[4] So it is! I've deserved it. Why did I dispense with myself and my worth and trust in demigods? I want to go home! – At least, not yet at the moment. I now have new wares for my spoiled designs. It may be that these are also bubbles; but it can also be that they will succeed. I am now making an opera[5] – it has been accepted; but how it will be received must depend upon the first stroke. If it is good, I'll have what I want – if otherwise, at least I will receive traveling funds and therefore certainly be home early in the year! I can give better and more detailed news about all this only in a few weeks. I now have a black Swedish costume.[6] I would give anything if you could see me! Don't I look like a Dutch seaman! Further, I have not received a single one of any of your letters (I mean the others), much less *Vogler's* book[7] about which I am so extraordinarily curious. God knows what has become of it. But – but – 40 foxes?[8] Oh dear! I certainly believe that I would be able to relieve my debts; why did you give me so little in my great need? – Yes, I know, where would I take it? Good, you are right. But listen! – at once I had decided not to borrow anything from Kämmerer. I have to have clothes made for me, and because I once sought service, I shouldn't be stingy – truly, I need more – Oh! Can you not spare another 40, and I'll earn it [back] with sketches. If you want to do yourselves and my brother a small favor, buy the *Etwas von und über Musik* in Frankfurt. It is the little work that Kessler didn't want to accept. But, please tell no one around you that it is by me. Why? Just read it.

Love me, as always – continue to love me

Your

most obedient Joseph

COMMENTARY

Original Buchen, Bezirksmuseum. It is clear that, pursuant to the previous letter, Kraus sought out Kämmerer, who subsequently became a conduit for Kraus to obtain funds, both from his parents and possibly elsewhere, though the composer takes great pains to assure his parents that he has not borrowed from him. His financial situation was also probably aided by the publication of his treatise by the Eichenbergischen Erben, which even though published anonymously, would have resulted in some royalties. He also implies that his opera project was accepted as a trial piece for furthering his career.

1. Orig. *keinen roten Heller mehr im Sak,* the Heller being a small coin akin to the Stüber. Reading between the lines, Kraus did not have enough funds to redeem the two letters of credit sent by his parents.

2. Orig. *eine halbe deutsche Stunde,* or about 4½ kilometers or 3 miles.

3. His parents have obviously sent a message through Kämmerer that he might be in need of official recommendations to obtain a post.

4. Orig. *Krebsgang,* or sideways without much forward progress.

5. The opera, as noted in the previous letter, is *Azire,* but Kraus seems to think that its acceptance automatically meant a performance; he was unaware of the need in Sweden for a test piece, generally created by one of the official members of the Vitterhetsakademie and further adjudicated by the Royal Academy of Music.

6. This is the Swedish national dress introduced by Gustav III in 1778.

7. This is Vogler's treatise *Pfälzische Musiklehrbuch* noted previously.

8. Orig. *Fuchse,* a colloquial term for Ducats.

20. Letter to his parents dated Stockholm, 18 January 1779

Dearest Parents!

Today I received your two letters of the 8th of October and the 14th of December. The fault lay with the post office here. I don't know anything about the books, however.[1] I didn't think it necessary to answer everybody under the circumstances, because I've already done it in my other letters. The letter to *Kämmerer,* which was enclosed in the first of these, is probably already too late, [but] I shall deliver it tomorrow.

It was pleasant to receive the enclosed copy of the review of my little missive by that fellow from Frankfurt.[2] And not just because he treated me so gently and thus conveniently danced to my tune, but rather he perceived why I was right. I believe that he is more than just a stupid fellow. I am not afraid of having my hair pulled, and even if Herr Vogler himself, as well as the chamberlain of the Apostolic Palace,[3] is to be placed ahead of me, I am certain that I do not lack knowledge or argument in order to be able to be responsible for my own things even in the end. Of course, much – much too much has been said in earnest – let it be! I had nonetheless decided when *Kessler* sent back my manuscript to alter many things. One of my friends took it on to have it printed in Saxony, but every one of the louts was afraid to make an enemy of the musical stable hands through the truth, until finally my piece wound up in *Darmstadt,* where a very prescient man[4] took it on and hunted it to publication. In this way it was as gross as it had been before, and I don't regret it – even grosser things are [yet] to come.

Fare you all well and love

Your most obedient Joseph

P.S. The reason for the letter coming so late is that I diligently waited to be able to tell you something new from me. But I have waited now in vain. My little opera[5] is now accepted, only I do not have the final word yet. I made it understood that I do not have time to hang around until the new year – therefore I hope to be able to write more in the next one. About the recommendation from Regensburg – you know that I cannot abide anything worse than recommendations from people who do not understand my profession.

Once more, fare you all well –

The enclosed letter is to my sister in Mainz.

COMMENTARY

Original Buchen, Bezirksmuseum. His parents seem to have sent along the first review of the treatise. They also appear to have been working behind the scenes to find Kraus a secure position, though it would seem as a state official rather than as a composer. This would explain his contempt for their approaching some acquaintance in Regensburg, presumably at the court of Thurn und Taxis.

1. Kraus's parents have apparently informed him that they have sent a number of books.

2. The reviewer from Frankfurt is unidentified; Johann Nikolaus Forkel (1749–1790), who was criticized in the treatise, wrote in the *Allgemeine Literatur der Musik* (1780): "It appears to have been written by a doubtlessly sensitive man who is nonetheless completely lacking judgment. . . . It is a diatribe filled with bitterness and invidiousness against English composers." As Schreiber (Sch-JMK, 39) stated, he wondered if Forkel had actually read the work.

3. The reference to Vogler and the "Apostolic Palace" (i.e., the Vatican) is a comment on that composer's sometimes obnoxious habit of flaunting his clerical rank and trappings.

4. The *vornehmer Mann* in Johann Heinrich Merck (1741–1791), chief editor of the *Eichenbergischen Erben*.

5. This refers to *Azire* (VB 18).

21. Letter to his parents dated Stockholm, 2 March 1779

It is almost half incomprehensible to me that I still have some small wit left among the throng that doesn't once make the effort to connect to the heart, [but] who always has to lend a pair of ears to one's neighbors in order to listen and thus not lose his patience! Do they make a fool of me or what? That would be nice. I have all at once begun the dance, and I cannot now give it up without sacrificing my honor. My music has approval, but the librettist[1] has enemies, and although I would bet life and limb that it is the best piece, that Sweden now has something original, it was neatly suppressed. Now what to do? The director[2] asked me to await the King's mood – subservience half forces me to do it. *Kämmerer* is leaving here and has offered me to take care of the baggage[3] as far as Hamburg if I will accompany him, but to help me out with money is now impossible for him. What does that help me now? If I were to leave here, then I need, above and beyond this, greater support, although I already live so wretchedly that I cannot tell anyone else but you, because you know my circumstances. Now this is my fate, and because the shitheads want to be flattered, do me a favor and put in a good word with Herr v[on] Benzel to provide me with a recommendation very quickly, for *Hessenstein*[4] is now here.

My sister should attribute my letter to my conditions, as good as she is.

Your Joseph

COMMENTARY

Original Buchen, Bezirksmuseum. The subtext of the letter is that his parents have asked Herr Kämmerer to accompany Kraus back home to Germany. The opening expostulation may reflect his views on the reactions to his opera by the Stockholm cultural establishment. See Letter 23.

1. Carl Stridsberg; see Letter 23.

2. The director of the Royal Spectacles, i.e., Barnekow.

3. Orig. *Reisekiste,* or literally "travel chest." Leux-Henschen read it as "nach Hause" but the original letter clearly states Hamburg.

4. Count Fredrik Vilhelm von Hessenstein (1735–1808), governor-general of Swedish Pomerania. See Letter 23.

22. Letter to Johann Friedrich Hahn
dated Stockholm, 4 March 1779

I migrated up and down the north, turned against the phenomenon of a lesser inscribed page; lost against the few that I sought; hit myself on the head when I found them; won against the crowd, and that has made me a fool. I had nothing to do here, could have gone and didn't, incurred debts and now cannot go; this is the reason why I am writing to you now what I would like to say to you.

For I have often thought of you – thought only of you – [and] for you I forgot father and mother who whine about me as a refugee.

Your Kraus

COMMENTARY

Original lost; published in Si-JMK (70) as "Till Theologie Candidaten Hahn uti Zweybrücken" (To theology student Hahn in Zweibrücken). The letter remains a torso, lacking an indeterminate amount of beginning text and salutation. Silverstolpe apparently used only a small excerpt of the letter, noting: "Concerning the latter [i.e., this letter], a Swedish translation follows, excerpting only the most pertinent section" (*Af desse sednare följa här i svensk öfversättning, och stundom i utdrag, de väsentligaste*). The letter was sent to Silverstolpe with the comment that Hahn[L] had recently passed away in Zweibrücken. Why the diplomat destroyed the remainder of the letter cannot be determined, though it is clear that he thought it superfluous, save as an indicator of the composer's mood. The final paragraph, seemingly couched in intimate language, is really no more than friendly *Schwärmerei*, effusiveness without much substance.

23. Letter to his parents dated Stockholm, 9 March 1779

Dearest Parents!

If the letters are so old, it depends for the most part upon my calendar. Often, I hardly know the year in which I live, much less the date. I forgive myself this and hopefully so do you, because it has become my custom from way back. I am often so distracted that I have to make my way back more or less piecemeal whenever I want to think. A great plague but never an epidemic; thanks to our loving Lord God! For then it would be lovely cabbage patches and cauliflower plots hither and yon. Whenever I become like this, people say I am unchristianly strange and shockingly unclear. Then I remember Papa's favorite saying: "You have *spiritum contradictionis*," but nonetheless do what I can *rebus sic stantibus*,[1] and always retain my little catechism.

I cannot tell you anything more specific about my trade than before. The review of the text at the Musical Academy[2] is going very slowly, although the music has been completely approved. Of course, patience is the best thing now. I'd have been bored silly by all this had I not had a half-Swedish and half-German living library at my back and call. – This is a Swedish postmaster in Wismar,[3] who is quite knowledgeable about music, literature, and art. He is here partly for numerous official reasons and has a bunch of music books with him that he has placed at my disposal as a favor in my hermitage. We converse about them in the evenings. It is something quite nice if one has to visit such an uncle or aunt during the evenings – I can demonstrate this. Good! At least I have

L. See Si-JMK, 70, Note 1: "This short letter, notable only for the character impression that it outlines, was delivered by Kraus's parents with the comment that Hr. Hahn had just died when it arrived at the place" [*Detta kort bref, märkvärdig endast för den sinnesstämning det afskildrar, är af Kraues Föräldrar meddeladt med den anmärkning, att Hr. Hahn var nyss afliden när det till orten ankom*].

some leisure with my dear postmaster. The most patriotic Swede and a rather patriotic German together in one – it might be suggested that something can drop out of this, for he has the honor of being a member of the Music Academy here. I would gladly let it be admitted, if one is able to be knowledgeable about such things, that Swedes ought to be sophisticates in the literary sciences – heroes, like myself in finances, and the Good Lord knows that I can only multiply one times one up to six times six is thirty-six. That is on no account to say that one cannot find folk here and there, like anywhere else, who aren't convinced by their own feelings about that which they speak. I've nothing against it, for one of the *Superum*[4] can bear in mind my insignificance with Herr Count von Hessenstein as the current Governor of Pomerania and would sing my praises, although he doesn't know whether I deserve it – thus all the better – but for that reason I have nothing more than nothing against it, and therefore to me it is of no consequence if he lets things alone. The reason is something one cannot write about gladly. To preserve my calling to speak with the poets of the Rhineland, to put down roots in the cities of the Rhine and Main – or to let myself be settled down in any case between four tapestry-covered walls – I have composed a small keyboard sonata[5] slickly and cleanly for Countess I.: thus I've done what I ought and only await a ship to Wismar or Stralsund in order to practice it over there. Just now I received the 79th Theater Calendar,[6] where a rondo by H[err] *v*[*on*] *Kerpen* is announced. Now I believe as I have never before believed that the Last Judgment is imminent. *Proh sup!*[7]

I was called by orders from on high to the post office and solemnly notified that a packet from Copenhagen had been waiting for me since the end of the summer, which I ought now to redeem at my immediate leisure. These will be *Vogler's* books. The blackguards in Denmark should have told me earlier, without it coming at such a high cost to me. I've already read all of the thing(s), moreover, for I was able to borrow them from my postmaster. As little approval as it found in its own country, it is nonetheless certain that he is among the best of the mathematical theoreticians. But, his so famous fundamentals are and will ever be rules for use as they have been for each genius – nonsense. Of course, there would be feuds throughout the entire Holy Roman Empire if one would bray something so definitive from the pulpit, for the majority would still suck it up into their faces like children do their little pacifiers. I am therefore utterly convinced by the affair that one can write whatever one wants, if one can find a printer – and a printer if there be a salesman. Oh Madonna!

To go home and to *"Actum* of such and such" – I would rather become an abbot in a monastery, something I don't need to be afraid of just now.

Your

Most humble Joseph

[P.S.]

1. What is my dear sister in Mainz and the others doing?
2. Has the money been sent to Doctor Jäger?
3. Please be so kind as to forward the enclosed letter.[8]

COMMENTARY

Original Buchen, Bezirksmuseum. Reading between the lines, Kraus has been informed that *Azire* has been adjudicated musically but not textually, though the tone remains upbeat. This is the first indication that he has made the acquaintance of Johann Friedrich Hallardt (1726–1794), who was later to become one of his closest friends. He is also attempting to forge some sort of contact with the powers that be in the Electorate of Mainz, possibly with the intention of returning home if his plans do not work out. Kraus is also less than impressed by Vogler's multivolume treatise.

1. *Spiritum contradictionis* = contradictory spirit; *rebus sic stantibus* = as things stand. The last is a legal term that allows for a situation to become inapplicable due to changing circumstances. He calls his father's epithet *Leibschüchelchen,* or literally, "his own favorite proverb."

2. Recte, the Kungliga Musikaliska Akademien, or Royal Swedish Academy of Music.

3. The postmaster is, as noted in the commentary, Hallardt.

4. *Superum* = superior beings.

5. The sonata is lost (VB 189), but was written probably as a means of bringing his talent to the attention of a noble family in the Mainz region. Schreiber (Sch-JMK, 59) calls the family "Ingelheim," no doubt based upon Kraus's spelling of the name in later letters. No aristocratic family with this name can be found at the time in this region, although there is a family by the name of Ingenheim.

6. The reference is to the *Gotha Theater Calendar.* The work is a rondeau based upon "an operetta by Count von Spauer" entitled "Schlafe, schönes Götteskind" by Friedrich Hugo Freiherr von Kerpen (1749–1810), a musical amateur from Würzburg and Heilbronn.

7. *Proh sup* = Prosit!

8. The "enclosed letter" has not survived; the identity of its recipient remains unknown.

24. Letter to his parents dated Stockholm, 8 May 1779

Dearest Parents!

I received your letter this very moment, for which I thirsted more for your well-being than news of the recommendation. Dear ones! God be praised: for my part I am now quite calmed, even though there are more and more obstacles. When the soul has worked off its acute distress, become secure in its independence, and stands there still trembling from the recent storm just like a newly exhausted wild animal and sees how fools try to outdo him; that is a comfort, as if it were [like] the same type that belongs to all lungs – that are consumptive. My body now lacks nothing: on the contrary I am now more healthy and robust than before; this makes me live like a Turk. But!!! Yes, if there were people, I wouldn't say to a point, [but] if they only would have a straightforward dose of healthy human understanding that is found today only seldom, [then] they would recognize that they would be required [to give] at least a little approval to my work. Now the oxen have stood up, praised it forward and backward, lauded it more than it was worth, and – given me nothing. Now everything is good. If the devils come around with their "an immature young man – a peculiar way of thinking, etc.," there is nothing more fitting than to wish them all to hell and himself in heaven, so that one can depart from the world in a good fashion. With all this you won't understand me, if I don't become more clear. You would see that *now* my remaining here is at least not an absolute consequence of my unhappy temperament.

When I came here I was unknown. My manner of making acquaintances, a certain something that in my nature is as old as I am myself, always keeps me somewhat distant from interacting. I would certainly not have sought my fortune here, but rather I depended upon the entire strength of my imagination, which runs so very much after honor to the point of being reduced to the most necessary maintenance. Thus, this is an entirely different motivation than has been made known to you since my departure. I kept quiet about it, because I was able to know in advance that you would not like it if it was the result of consideration that, after so many expensive years, I would be occupied with, [or] ensconced in a profession for which I had not the slightest liking.

I will not justify it so completely, either. It is enough that in the first days after my arrival virtually nothing was accomplished. Certain circumstances led me unnoticeably on my former path, and I found myself in the middle of it before I was aware of it. Then I went from one thing to the next and decided I would rather be destroyed than remain standing halfway. The notion that it is impossible to study a nation and its tastes, attributes, customs, etc., without the knowledge of its language was accompanied by something even more difficult that I didn't want to get involved in, and my most marvelously sufficient foundation, about which I was almost half-convinced of its certainty as were the horrible people as well, allowed me to consider every appearance of politeness as importunity. This difficulty was finally overcome. Due to quite a grasp of the language, I was finally put in the position of being able to judge the country, and I found not from one attempt but rather a hundred that the people about which I promised so much – were a cold, half-polarized, and all the more frustrating above all else, a French-loving, enervated folk.[1] Now upon a stage filled with such fauns and apes I once made my decision to dance. God knows what I would rather have done in all possible silence. But the gains of the wayward set hard conditions on it: one must of necessity dissemble if one wants to use it. I would have liked to impart all of my experiences to you if I were able to make them quite clear; this would be material for a book, not a letter. I finally dared to walk this path of burning embers and still retain a forthright mind. I worked. *The man*[2] who was to judge my work and, in my opinion at the beginning, was of course not able to let me experience something other than fairness (because he didn't understand it) and ease the path to the fulfillment of my hopes through his flattering opinions. Now my work was known, but the long and short of it was, that it occurred to the court that I aspired to be the director of the theater – and that was the last thing that the *man* desired. A specific difference was that, to him, I was certainly not fawning enough in my demeanor in order to have my work accepted, [which was] evidence to him of the complete antipathy between us. He did whatever he could in all secrecy to foment intrigues against the poet and consequently against me. What happened? The Imperial ambassador recommended a certain *Mysliveček*[3] – whether it happened under the influence of information provided by his wife, who also worked in his office, or through the friendship of Herr Captain *Kämmerer* for me, I do not know. This is certain; *Kämmerer* promised me at the beginning to make the acquaintance of his Count – and I was honest enough to confide in my dear countryman my views. – All at once my dear Captain was left out in the cold, and I learned [this] from one of the *high and mighty* here whom I had to thank for the cabals. Whatever will be with all of this will be, but at least I now know what sort of rival I have to contend with, and, moreover, I must ask you to keep the entire story secret. The recommended *Mysliveček* is at present in Italy; they wrote to him, and he immediately sent a trial piece that was performed and *whistled off* the stage. Now I am working on something a little less secret.[4] My work was accepted well but not rewarded. Because the King doesn't love music at all, there was nothing for me to hope for by the direct path. – There were still prospects, but which ones? Take this one – the basic reason – accept it that I must of necessity accept credit from good people, who have at times been so nice to me to provide for myself until better fortune comes along. – My desire to restore what is theirs to the good people – is this not reason enough that I would rather suffer through it – patiently suffer through it rather than vex myself as a day laborer in the future over my weakness?

Let me suffer, I ask you above all else, let me be right in this matter. Things are wretched enough without it, for I would not have thought that I would encounter so much misfortune so early. And, if it is the Good Lord's will that it is my fate gladly to endure such tribulation of necessity as I am guilty of, then I would rather suffer alone than share my pain through empathy, even if it means that I am lost forever.

Your Joseph

[P.S.] The music for Frau Countess Ingelheim[5] is on board a German ship.

COMMENTARY

Original Buchen, Bezirksmuseum. This rambling letter is a way of letting his parents know that his opera *Azire* has been rejected, the result of which is a venting of his spleen against his enemies and the Swedish court establishment in a way that will not jeopardize his future prospects.

1. Orig. *ein kaltes, halpolirtes, und was ärger als das all ist, ein französirtes, entnervtes Volk.*

2. *Der Mann* is a direct reference to the intendant of the Royal Spectacles,

Adolf Fredrik friherr von Barnekow. See Letter 35.

3. Joseph Mysliveček (1736–1781), a Bohemian composer resident in Italy. Though no official letter of invitation has survived, an aria, probably the trial work mentioned by Kraus, was performed at a public concert in Stockholm on 11 April 1779, according to a program published in *Stockholms Posten*.

4. The new project is not identified, though the implication is that it is another opera text.

5. The aforementioned keyboard sonata.

25. Letter to his parents dated Stockholm, 28 May 1779

Dearest Parents!

I waited and waited, but for all that, I have seen nothing practical in a recommendation. Of course, each week my debts climb – the greater and lesser have made it a business to preach patience to me, and I can think, hope of nothing else but that [there will be] an end to it soon, though God knows when that will be. It has cost me much until I had convinced myself that it is not my fault, but rather simply true bad luck. Now I have. – How would I not be if I were to see so much in motion about me, and all of it fruitless? – I wished you could see this by giving you a description of my life – how I have helped myself[1] and even with all of that I am indebted for 100 Ducats. How is it possible? God, I hardly know myself. Of the 40 Ducats I received from you, I had of necessity to buy clothes, and, listen, what my equipage consists of. I had to have a black waistcoat made for me due to the edict[2] – it cost me more than 20 Ducats (NB) including my old little clothes that I had to have retailored to conform to the fashion. A hat – don't laugh, cost me 2 Ducats. *Kämmerer* can attest to the price, if needed. I had made for me one pair of the so-called *Kjängor*,[3] one pair of shoes and one pair of boots, and my old things resoled, all at once a bill of 5–6 Riksdalers in coin. However much I had left over – I had to procure small items, tobacco, etc. – that it hasn't given me any pleasure to do all of this, not even once, I can prove, and by the fact that for weeks on end I don't even leave the house at all. Of course, there are reasons that did make me sorry, and because I wasn't used to it previously, naturally had to cause me harm. My clothes[4] are subsequently going to ruin. My landlords, who are otherwise good people, show respect only for money, and now not to be totally lost, I've had to make my watch run to the pawn shop, and because I didn't want to do it, a good friend had to do it for me. If I cannot redeem it in four weeks, both are lost.[5] Think about my present wretched situation. I am sometimes forced not to go out simply for this reason, for perhaps my neckerchief was not washed or I lack stockings. I have never been in such poverty-stricken circumstances, and if you are not in a position to help me, even more hard times are in store for me.[6] Good – I can then still say that I've tried. How gladly I would have avoided this situation!

If it is possible for you to free me from the debts, I'll run to be with you, and even if I would have ten times more hope than present, I would promise you. If it is not possible – well, so be it: it is hard not to have a penny to my name, which reminds me of my misery, but to be able to bear it must be a consolation for a boy who has two healthy legs, and that is to my credit. For the most part, if the matter is so involved that one cannot believe that a human being can be more denigrated or made whole, – then dear God comes along and ends the little song. . . . May he also do it with me.

To owe a hundred Ducats – and not to have a penny to my name – I don't know where my head is!

Live well and better than
I

COMMENTARY

Original Buchen, Bezirksmuseum. At the bottom of the letter someone, probably one of Kraus's parents, has written: "Delivered an answer to the post office on 11 June." This indicates that Kraus's letter made the trip from Stockholm in about two weeks. While it takes on an urgent tone in begging for money, it is clear from the enumeration of his clothing and other expenses that he was hardly living an impoverished existence; indeed, it seems to present the portrait of somewhat of a spendthrift.

1. Probably meaning the earning of some money through his music, though Kraus is vague.

2. The edict was one made by Gustav III for all officials to wear the national costume.

3. *Kjängor* = special boots belonging to the national costume.

4. Orig. *Wäsche,* or laundry.

5. The watch was made to "run" to the pawn shop numerous times, but eventually it was redeemed and returned after Kraus's death to his parents.

6. Orig. *Wie gern that ich auf diese Wissenschaft Verzicht!* or How gladly I would have resisted this knowledge.

26. Letter to his parents dated Stockholm, 22 June 1779

Dearest Parents!

My circumstances are now horribly bad. In my last letter I already told you that I am completely without money – and [I] am now even more so, if one can be more poor than to have nothing and thus [be] without hope. Perhaps this last would have been in view had not the mountain of debts oppressed me so much. If I wish to otherwise save myself, I must enter into an agreement[1] with my landlord to meet his demand by the end of *July.* If I am not to be arrested, I have to ask you to help me out with everything, and in the fastest manner possible. My debts have risen to 100 Ducats – I am almost ashamed to say that I have not enjoyed a single good day for all of it. But now it is a real emergency. I have no way out – either I have to pay back the sum by the end of July or I shall be arrested and with this lose what little reputation is left to my honor – and I would certainly have anything happen but this. Today I received exactly that sort of little thing that aroused my ire. On 13 April I gave a Hamburg shipper a packet for you. – Today I received it back from *London,* where it had been brought as a prize.[2] I would have preferred that they would have kept it, [for] it cost me half a Ducat. It was the music for Frau Countess *Ingelheim.* Now I will have to put it on board another ship.

There is nothing to the history of *Greistenheim*[3] – only bald-faced lies. If it is possible, please help me – I am convinced of it – and God! How often I wished and worked at (to be sure with a wretched result) being able to make things known to you through anything but a signature

Your most obedient son
Joseph

COMMENTARY

Original Buchen, Bezirksmuseum. This letter outlines a clash of cultures. Kraus, who regarded his debts as loans to be repaid, was apparently unaware that in Stockholm it was customary for even court-supported artists to accumulate debts and even spend time in jail (in relatively confined but not dungeon-like cells), after which their debts were considered absolved or paid in full by the king. Gustavian luminaries such as poet-singer Carl Michael Bellman (1740–1795) endured their sentences in relative comfort and apparently without social stigma, and had Kraus been less anxious, no doubt due to the lingering Göttingen indebtedness, he would have realized that it was par for the course for such employees to spend time in debtor's prison.

1. Orig. *mit einem Revers* [*sic*] … *verbinden*. A *Reverse* is a promissory note, and the "arrest" refers to debtor's prison.

2. The German ship was evidently commandeered by an English privateer, but since the music had no intrinsic value, it was returned to Stockholm postage due, thus adding insult to injury.

3. Recte Greiffenheim. The issue refers to the declaration of 1757 of the Swedish ambassador to the Imperial Diet at Regensburg, Johan August von Greiffensheim (1712–1789), that reaffirmed Sweden's right to Pomerania.

27. Letter to his parents dated Stockholm, 25 June 1779

Dearest Parents!

Just this moment I received your letter and this moment I have to answer it, even if I should not be so short. The debt of 100 Ducats is only my liquid debt for my landlord and the main post, but apart from them it is not possible therefore to return home, and I cannot count on the Court under the circumstances. If I am to embrace you, I must have an additional 50 Ducats. My dear ones, my dear ones, don't abandon your unfortunate one who has almost gone crazy without it. Surely, if it would not be God's work and hand in it, I would already be insane. I thank you a thousand times for the Ducats, for they were worth more than 200. But dearest [ones], if I am to leave this damned Sweden, I have to have 150 Ducats. Would that I could make for you a single happy hour for all the misfortune that I have caused you! – Now my desperate hours have come again – do not abandon me!

Your most unfortunate Joseph

COMMENTARY

Original Buchen, Bezirksmuseum. As usual, the plea for specific help is not reflected in the various sums he requests, although it is clear that his parents have sent him 100 Ducats.

28. Letter to his parents dated Stockholm, 2 July 1779

Dearest Parents!

I received your generous letter of credit – the 30th [of June]. I have absolved my debts immediately, as far as was possible. But to be free of them completely was impossible. *Kämmerer* himself went with me to the best money changer, but I had to accept 33 RD [Riksdalers] per Ducat. With a loss of 300 copper Dalers along with some smaller debts and the cost of travel all counted in total, it is of course not natural that I can depart. Moreover, add to that the fact that I am at the least so sickly that it seems impossible for me to travel on the water.[1] I have the opportunity to travel a bit cheaper nonetheless, for at the end of this month the Imperial Minister goes to Copenhagen.[2] I thank you in tears for your generosity, but with the selfsame tears I ask you for yet another 50 Ducats to release me from this misery. I will travel as lightly as possible and only drink wine two or three times every eight days. – Dispatch to me for my well-being this last help that will allow me to depart this damned nest.

Your

obedient son

Joseph

COMMENTARY

Original Buchen, Bezirksmuseum. Kraus's parents evidently responded to his plea (see the previous letter), but it seems that he is unable to navigate the ever-changing and very complex exchange rates. This is, of course, his main excuse used to stay in Stockholm, and to ask for even further funds due to his "ill health."

1. Orig. *zu Wasser zu reisen*, meaning to travel by sea.

2. The implication is that he will be allowed to tag along, possibly due to Kämmerer's influence.

29. Letter to his parents dated Stockholm, 27 July 1779

Dearest Parents!

Early today *Kämmerer* departed with his retinue. He was at my place yesterday and took his leave of me – we parted as good friends. We shall see whether it will go better there with the good folks in Copenhagen than here. Here, one was immensely glad to be rid of [him], at least on the part of the Court. I will accelerate my departure as soon as possible, that is – as soon as a ship comes; the mail boat[1] costs too much. God forgive my sins, for outside there is thunder and lightning as if the Last Judgment were upon us, and I have to laugh, and laugh out loud as only

I can – at all of the projects and intrigues of my acquaintances, done in order to keep me here – that everything should be against me, which it is not. I have also not deserved it, and for the most part I think that, according to my nature, I have dammed few obligations toward the people for whom I at least do everything within my ability, and – just when I don't have a penny, they offer me money for music – I become embarrassed, as if I did not have good sense. At least (thank God!) I was not born to be a merchant. Furthermore, they of course now had to learn that I wished to leave. Now they come [and say] – I should have – done such and such – turned to this one or that – and demanded satisfaction from the King.[2] God knows what all I had to do and should still do. Finally, I was tired of creeping about and assured the gentlemen honestly that I would not let myself be bossed about[3] by someone who doesn't understand my profession (even if he has total authority over all of the luminaries of the Sultan's court down to the least landed Count in Germany) – "But that is what all great men, Kapellmeisters, etc. have done."[4] Well and good – despite their titles, they can be great rogues. That didn't happen and even up to this hour they've spared no effort to bring me around to another view. Last Sunday we were at the home of an assessor,[5] where I declared openly that I would consider it justified for myself as soon as I was home again in my fatherland to bear witness to the entire world in writing about the poor treatment I have received. One blamed it on the others. Each and every one took it seriously. Everyone wants to be my physician. I thank God that I count doctors along with lawyers among the lowest form of insects – and thus I am acquitted of them.

There is enough news here – but it is related better in person with a pipe full of tobacco than here.

The money needed to depart – 50 Ducats – and the ship I await with longing.

Soon, soon I shall embrace you all, and you

Your Joseph

COMMENTARY

Original Buchen, Bezirksmuseum. Clearly, Kraus is playing a sort of game of poker or blind man's bluff with both his parents and his Swedish friends, attempting to leverage them into a position to support him.

1. The mail boat would have been direct to Germany, while other ships would have taken a more roundabout route, and thus would have been less expensive.

2. Orig. *beim König Satisfaction begehren.* To demand satisfaction normally would have meant to challenge him to a duel, which would have been an impossibility; what Kraus means is "to demand restitution."

3. Orig. *hofmeistern lassen,* or literally "to be dictated to by a chamberlain." It is unclear whether Kraus means the king or Barnekow.

4. He is probably reporting a statement from one of his Swedish acquaintances.

5. The identity of the assessor is unknown.

30. Letter to his parents dated Stockholm, 3 August 1779

Dearest Parents!

I am still sitting here and awaiting an opportunity by sea. In all my days I have not lived with such boredom and so fearfully. Previously, I stamped about an entire year, and no one wanted to prove that he was actually a connoisseur of art – naturally, I was finally forced into a position from out of which only your generosity could extract me. Now – just listen! Herr von Benzel, whose generosity toward me I can never treasure enough, had the good will to allow me to be recommended by way of the Herr Agent in *Aachen* to the *notary Säfström*[1] at the Chamber of Commerce here.

This gentleman showed himself to be extraordinarily polite and offered me his complete friendship. He knew from the letters of my situation and my vocation. "You have to remain here; it cannot be helped." Too late, I answered him, because my economic circumstances do not allow me to stay in so expensive a place. Good. Today I visited him again. All the same, he said, you have to at least meet the Herr President of the Finnish government, *Baron Lejonhuvud,*[2] who is simultaneously the director of the Academy of Music. I had previously already placed my faith in the Swedish Herr Conduit, but all the greater was my wonderment to be, when I met in Herr President a man who was not only extraordinarily polite and agreeable, but who was also a connoisseur and possessed a great soul. In three or four minutes he had me completely. He could not understand how it was possible that I had not been fortunate. I made known to him the entire situation. He understood and was so honest to tell me that I had been entirely too honest in dealing with my enemies with my project. His advice was this finally, that I should stay at least until the next year. I presented him with the impossibility – my reduced circumstances – my father, for whom my little bit of jurisprudence had cost so much, and who now waits for me, so that I would like to work beside him on his many business affairs – in short, I told him everything, for I could not be silent before one whose soul was so open to me. In vain! Your parents, he said to me, "would not begrudge you your happiness. The money that it has cost them can be earned back, and I will ensure at court everything that will satisfy them. We desperately need a composer, for ours are old – the King himself told me this – and it was only the intrigues of your enemies that sent you running from one person to the next – people who either could do nothing in the situation or didn't want to." These were his words. His Excellency was so generous to say to me that "as soon as the membership has returned from the country, the Academy of Music would extend the honor of naming me as a regular member in a public document."[3] Immediately after this audience, the Herr President said to Herr *Sefström* that he wanted to clothe me in the Chamber of Commerce in order for me to make the acquaintance of several economic councilors. What was most marvelous was the fact that I was led to the councilor's office and solemnly presented in the name of His Excellency and well treated. Two of the councilors approached me and wondered whether I might have the desire to establish myself permanently in Sweden? I answered the question that, due to the few prospects I had and the little attachments that I had formed, I was not able to consider this. They assured me that they would spare no effort to present this to His Majesty himself – but – I had to give them my word that I would not depart until I had seen the effect of their promise. I gave it – May God bless it! And

> *Your*
>
> *Obedient Joseph*

[P.S.] A greeting to all.

Write me your advice as soon as possible. If you are of one mind with me, then I would ask you [to ask] Herr Court Chancellor von Benzel[4] to recommend me once more.

P.S. The music for Frau Countess Ingelheim has been taken by the post-master from Wismar with the promise that he will take care of it.

COMMENTARY

Original Buchen, Bezirksmuseum. It is clear that Kraus has had enough of a turn of fortune to decide to stay in Sweden, which he attempts to tell them in as an-ecdotal a manner as possible. The recom-mendation from Benzel, the Kurmainz chancellor, was for him to join the Swed-ish bureaucracy as a commerce secretary. Such an "official" position was common-place for artists in Gustav's cultural es-tablishment; for example, Carl Michael Bellman was officially a secretary in the office of the state lottery, even though there is little evidence that he actually did any work there. For Kraus, after months of desperate pleas for funds, the sea change could hardly have consoled his parents.

1. The identity of *Säfström/Sefström* is not known, but it could refer to Anders Säfström (fl. 1745–1785), who was an author and state official. He left Sweden in 1756 to avoid debtor's prison, traveling to Germany, where he served as a leg-ate to several German principalities. He translated Prévost and wrote novels, all published in Stockholm between 1774 and 1783, and may have been the father of Swedish singer-actress Ulrika Eleonora Säfström (1770–1857).

2. The reference is to Axel Gabriel friherr Lejonhuvud, referred to in Letter 9. He was one of the founders and first president of the Royal Swedish Academy of Music.

3. Lejonhuvud was as good as his word. On 2 November 1779, according to the protocols of the Royal Academy of Music, Kraus was nominated for membership; following the normal vetting of his credentials, he was admit-ted on 29 November as a Swedish (not foreign) member, being *beneventerade* (i.e., welcomed in person) as "*Herr Hofkapellmästaren* Kraus" on 4 April 1781, some two months before Gustav III named him to an official post.

4. It is not known what further "rec-ommendation" Kraus would have re-quired from Benzel, save that it may have been an official one for him to obtain his "clothing" as a commerce secretary.

31. Letter to his parents dated Stockholm, 12 October 1779

Dearest Parents!

I have now just returned from the country and find both your letters. It is a shame that I desired gladly to say so much that is now unneces-sary to reply to and would be more easily saved until another time; and moreover so little about the principal matter. Due to my health, I made use of an opportunity given me by a friend, which of course cost neither more nor less than my being here. I have not yet been restored through it. I am not ill, but I have something that is more annoying than true illness – scabies. Only God knows how this will eventuate, for despite eternal laxatives and the imbibing of blood purification tea, I am not able to get rid of them. Whenever I go out, I have to stick my hands in my pockets, and I dare not go to my friends, for they will insist that my fingers ought to walk about the keyboard in plain sight – and I really don't want to do that. Let it be! I've purchased gloves – as soon as I hear that I can put them on, I'll march straight over, but before then it is not possible to be able to say anything more clearly and with certainty. I have to wait until the next time, therefore. We have three churches here, a German, French, and Spanish;[1] thus, there is no lack of opportunity, at least not in my conviction that I have to make for myself to God, like my consolation in the matter that neither you nor anyone else in the world can give me. I have received the last 50 Ducats and have already thanked you for them twice in two letters; it is incomprehensible to me that you have not received my letters.[2] The reason for the unequal postage is that sometimes one must pay postage only to Frankfurt. One of my letters was misdirected to Königstein in Saxony,[3] but which one I don't know. I learned of it, because all outgoing letters are written out on a chart here. I will complete everything together with the letters to H[err] v[on] Benzel and H[err] Häussler. At this very moment the post is departing – NB – I am writing this just now at the post office. The postmaster sends you his compliments, though he doesn't know you. I send my greetings to everyone most lovingly and remain

Your obedient son
Joseph

COMMENTRY

Original Buchen, Bezirksmuseum. It is telling that Kraus writes this letter, literally posthaste, after just returning *vom Lande,* that is from vacation, which undermines his former description of his poverty-stricken state. The scabies were probably not the same as that today, caused by a mite infection. Rather, during the fall, the dry air probably caused extreme eczema or chapping, which is not uncommon in northern climes even today.

1. The churches were at the embassies of the countries; the German was the imperial embassy of the Holy Roman Empire.

2. It is difficult to determine whether these are lost letters.

3. His parents were, of course, residents of Königstein in *Taunus.*

32. Letter to his parents dated Stockholm, 15 November 1779

Dearest Parents!

Was it really my own fault that you've heard nothing from me for three months? If I really have to accept the anxiety that I have caused you only on my account, surely I could not forgive myself. As deeply as you love me, I am convinced of it equally as deeply, and it gave me so much pain inside when I heard from my friend *Hallardt* in *Wismar* how concerned you were for me. No, my dearest ones, I am very much aware that I need to be worthy enough of your love so that I don't cause you unnecessary worry. You must have had so often enough tribulation that I could not allay. Two months ago you must have received a letter from me (dated the day before my departure to the country), as well as fourteen days ago an answer to your two letters that I found when I returned. I promised in that one to write more in the next. Of course, I would gladly have kept my promise, so deeply and happily I wished to write something new. Alone, you would rather be astonished at my stubbornness on something that I have set my sights upon rather than about the barriers that lie in the way of my desires. Do not think ill of my silence, but rather how it rhymes with my heart that you know so well. I babble on day and night with you, as if I had you here with me – [I] lament my distress and sometimes weep, as well. It does me good that I can thus explain away my inner cares that a fellow like me can never wipe away. There are people all about me who believe me marvelously happy with my temperament, because they've never tasted the bitterness of it. But, thank God, there is something that lies within my soul that I nonetheless am able at times to oppose my fate – it should simply be impossible to be able to help myself.

This week, I think, I will have at least some news, for President Lejonhuvud is once again back in the city. As soon as I know, it is self-understood that I shall write on the next post day. Keep your old love for me and have patience with

Your

Most obedient Joseph's destiny

[P.S.] Greet everyone who is dear to you and me. The King is now at one of his country estates[1] and at the moment no one knows when he will return to the city. There are various Germans[2] here at the present, some who serve at court, or [others] who simply go around begging for their craft; but these, God knows, do me the most harm. If I were only a bit practical, I would have succeeded better – but then I would have been a less honorable fellow. Of course, one doesn't progress much for all that – unfortunately!

COMMENTARY

Original Buchen, Bezirksmuseum. Apparently, his parents have asked Hallardt to provide them with information on their son, since the correspondence seems to have been interrupted. Kraus is thus answering their inquiries passed on through a third party, as well as the delayed letters from home.

    1. Gustav III usually retreated to Gripsholm on the southern shores of Lake Mälar at this time of year.

    2. Kraus implies that he is in competition with fellow countrymen, with the implication that they too are seeking musical employment. He is being disingenuous, particularly since there is no evidence of any other applicant from Germany at the court in Sweden at this time.

33. Letter to his parents dated Stockholm, 10 January 1780

Dearest Parents!

Happy New Year! And the most heartfelt thanks for all the love that you have had for me up to now! Would that I were still in the position of repaying it as I would wish! This year vanished like the others, only I am now a year older and closer to my vocation, which is in God's hands, for equally as long. It makes me happy or unhappy, as it pleases Him – only if He would give me the great gift of being able to be resigned to His will – I need it. The court finally returned to the city on the seventh of this month after an absence of six months. During this time there wasn't much for me to do, other than I had to exert every possible effort to disperse the intrigues against me. My patron, Baron *Lejonhuvud,* has suddenly disappeared. He is said to be making a secret journey on the orders of the court. One person rumors this, and another something else. So much is certain; that he has obtained travel funds in *Hamburg* on assignment for the King. I lost in him a supporter, who was more precious to me because he was one of the few that combined a good heart with insights into science and taste as a Mæcenas.[1] But I am on the way to obtaining a new and now more important one. Perhaps then things will be better. At least I have not advanced a step further in pursuit of my quest, and thus [I] stand on the same speck [of ground] where I stood half a year ago, and therefore I really need another pair of horses on the team. The entire winter through I have had to endure the cure. God grant that it does well! Of course, I am very much in need of money, for I am poor enough to appeal to good people for credit, if I am able. Send me something so that I can buy a winter waistcoat, for this winter is extraordinarily cold. Many a Swede has already frozen his little nose off months ago; it's no wonder if the German whistles. Tobacco is also expensive, and I cannot do without it, for my pipe has now become my best friend.

I have enclosed herewith a letter to H[err] v[on] Benzel. Due to the postage and because I no longer know the address, it is open. There are also two scraps of paper to my brother[2] and sister, Anna Barbara. Next I shall write to the nun. Truly, it is abominable that I haven't written to her[3] yet, but it is just as terrible that she hasn't written to me; and perhaps she has more time for it than I. I would gladly send my little Marianne some music;[4] but as long as the passage is not open, the postage is too expensive.

Fare you all well! Lovingly well!

Your most obedient Joseph

COMMENTARY

Original Buchen, Bezirksmuseum. Kraus is no doubt responding to a further inquiry as to his state of affairs, especially given the optimistic tone of his previous letter.

1. This is a reference to Caius Cilnius Mæcenas, a favorite courtier to Caesar Augustus and wealthy intellectual and supporter of the arts in Ancient Rome.

2. He means his brother Franz, not his youngest Alois.

3. Kraus uses the neutral pronoun "*es*" for his sister at the Mainz cloister, no doubt due to her vow of celibacy.

4. Kraus seems to have written compositions for his sister to perform, though their identity is not known.

34. Letter to his parents dated Stockholm, 14 April 1780

Dearest Parents!

Last Monday I received payment of the 20 Ducats from the Royal Librarian, *Björnstjerna,* whereupon the following post day the receipt was transmitted along with a little letter to *Seiz*[1] to the brother of this gentleman. I thank you with all my heart for this. I would gladly make this my traveling funds, if it were possible; but I am so involved that I have to delay it for a few months. My former supporter *Lejonhuvud* is back once more, and I have as many promises as before; even with all these, I had to see in the end that the entire value of his intentions toward me consisted simply of compliments; and the word of honor of this sort of gentleman is valid only as much as it suits their comfort level or influence at court. That I recognized this in the end means much, for I treasured all of his efforts on my behalf and took everyone for an honest fellow, because I am one myself. This revelation and the critical state of my economic circumstances finally made me seek a path myself that previously no recommendation could have accomplished; and it was quite successful. My ultimate goal is simple; at least to demand some sort of reasonable restitution for my damages. With all of the exacting household expenses that I have incurred, and about which all of my countrymen themselves marvel, I have a sum to pay out that I would not like to be burdened with, for I have already been most careful about it. In a few days I expect a result that must determine my fortune for better or worse. As soon as everything is set to rights, I will write you. Live well with this [knowledge] as I wish and greet all friends. I love my dear siblings with all my heart.

Your most obedient son Joseph

P.S. I will take care of the small commission that Herr *Seiler*[2] gave me and write to him myself the next time. The letter by way of Regensburg is a costly thing; it cost me over a Gulden.

COMMENTARY

Original Buchen, Bezirksmuseum. The tone is now hopeful and assertive, but it is clear that he is responding to yet another call from his parents to return to Germany.

1. The "Royal Librarian" is Johan Björnstjerna (1729–1797), a scholar whose work on Emanuel Swedenborg was considered seminal at the time. The identity of Seiz (recte Seitz?) cannot be determined.

2. Neither the identity of "Herr Seiler" nor the music that Kraus wrote for him is identifiable, though it is likely that the commission was brokered by his parents.

35. Letter to his parents dated Stockholm, 20 June 1780

I would rather wish that I was in the position to be able to give you an answer as to the day of my departure, and in that way I would both alleviate my worries for you and satisfy my friend *Hallardt.* I have finally obtained the government councilor *Ziebeth*[1] as my supporter, and it was just this, which all of my efforts and all of the recommendations could not accomplish. This man is the King's First Privy Secretary and an absolute dictator regarding whatever concerns the theater. As long as the former Intendant of the Royal Theater, Baron von *Barnekow,* was on board, there was no hope for me, because he publically showed himself to be my enemy. His replacement was Count *Fersen,*[2] a man of much knowledge and at the same time warm patriotism for the stage. Both of these men now sought me out in order to help me in the best possible way. The beginning is done. I have received a libretto from the former, which owes its existence to the best poet in Sweden.[3] I hope to be finished with the musical portion by the return of the King, if dear God keeps me healthy, after which the entire matter will be decided and then what will happen will happen. Because the libretto is already approved by the King,[4] they at least will have to pay me, even if they don't want to keep me. Now I am working steadily on it, and there is nothing lacking for me to have the right courage except – money. Money again? I would not need it if I was able to get away with it, but that won't do. Now once more I have to deal with the fellows;[5] thus I have to do myself a favor and make the rounds often. I have had made for myself a small suit, but God knows that I hardly have a single pair of shoes that are appropriate, and all the rest, etc., etc., is lacking, but in addition there is, that these dear people should not notice my poverty, for otherwise it would be said: that which was not appropriate for Germany would work in Sweden, and such thoughts would ruin the entire game for me. Dearest parents! This is now the last step needed to make all of my circumstances change for me. I hope upon your love that you will support me, so help me with as much as you are able: and then I shall have you and the dear God to thank for my happiness. My underclothes, stockings, in short, all of the accessories including the hat are rickety furnishings, with which (by my poor soul) I dare not go with to any honest man. If it is possible, I ask you to send me 40 Ducats; perhaps I can pay it back again over the course of the year – it would be a *Gaudeum*[6] for me. Fare well, heartfelt well, and greet my dear siblings and friends

Your most obedient son Joseph

35a. Letter from Postmaster Hallardt to Kraus parents dated Wismar, 10 July 1780

S.S:

With greatest pleasure I have the honor to report that your Herr Son is both healthy and well in Stockholm, and now has achieved his desire, in that he has now been commissioned to write an opera, as he has told me. Probably Herr Krause will show off his talent at the first rehearsal, and because he had made himself known and loved through all sorts of compositions when I was in Stockholm, and thus [he] had learned the Swedish language with such fluency and diligence that he both understands and speaks it well. And thus it is only natural that he will take advantage of this opportunity that has cost him so much time and money in order to seek to become even more known through an opera. Perhaps, through this he will reawaken his desire to achieve his goal; through his quiet and well-bred manner he really has obtained many friends, and now I've heard that he has persuaded Herr Count Fersen to be his patron, a man who appreciates talent and who can be very helpful to Herr Krause. The news that he has taken over the setting of a new opera[7] into music is very pleasing to me, especially since through it he has received the support of a very insightful man with respect to music. Because the opera does not have to be ready until the fall, he will probably have to remain in Stockholm throughout the winter. Perhaps he will ease his way to his fortune through it, something I wish for him with all of my heart. I have the honor with all respect to proclaim myself

Your most obedient servant
J. F. Hallardt

COMMENTARY

Originals lost, but copies survive together in Buchen, Bezirksmuseum. Kraus's letter is missing the salutation and perhaps the opening paragraphs. The implication of Hallardt's appended missive is to inform his parents that their son's apparent solitary existence and inability to penetrate Stockholm's musical establishment so often reported in the composer's letters was, to say the least, somewhat exaggerated. He clearly notes the progress Kraus has made in becoming known for his music and conviviality among his new Swedish friends. It also substantiates the claim Kraus made in an earlier letter about his linguistic ability.

1. The new patron is Cristoffer Bogislaus Zibet (1740–1809), later royal secretary, chamberlain, and vice-director of the Royal Spectacles 1773–1786.

2. Count Carl Reinhold von Fersen (1716–1786), intendant of the Royal Spectacles from 1780 until his death. His patronage is verified by Hallardt's letter.

3. The libretto refers to the opera *Proserpin* by Johan Henrik Kellgren (1751–1795).

4. The text to *Proserpin* was based upon an outline by Gustav III himself, and therefore its approval by the Royal Academy of Music was a given.

5. Orig. *den Kerls,* or the boys. Kraus is referring to the various people with whom he is courting favor as he did in the past.

6. *Gaudium* = joy or delight.

7. Hallardt notes specifically that Kraus has "taken over" (*eine Neue oper in Musik zu sezten übernommen habe*) the composition of the opera, implying that it was originally given to someone else. There exists a manuscript score of a recitative and aria by Pehr Frigel (1750–1842), a composer recently arrived in Stockholm from Kalmar in southern Sweden (Stockholm, Kungliga Biblioteket). He had some success at the Utile dulci public concerts with a number of compositions. The text is taken from an earlier draft of the opera *Adonis och Proserpin* by Kellgren, and while the accompanied recitative is dramatic, the aria is quite amateurish. Frigel was originally a protégé of Barnekow, but after they had a falling out, he became a pupil and friend of Kraus. He was also commissioned to compose an opera, *Zoroastre,* about this same time, but his work was neither produced nor performed.

36. Letter to his parents dated Stockholm, 14 September 1780

Dearest Parents!

I thank you from the bottom of my heart for your good arrangements, and I hope that H[err] *Cunoy*[1] in Hamburg will soon expedite the matter. My work is now virtually finished, and I am only waiting upon the King. God grant it that I put my best foot forward![2] Moreover,

it should not be demanded that I bow and scrape, if it is not required;
for I cannot do it, even if I am to be rewarded for doing with a golden
apple. I am very sorry for my dear brother, as it becomes all the more
probable that all methods of help are in vain.[3] I would wish to be with
him; perhaps I could be able to ease things for him in one or another moment yet. But – thus fate divides those who have been bound the closest
together by nature. The letter to H[err] Häussler is already a month old.
But the letter by my sister – Holy God! I believe – I don't know what? At
least, I assume that it was a letter that a nun of forty years of age once
had written to her father.[4] If I weren't so very much convinced, or had yet
accepted the expression that she loved me, I believe I would have broken
out in a cold sweat over it. Concerning the music, I will see whether I
have the opportunity, namely to send it by way of a ship to Wismar.[5]
Greetings to you, my beloved siblings, who I, God knows, love with all
my heart, as you do me

Your

Most obedient son Joseph

Please present by most obedient salutation to Herr *Würdtwein*.[6]

P.S. I cannot answer Herr Seiler yet, which annoys me, for neither I nor
the postmaster can figure out the person who should receive payment.

COMMENTARY

Original Buchen, Bezirksmuseum. The
fragmentary statements of this letter
make it clear that Kraus was responding to various questions and letters
received during the intervening three
months.

1. The identity of Cunoy in Hamburg
is unknown, although he may have been
either a banker or a merchant through
whom Kraus's parents have arranged another letter of credit.

2. The work (*Meine Arbeit*) is *Proserpin*. The last statement reads in the original: *daß sich das Glük zu meinem Besten
wendet!* or "that fortune turns toward my
favor or best." This has been translated in

a more idiomatic manner to fit the context of Kraus's description.

3. The reference is to the institution-
alizing of Kraus's brother Franz for his
mental instability.

4. Kraus's sister Katharina Josepha has
evidently written a cold and dispassionate
letter to her brother that was, in Kraus's
eyes, devoid of any family connection.

5. The music, probably one or more
original compositions, are unidentified.

6. The identity of Herr Würdtwein
(recte Würthwein?) is unknown, but
possibly a local Buchen patron for whom
his parents have arranged a commission
by their son.

37. Letter to his parents dated Stockholm, 11 March 1781

Dearest Parents!

Not counting the replies to your letters, my last missive is not yet three weeks old. Where in the world have all the letters gone? If you have not yet received a single one of them, I will thank you for the fourth time for the money that I received from Hamburg, as well as the missive that has such a nice seal;[1] both will be uncommonly put to use. My position has not yet been determined, but I still hope that it will soon happen. My opera is now on the stage and the rehearsals are in progress. In short order a performance can be considered, and thus my fate will be decided, and I am – God knows, what? Of course, a little place with the Count would not be amiss, and if all at once his horns can be heard at the uttermost corners of the earth, it is always such a nice refuge to become a bungling secretary.[2] So be it! I am resigned to everything, at least more than that. And, if it all at once should be a pure impossibility to wish to be with one's head above the world, it makes no difference in what type of office one works oneself to death. But long enough until my tribulations here run their course. I have to apologize. You have had patience for so long!

I don't know what else new to write, but I nonetheless would wish to be able to soon. Soon I shall lick myself all over, soon I'll bite myself, and thus I shall become what is normal with dogs. The whelps are not able to suffer, whether or not they are friends or foes. It has been thus since the beginning of the world, and thus it probably will always be, and therefore everyone should be comforted that the world cannot be reformed – no one can. Fare you well, lovingly well, as I also wish for my siblings. Love me always

Your

Most obedient son

Joseph

P.S. The Archbishop of Uppsala[3] has a cough – so do I.

COMMENTARY

Original Buchen, Bezirksmuseum. It is clear from the context that over half a year's worth of correspondence has gone missing. What can be surmised is that Kraus

has once more been importuned by his
parents to return to Germany and accept a
bureaucratic position they have arranged,
probably at one of the minor courts.

1. The seal (*Sigill*) refers probably to
the official offer of a court position as a
secretary.

2. The count is not identified, but
perhaps it could be Benzel, with whom
Kraus's parents and Kraus himself
were in contact. Kraus is being sarcastic
here.

3. The archbishop of Uppsala was
Carl Fredrik Menander (1712–1786).

38. Letter to his parents dated Stockholm, 14 May 1781

Dearest Parents!

"Never to see my fatherland, my beloved parents, siblings, and friends
again?" That is not the desire of my heart. I truly believe that Stockholm
is not the only place on earth where one can learn patience, moreover.
That was, however, not the real reason that I remained here for so long,
for – if I had nothing more in my head but to learn patience, in that moment I would resign myself and cobble together small reports, requisi-
tions, and duplicates. Submission – castrated up to the last nerve of my
soul – to be deaf and dumb and accept the entire bundle of stuff that is
laid upon me with all patience without once daring to question whether
they contain hay or oats? And then to be forced to fashion all of my
little steps under the watchful eye of the nobly born – by God, this is
a *requisite* that I don't have, nor do I want to, and I would be destroyed
by it – it would be better to let oneself in all Christian resignation be
driven insane. For that – no, for that there is a solution, God be praised!
He – who has planted all of the seeds within me that do not change and,
unnoticed by myself, develop by and by; He, who awakened first within
me the longing for a wider world, the web and taste for that thing people
call fame; [He] who did not give me the patience, not the resignation,
and not the insensible indifference to be able to philosophize away the
annoyances all about me – No, [He] who gave me nothing of all the rubbish, nothing for comfort save a little frivolity so that I did not destroy
myself – Hmm – to Him I thank with my entire soul for that which He
gave and did not give to me, and I know that He is pleased with the
warm gratitude of his child – that He demands nothing from me that is
opposite to my nature; and – He calls – happy is he who understands His
gesture and thus, I believe, it is really less of an art to resign oneself. Now

He sends me tears, whose inner sorrow does not destroy me; for the fact that I have had miserable days is obvious; but He alone also knows how difficult and oppressive they have been sometimes. To whom else should I complain? Whom should I afflict with my whining at some point without daring to hope for aid? I myself have thousands of points of view and pathways in my heart that are unknown and hidden – thousands of times I don't understand myself at all – who then is to better understand me? God knows, there is something miraculous about all this; to want to, to have to, and unfortunately to be able to say something in certainty with a not too happy disposition: ["]Boy! Look, here is the link in the chain that now binds you, and you forge this over here and the other over there; the lock you bought at the marketplace, the ankle fetters at the other!" I am thus always reminded of the poor prince who so willingly embalmed his heart and brains in a casket and entrusted it to the keeping of a fairy;[1] and when he was no longer happy with his servitude, he demanded his casket back. But look! The key was lost, and the chronicles say that the poor devil wandered about the entire earth until the end of his miserable life without brains or heart, a punishment to himself and hideous to others.... Comrade! You are simultaneously more fortunate than he whose head and heart have been stuffed with kitchen salt and finally *confiscated* in its *totality* under the law.

I have nothing but a single shirt left of my underclothing; the rest look like old shredded banners – Dear God should keep those healthy a little while yet until I have organized things differently; and for that much still needs to be done. My economic circumstances are all so confused with respect to the details, with which I live, that for at least a year I would not be in a free position, even if I obtain employment. Listen to my recommendation! I have debts, and about these I am not the least concerned and no man who can add up what it costs to live for 365 days would be concerned either. Now I not only have hope, but rather more than a possible hope that I would be better off staying here. In every case I will receive payment, with which I won't achieve the position that I would have desired, however. My opinion would be this at this point: if I am engaged, I would entreat you to raise money for me in Germany, which I would certainly be able to pay back by and by, so that I would be without debts immediately at the beginning of my employment. If I would not

be employed: as [I] already said, I will at least be paid for my work – but
whatever is subsequently lacking is "of course clearly unforeseen," and
that is all that one can say about the weighty issue; but – Why must I be
like this? Why am I like this? – The fact that I cannot leave before the opera is performed is obvious, and, as I believe besides, the timing is of no
importance whether or not it will occur in this or some future week, that
is, NB, the performance of the music before the King. But that in case
people don't want me further and give me dessert of a certain amount
of payment so that I would thus be free at that moment to be able to begin
my journey back to you, there would still certainly be 200 Ducats missing. It is a sum that gives me fear and palpitations, for then – How would
I earn it back? And – perhaps it is impossible for you to raise, however
much you would desire to for the love you have for me? And then – God
knows that I believe the entire thing makes me half-crazy in the end.

Dearest parents, fare you well. Withdraw from me your aid – but not
your love!

Your Joseph

[P.S.] Please tell my dear H[err] Godfather that I love him with all my
heart. All my siblings I greet from the bottom of my soul.

COMMENTARY

Original Buchen, Bezirksmuseum. Kraus
is marking time until the first performance of his opera, but it is clear from
the inference that his parents have sent
him an ultimatum to return home and
enter into service as a bureaucrat. The
rant demonstrates how abhorrent the
thought is to Kraus.

1. Kraus is clearly paraphrasing a
folktale at this point.

39. Letter to his parents dated 14 June 1781

Dearest Parents!

Finally my work was performed before the King at the royal country
estate of *Ulrichsthal*,[1] and I received permission to conduct it myself. The
court was extraordinarily pleased with it, and the manner in which the
King declared his satisfaction exceeded my expectations. As soon as the
music ended, the King conversed with me for over a quarter of an hour:
he first complimented me quite politely, asked me about this and that,

and measured me with his large eyes from head to toe, and in my usual fashion I allowed myself the freedom to gape at the monarch through and through, and that – as I learned later, pleased him immensely. Because the divisions in the libretto have to be altered somewhat, the opera cannot be given until fall, of course; but then I can hope for quite a pretty present as well.[2] But – for the rest of this year there will be no traveling home, and if I would be quite honest, I have at the moment no really great appetite to do so – and furthermore, because I – can't. In short, I have been tied in quite firmly for the rest of my days. Yesterday I was engaged and that for the first and last time of my life in all probability. Of course, I did not receive a grand title, neither confidential religious councilor nor Chamberlain of the Apostolic See, or some such – nothing of such high import, but rather – for the short and tall of it, *Kapellmeister.*[3] The salary is 300 Ducats, and what is worth more than 600 is the grace that this coming year I must make a brief journey at the King's expense throughout Germany, France, and Italy – not to study music, as the King says, but rather simply to observe the latest trends in the theater. And, just think – they thought the conditions marvelous, that they would be unacceptable for me, and at the same time just at this point, which pleased me to the bottom of my soul. All my works that I am able to make for the stage will be specially paid for by the King – therefore – what better could I expect or desire?

This coming year I will thus see you, see you and embrace you all. That really will be a *Gaudium!* – I'm as happy as a child about this. Now, on to my economic circumstances. As I wrote to you in my previous letter, I have debts. These I can absolve by and by. But, you know how it is to keep house beginning with debts. I therefore would wish happily that I could arrange things as soon as possible. The reasons for which I repeated in my request that I wrote you about in my last missive, to send me as soon as possible 200 Ducats, that I can soon repay you, for now in the best possible fashion, if dear God grants me life. You have helped me out so often, and I thank my Creator a thousand times that he has now placed me in a position to be able to give you joy with time. If you are in the position of helping me out with the requested sum, I ask you to do so out of your love for me, so that I will receive in the coming month at least the funds. Think – in all seriousness I have only two single shirts that are whole – Greet all my dear siblings. This coming year I shall see you all – all. Love me always

Your

Most obedient son

Joseph

COMMENTARY

Original Buchen, Bezirksmuseum. Although Kraus's joy is palpable, he still includes a mocking allusion to the attempts by his parents to lure him back to Germany to take on a governmental sinecure.

1. *Proserpin* was performed in a private performance at Confidencen, the small theater at the summer estate of Ulriksdal north of Stockholm.

2. By "divisions" (*Eintheilung*) Kraus means scene arrangements or staging.

3. According to Kraus's initial contract (see below, Letter 39a), the position was actually Vize-Kapellmästare; Uttini still retained the position of official Kapellmästare.

39a. Contract between Joseph Martin Kraus and the Royal Spectacles dated Stockholm, 23 June 1781

I, Joseph Krause, acknowledge that I have been engaged by the Administration of His Royal Majesty's Hof-Capell and Spectacles as Second Capellmästare upon the following conditions:

1) I, Krause, bind myself on all the occasions required of me by the Administration to undertake all of the responsibilities pertaining to a Capellmästare with respect to the court orchestra, as well as His Majesty's Royal Theaters.

2) Of every new opera that I compose, the third performance will be for my own benefit.

3) To perfect further my taste and insights, I am assured that next year 1782 for up to a year and a half I will undertake a journey to foreign places where music, especially with respect to the dramatic, flourishes, and there I will use every opportunity to study the stage and theater. And I shall receive outside of my salary a subsidy of 500 Riksdalers specie.

When I have returned from this journey I bind myself for at least 10 years to remain in His Royal Majesty's service and to undertake during this time to develop and organize the educational system at the Royal Academy of Music or the Opera, and for that purpose to recommend talented and appropriate teachers and to institute such subjects that are naturally suitable and appropriate, and will be responsible for these conditions so that good singers are not lacking for the roles consequentially.

Furthermore, I agree always to have a student in music theory, and moreover to take all care and spare no effort to contribute to the function and appearance of the Royal Theater, and by this measure complete everything that has been entrusted to me and required of me for my own honor.

This contract shall be kept without alteration. But, if before my foreign travel is begun I do not receive at my recognizance the assurance of being the successor to the present Kapellmästare Uttini, I have the right then but not later to break this agreement and in the case shall declare myself free and unbound from my contract.

To make doubly sure, two examples of this have been authored and this one signed with my name in Stockholm on the 23rd of June 1781.

Joseph Kraus[M]

COMMENTARY

Original Stockholm, Riksarkiv, Kungliga Teaterns Protocoller. The formal contract was signed about a week after the last letter above to his parents, indicating that the offer of employment was only oral up to that point. Despite the legalese, the contract is quite precise and clear as to his duties and future with the Royal Spectacles. He apparently did receive at least verbal confirmation of his position as Uttini's successor prior to his departure for continental Europe in 1782, though there is no documentation of this fact.

40. Letter to his parents dated Stockholm, 26 June 1781

Dearest Parents!

Those who believe in presentiment can do so; I never will. At the same time, it was nonetheless one of my favorite notions; but – on the

M. This contract contains one of the few actual complete signatures of the composer, who generally used either his first or last name, but not both.

self-same hour that I drunkenly thought through my happy day that was the only one meted out to me in three years – that self-same hour I was so filled with delight, enjoyed so inwardly that I could be able to share with you, with all of my siblings, my fortune – should not this hour have been a sign for me? Is there no more terror than a presentiment of approaching misfortune? – Nothing – Nothing – and she vanished as I was imagining embraces – embraces of the most holy love – I will find nothing but stone that covers her cold remains![1] In *Weilbach*! God! And that would be the last time that I saw her – that I wept after her. The last time? When I tore myself from her, angry about everything to do with a cloister – she left me with all of the sweet melancholy of her spirit – and that was to be the last farewell, parted, thrown apart from each other, never more to see her on this earth? For three days my loss has grown more plain, and at the same time it is still incomprehensible to me simply how this was possible. "What was I doing," she asked as she lay on her deathbed, "How did I live? Whether I would come soon?" Dear Angel! You asked this in the very hour that I was in rapture over the thought of answering everything in person – in the hour that no substitution would now be possible, but I still thank our beloved God that, in the place where He takes all of His beloved children, He was able to mitigate her pain a bit through the thought that He wishes to make the others on this earth happy. Yes, my dearest parents. Our good God knows that I would gladly give up all my fortune, all my fortune that he has given me in order to be able to make just a single happy day for you. And certainly! Beloved God once gave me the joy of those things that my heart makes and dares to make demands without affectation. You have without doubt received my last letter from Wismar, and thus you know that I have been employed, that I have to make a journey to Germany, France, and Italy this coming year, that I shall receive a good salary, and am to expect even more in the time to come, and the best – that this coming year I will see and embrace you. Because I was rather dark in my letters regarding my economic circumstances, I shall make it more clear. I have two running tabs – that is to say – two written promissory notes, one for 60 Ducats and another for 65 Ducats. I don't need Jews to become placed in a precarious situation and to incur these debts, for one of the notes is held by my landlord, and the other a man who subsidized me in my exigency.[2] – These two sums, including the interest of six percent, make: 132½ Ducats, and the unfortunate thing is that both promissory notes will fall due already in the coming month. My watch has been pawned for them, and I must redeem it again around the same time, if I don't want it to be auctioned off to my disgrace. I lack everything down to the most necessary least bit of my underclothing, and naturally it is not possible to count on a portion of my salary before the quarter is concluded first. If I wish to avoid the vexation of becoming prostituted with citations and lawsuits, and moreover (and what is the most annoying) receiving a bad name right at the beginning of my service, there are no other means left other than that I have recommended to you. By everything in the world, I ask you, insofar as it is possible for you, to come up with the desired sum of 200 Ducats for me, and the sooner the better; I should certainly be able to pay you back again in a few years. My honor depends upon it, and this is sacred to me; and if it is finally the case that you are not able to help me, I shall be forced to borrow money from a usurer with a high interest rate, and then subsequently borrow on the high interest with an even higher interest, so that I predict that my shade will remain an eternal beggar. Once more! I ask you for everything that I am able to ask for, to help me out this time and in the coming month, for after that it is too late. I will also write to *Hallardt* today as well, as to whether he is able to accept some money and pay it out to me here again? I will immediately give you an answer about this.

I have heard nothing yet about the recommendation from H[err] v[on] Benzel to the Russian minister here.[3]

I thank you a thousand times for your usual intercessions; they were quite welcomed.

Fare well and greet all my siblings and our few friends; and if possible please help

Your

Most obedient son Joseph

COMMENTARY

Original Buchen, Bezirksmuseum. The emotional beginning of the letter is no doubt a response to one from his parents announcing the death of Kraus's sister, Katharina Josepha, with whom the composer was particularly close in all but the last letter. As a nun, she was buried in the cloister graveyard in Weilbach. The total sum of his debts has now been revealed to be a fraction of that previously reported to his parents, though one might well question Kraus's accounting at all levels.

1. Katharina Josepha Kraus died on 1 June 1781 at the age of 23.

2. The identity of this "other man" is not clear, though it was probably one of his Swedish friends.

3. It is not clear why Kraus would have solicited or received a recommendation to the Russian ambassador, given that he was already friends with him. As will be noted in Letter 42, he may have been approached regarding a further post in St. Petersburg at the court of Empress Catherine, though this remains speculative.

41. Letter to his parents dated Stockholm, 26 August 1781

Dearest Parents!

I received your letter of the second of this month on the twenty-second, and on the twenty-fourth the funds of 209 Swedish Riksdalers and 18 Schillings, as well. I thank you from the bottom of my heart for the love that you have shown me; and – if it is not possible to help me out all at once with the matter, it can happen eventually. But – of course I have to learn how to economize – an art that I have understood little or not at all my entire life and that had to become an annoyance to me in the beginning, for custom and honor demanded many times disbursements that really did not rhyme with my situation. In all of this, I console myself with the old proverb: if it has to happen, it will. That which you counseled me about regarding the underclothing[1] was also my thought as well, for I was certain by my [own] calculation long ago that I would have been able to resolve the circumstances more cheaply if I came home than [if I had stayed] here, but – something – and I would have liked to have known what I would not have needed, [for] I had to purchase everything everywhere, for, in all seriousness, I don't have a single shirt remaining in my possession.[2] I would dearly like to write my dear godfather, H[err] Häussler, if I were not enclosing this letter for Hallardt, for then the packet would become too thick; I will save it for another time, however. He does me an injustice if he thinks that it would have annoyed me for him to have advised me to come home. Was he able to know my situation? Did you know better? I may now honestly admit to him that only an extraordinary degree of obstinacy held me back – a favorite *Dosis Galle*,[3] that once had determined for me accordingly to oppose every destiny of God's green earth that I could not endure. And rather than telling people that they ought to give me bread, I would rather have starved. "Strange!" – as far as I'm concerned – it was no less strange that a fellow was not able to remain in the small circle and lust contentedly after other honorable people in this lame devilish play up to the end of his days – to lie about this to one's self as if there existed roast quail on the other side of the ocean – and to journey toward a goal without purpose for this, so that with each step it was moved another ten ahead – and then to stick one's hands calmly into one's pockets and wait until the roast was served up and then eat with as much appetite as any other wanderer. No – you will allow me the opportunity, and even if I currently would only have a single pair of pants and stockings that perhaps an honorable fellow ought to have, I would still show an attitude and demand time for reflection – Ha! How sweet it tastes not to have a single small devil on this earth to thank for his fortune!

The new opera house, which has been under construction since 1773, will be ready at the end of this coming year and is intended to be one of the largest, most solid, and most expensive in Europe. And I received the honor of crafting the new piece with which the new theater will be dedicated. I now have my hands full to bring the matter to fruition. The title of the opera is *Äneas i Cartago,* the outline of the story, the plot, and the episodes are by the King himself, and only the versification is by the poet who did my last opera.[4] *Hallardt* was not like you said; for he immediately gave the appearance of driving as much my way as he was able; because I really want to await your answer first, I made no use of his opportunities.

Concerning the sealing wax, I will see if I can't get something better.
Greet everyone – all my siblings and friends – Fare well and love
Your
Most obedient son
Joseph
P.S. My address is:
Maître de Musique de la Chapelle de Sa Majesté Royale de Suede. From this moment on you don't need to write anything else on the letter, for I have moved to another lodging.

COMMENTARY

Original Buchen, Bezirksmuseum. The response at the beginning seems to be one to his parents admonishing him for his lack of economy, perhaps even reading sub rosa that they still did not believe he had obtained such a prestigious position and that he ought to return home to Germany. Apparently, his godfather Häussler was of the same opinion, blaming Hallardt for not allowing his departure. Both of course are dismissed with the usual diatribe, though for the first time Kraus admits his own spendthrift ways.

1. Orig. *Wäsche,* or laundry, but here taken to mean his general underclothes.

2. That he was down to a single shirt is patent nonsense, which his parents must have realized.

3. *Dosis Galle* = a dose of bile.

4. Kraus is referring to Kellgren. This is the first mention of *Æneas i Cartago,* an opera that was to occupy the composer for the next decade.

42. Letter to his parents dated Stockholm, 16 November 1781

Dearest Parents!

Just today I returned from Drottningholm,[1] where I had to do my service from September onward. From one post day to the next I thought to come to Stockholm in between in order to be able to write to you, but partly this was impossible for me due to my small business at court, and partly because my head was filled continually with a hundred tasks that I had to do in the city and for which there was always too little time. Of course, I love you, my dearest [ones], always as much as ever, and I'm sorry that I was placed outside the city, not least so that I would be able to converse with you by letters – an obligation that I would gladly fulfill! I received both of your letters only today, for here one has to obtain the letters oneself from the post office. Nothing pleases me more than that you are all well. It is always the most precious thing that I read in all of your letters; for, the fact that you love me – do I need to tell you? My journey that was intended for early next year has had to be put off until the following autumn, for the new opera house is not yet finished. I would gladly have nothing to say against it, if not because of it I have to relinquish the happiness of seeing you a few months earlier – but – it is of no use, and I have to be content. I now have made the acquaintance of the Russian ambassador. He himself sought me out in Drottningholm and was extraordinarily friendly toward me and from this moment forward

I am to be with him at his home every Friday. His wife is the daughter of the Dutch envoy to Mainz – Count *Wartensleben*.[2]

How did I feel when I received my first quarterly salary? Hmm – just think. He, the poor devil, was half embarrassed when he signed his receipt: for this quarter I have by my signature received this and so much, and for this my freedom has been purchased for this long. Lots of luck!

Greet all of my dear siblings and especially my eldest sister – God grant that we can once more live together.

Fare well and always love
Your
Most obedient
Joseph

COMMENTARY

Original Buchen, Bezirksmuseum. The composer is responding to an obvious inquiry from his parents whether or not he has been paid his salary and how he plans to travel to see them.

1. Kraus's service at the country palace of Drottningholm would have been conducting works at the court theater there, which, as Åstrand has pointed out (HÅ-JMK, 91), would have been unheated and unbearably cold in the various outer rooms. It is therefore probable that Kraus was assigned quarters in Canton, a village established near the palace especially for the artisans of all kinds, where a reasonable degree of comfort could be maintained. The exact quarters he occupied, however, have not been identified.

2. The Dutch envoy was Karl Friedrich Graf von Wartensleben (1710–1776), who was involved in the various political maneuverings of the Prussian, Scandinavian, and Russian courts. The Russian ambassador was Andrej Razumovsky (1752–1836), and it is a curious statement that he personally sought out Kraus to make his acquaintance. While friendship was no doubt on his mind, Razumovsky was also on the lookout for musicians who might be persuaded to relocate to St. Petersburg, which would have caused a diplomatic incident at this point in time, given Kraus's recent appointment in Sweden.

43. Letter to his parents dated Stockholm, 17 February 1782

Dearest Parents!

The summary list for the resolution of my Göttingen debts is, save for a few changes, the same one you recently sent me. I will append it to the end of this letter so that I shall better be able to answer the remaining points of your missive more precisely. Did I win or lose in the exchange between my fatherland and my present employment? One can only learn that in time, or I would have had to have prophetic foresight to be in the position to be able to weave together everything possible in this or at each stage of my fate. Perhaps I would have been able to be greater in my fatherland, but never more satisfied – and that is exactly the struggle between fortune and misfortune. And I know that it will make you happier to embrace a satisfied rather than a great me, and certainly, if I simply remain healthy, things won't go awry. The only thought that would distress me would be that I would have seen you for the last time. But – fundamentally, it is not such a great distance over the sea, and even if the thing still appears far on a map, it doesn't terrify me. You ask me about the state of my inner being. I am reassured by this, for you half ask only about my own health due to the opportunity of the matter; and because of this self-same reason, I am glad that I am able to answer you so easily about it. We have here three places of worship for our religion, which anyone is able to use enough in the requirement of one's religious duty. The first is in the palace of the Spanish [ambassador], the second in the palace of the French ambassador, and finally the third in one of the southern suburbs. The French is closest to me; but it is impossible for me to visit it more than once a week, namely on Sundays and holidays, due to my affairs. It is more difficult in the country, where, if one of the aforementioned ambassadors is not in the vicinity, there is no access for the practicing of our worship service at all. Both of these inconveniences affect those employed by the legations, the other Kapellmeister who is Italian, and four composers of the Kapelle who are Bohemian;[1] and the French ambassadorial preacher always gives us permission for it. Around Easter we go to confession and communion, and for this we have to pay the priest two Riksdalers apiece; otherwise he would have only a small subvention without it. Now you have my religious practice for the entire year. Concerning my economy, I will make you acquainted with it as succinctly and as completely as possible. My apartment consisting of a music salon and two rooms costs me 150 Fl [Florins] with the necessary accoutrements and wood, my dinner at noon for the year 160 Fl, for I am not yet set up enough for eating in. The servant costs me monthly a bit more than 5 Fl in wages. Coffee, tobacco, etc., according to my calculations for this half year have cost me approximately somewhere around 50 Fl. I have not noted down my other expenses so exactly, apart from those that I have put toward paying off my debts – a sum of about 500 Fl – but there is a bit left over that I would have been able to deduct for small comforts had not an idiotic blow come in between. And this consisted of the fact that our prima donna, *Müller,* along with her husband who is a German,[2] have up and left, and this has had the most unpleasant influence upon my situation. For she had the primary role in the opera, with which the new opera house was to have been dedicated. With her flight all my hopes were dashed, for the third performance was my own and a sum of at least 7[00] to 800 Fl has slipped through my fingers. Of course, the sum will remain with me for another time, but I'd have preferred to have it now threefold more than another time, for with it I would have been able to absolve my entire debt. This unpleasant incident was nonetheless good for me, for I have hopes of being able to begin my journey sooner. The King has not yet expressed this precisely. But I have let it be put forward and hope to obtain a completely decisive answer in a few weeks. It is for this reason that it will depend upon whether I send the already finished music for my dear siblings by sea or bring it to them myself.[3] Before I come to my little accounting, I have to assure you first that the golden watch from Göttingen is still retained firmly in my possession,[4] and I believe that I would not like to be caught short if I were able to exchange it for a better one. Gifts of this sort have not been received, for none of my pieces have yet been put on the stage, and certainly won't be until the new theater is finished.

Greet with affection all of my dear siblings and my dear godfather, Herr Häussler, for I love them all. Fare well my dearest parents and love me always

Your

Most obedient son

Joseph

[P.S.] Invoice

1) for the notary Müller for the tailor's bill 2 Rth [Reichthalers]
2) for the landlord Leuburg 7 Rth
3) for Mrs. Sothin 15 Rth

4) [for] the wigmaker 3 Rth
5) [for] the deaf Schröder or boot polisher 5 Rth
   Total   32 Rth
   Or 6 Louis d'ors and 2 Rth

I am writing to notary Müller with this same post. If he is satisfied with this, everything is good; if he isn't, then it is his own fault.

COMMENTARY

Original Buchen, Bezirksmuseum. This letter marks the first indication of the fate of his opera *Æneas*, whose circumstances continually prevented its performance. The two performers mentioned fled the country to escape their debts, even though Gustav sent military forces after them to prevent their escape. The letter is largely in response to a rather focused series of questions posed by his parents, no doubt worried that his position was less secure than he makes it out to be.

1. The Kapellmästare is Francesco Antonio Baldassare Uttini (1723–1795); the "Bohemian" composers are probably Johann Friedrich Grenser (1757–1795), Carl Megelin (1763–1836), and Christian Gottfried Scherber (ca. 1750–1831), all from Dresden, and Johann Caspar Meckel (ca. 1734–1804) from Vienna.

2. The reference is to mezzo-soprano Caroline Halle Walther Müller (1755–1826) and violinist Christian Friedrich Müller (1752–1827).

3. Yet another indication that Kraus has been composing music especially for his family, though the works cannot be identified.

4. An indication that the much-pawned watch has been redeemed, though Kraus is clearly anxious to have it replaced by a gift from the king.

44. Letter to his parents dated Stockholm, 24 June 1782

Dearest Parents

Now this really is entirely too much. No letter from me since February? And my last one is hardly more than a month old? God knows! That is crazy! I, like all other honorable people in your business, have three valid reasons that I didn't write to you at the beginning of this month. *Pro primo,* I could not then give you so certain news about a matter that I now can. *Pro secundo,* I had resolved to try already at the end of last month, as one would have written in the letter, when one has the honor of becoming 26 years old. *Pro tertio,* and now I can truly tell you – I was out in the country and wandering about a little and experienced, as did

the entire Christian world, renewal and joy. Are these not 3 valid reasons? Now, my dears, I can tell you in all certainty that I shall yet see you
this year. My departure depends solely upon the arrival of Saxon Kapellmeister *Nauman*[n], who has been invited here to perform himself in all
his glory his opera[1] that he fabricated four years ago at the request of the
King. I await him daily with longing; less in order to become acquainted
with him, for all that he is entirely a nice fellow, and even if it wouldn't
please me a hundredfold that he would come into my place, at least I say
so that I can make tracks and shortly be able to eat Hasenpfeffer with
all of the trimmings with you. God knows, how good this thought does
me. Therefore – today the gentleman entered into his twenty-seventh
year – Cheers! – I would in any case have intended to congratulate myself with quite a pretty nice compliment, even if I always had to keep
my hands in my pockets. Knock, knock. – Come in! – and was met with
someone in a blue waistcoat lined with silver, who had the honor of celebrating my birthday with a little good wish – it's only a member of the
orchestra – many thanks, my friend – and I know what he wants – and
that's money. So the entire morning went by so quickly and now I would
have sweated a bit less with the hard work, if the most annoying notion
of what was to come didn't run around inside my head. Look! My dear
performers have brought me a small trifle so early in the day, and I ought
to pay with a little supper. Just listen to what they organized: 1) a large
sausage of 2 Marks à 12 Thalers copper coin; 2) roast veal à 27 Thalers
ditto coin; 3) a flask of brandy à 6 Th[alers] ditto; 4) 3 bottles of Arak for
3 punch bowls à 45 Thaler[s] ditto, 12 lemons for it à 9 Thalers, 2 Marks
[and] sugar à 8 Thaler[s]; 5) butter, cheese, bread, etc.: 12 Thalers; 6) beer
and a few bottles of wine, 30 Thalers, in *Summa sumarum*[2] 149 Thalers,
or in our money, 4 Ducats and 17 Bazen. It couldn't be helped; it had to
be paid. If it is to be that the sons of bitches simply drink to my health
quite handsomely, I will be satisfied for this time. Concerning the people
of Göttingen, here is my opinion. The Herr Solicitor Müller is a rogue
and the rest sluggards. If they aren't satisfied with what has been offered
them, then I'll do the same thing as Götz von Berlichingen; I'll slam
the window shut and say to them what Götz said to the captain.[3] Herr
Procurator will not accomplish anything with his high and mighty tone.
I will bring the watch back again, naturally, and then we will wish to con-

sider how to bring the entire matter to a close. That H[err] v[on] Stuber-auch[4] must bear the brunt of the most misfortune from the revolution in Mainz – pains me in my soul, for I have always been good to him from the bottom of my heart. But – a comforting notion always intercedes: Dear God, how thankful I am to You, that You wrote in Your great book before I existed "a fellow ought not to become a lawyer *par tout,* or otherwise a laborer in the political council."[5]

[Continuation dated] 19 July 1782

I have just now returned from Drottningholm, where I did my tour of duty. This was precisely the reason that the letter wasn't finished earlier. Naumann has now arrived, and they will give me permission to travel as soon as the burial of the dowager Queen[6] is over. I greet all of my friends with affection

And am always
Your
Most obedient Joseph

COMMENTARY

Original lost, contemporaneous copy Buchen, Bezirksmuseum. The transcription was apparently made for Silverstolpe, but since the original is lost, it is impossible to say if it is complete in every detail.

1. The opera is *Cora och Alonzo.*

2. *Summa sumarum* = grand total; the cost of the birthday feast was approximately US$300 in modern currency. The identity of the man in blue with silver trim is unknown, but given the importance of the occasion, it may well have been concertmaster Erik Ferling (1733–1808).

3. As in Letter 16, the epithet from Goethe is "*Leck mich im Arsch* [Lick my ass]!" The entire insouciant attitude is directed toward Kraus's Göttingen creditors, who have apparently rejected the settlement offer in quite an arrogant manner.

4. The identity of Stuberauch is unknown.

5. The quote does not, however, appear to have been taken from the Bible, as Kraus implies.

6. The reference is to the funeral of Gustav III's mother, Lovisa Ulrika, who died on 16 July 1782.

Interludium

The last letter was posted probably on 19 July (or shortly thereafter) and was the final missive sent by Kraus to his parents during his first period in Stockholm. On 7 October 1782 he set off on his grand tour that was initially intended to last only a year or two. The new opera house, the dedication for which his opera *Æneas i Cartago* was to have been performed, was finally inaugurated on 30 September with the premiere of Naumann's much delayed opera *Cora och Alonzo*, to great public acclaim. Kraus must have witnessed this with a degree of disappointment, but given that his own work was incomplete – only three of the six acts had actually been composed – this must have been tempered with the knowledge that he could use the time to his advantage to perfect his complex and monumental work. Thus it would be even more powerful, given a longer germination time. Now free to travel at the King's expense, he focused upon his main purpose: to observe the latest trends in both music and the stage in the cultural centers of Europe. This was no random journey, although he clearly had some freedom as to his initial itinerary. He maintained from the start a succinct diary in which he noted down his route and various thoughts. This document was primarily meant to serve as a private memorandum that he could draw upon later for a more official description of his observations and comments to be sent back to Stockholm. It was therefore not intended as a detailed travel diary in the ordinary sense. Gaps in the sequence of entries gloss over items that were not germane to his principal purpose, thus making it a lacunar document. Moreover, there exist drafts of official letters back to his employers in Sweden, as well as the aforementioned list of "official correspondence" and graphic information on the journey, all of which confirm that this was more of a general notebook than travelogue.

Initially, his journey back to Germany retraced the route he took several years earlier in coming to Sweden. From Stockholm south to the town of Eksjö he traveled on the main north–south road, but thereafter he diverted directly to the southern tip of the country in Ystad, from which he took a ship over the Baltic to the Swedish Pomeranian port of Stralsund. His first continental stop was in the provincial town of Wismar, where his friend Hallardt was postmaster. This first stage was, according to his precise calculations, a distance of 97 Meilen, or about 970 kilometers in today's distances. His second stage took him by way of Rheinsburg, an important Prussian court and university town, to Berlin and finally to Dresden. He may have been invited to go there through his immediate contact with Naumann back in Stockholm, but in any case it was also the hometown of one of his colleagues, wood-wind player Johann Friedrich Grenser (1757–1795), whose father was one of Europe's leading manufacturers of wind instruments. This may indicate an ancillary purpose to obtain the best musical instruments for use back in Sweden, although there is no documentation of such procurement. Afterward, he went via Leipzig, Eisenach, Erfurt, and Gotha to his parents' house in Königstein, visiting them twice, once there and a few weeks later in their new home in Amorbach, before continuing on by coach and boat to Vienna by way of Regensburg.

Over the next several years, the tour, begun so diligently, did not go as planned. Kraus spent over six months in Vienna, an extraordinary length of time with which Gustav III was not entirely pleased. But he did make good use of it by befriending important Viennese colleagues, including his idol Christoph Willibald von Gluck and Joseph Haydn, both figures of international stature. In October of 1783 he was ordered to meet up with the king's party in Italy, eventually following his sovereign to France in June of 1784, some eight months later. Having regained the confidence of Gustav, he was to have remained in Paris for a year before returning home. He made good use of this time by becoming involved in the vibrant Parisian concert life and even taking a month-long journey to London in 1785 to witness the Handel Centenary Festival. His absence became the fodder for intrigue, however, and he was forced to remain in Paris over a year longer than planned as the situation in Stockholm rectified itself. The next series of letters (and the diary) therefore constitute a rich and varied travelogue of his grand tour.

45. Travel Diary, dated 7 October 1782 to 23 April 1783

In Stockholm received from R[egerings]r[ådet] and signed for 464 R[iksdalers].

7th October journey from there via Ystad to Stralsund and Wismar, where arrived on the 31st. I stayed there for three weeks.

Underway in Rostock I met H[err] Schmidt, who built the large organ work with five keyboards, pedals, and ninety-plus stops, among which is to be found a trumpet stop also, for which the timpani voice is in the pedal, all in the large, tall, and antique Maria Church. At his house

I saw his own invention of a sort of harmonium. The frame above the usual box containing the keys, whose insides enclosed the secret mechanism, represents the upper half of a harp. The strings consisted of simple brass and steel, the former for the lower, the latter for the higher tones. The mechanism of the instrument was set into motion by means of a machine that is to be regulated by the feet according to the rules of the violin strings. The tone is quite transparent and rather equal from FF to f'''' and is similar to an extraordinarily fine cello tone. The only disadvantage that I noticed was that the tone had too long a reverberation, and this seems to derive from the nature of its invention. A fortepiano with two keyboards, among which the lower had a pipe voicing, pleased me less. The main invention of the above consisted mainly of an imitation of a quilled harpsichord with hammers. I did not like either the elasticity of the tone or its purity.

In Stralsund at the house of the merchant Ramsdahl I met a pretty girl with the most beautiful feet ever, a Frederician keyboard with a good tone, and a performer on the piano [named] *Mattstedt*. The sonata he composed was commonplace, and he lacked precision and a certain touch in his manner of playing. On the other hand, [there were] overblown affectations in the fast passages.

In Wismar I did more of the same and made the acquaintance with both of the *Gröning* [brothers], the youngest one's wife, their two sisters, and father: Doctor Nürnberg, Master Kühl, [and] Assessor Breitsprecher. During the visit I composed music on a text *by Gröning* for the King's birthday, the 24th of January. The majority of the time I passed with reading. At the house of my f[riend] Hallardt we had a concert early on. Frau Gröning sang a Largo in E-flat by Piccinni. The performance and compositions were good. The new books I became acquainted with were:

1) *Über Musik und ihre Wirkungen* with annotations by J. A. Hiller, in octavo, Leipzig, 1781. The piece is original and contains much that is good, and belongs to aesthetics. In his annotations Herr H[iller] has shown himself to be nothing less than a good *disciple of Gluck.*

2) *Briefe die Musik betreffend,* especially *Cora,* in Halle, octavo, Quedlinburg. Wretched garbage.

3) *Anweisung zum musikalischen zierlichen Gesänge* with appended
   examples by Johann Adam Hiller. Leip[zig], 1780.

4) *Anweisung zum musikalisch richtigen Gesange*, Leipzig, 177, by
   Hiller. Is good but not new.

5) *Anweisung zur praktischen Musik* by Petri, Leip[zig], 1782.

I didn't have time to read it through, but in all truthfulness, it has
to be a very useful book. The author has reworked it, for it formerly consisted of a small piece in octavo.

The remaining books I obtained myself.

Regarding the musical pieces I heard, several symphonies by Ditters,
Haydn, and Cambini. In concert Benda's *Flucht der Lalage,* and several
arias by Grétry, together with an aria in B-flat from Naumann's *Cora.*
Several concertos by a certain Schmid from England – that said nothing.
There is always a concert Tuesdays and a rehearsal the Tuesday before.[N]

[In the margin] Lodged at the Hotel de Saxe, formerly called Die
weisse Taube at Richters': – expensive.

Novemb[er] the 23rd I traveled from here via Büzow, Gustrow, where
I had to remain from Sunday evening until Thursday afternoon. During
the night between 30 Nov[ember] and 1 December I arrived in Berlin.

My acquaintances I made were H[err] Hummel, a certain Müller,
H[err] Bachmann. In a *Li[e]bhab[er]* concert I heard Rolle's *Tirza.* The
composition had certainly quite a lot of fire, especially the choruses.
The instrumental execution was rather good, but the singers less than
mediocre. A certain M[on]s[i]eur Sten, L . . . ten, who was formerly a
singer with Prince Heinrich, a certain Braun from Mannheim, also
did an aria. The daughters of the court counselor made up the voices.
The German National Theater is wretchedly built and wretchedly appointed. I heard here *Zémire et Azor, Der seltne Freier;* M[ademoi]selle
Niclas sang well but without feeling, and moreover she is not an actress
in the least. Langans did Azor as extraordinarily awfully as the role
could be performed. I wrote a letter to R[egerings]r[ådet] from here and
delivered the letter to Minister B[aron] Ehrensvärd.

N. Here follows in the margins the route and mileage: "Via Büzow – 4/Gustrow –
2/Witstock – 8½/Rheinsburg – 2/Ruppin – 2/Ferbellin – 1/Botzow – 2/Berlin –
4 – 4 S[um]ma (i.e., in total) 26½."

I promised Hummel the remaining sixth quartet.

Dresden 20 [Meilen]

Lodged at the Post, awful.

The 7th I traveled from Berlin to Dresden. I delivered the letter from Grenser to his father, who along with his son-in-law visited me in my lodgings and gave me a letter that I sent with the one to Wikmanson from Amorbach. In the tavern I made the acquaintance of the young Gözel. I heard a Mass in the Cathedral. Nothing special, [and] the building reverberated too much.

From there after a sojourn of two and a half days I traveled with a wagon driver from Eisenach in a post coach to Leipzig, where I spent the night with the Zimmermanns (a female cousin of Ficker) across from the post office – was quite expensive. The next morning [I traveled] to Jena via Naumburg – lodged a few days at the Sonne, where one had cheap sustenance. From there to Erfurt. Visited Cantor Weimar. Met the city chief of police, Wirt, etc., at the Römische Kaiser (run by Hoffmann's widow) and learned that Weissenborn had gone insane, etc.

I arrived in Königstein on 24 December.

7 January [1783] I traveled to F[rank]furt. Here *Orphé* was playing at the new comedy house. Several bravura arias were inserted for Orpheus. Eurydice was the wife of the director, fat as a priest's cook. The orchestral execution was all right, but the tempos were often incorrect. The theater is too small. A few of the decorations by Quaglio from Mannheim are well-executed, and the curtain by Schüz likewise was good. Here I met Pfeiffer. In the public concerts for which Kaiser (as conductor) gave me tickets, I heard Bäumel, M[a]dame Hi[t]zinger, from Bamberg and Würzburg. Her voice was too strident for me. Pfeiffer blew a concerto, as did a clarinetist *Hesse*. The tone of the former was somewhat un-bassoon-like.

The 12th I arrived in Mainz. I saw *Die seltsam Freyer* again, *Der Schornsteinfeger* by Salieri, and *Macbeth*.[O]

Arrived in Vienna on the first of April. The same day an Academy was held at the Burgtheater. The Symphony in D by Rosetti was an imitation of Haydn's symphony I heard in Regensburg. Herr Umlauf conducted from the keyboard. M[a]d[ame] N, M[ademoi]selle Cavalieri,

---

O. Hereafter follows concepts for two letters, reproduced here as nos. 46 and 47.

and H[err Adamberger] made up the voices. The performance was very mediocre with the exception of the first violin and oboe. Md [Madame Le] B[run] was heard for the first time. The voice was strong and in-elastic; and the coloratura was always the same, which was especially noticeable when she repeated her last rondo on demand. M[ademoi]selle Cavalieri has a quite flexible and a tight but well-sounding voice. The bravura in the first aria in A major by Salieri was well-composed and well-sung. The location did not seem to me to be well-suited to music. The theater has four banks of loges.

The 2nd I stayed home and gawked at the people.

The 3rd I ate dinner at Counselor v[on] Schick's place.

The 4th I was at the home of the chargé d'affaires v[on] Engström; received a letter for Z[ibet] dated 14 February, and went with him to the Prater and the Augarten. Dined with him. Was at Süsemihl's house in the morning. In the afternoon went to the Prater in Bülow's equipage.

The 5th was at home all day.

The 6th there was an Academy for the benefit of one of the recently established musical societies; *Die Israeliten in der Wüste* composed by Max[imilian] Ulbrich was performed. The orchestra was strong, but did not consist of the promised number of 180, but rather some 70 odd persons. The music had much fire throughout. The overture, in D minor, had three movements. The first represented the liberation of the people. The second movement, in A major, and the last in D major didn't belong at all. He proceeds into the first chorus with ideas from the first movement. I believe Bach has understood the true meaning of the text in this chorus. The role of the First Israelite was sung by M[a]d[ame] Theresia Täuber. The aria *"Will er, etc."* was too modern, and the performance of the singer was very poor, and her lack of understanding [of the text] was made more apparent still through the ill-suited cadenza on the last line (*"Ach, wie seyd ihr so beglückt"*). Aaron was Hofmann, a wretched bass. His aria was also too modern, and [in] both of these arias the main mistake was an accompaniment that was too strong. And the same could be said of the third aria of the Second Israelite, sung by M[ademoise]lle Cavalieri, for it was too much like a concerto, and the accompaniment of the vocal coloratura by the English horn was not terribly successful in its expression.

The Chorus of the Israelites (*"Du bist der Ursprung,"* etc.), on the other hand, far exceeded what came before, and indeed Bach's entire work (insofar as the arias and choruses require fire). The movement is in C major and fugal. Moses comes in with the chorus in a very successful balance, and nothing could be thought more appropriate than the answer of the people to M[o]ses['s] question: (*"Has du die Werke und Wunder schon vergessen, die für dich dein Gott gethan?"*) *"Gott schlummerte"* (ungrateful people!); *"Er erwache!"* – the composer has altered the words according to the circumstances – in this chorus as well, [but] with an apparent large gap. However, the aria of Moses that follows immediately after is quite trivial.

The duet of both Israelites with another text would be appropriate for any concert. I have to note that both singers competed with each other quite prettily as to who could be the most raging. The next [one] with Moses reciting [versus] a mixed chorus is pretty, but less modern. Too, the last movement of Moses's prayer, in which the poet and the nature of the thing should certainly have demanded the largest tension, fell flat. The chorus following the great miracle, in C major, was well worked out, and the painting of the pouring forth of the fountain completely forgivable. The first act ends with this. The same comments are valid for the second act, with the difference that the music is even less worthy for the church. The theme of the first recitative is quite childish for both the subject and characters. The chorus that begins with a solo by M[oses], ditto, the aria of the First Israelite in G major, ditto, and Moses's aria with an obbligato violoncello is extra trivial. The accompaniment for the second part (*"Dies ist der Held,"* etc.) is too strong, so that one cannot hear the voices.

In the recitative that precedes the aria the composer has painted *"Doch einst vor meinen Blicken she ich die Zukunft aufgehellt"* like this: first comes a crescendo in the timpani, followed by one woodwind instrument after the other in a row. The recitative closes the same [way], but with less effect.

The following aria for M[ademoi]sell[e] Cavalieri with obl[igato] oboe, flute, bassoon, and horns is a blend of garlic and onions. The final chorus is mediocre. For the most part, the first is far beyond the second. The fault lies halfway with the text itself. The composer too has here and there in the last part thoughts that one has heard in the first. The performance was rather spirited – but not precise. Piano was not really observed, and even less the crescendo, and in the triplets every stand had its own bowing. The basses were also not clear enough for the size of the contrabass [section] – there was a lack of violoncellos. The composer has, moreover, overloaded the basses too much.

Between the two acts was heard the Emperor's own wind instrument ensemble consisting of 2 oboes, 2 clarinets, 2 horns, 2 bassoons. The composition was by *Johann Went,* and quite well set for the nature of the instruments, but not for novel thoughts. The performance was as animated as one could wish for.

The 7th Süsemihl was at my place, and I toward evening at his (and I sent off a letter to my parents).

8th was held the same Academy. All of my former comments are valid here too. Instead of the earlier musical interlude, H[err] *Gehring* performed on the flute. The tuning of his instrument was a half-tone too high, and I didn't think that the years he was gone from G[öttingen] had done as much for him as they could have. The movement by Graf was more remarkable than common.

Began learning French today.

The 9th from yesterday midday and today for the entire day I had such a powerful cold that I could hardly speak and passed the time with lectures.

The 10th I was visited by H[err] Gehring. Through him I learned that 1) Schmidt (who I knew from G[öttingen]) is a city musician in Frankenhausen and married; 2) that Graf from A[ugsburg] is in London with an excellent position and returns in the fall; 3) that Salieri travels to Paris.

The 11th I remained at home all day. H[err] Süsemihl visited me, and I passed the time just like the first.

The 12th [was spent] with reading. The books so far are: 1) *Les memoirs du Comte de Grammont;* 2) *Die Bestimmung des Menschen* by Spaulding; 3) *Der Philosoph der Welt* 1st part; 4) Blum[auer]'s poetry; 5) the Swedish translation of *The Vicar of Wakefield;* 6) M[a]d[emoisell]e Rowe's letters of friendship, a miserable book of which I could hardly read three pages; 7) *Lesebuch für all Stände* – a selection of philosophical miscellanea by a priest; 8) *Le process des trois Rois* – quite satirical, but in miserable French.

The evening of the 13th I visited Frau Süsemihl and took with me the latest edition of Klopstock's *Messias.*

The 14th I finally visited *Gluck*. He was quite gracious but told me himself that, following his illness, he had difficulty expressing himself. His right hand did not possess entirely the former necessary flexibility as earlier, as well. Klopst[ock]'s *Hermannschlacht* is not yet written down, and according to what he said about the Emperor often asking him about *Danaïdes,* this as well. In the beginning he intended to use Salieri to set this down on paper – but then he noticed that he would have to make too many interventions, and on doctor's orders he left it alone. Salieri is therefore to set this opera in Paris under his own name. Gl[uck] has rather clearly let it be known that Salieri has rather retained his thoughts, but that he likewise did not like that it would appear under his [i.e., Gluck's] name.

He presented me with his portrait and showed me the original painting, which is a masterpiece of expression. He repeated often his contention that a simple singing [style] belonged of necessity to a stage piece. He was the first to use the chorus as actors in Paris, for formerly they just stood there like statues. He allowed *Orphé* to be translated then, but he was not satisfied with the greatest poets, but rather took on someone mediocre, who did things more according to his liking. He was quite satisfied with the scene *"Un seul guerrier?"* etc., *"pousuivons notre ennemi jusq'au trépas,"* etc., in *Armide.*

Toward the evening I paid a visit to N[iklas Lars von] Engström and read at his house from the poetry of [gap in the text] by M[ademoi]selle Clairon, of which I was most pleased with the opera – *Les Bacchanales.*[P]

The 16th

17

18   I heard the famous *Stabat mater dolorosa* by Haydn at the Barmherzigen Brüdern in Leopoldstadt – but I expected much more. The performance was mediocre.

19

20   I was at the Prater with Gehring.

21   I was at a concert at Liedemann's place, in which a good violinist [gap in text] by name and Catrani also played – I heard quartets by a certain violinist Tiz – that had – a rather modern structure.

P. At this point in the text are two draft letters, one to Zibet and one to Kellgren. See Letters 50 and 51.

22   Ate dinner at Gluck's place and met H[err] Greybel, who had
conducted *Iphigenie.* G[luck] was quite satisfied with the translation.
    23[Q]

COMMENTARY

Original Uppsala, Universitetsbiliotek, Folio X270f. As noted earlier, this lacunar diary was clearly intended as a sort of private notebook intended to provide information for a more thorough and comprehensive report home. The language makes it clear that much of it was compiled after the fact in many instances, and not as Kraus encountered the people or made his observations on a daily basis. It also contains several draft letters, the originals of which have not survived; it is therefore impossible to say whether or not these drafts corresponded completely with the final versions sent to their recipients. While there is still a plethora of information contained therein, extensive annotated reproductions and analysis of this diary already exist with the scholarly literature (and is not repeated here).[R]

46. Letter to Cristoffer Zibet dated Würzburg, 12 February 1783

From the time according to my calculations that my second letter could have reached you, I have longed every post day for a notification from the main post office in F[rank]furt of a letter of credit to R[egensburg], for which I asked H[err] Zi[bet] in my last letter but have not yet had my wishes fulfilled. The only way left to me, therefore, is to make a written request in advance to our minister in R[egensburg], Björnstjerna,[1] to provide a subsidy for me for a longer sojourn at a place that is without doubt quite expensive but not interesting for my purposes, and for this reason has been interminably tedious for me. I must humbly petition H[err] R[oyal Counselor] to relieve me as soon as possible of the necessity of pausing my journey. The many twisted paths and the visiting of places that were important for my objective are the cause of me having to plague

Q. The diary ends at this point without an entry.
R. See Helmut Brosch, "Quellen zur Biographie von Joseph Martin Kraus: d) Fragment des Reisetagebuchs von Joseph Martin Kraus 1783/1783," *Mitteilungen der Internationalen Joseph Martin Kraus Gesellschaft* 9/10 (1989): 8–20, with comprehensive annotations and commentary, and HÅ-JMK, 96–107. The present author has also analyzed the work in "The Travel Diary of Joseph Martin Kraus." There also exists a further, if lacunar, translation/transcription by Schreiber in Berlin, Deutsche Staatsbibliothek, Mus. Ms. theor. 501.

H[err] R[oyal] Counselor with this request earlier than I had thought. However, I must await the requested aid in order to continue the journey onward to Vienna. I have not been idle in the meantime, for I am now editing with all diligence the outline for the plan of instruction that I have made and that I have communicated to Holzbauer[2] and many other professionals in parts, and who passed on to me comments and experiences that I must incorporate in order to give my work in time the perfection that a work demands, and that will win the H[err] R[oyal Counselor's] approval. As soon as it has run the gauntlet in Vienna I shall allow myself the freedom to pass it before the H[err] R[oyal Counselor's] informed view.

My observations of the theatrical performances in F[rank]furt, Mainz, and Mannheim are too extensive for a letter![3] I reserve the right therefore to send along the highlights thereof at the first opportunity, along with several small musical pieces[4] that will deserve a connoisseur's attention in some fashion. – The design of the Mannheim theater (by Lessing[5]) has especially interested me.

COMMENTARY

Original lost, formerly Stockholm, Riksarkiv? The letter is preserved as a draft in the travel diary. Kraus annotates it: "written in Amor[bach]" and "sent off on 15 February."

1. Magnus Olof Björnstjerna (1738–1785), Swedish ambassador to the court of Thurn und Taxis.

2. This curricular plan has not survived, but it is clear that it must have been extensive, and perhaps it was later used at the Royal Swedish Academy of Music. The composer is Ignaz Holzbauer (1711–1783), the former Kapellmeister who had retired the previous year. He was in a position of a colleague with whom Kraus could communicate his musical mission. It is not known who the "other" people were.

3. These observations have not survived, but must have been a formal report.

4. The identity of these *små musikaliska piecer* is unknown.

5. Ephraim Gotthold Lessing (1729–1781), German author and playwright. In 1778 Lessing was offered the position as theater director in Mannheim, which he turned down, but Kraus's letter indicates that he at least provided a design that was still used some five years later.

47. Letter to Magnus Olof Björnstjerna
dated Würzburg, 12 February 1783

The enclosed letter should excuse my taking the liberty of bringing to the attention in writing to Your Most Noble Worship of an urgency. A longer stay in Berlin, Dresden, Mannheim, and many other places in the fulfillment of my objective held me back, as did the poor roads, which have heretofore denied me the pleasure of proving my worthiness in person. To complete my obligation would be my greatest desire, if only another economic circumstance had not delayed me. I have already written to H[err] R[oyal Counselor] Zib[et] from F[rank]furt regarding a new disbursement of funds, either by letter of credit to R[egensburg] or by another efficient way, in order to be able to continue onward on my travels to Vienna unhindered. Because I have not yet received an answer from [him], perhaps because the post has been incorrectly delivered, I request of Your Most Noble Worship the grace to present to me therefore favorable news. Here in W[ürzburg], where I have already become known to some extent, the sojourn has not been as expensive as it in all likelihood would be at a place where I was a foreigner. [I am] completely with the most humble expectation of Your Most Noble Worship's gracious answer in an envelope to Professor H:[1] in Würzburg and with the greatest admiration

> *Your Most Noble Worship's*
> *Most humble servant*

COMMENTARY

Original lost, formerly Stockholm, Riksarkiv? The draft letter has been preserved in the travel diary; see the previous letter. It is clear that he expected the ambassador to have some knowledge of his journey. Björnstjerna's reply, if any, has not been preserved, but it must have been favorable, since Kraus arrived in Regensburg in the middle of March and stayed for about two weeks. See the following letter.

1. Professor H: is his godfather Häussler, who had moved to Würzburg from Mundau. See Letter 58.

48. Letter to his parents dated Regensburg, 23 March 1783

Dearest Parents!

I have certainly not expected so much pleasure as I have enjoyed here, and could not even have expected it had not Herr Schmidt[1] hurried me along on the departure. H[err] v[on] Björnstjerna immediately offered me lodging and everything, and presented me to the Prince,[2] who was completely gracious, on Joseph's Day, when there is always a celebration here because of the Emperor.[3] That which exceeded all of my expectations was that every day concerts were organized at the court on my behalf, where I could not marvel enough at the perfection of the orchestra. Our ambassador immediately made me acquainted with a few other ambassadors, among which I am especially taken with the Saxon, Danish, and Bohemian. In the house of H[err] von *Dithmar*,[4] where H[err] Schmidt had introduced me, as well as the houses of the aforementioned ambassadors, I was so well-treated this past week that it truly pains me that I must leave such a pleasant place. Yesterday I had the grace to be received by the Prince, and today we travel by water to Vienna, where I shall meet *Glück*.[5] Fare you well – you and my siblings are beloved from the bottom of my heart

Your

Most obedient son

Joseph

[P.S.] Greet all good friends, especially the F[athers] Roman and Aegidi.[6] The Seifrids are to be greeted.

COMMENTARY

Original Buchen, Bezirksmuseum. Kraus has reduced by half the time that he has spent in Regensburg; he remained there two weeks instead of one, according to the court protocols for the Swedish embassy.

1. Kraus's cousin Ludwig Schmidt, a merchant who was relocating to Wölkersdorf outside of Vienna, according to Silverstolpe (Si-JMK, 61).

2. The Prince is Carl Anselm Prince von Thurn und Taxis (1733–1811).

3. St. Joseph's Day occurs on March 19,

and the Emperor is Joseph II.

4. Joachim von Dittmar, a member of the Thurn und Taxis court.

5. Christoph Willibald von Gluck (1714–1787), but spelled as a pun, meaning both the composer and meeting his fortune or luck (*Glück*).

6. Pater Roman Hoffstetter and Pater Aegidius were Benedictine monks in Amorbach (see Appendix D). The "Seifrids" (recte Seyfried?) are unidentified friends in Amorbach.

49. Letter to his parents dated Vienna, 5 April 1783

Dearest Parents!

This time I'm only writing to write; for I am much too much a neophyte here to be able to tell you or myself something interesting. I have describe to you the morning before my departure from Regensburg on the 23rd of the month, of course, in brief – for it is my usual habit in writing letters that I always wait until the last minute. With heavy heart I left a place that offered me such unexpected pleasure. And certainly (God knows, [though] I have often desired him to be placed among all of the angels) it was not because of *Schmid;* no devil should have to care for me for six weeks. Our ambassador and his much-beloved wife gave me the most sorrow. The agreement of our characters was special. Such unselfish souls do not exist. At our farewells, the ambassador wept and gave me in remembrance a ring that I now wear, and his wife – God! It is impossible for me to describe it to you. *Such a Swede is worth more than ten Germans to me!* Otherwise, the passing of time at the court and with the other ambassadors I have, I believe, already mentioned in my last letter. Regensburg!!! Amen . . .

The morning before I was visited by Baron [von] *Schak,* Captain Küfer, and our new Herr cousin, *Saolo* with his lovely wife (*Spes*), her Herr brother with his other married half.[1] After a threefold repeated farewell at the house of our ambassador and a magnificent dinner at the house of Frau von Dithmar, I finally began my journey on the Danube with my dear Herr Schmidt, provided by this lovely woman with roasts and Rhine wine in abundance. The continuing beautiful weather for several days was the reason that I decided upon traveling by water. And, of course, if only it had continued for another week, I would have had the most pleasant trip. But the first evening it began to rain and storm, and with this the joy received a terrible blow. The country on both sides of the Danube is magnificent and has a certain majesty about it that is lacking in other mountainous rivers. Hill vineyards, which on one side one can lose one's vision in their expanse – here and there half-ruined castles are lost in the folds of the rocks – brilliantly on the opposite side the magnificence of the newer monasteries, the like of which I have never seen in all my days. It is true that, had not the ship's captain demanded so much all at once, I would have gladly have given half again for this brilliant interplay. 9 Sch[illings] was the cost of freight for myself and Stålberg[2] to Linz (half the journey), but it was agreed that this included both trunks all the way to Vienna. Everything is Bavarian from Regens[burg] to Passau. We stopped every evening and then – Merciful God! It is a shame that I am no theologian – for I could prove categorically that the swine in the Gospels, in which the possessed devils were so unmercifully housed and then made to undertake a journey into the abyss of the sea, were not drowned but were well baptized so that they and their inhabitants were transported to Bavaria in order to become innkeepers. Worse lodgings do not exist, nor does a more gross and superstitious people. The entire night the innkeeper patrolled with his rosary about the half-fouled straw upon which we sixty were placed and said his Pater Nosters. In the morning the bill was presented with the same devotion. For two pancakes and three bundles of straw, 6 Fl[orins] 36 Kr[eutzer]; *O dio,* what for? "No answer" – for the innkeeper took up his rosary in aid and did not trouble himself with our complaints in the slightest. Finally we arrived at the first Imperial customs house at Engelthalzell.[3] The inspection was quite thorough, but nothing was found on me. Simultaneously, we had to remain there the better half of a day while the entire ship was searched. By noon on Friday we finally had achieved the halfway mark. As I visited Linz with several good friends from Sweden who were studying there at the Nordic College,[4] we decided anew to continue likewise the second half of the journey by water, when suddenly the wind rose. Then all patience left me, and I convinced my traveling companions to proceed from there by land; and our baggage we could allow to follow later by water. For 18 Sk[illings] in Imperial coin we obtained a good opportunity. Thus, on Sunday afternoon at three o'clock we departed Linz and made a detour through Steiermark in order to visit Schmidt's brother-in-law, who is an official there overseeing Colloredo's possessions.[5] Here I enjoyed much honor. From there we traveled through magnificent country to Vienna, where we arrived on the first of April in the morning in good health and with straight limbs. Schmidt immediately made the effort to procure a certain lodging for me. Damned,[6] how expensive! Six Ducats per month and one Gulden for each dinner without wine. When I become a bit better known here, I will see if I can make my bill a bit more Christian. Of course, the lodging is very good and across from the palace, thus in the best place; *Glück* is my neighbor – I have not yet visited him – but I have our chargé d'affaires v[on] Engström[7] – a nice fellow. I immediately met an acquaintance from Göttingen here, Chamberlain von Bülow, who is at the Danish embassy. In this company, my Swede drove the entire day around the Prater and the Augarten, etc., so that I would at least know about a few of the prominent sites of Vienna – and I was quite satisfied with this. Already on the first day of my arrival an Academy (or concert) was held at the Burgtheater, for there is no stage performance during Lent. The music did not come up to my expectations.[8] That which pleased me above all else was the letter from my director, Zibet, which awaited me here. One cannot write more friendly and politely. Accept this little amount for now and love me always as before

Your

Most obedient son Joseph

P.S. The requested order for my sisters is not able to be immediately forthcoming, of course; for here I am still a *peregrinus in patria*,[9] and the little necessities that I have to obtain have made me so fearful due to the high prices, so that I lack all desire to shop further for something before I have first learned the Austrian tricks of the trade. Until then, I ask that my dear girls exercise patience. I greet my remaining good friends I left behind fondly. *À propos: Schmid* desires to make one of the girls in our neighborhood his wife. He has heard something of the beauty of the youngest Mademoiselle Wiese from Reinsaker, who is staying in Zelle.[10] Do me a favor and poke about a bit to find out what her circumstances are? – He has asked me about it quite a lot, and I consider it my obligation to extend to him this friendship. My address is Kraus, Maître de Chapelle au Service de la Cour de Suede à Vienne.

[I am] living on the Kohlmarkt across from the Michaelskirche in No. 134 on the third floor.[11]

COMMENTARY

Original Buchen, Bezirksmuseum. One must savor the irony of Kraus proclaiming this lengthy letter "a short one."

1. Baron Theodor von Schacht (1748–1823), Kapellmeister in Regensburg. Captain Küfer is unidentified but was no doubt a military man in the service of the Thurn und Taxis court. The other people are also unidentified, though the implication is that they are Kraus's distant relatives.

2. Stålberg = Kraus's personal man servant.

3. Engelthalzell = Engeltal along the Danube and site of a large monastery.

4. Known then as the *Nordische Stift,* which was intended to transform boys from the Scandinavian countries into good Catholics. It was founded in 1675, and today is the Nordico Museum.

5. The reference is to Hieronymus Colloredo (1732–1812), the prince-archbishop of Salzburg and a personage who figures prominently in the life of Wolfgang Amadeus Mozart. Steiermark is in central Austria.

6. Orig. *Blitz* or lightning, but translated here idiomatically.

7. Niklas Lars von Engström (1752–1826); the Danish chargé is Franz Christian von Bülow (1756–1835). The Prater and Augarten are the main city parks in Vienna at the time.

8. See his criticism in the travel diary; this dismissive judgment contrasts with his earlier comments.

9. *Peregrinus in patria* = a pilgrim in one's own country.

10. Kraus means Mariazell outside of Vienna.

11. No. 134 on the Kohlmarkt was around the corner from where Wolfgang Amadeus Mozart lived at No. 1179; there is no rhyme or reason to the eighteenth-century Viennese address numbering, of course.

50. Letter to Cristoffer Zibet dated Vienna, 15 [April 1783]

I finally met Pan Gluck. Certainly no pilgrim expressed more devotion toward the remnants of the Holy Land than I toward this great patriarch. His eyes, with which I believe he could have delved into my most secret musical sins, must have read in mine the perfect agreement with his sentiments. For, in less than two minutes, I had won his admiration and, moreover, something that makes me even more proud, his love. The last illness[1] has affected him sorely, so that he has difficulty expressing his thoughts and is obliged sometimes to search for words. But familiarity in a subject that has been the goal of his thoughts for half a lifetime soon offered him another [mode of] expression if the previous did not work. His right hand also lacks its former flexibility. That was the reason that Salieri[2] was to have set down his *Danaïdes* on paper, but even this stressed him too much so that the doctors feared a new onset of apoplexy; he has given up on this opera, and Salieri has been called to Paris in his stead to compose it. Gl[uck] believes that the music ought to be very much according to his own ideas, that S[alieri] often enough had the opportunity to hear [them] so that it could be Salieri's – but equally he did not have entirely complete confidence in this young man's ability to allow it to pass under his name. The newspapers have already known half a year ago enough to proclaim the agreement of the French Music Academy regarding this piece and spoke of it as if it were already a completed work, which has thus been delayed. It is something peculiar with this great composer that he has time and time again completed numerous operas in his head without writing them down, and is accustomed to retaining them in his memory unchanged for many years. I also heard many scenes from Klopstock's epics and great odes, complete acts from French and Italian musical dramas, all of which were performed in that manner. He has a grace without equal when he is at ease to introduce in an instant whatever passion he wants. He thus carries along his listeners with him like a storm, and it is purely impossible to recover until he desists. I would have wished that H[err] R[oyal Counselor] could have heard the scene in *Armide* "*Un seul guerrier,*" etc., and the chorus "*Pousuivons notre ennemi,*" etc. – I forgot myself and hunted all over the entire room for a weapon to help Armide. He is the perfect master of declamation, and his first fundamental is that the actors (not excepting the chorus) must first learn to declaim correctly before they dare to learn to sing. He was not entirely satisfied with the Swedish translation of his operas, for he sought in vain so many of the finer nuances that he had in the original. He liked *Orphé* the least, for within he thought he found unending (his own expression) absurdities. Unfortunately, I did not have the translation of *Alceste* and the reduction of his score with me in order to be able to hear his further judgments. In all this, he was nonetheless so reasonable in excusing us, for he was reminded how the same sort of thing had gone in Paris, where he, moreover, had abundant access to the translator. The praise of the Swedish court and public flattered him so much that he wished himself a few years younger so that he could see his children in Swedish dress. But, merciful God, there was our beloved S[tenborg], who made so much effort to sew his wide gold braid onto their simple clothing.[3] I made a single attempt as a jest to do the aria ("Grymma vän" from *Alceste*) according to H[err] Secretary's manner, which terrified me from tempting him a second time, for he became half raging, and to mollify his tortured soul, I needed nothing less than to tell the anecdote of the poor cantor in Saxony;[4] he finally forgave him, as if [he were] a lost soul. He has been painted by Duplessis,[5] royal painter in Paris, in a paroxysm of enthusiasm, as well. It is a masterpiece, and the painter had studied him daily a year in advance in order to succeed. The engraving that was made from the original is not so perfectly executed but equally very similar. With the example that he gave me, I have taken the liberty of acquainting your most worthy H[err] R[oyal Counselor] with it, as soon as H[err] v[on] Engström can forward it to Sweden. In my forthcoming letter, I will make the H[err] Royal Counselor aware of the theater and music in this place. I thank the H[err] R[oyal Counselor] for the letter and letter of credit, and assure the H[err] R[oyal] C[ounselor] without further ado that he can believe that I shall not remain silent in the slightest regarding anything that can enhance my limited insights and abilities. For the sake of M[a]d[emoiselle] St[ading][6] I shall not spare any effort to seek something appropriate for her voice. With greatest obeisance and submission I have the honor to be

[Your most] W[orthy] H[err] R[oyal Counselor's servant]

[P.S.] I would like humbly to request at the first [opportunity] to know from your most W[orshipful] H[err] R[oyal Counselor] if it would be allowed for me to dedicate to His Majesty 6 quartets[7] that I left in Berlin to be printed?

COMMENTARY

Original lost; formerly Stockholm, Riksarkiv. The letter in draft form is preserved in the travel diary. As Åstrand (HÅ-JMK, 114) notes, the Swedish draft version was somewhat freely interpreted by Kraus, resulting in a number of words and concepts that are unclear in the language. It was "improved" by Silverstolpe (Si-JMK, Letter 42), but it is unknown whether this rough draft was corrected by the composer before being sent off to Zibet. The use of the third person and repeated titles of his superior indicates that this was to be an official missive, possibly to be shared with Gustav himself.

1. This illness was a stroke.

2. Antonio Salieri (1750–1825), imperial Kapellmeister. His opera *Les Danaïdes* premiered in Paris at the Opéra on 26 April 1784.

3. Orig. *Sy hans bruna Galoner på deras enfaldiga klädningar*, meaning to ornament extensively the original vocal line.

4. This anecdote is not further identified, but may have been somewhat off-color.

5. Joseph-Siffred Duplessis (1725–1802).

6. Franziska Stading (1763–1837), one of the principal singers at the Royal Spectacles and possibly a very intimate friend of Kraus, according to Leux-Henschen.

7. These are the Six Quatours Concertants a deux violons, viola et violoncelle. Tres humlement dédiés à sa Majesté le Roi de Suede. Par J. Kraus, Maître de Chapelle de la Sus-dite Majesté. Oeuvre Premiere. Chès J. J. Hummel. Berlin (VB 181–185, 187). It is clear from this title page that the permission for the dedication was received.

51. Letter to Johan Henrik Kellgren dated Vienna, 20 [April 1783]

Best Friend!

I would gladly write much and simultaneously something that would deserve my f[riend's] attention, and things have gone as usual. Today I noticed something that was worth reporting, but already this morning I perceived it as trivial, and had not Gluck wakened me from my stupor, I would certainly have let it lie until my return home.[1] For the most part, there were the usual puppets that stood in my path; it would most naturally have been worth the effort to seek out the originals at home in a book, rather than trot all over the world and look up to caricatures at the end. The greatest harm in one doing this is that one becomes seemingly without emotions at the end, when one once tires of laughing and mocking all of the bizarre notions that bedevil a Christian man. Thus, I traveled half-awake and half-asleep throughout half of my fatherland, and swore at each street corner that I recognized every window and every roof, as similar as they were [to each other]. Wigs, feathered hats, shoes, stockings – everything, everything [was] still so embedded [in my] literary birth nest that I fled. For this reason, I accepted it as both advisable and healthy to plug the holes in order to preserve what little I possessed against this influenza. The cure was fine, but my consciousness was so hard tested by this, that nothing more could be added to it – much less to remember the promises I had given to write to my f[riend]. But now in the present Holy Week, when dear God softens so many recalcitrant souls, mine too has been thawed out, much to the great relief of my father and mother.

First, I have to report that I have seen theaters in Berlin, Dresden, Leipzig, F[rank]furt, Mainz, Mannheim, Würzburg, Munich,[2] Regensburg, Linz, and finally Vienna, and thus [I] can tell you within a hair's breadth how tall, how wide they are, how their sets are created – how many ranks the loges have – how many chandeliers – how many backdrops on each side, everything that is certainly of much value, but to the misfortune of my important education, [such] can be found in the travel description of every charlatan – and secondly, the few lines will not allow me to inform my patron that at all of these theaters I saw and heard mono- and duodramas,[3] comedies and tragedies, operas and Singspiels. Also, in truth I saw there many small and wide women's shoes – all *utriusque generis*[4] – and I also in truth collected a very pretty compendium of the distinctions regarding voices.

Thirdly, it would be a sin not to admit that the majority of these things pleased me very little – a few somewhat – and among the fifty-odd only *siliciet: Ariadne* in Berlin – *Macbeth* in Mainz – *Agnes Bernauer* in Mannheim – *Lear* in Vienna.[5] A few of the comedies were bearable, and the remaining historical pieces, which were interesting only with respect to music – are likewise not included – as well as those uncounted that I shall have the pleasure of liking in the future. Here at the moment the greater part of our poets, rhymesters, and epistle/epigram-makers, along with the moral scribblers, are visiting and like it here so much that I believe the climate has been uniquely made for them. Those who deserve to be known are, my f[riend], already acquaintances. Denis, Blumauer (one of the most witty), Schink (a lyrical genius), Wezel, etc. – these are all names that do honor to German literature.[6]

Further, I must confirm with tears that the sorrowful news that has already been for so long the fodder of all newspaper correspondents regarding the great persecution against the black-clothed servants in the vineyard of our Lord[7] is unfortunately more than true. The thing that truly proclaims most assuredly the imminence of the Last Judgment is that poets are so unashamed as to tell them the truth daily, one more bitter than another, without being invited to appear before the bench or being fined for this horrible crime.

The thing that annoys me no end is that I have embarrassingly forgotten the wonderful exclamation of His Eminence in *Le process des trois rois*[8] – that would certainly have come to pass here. I now charge my [friend] to answer me at the first opportunity, or more correctly, to write me a letter containing questions only – NB, those that I can answer – Blast and damn![9] In all of this hoi-polloi I forgot to say that Gl[uck] is a terrific fellow – that I love more than the tenth commandment.

With greatest admiration I remain
My best friend's . . .
[P.S.] Where the hell is the libretto for *Æneas*?

COMMENTARY

Original lost; draft preserved in the travel diary. There is no indication that this letter was actually sent in a redrafted form, though it does seem likely, since Kraus apparently received a reply from Kellgren during his visit to Vienna, presumably including the latest draft of the opera text.

1. The reference is difficult to fathom, given the lacunar state of the running commentary. He may mean, however, that he is tiring of keeping up with his travel diary draft.

2. If this list of cities is accurate, then Kraus made a side trip to Munich, a place that is mentioned in neither his letters home nor his travel diary.

3. Mono- and duodramas refer to a German style of stage work wherein spoken theater is embedded within a musical score.

4. *Utriusque generis* = of various sorts. Given the comment in his travel diary and this statement, it would appear that Kraus was fascinated by women's feet and footwear.

5. *Silicet* = rightly so. The works mentioned are probably *Ariadne auf Naxos* by Georg Anton Benda, Lessing's drama *Agnes Bernauer,* and two Shakespeare plays in translations by Christoph Martin Wieland.

6. These literary figures are Johann Nepomuk Denis (1729–1800), Aloys Blumauer (1755–1798), Johann Friedrich Schink (1755–1835), and Johann Karl Wezel (1749–1819).

7. Kraus is referring to the suppression of the Jesuit order that had begun already in 1750 and was reaching its peak in the capital of the Holy Roman Empire as part of the so-called Josephian reforms.

8. This refers to *Le process des trois rois, Louis XVI de Franco-Bourbon et George III d'Espagne-Bourbon et George II d'Hannover, fabricant des boutons. Plaidé au tribunal des puissances-européenes. Par appendix L'appel au pape,* a significant revolutionary political treatise written by Bouffonidor (pseudonym for authors Ange Goudar and Simon Nicolas Henri Linguet) and published in Paris in 1781.

9. Orig. *Donner und Blitzen,* or Thunder and Lightning. The translation is closer to Kraus's sense of the euphemism.

52. Letter to his parents dated Vienna, 15 May 1783

Dearest Parents!

If something is put in front of me, I would rather set it to rhyme, for it is well-known that I am no regular correspondent. But – still no answer to two letters? – God! How that terrifies me! Perhaps you are ill – May Heaven forfend it! Or – what is more plausible to me, my letters have gone astray. At least I have followed up a few times per week at the post office – of course, in vain. I know that they wouldn't wait for me long, and, because my former lodgings have been changed, it is the safest to let the letters be sent to *Schmidt,* or on the letter to write expressly that they ought to remain at the post office as long as it takes to reach me. How this can be accomplished is easiest and best learned in Miltenberg. For the forwarding of the Swedish letters I thank you profusely. These were, of course, filled with news, but nothing that subsequently had anything to do with me or would interest you.[1] Enclosed within is a little letter to our dear cousin Jakob. I will send the gift along with other little considerations to my siblings all together, because I am involved with business affairs all day long[2] – you understand that [it] concerns my handicraft. I am sorry for the Neumann children from the bottom of my heart, for even now the thought – to lose a mother – lies upon me so heavily and painfully that I would gladly give every poor orphan my sympathy and my tears. Pardon me that I write so little until such time as I know you have received my letters in good order. Schmidt and I have long waited with yearning for an answer. Then I shall write quite a long letter. I shall travel to Hungary[3] next month – but I won't stay there for long. Our chargé d'affaires will no doubt travel with me. I anticipate your love. Write soon

    Your

    Joseph

COMMENTARY

Original Buchen, Bezirksmuseum. Reading between the lines, it is apparent that there is a gap in the correspondence home, with a number of letters that may have gone missing or crossed in the mail.

1. The letters forwarded from his parents were, of course, in Swedish, which neither of them could read. They no doubt asked Kraus about the contents.

2. His business was no doubt something to do with musical composition and arranging to sell his works to the broader public. About this time he made the acquaintance of Johann Traeg, a music seller who largely dealt in manuscript copies.

3. This may be the first intimation that Kraus has received an official invitation to visit the Esterházy court, probably extended by way of Joseph Haydn. See Letter 57.

53. Letter to his parents dated Vienna, 28 June 1783

Dearest Parents!

    God's greetings, dear father!

    Of course, this time the fault lies with me. But this time the road to hell being paved with good intentions[1] was not the original reason for my delay, but rather a truly excusable confusion. For the entire month I traveled by coach throughout the countryside especially to look at the brooks, hills, and dales, all of which were quite enjoyable. The Viennese truly have quite a pretty countryside all about them, which they make use of with a healthy conscience. I too have *profited* from this bucolic *Gaudium* and have *toasted* it. I spent the beginning of this month at the house of *Schmidt,* who sends his most sincerest regards. He should have done it himself, but it was such a long time ago. He lives very well, as well as one could always desire in the country. From there I wrote off to Heinbach from Zell on his behalf but have not yet received an *answer,* which therefore makes the lover squirm most terribly with impatience. Let us wish that everything succeeds! From there the staff was carried further to the forehead of Hungary, which I wandered throughout a bit. Nothing came of my journey to Esterháza,[2] however, because our chargé d'affaires wanted to come along, and I therefore had to wait upon him; but this will nevertheless occur rather soon. Your news saddened me very much when I learned that in the little city of Amorbach, the unfortunate contagion of trifling with free thinkers has also reasserted itself. I am the most sorry for the old Hans Kaspar, for I believe myself to still be obliged to him for his game of draughts. Otherwise, I would suggest a good recipe: *Scilicet* a philosophical trial at the home of Herr Pastor *nunc temporis.*[3] *Probatum est*! For the rest, I would like to assure with all good intentions Herr Cousin Steffe that the free-thinkers have always left out Odenwald on their maps; which thusly clearly shows that insects of this sort do not like it there. Concerning your humble servant, I find myself tolerably well enough to be able to say: *Stat bene.*[4] Damned! That is a *phrasis* for my Latin Alois, to whom God give a long life, health, and – that which I would ask Him first and foremost – diligence and puberty soonest! I have found my *Glück* – he treasures me, and that is good, but he also loves me, and that is better. A most excellent man, but fiery like the Devil, and I am nothing but a joke in comparison to him. When he focuses on something – Ha! Everything sparkles and every nerve is tensed and resounds. I have also met the most honorable Albrechtsberger,[5] to whom Hummel in Berlin sent a letter through me. Tell my dear friend P[ater] Roman[6] that A[lbrechtsberger] is one of the greatest *contrapuntists* of our age – that, moreover, he is one of the most honorable fugal souls on God's green earth – it will please him. Our Emperor is now off on his travels, and no one knows when he will return. Our citizens shut their mouths and await the outcome of the rather learned debates of certain wise people with the most honorably worthy Herr *Cardinal* and Archbishops, in which therefore many innocent arks of white and grey paper have been filled with scribbling.[7] But I have the honor – to hell with it! No – With my innermost tenderness I remain to my beloved parents

Joseph

[P.S.] *À propos* to me, sisters Bärbel – Mariangen – Treschen! Are you not able to make your little-corresponding brother happy with a small letter?

COMMENTARY

Original Buchen, Bezirksmuseum. Apparently the letter was intended as a special greeting to Kraus's father for a special occasion. From the content, however, it would seem that Kraus felt quite enamored of the Viennese countryside, and he appears to have wandered as far afield as the region near today's Sopron in Hungary.

1. Orig. *Nicht eben Leichtsinn schlecht Weg,* or literally, "not precisely a poor route by reason of thoughtlessness." The translation is more idiomatic in the sense of what Kraus is saying.

2. This is an indication that the visit to Haydn was originally scheduled for May or June, though it has now been postponed.

3. Kraus has evidently received news of some sort of polemical fracas back in Amorbach, the precise nature of which remains elusive. Calling the protagonist "Hans Caspar," which if it isn't the true name seems to be that of a foolish street theater character, he recommends that the debate (religious?) continue at the home of the parish priest *nunc temporis* (or of the moment). The expostulation seems to suggest that the issue can be resolved as a convivial occasion.

4. *Stat bene* = in a good state.

5. Johann Georg Albrechtsberger (1736–1809), later a teacher of Ludwig van Beethoven.

6. Pater Roman = Pater Roman Hoffstetter (1742–1815), here mentioned for the first time.

7. This seems to be another allusion to the Josephian reform theological debates, but the context is far from clear.

54. Letter to his parents dated Vienna, 3 September 1783

Dearest Parents,

I would have had an excuse for not having written before now, but I think that even if I had none or at least only a very lame one, you would still be all right. The intent is always truly the most immediate to learn how one lives and whether one is healthy. This time I will certainly write something more than merely just writing to write. The next letter may in fact be somewhat more interesting, if I receive my instructions from Sweden rather soon. I have had the grace to speak with His Maj-esty[1] – but to me he really does not have the true physiognomy of an artist, something from which I would like to expect greatness. Further, there is something to be done for those like us; for – by my soul, I would really like to see the charlatan who was so fundamentally stupid that he could not at least be able to make a noise here in a short time! It is also so completely understandable among a population in a city of 400,000 to 500,000 souls, that there must be among the most moral and Christian number indisputably more than three-quarters of them fools or idiots.

I greet my siblings from the bottom of my heart – I shall certainly not forget my promise to you to [send] you a piece, if only I am to remain here a few weeks.[2]

Your

Most obedient son

Joseph

P.S. I certainly have a couple of pieces of news to pass on. I have now met Herr Bauer[3] – this is how it is. . . . He has promised to send over a little letter for today; I am to wait for it –

2nd I have been acquainted with a chancellor from Kaiserheim, Herr v[on] Bessel[4] for a few months – quite a good fellow. He is the brother-in-law of Haydn in Bischofsheim and of the Imperial Counselor Heger here – He knows our entire budget on his fingers – *prosit*!

3rd Sikingen[5] was here and made a horrible impression.

COMMENTARY

Original Buchen, Bezirksmuseum. Apart from the gossip in the postscript, the letter is the third noninformative communication that Kraus has sent his parents. It is clear that he is marking time, but he veils his activities. It is known, however, that much of the summer included visits about the town in the company of a fellow composer, Johann Friedrich Reichardt, whom he may have met while in Berlin several months earlier. He also interacted with important Viennese households (including the imperial court) and formed an association with the freemasons at the lodge of Zur wahre Hoffnung.

1. "His Majesty" refers to Joseph II.

2. The promised piece of music is unidentified.

3. The identity of Bauer is not known, but from the tone he was evidently an official.

4. This refers to Abt Gottfried von Bessel, imperial minister in Kaiser-heim, whom Kraus probably met through Haydn. Heger is unidentified.

5. See Letter 12.

55. Letter to his parents dated Vienna, 3 October 1783

Dearest Parents!

This is probably the last letter that I shall write to you from here. Yesterday I received my *orders* from home to follow the King, who has undertaken a journey to Italy, instantly upon the first news of his whereabouts. I shall now visit our Schmidt, who delivered your last letter personally the day before yesterday, for a few days – and thereafter [I] will take myself off for a short time to Esterháza to take farewell of my *Haydn*.[1] During this period I must forgo the pleasure of your letters until I am in the position of sending you a more secure address on my journey. In case you would need to write me something important that cannot wait – deliver the letter to the address of our resident [ambassador] as follows: *a Monsieur d'Engström chargé des affaires de la Cour de Suede pres de Sa Majesté Imper: et royale à Vienne.*[2] In this case the letter contained therein should be sealed only with a simple seal. Probably you don't expect me to make excuses because of the *prodicat*[3] of your last letter. That I am a lazy correspondent tells me what I already know; but I can equally assure you, if you will allow my testimony, that I do not depend upon anyone with a warmer love than my parents. Yes – dear mother, if it is allowed for you to experience in the fall what happened about six months ago,[4] I can calm you [by saying] that perhaps no other Amorbach youth is more devout than I. Of course, this (unfortunately) doesn't say much. I would, however, have no credibility on that score if I were not able to assure [you] without bragging that I have practiced the duties of an honest Christian with a perfect thoroughness. And thus I hope that both you and our Dear God can be satisfied with me. I am only half-pleased with my dearest father's tour about the Odenwald – God grant him health and many good days ahead, now that he has achieved this in spite of the tribulation. Before my departure I shall still hand over a package to the mail coach. It contains some small treats for my beloved siblings – I wish that I am able to give them a bit of joy therewith. Live happily and love me always

Your most obedient son

Joseph

P.S. Our director has told me in all secrecy that he expects me about the middle of February in person in Paris, and then we shall have quite fine days together. I greet my dear *Hoffstetter* from the bottom of my heart – Vanhal[5] also sends his greetings; for I have told him that he was as sympathetic a person as himself.

Hopefully, you have received my last letter with the enclosure to my friend Roman?

NB. Greetings from me to my fat *cousin* in Miltenberg. The scum have sold you a bill of goods.[6] At least all of the lies that *Wiese's* mother wrote to her brother here and about which was bandied about publically that I had written such things to my parents, are able to be traced back to none other than [Wiese] himself. For example, it is stated by Frau *Wiese* in her letter – Kraus has written his parents that Schmidt was now in the service of the Emperor – and had received; God knows how many thousands of Gulden in salary, etc.

COMMENTARY

Original Buchen, Bezirksmuseum. Kraus is being extremely vague about his plans, probably due to the nebulous nature of the command from Stockholm to join the entourage of Gustav III, who was on a state visit to Italy.

1. Joseph Haydn, of course.

2. To Mr. Engström, chargé d'affaires of the court of Sweden to His Imperial Royal Majesty in Vienna.

3. *Prodicat* = to give notice.

4. Kraus is referring to his visit home and his mother's worry about his religious duty.

5. Johann Baptist Vanhal (1739–1813), composer and violoncellist.

6. Orig. *Der Schwerenöter hat wider gelogen, daß es ein wahres Kreuz ist,* = The credulous have lied again that it is [part] of the true cross. Kraus is referring to the continual conning of the unsophisticated by people claiming to have and sell a portion of the cross, one of the ultimate religious relics. The reference to his "fat" cousin is a pointed and sarcastic comment on the rumormongering that one of his relatives did in Germany.

56. Letter to his parents dated Wöllersdorf, 7 October 1783

Dearest Parents!

This is certainly the first red letter on blue paper that will have come into your hands. And – just why the notion occurred to me to make such a nonsensical joke? *Cum pace!*[1] This time I've got two – or rather I could say three reasons – all of equal validity and weight. The first and most basic is without doubt because I didn't have any black ink or white paper – and – because cousin Schmidt and cousin Wiese dragged me outside this morning at 4 AM to go hunting – it is most probable that I will not be able to obtain other writing materials today. The second no less important matter is – that today it is the best way to celebrate that it will have been one year since I traveled forth from Stockholm. And for this it goes without saying that red ink and blue paper are mandatory. *Enfin,*[2] the third reason, if there are to be three – is to say that once in my lifetime I've also had to write a red letter on blue rags. And – this last reason for doing so is certainly the most logical. Of course, there is also a little gloating as well. It should be said about this gentleman that he would have been a very lazy correspondent. The worst thing about it is that he would also have to put up with it. The day after his disgraceful confession, he read in a book how there once was a very highborn nobleman, who was so extraordinarily endowed by nature that his legs were resplendent with double calves and his back was a true copy of a camel's hump – he, however, did not want for the life of him that such people would notice it – and – forbade all talk about it on pain of death. It also occurred to this gentleman that in a fit of generous mood to *revoce optima forma* the aforementioned vow and thus to encourage all who *qua recursum petentem*[3] not to consider him a lazy writer – all the more so because of the following damaging consequences that might exist, for example, "his future children would like to read such a letter from their dear grandparents simply about where their Herr Papa had obtained such a fine title – then they would believe themselves obligated to the bottom of their souls to make amends for it["] – something I would gladly forgo.

Moreover, I have thus *advertised* according to the most praiseworthy merchant's style how the sojourn here was short and sweet. I still have to take my farewells from three or four of my neighbors, after which a little *excursus* in foreign regions will follow under God's guidance. I shall simultaneously leave no stone unturned in order to *notify* all of my relatives from Hungary with black ink on pretty white mailing paper how their Herr Son, Brother, Cousin, *amicus,* etc., etc., finds himself in good shape and recommends the best to everyone – which thus completely shows and proves his good intentions. Furthermore, there are vineyards all about, and wherever one has not been in company, it will eventually no doubt be rectified. Further, there have been a monstrous number of plums, from which here in the country and especially in Hungary a really good brandy called *Slipowiz* is made.[4] I tasted the vintage today and yesterday and found it *probatum*. Today is also notable in that the first frost has fallen – but I played a trick on it and didn't get up until the sun had already melted it. My Stålberg looked at it lovingly and found that it was every bit as white here in Germany as in Sweden – which betrays the spirit of a keen observer. A year ago this day, night fell early on in Stockholm, but it doesn't today, but rather the sun still shines brightly, which this is really pretty to see. Friend Schmidt has *reported* to me most loyally how last week he had shot a fox while hunting (I believe it was Wednesday about 9:30 in the morning) so thoroughly that not a piece of buckshot was lost; the fox *in questionis* got to his feet after a short *soliloquo*,[5] however, and marched off; according to Schmidt's reckoning, such behavior should not have been the fashion at all; therefore, he had a mind to further prosecute the poor fox. [I] have also become aware from the newspaper that the *Universitas Patrice à Maience*[6] has now become plagued with an extraordinarily voracious appetite, called gluttonous fever here in the countryside, following a long and difficult illness, and thus has devoured already 600 volumes of dissertations in total from the bequest of the immortal executioner of Roman law, *Hellfeld* in Jena. Because I am of a mind to be patriotic and fear a possible bout of indigestion, I take the liberty of recommending without reservation Halle bitters, which among Christians and heathen, *respectively* upper and lower nobility and commoners, have the best credit and do the best incomparably to aid in the business of digestion. I cannot help making the pronouncement, and I have had the *obligation* to pass this on to you, but which I forgot to do. H[err] Ludwig[7] sends his regards – I too

> *In the morning about 9:30*
> *Your*
> *Joseph*

P.S. I have at this moment four *well-broken-in* pipe heads in my possession – ditto a young dog or rather a young bitch who has taken the place of my black poodle which a good friend of mine stole from me on the street.

COMMENTARY

Original Buchen, Bezirksmuseum. The frivolous and jesting tone of this letter, along with an obvious tall tale, was apparently not well-taken by his parents; see the next letter. Indeed, the incoherency of it may indicate that Kraus was writing after having imbibed a bit too much. It does, however, preserve some indication of his personal interests: good drink, hunting, and dogs.

1. *Cum pace* = with peace; here idiomatically meaning "Calm down!"

2. *Enfin* = finally.

3. *Revoce optima forma* = to call back from; *qua recursum petentum* = in the course of applying this.

4. *Slipowiz* = Slivovitz, or a distilled plum brandy; *probatum* = excellent.

5. This is Kraus's way of saying either that the fox was superficially wounded or that his cousin missed his shot. *Soliloquo* = short nap.

6. *Universitas Patrice à Maience* = Mainz University; the professor of Canonicum or Roman Law in Jena, Johann August Hellfeld (1717–1782), donated or left his collection of dissertations, probably to his own university, but Kraus implies that the collection was absconded with by Mainz University.

7. Herr Ludwig is unidentified.

57. Letter to his parents dated Esterháza, 18 October 1783

Dearest Parents!

You will have received my last letter along with that of Herr *Schmidt* from Wiener Neustadt. To fulfill my promise, I write once again from a place where I have enjoyed pleasures in full abundance and where I am around a hundred miles closer to you than I soon will be. The Prince[1] here was very condescending toward me and was inevitably going to do something for me economically if I had the time and energy for it – and was able to bear the living standards of the Hungarians better. To give you a small impression of Hungary I only need to tell you briefly: without exception everything is dirty and unclean, and the spirit of the nation unbearably proud. They have all sorts of wine in abundance, and I have traveled through places like *Oedenburg, St. Jörgen, Rasersdorf, Seele*, etc.,[2] where one would gladly desire to fill a few casks in order to receive an empty one for them; thus the local Hungarian vineyards were blessed. The theater here has been built with unequaled magnificence – but with little taste and even less reflection. The orchestra is exactly what one can expect under the direction of a Haydn – namely one of the best. It is nonetheless no larger than 24 men, but still makes a magnificent effect – the first two violinists and the cellist are Italians[3] – the remainder are almost all Bohemians. In Haydn I have met quite a decent soul, save for one point – [and] that is money. He could not comprehend that I had not equipped myself with a selection of scores for my travel in order to present them to people as opportunity arose. I answered quite drily that I was not cut out to be a Jewish merchant; *Enough! Sterkel*[4] wrote to him and requested from him several arias for his sister and offered him an equivalent number of arias from his Neapolitan opera. Haydn shook his head, for there were no jingling coins. This is the most marvelous thing about the majority of artists. The closer one illuminates them, the more they lose the halos that the Herr amateurs, critics, etc., etc., have painted around them like saints. Give my regards to my dear Hoffstetter and ask him to have a copy made of the score of the *Stella coeli*[5] for me and to send it as soon as possible to a certain friend whose address is: Monsieur Joh[ann] Traeg in the *Pilatischen* House on the Prater in Vienna. I will then be of service to him again in every other matter.

Greet my siblings and love me
Your
Joseph

COMMENTARY

Original Buchen, Bezirksmuseum. From the previous letters it is clear that Haydn had met Kraus earlier in Vienna and tendered the invitation to visit the Esterházy estate; see Letter 55. Haydn himself noted many years later that Kraus had written a symphony especially for him, possibly on the occasion of this visit. Which work this was is still a matter of debate; tradition has it that it was the Symphony in C minor (VB 143), based upon the reminiscences of Silverstolpe in 1842, but during Kraus's lifetime a more "Haydnesque" symphony, in D major (VB 144), was published in Paris under Haydn's name. Kraus, of course, provides no information that would help in this matter.

1. The Prince is Nicholas I (1714–1790).
2. Ödenburg is now Sopron, Hungary, and the others are small villages in the surrounding area.
3. The violinists Kraus means are Luigi Tomasini and Niccolò Mestrino; the cellist is probably Valentino Bertoja.
4. Orig. *Satis*! The composer is Abbé Johann Franz Xaver Sterkel (1750–1817). The opera is unidentified, but was probably *Farnace,* produced in Naples in 1782.
5. The *Stella coeli* (VB 11) was written for the dedication of the Stumm organ in the Benedictine monastery in Amorbach earlier in the year; Johann Traeg (1747–1805) was the music publisher and distributor in Vienna. It is ironic that Kraus, who rejects Haydn's astonishment at not

scattering about his music, has apparently done just that. His comment to be
passed on to Hoffstetter is enigmatic, for
it cannot be determined what he means
by *in jedem andern Falle* (or "in every
other matter or case").

58. Letter to his parents dated Graz in Steiermark, 2 November 1783

Dearest Parents!

I received your letter forwarded to the post office. Of course, it was not written in the best of moods – but I don't have the desire to answer you in the same tone, and because I already took the opportunity myself to do so in my dumb letter of the 7th of October. The idiocy has now been done, and if only the Jewish bastard had reminded me of it earlier, I would have taken pains to bring the matter to an honest conclusion. Now I see that for the sake of my honor it is the most advantageous to repay the debt in the most quiet way possible. Of course, I fear little from the Stockholm court; for it is not my forum. But I also wouldn't like for the King to learn about the matter *per accidens*[1] on his travels, during which every little detail is written out for him from home. By all that is sacred, I don't want my siblings to imitate me, and moreover, I would rather that everything happen to me than to incur a reproach from a mother who loves me without question. My suggestion is this, that the *remaining* debts are resolved entirely and completely, after which I will spare no effort to give restitution to you for the sum myself by and by. I ask that you and my siblings be satisfied with this, my suggestion. The sum runs to about 132 R[iks] d[alers],[2] and putting all jesting aside, I will seriously direct all of my efforts and in all gratitude to restore this as soon as possible. I am now on a journey to *Trieste*.[3] I scarcely believe that I will receive another of your letters until my first stop, most likely in *Venice* or *Pisa,* for until then it is impossible for me to give you a specific address. The small packet with the little gifts for my siblings is to be sent by my commissioner in Vienna to Herr Professor *Heussler*[4] in Würzburg, who will then do me the favor of passing it on to you. Fare well and [give] my regards to my few friends

 Your
 Most obedient son
 Joseph

COMMENTARY

Original Buchen, Bezirksmuseum. It can be inferred from the content of this letter and the one that follows that Kraus's Göttingen creditors, in particular a Jewish moneylender from whom he borrowed funds many years earlier, have finally claimed restitution directly from Kraus's parents, probably with the threat of a lawsuit and going directly to his employer in Stockholm thrown in for good measure. Kraus's own glibness in writing cannot have helped matters, and the now-lost letter from his parents was probably filled with recriminations, especially from his mother. Implied is that he is setting a poor example for his brothers and sisters to follow.

1. *Per accidens* = accidentally or coincidentally.

2. 132 Riksdalers would have been about £2,830 or around US$5,000 today.

3. He means by way of Trieste, which was not one of the cities on his itinerary.

4. Kraus of course misspells Häussler, his godfather.

59. Letter to his parents dated Venice, 18 November 1783

Dearest Parents!

As much as I long for your letters, until now it has been impossible for me to indulge in this pleasure, because I could not determine a specific stopping point. But I shall use every opportunity to bring our exchange of letters back to life again. Please answer this letter immediately, but write as briefly as possible and on the finest and thinnest paper, and seal it then with good wax. The address is simply *"a Monsieur, etc. Kraus, Maitre de chapelle au Service de la Cour de Suede"* – without noting a particular place of my sojourn. Then send this letter under separate cover by mail to our consul here. Here is his address: *a Monsieur de Lorth, Consul de Sa Majte le Roi de Suede à Venise.*[1] As soon as our consul then receives the letter, he will forward it along with the concurrent others intended for the King's party and the King's Chamberlain. This is the only possible way that I can receive something written from my loved ones at home right now. As soon as I reach *Pisa,* however, which will happen at the end of the coming week, I will be able perhaps to send you a better and easier address. Now, you will inevitably want to hear something about my journey and how I spent my time. I would gladly share with you a complete excerpt from my diary;[2] but much of it would be unimportant to you and the majority of it incomprehensible; moreover, I would hardly be able to include it in a letter. Therefore, please be satisfied with a rather brief description. You will have received my last missive from *Graz* (the capital of Steiermark), which was rather a response to the story in Göttingen; just as I hoped that you received my letter from Hungary and the small parcel with the silver trifles for my dear siblings, which were forwarded to H[err] Heussler in Würzburg by my commissioner in Vienna. Regarding the Göttingen business, I shall once more attempt to bring it to an end as soon as possible – and thus I repeat my promise about the damages as well. From Graz I thus traveled to *Trieste* through the Duchy of Carinthia. The way consisted of an eternal chain of smaller and larger mountains, and thus the otherwise good road made it difficult for the continual horse- and cattle-drawn wagons. The cost with incidentals ran to approximately 100 Sk[illings] Imperial money.[3] *Trieste* lies around 60 miles from Vienna on a gulf of the Adriatic Sea. The location is very important for trade by sea for Austria, but less pleasant for the perceptive eyes of an artist. There are mountains all around, upon which now and again there are vineyards, and here and there a couple of poor, thin trees. The 15th I traveled on a Venetian bark and landed toward evening in *Pirano*,[4] the first Venetian city in Istria, and the 17th I finally arrived in Venice. Normally, with a good wind one can make the journey in a single day. Of course, the first sight of Venice was a bit unusual for the eye of a foreigner, but it was not by a long shot the brilliance that all of the travelers have described in so much detail. The city lies on about 70 islands;[5] the city is uncommonly large in terms of population, the further one island lies from another. The Piazza *San Marco* and the palace next door are built right on the sea. One must undoubtedly marvel at the obstacles that stood in the way of human hands; and even more at the courage of the first inhabitants who were able to overcome them. Of the churches, there are innumerable bunches. The one I liked best was the Benedictine abbey[6] in which the Emperor and the Pope were both housed as they passed through. There is enough painting of value, and – by my soul, I do not think that I have ever in my life walked about and gone by gondola in a single day as much as here. For here one sees neither horses nor wagons. There is also no lack of music, for daily there are performances in six theaters, and during Carnival nine. Tell my dear Hoffstetter that every day one can hear one opera after another, but – seldom anything good. Yesterday I heard one by *Bianchi,* today one by *Cimarosa*.[7] The first was tolerably good, and there was fire now and again, but the latter was dull. The male and female singers were mostly mediocre. The other notable things you can read in every travelogue. Greet my dear siblings and friends and love me always

    Your

    Most obedient son Joseph

[P.S.] I am sending this letter enclosed with one to my friend in Nuremberg, the merchant *Kessler*.[8]

COMMENTARY

Original Buchen, Bezirksmuseum. It is clear that the previous letter was so emotionally fraught that Kraus sent nothing for a fortnight during his journey. It is implied, however, that his parents probably acceded to his "suggestion" on how to resolve the debts. The listing of cities identifies the route Kraus took to Italy. Since this was toward the end of November, the usual overland route to Venice through Klagenfurt and Udine was most likely blocked with snow in the high passes, forcing Kraus to travel via what is today Slovenia. An all-weather imperial road went south from Graz via Maribor to an important junction in Neustadt (today, Novo mesto), the site of a large Benedictine monastery, and there either via Laibach (Ljubljana) or more to the south directly to Trieste for the short final sea passage. That Kraus indeed took this route is supported by the rediscovery of a brief offertory, "O Maria, virgo pia" (VB 10a), the autograph parts of which are preserved in the monastic library at Novo mesto and bear a dedication to the abbey.

1. Lorth, about whom little is known, was Swedish consul to the Venetian Republic. The other concurrent letters were probably official dispatches.

2. Kraus seems to imply that he has kept or has started another travel diary; this has not survived.

3. 100 Skillings Imperial money = approximately £118 or US$188.

4. Pirano is a city now in Slovenia, at that time under Venetian rule.

5. Actually, Venice sits on 118 islands.

6. San Giorgio Monastery is meant; see the next letter.

7. Francesco Bianchi (1752–1810) and Domenico Cimarosa (1749–1801); see Letter 61.

8. This Herr Kessler remains unidentified.

60. Letter to his parents dated Florence, 4 December 1783

Dearest Parents!

    I enclosed a letter from Venice to you in one to an acquaintance in Nuremberg that has doubtless already arrived in Amorbach. The few moments I have at leisure I certainly could not use better than to discuss things with you. From Venice I traveled in the company of a Tyrolean Count – as poor and as good as I – to *Bologna*. Apart from the advantage that it cost only half the amount of passage, it was certainly not in the least [disadvantageous] for me that my traveling companion was fluent in the language of the country, and therefore [we] were not able to be so thoroughly conned as almost every other foreigner in Italy. Apart from a few miles, the journey was for the most part by water. From one place to the next, if one doesn't wish to pay extra for the trip, one has to come to an agreement with a so-called Vetjurino[1] regarding passage, lodging, and food. Of course, one does not travel very comfortably, but it would be bearable simply if there was better bread and tolerable wine in the countryside. In *Ferrara* I spent only as much time as it took me to view the most notable things in this city, but which is not even half as large as *Bologna*. The streets here are very wide and for that reason especially famous, for there are pavilions on both sides throughout the entire city for pedestrians, underneath of which one is safe from unpleasant storms – just like in Mannheim beneath the warehouse. There is a plethora of excellent paintings here that I of course would not leave unvisited; but the most important thing was the famed *Padre Martini*[2] – the greatest music theoretician alive, and the famous music academy here. It occurred so fortuitously that they were celebrating the feast day of their patron by performing in the church of *San Giovanni al Monte* 12 composers,[3] among whom I felt *respect* for only one. Padre Martini is now 78 years old and very feeble, but was nonetheless quite polite to me, as were all of his *compatriots,* and I have to have myself painted with the utmost expediency, for he has a collection of portraits of all of the now-living composers and would like for it to be complete – and [I] have also been quite well met by an Italian master named *Pomaroli*.[4] I have now been fortunate enough to have met my King in *Florence*. He was very gracious toward me according to his usual praiseworthy manner. He will travel to Rome at the end of the week; I will precede him, however. In my earlier letter I gave you an address for me via our *consul De Lorth* in Venice. Nonetheless, I have not yet received an answer, which is only natural; I will receive it forwarded to Pisa. From this point on, however, I cannot give you a secure address until I arrive in Paris. If I must wait until there for your loving and enjoyable letters, I shall nonetheless promise to write assiduously myself. Therefore, you will receive news from me from *Rome* and *Naples*. Be patient until then and don't write until I arrive in France; for otherwise the letters will most likely be lost. Love me and greet my siblings and P[ater] Roman

From your

Most obedient son

Joseph

COMMENTARY

Original Buchen, Bezirksmuseum. Kraus's letter includes the usual stereotype attitude that the Italians were conniving and untrustworthy. His companion, the poverty-stricken nobleman from the Tyrol, remains unidentified.

1. Kraus means a Vetturino, an open carriage drawn by four horses, usually chartered through a livery stable. The term also can refer to the owner of the stable, who acted as guide, driver, and travel manager. The travel by water means via the Po River.

2. Padre Giovanni Battista Martini (1706–1784); the musical academy is the famed Academia filarmonica. Kraus does not appear to have been inducted as many foreign composers were.

3. The next letter will provide a more exact description of this event.

4. The painter is Antonio Pomarolli (fl1770–1790). The painting was not entirely complete before Martini's death early the following year and was returned to the composer. It is currently housed in Buchen, Bezirksmuseum, Kraus Sammlung, and has been frequently reproduced.

61. Letter to Johann Samuel Liedemann dated Florence, 5 December 1783

Every travel writer will already have told you how charming the first sight of this world famous city[1] is for the eye of every foreigner. To me it appeared, however, as if the genius of some ancient ruined kingdom had escaped with the salvaged remains on his back, fled across the Adriatic Sea with his burden, and crammed it together piecemeal as soon as possible on the spot. The city sits upon some 70 odd small islands.[2] The buildings are for the most part bad and old, and the streets are to a large extent so tight that two people are barely able to pass by one another. Of course, the St. Marks plaza is here, as are several beautiful palaces and the Rialto bridge, as well (built in an arch), etc.; something that a traveler must harmlessly stop at. Here I wandered from one church and one palace to the next to look at the paintings and galleries. Here and there one finds magnificent things, but for the most part it is a *gustus mixtii*[3] – I have to make you more acquainted with one painting, a masterpiece by Paul Veronese,[4] and perhaps one of his best. It is a huge mural in a refectory of the Benedictines in San Giorgio Maggiore, painted on the wall and representing the Wedding at Cana. Christ sits with his mother and a few other guests at a table and acts as if the food is not to his liking. To his right is another table at which a Persian with his magnificent houris are placed. It thus appears that the Persians of that time were normally invited to participate in weddings in Galilee. In the background stand many of the onlookers who have come to look at the celebration, and finally a few church towers upon which very artfully the Herr Christus himself parades about as resurrected, instead of the usual weathervanes. While the ceremony goes on in silence, the painter desires for his guests a better mood and thus paints into the foreground another small table. At this he places himself with a viola, Tintoretto with a violin, Titian with a contrabass, and Bassano with a flute.[5] These portraits of the greatest contemporary artists are well-liked by all, and there is no less clarity in that Paul Veronese also portrays his pair of hunting dogs that he places into many of his paintings, and Tintoretto bears his usual silver crucifix. Of course, the head of Paul is wonderful and a masterpiece – but one should not be so critical about the costume. – Please excuse that I have nothing else to say about Venice, for you can find it all in Richard, Lalande, etc.[6] Only this, however, that I have heard two operas at two theaters, one by *Cimarosa* and the other by *Bianchi*. *Il pittore parigino* by the former wasn't much; *La villanelle rapita* by the latter on the other hand was good.[7] The performance of both [was] miserable. – In Bologna the stage is not worth seeing. The composition for this fall was by an inconsequential master and for Aglaurus[8] the Devil would certainly not have made progress. Apart from this, the place was incomparably more important for my handiwork than Venice. I do not need to remind you that here is the home of the well-known *Academia filarmonica,* and furthermore the even more famous Pater Martini. It was quite a good coincidence for me that this honorable *academy* celebrated the feast of their patron St. Antonius in San Giovanni in Monte, in which it is common that various masters present their works on display. From the following list you can learn the number and names of the authors:

Messa: Introito;	del Sigr: Gabriele Vignali
Kyrie;	Lorenzo Gibelli
Gloria;	Vincenzo Cavadagna
Graduale;	Ignazio Fontana
Credo;	Valerio Tesci
Concerto; essegnito del Sigr:	Melchiore Ronci
Vespro Domine;	del Sigr: Gio[vanni] Battista Gaiani
Dixit;	Petronio Lanzi
Confetibor;	Carlo Zanolini
Beatus vir;	Antonio Mazzoni
Laudate pueri;	Angelo Galeassi
Laudate dominum;	Lorenzo Gibelli
Hymnus;	Ercole Morigi
Magnificat;	del Sigr: Can. B. Pancrazio Morigi.[9]

All masters enough, but with the exception of the last three, the others did nothing more than induce a staggering boredom in me. The orchestra consisted of 200 people, but for all that made little effect. I found enough conversation with Pater Martini, even though he is 78 years old and appears very feeble. He still studies constantly, and [he] finds his greatest joy in his collection of portraits of all of the composers that he can obtain. Most of them are very poorly done, however.

Concerning painting, one can truly call Bologna rich. It is here in the Zampieri Palace on the Stada Maggiore that one can find Guido Renis's best work, *Pietro e Paolo,* hanging.[10] One seldom finds united in such good coloration, strong correct delineation, and pathos as in this great masterpiece. In the churches one often finds the most magnificent things by Carracci, Guercino, Albani, and Franceschini,[11] and I am able to assure you with all honesty that I would have found enough solace for my soul here – if only the Italians didn't have the damned custom of praising all of their rubbish at the expense of other nations.

P.S. I have been well-met here, for our King is here at the moment. He wasn't entirely satisfied with my long stay in Vienna, but now everything is back on track. The gallery here is heavenly; I have already studied it thoroughly three times.

COMMENTARY

Original lost; the excerpt was published in Si-JMK as Letter 37. This letter makes an interesting comparison with the preceding one to his parents in terms of the amount of information imparted.

1. Venice, as will become clear a few lines later.

2. See Letter 59. Kraus has evidently read the number of islands from a travelogue.

3. *Gustus mixtii* = mixed taste.

4. Paul Veronese (1528–1588).

5. The contemporaries (to Veronese, not Kraus) are Titian = Tiziano Vecellio (ca1488–1576); Tintoretto = Jacopo Comin (1518–2594); Bassano = Jacopo Bassano (ca1510–1592); Veronese has curiously made them a chamber ensemble.

6. The main reference is to Joseph-Jérôme de Lalande, *Voyage d'un français en Italie* (1769).

7. *Il pittore parigino* by Domenico Cimarosa was first produced at the Teatro Valle in Rome on 2 January 1781 and in Venice probably at the Teatro San Samuele. *La villanelle rapita* by Francesco Bianchi was produced at the Teatro San Moisé in the fall of 1783.

8. The passage is a reference to Dante's *Divine Comedy* where Aglaurus is a stone that foils the Devil in the 14th Canto of *Purgatorio*.

9. The composers are mainly clerical members of the Academia filarmonica. Largely unknown today, composers' dates can be assigned to the following: Gabriele Vignale (d. 1792), Lorenzo Gibelli (1718–1812), Battista Gaiani (1757–1819), Petronio Lanzi (d. 1791), Antonio Mazzoni (1717–1785), and Pancrazio Morigi (d. 1800). The number 200 most likely also includes singers.

10. Guido Reni (1575–1642).

11. Annibale Carracci (1560–1609), Guercini = Giovanni Francesco Barbieri (1591–1666), Francesco Albani (1578–1660), and Marc'antonio Franceschini (1648–1729).

62. Letter to his parents dated Rome, 25 December 1783

Both my sanity and stomach would play havoc with me if I had to lodge here for an entire year. On fasting days, butter, cheese, and God knows what else is all forbidden, and instead his Italian Holiness has given the good advice to melt everything with oil – by my soul, one is possessed at every moment with devotional thoughts, including Fridays, Sundays, and Wednesdays, [enough] to wish the lot to hell. God forgive my sins! – Of course, in a few places one can find unripe lemons and oranges, peasants, whores, beggars who speak six languages, saints, lean beef, female and male hermaphrodites, who are all used for things that nature did not intend, pious tightrope walkers who reek of perfume and musk, along with pickpockets, all dwelling quite nicely together here – I do not lie; whether the country should therefore be imagined to be closer to

God's heart than another authentic rubbish heap on the face of the earth is another question. Never have I eaten and drunk more awfully, slept more terribly, traveled more uncomfortably, and frozen more than in Italy; I have to report the truth of it in amazement – and yet the sons of bitches[1] who write travelogues one and all blather on as if they had discovered paradise hereabouts. I refuse to believe that these gentlemen arduously and against their better conscience desire to deceive another pilgrim, for it is clear enough to me that if one only wanders from one excellent kitchen to another and whiles away the evenings, which are often plagued with deathly boredom, with important affairs, he only licks the proffered hands of the Italian scum – I believe that in this manner one perceives few of the problems of a country, but even less gets to know the peculiarities of a people. I will tell you at once of one, and nonetheless certainly one of the most important commentaries about Rome that has resulted from my previous sentence, for you will not be able to read about it in any travelogue. The observation is this, that if one has not considered the reality of his religion enough and is not convinced of the truth of his true Christianity in advance and then arrives in this so-called holy city and sees how one mishandles the sacred customs of his religion, he must either be a ninny or a hypocrite, if he doesn't scream murder about a people that openly do asinine things without any shame. I am not the most devout, that I know – but if Turks and heathens had been put into the mix with me this night – they would have to have been devils if they had not been as angered as I. Think about one of the most prominent churches in Rome, the so-called center and archive of the most holy relics of the earliest Christians – in a temple where the true stable of Bethlehem is presented to be seen and kissed throughout the night – where the Pope himself says Mass[2] – one person is set upon by another with a knife, sticking it into his chest in cold blood. That one dies; and the perpetrator, knowing that he is not allowed to be arrested in church, stands by the corpse with calm face, protected by the superstition of a highly hypocritical rabble. God! If only there was one drop of true Christianity flowing through the veins of our newly purple-clad patriarchs; then I don't know whether Christendom or I am the thickest idiot on God's green earth. No beggar monk in Germany has said a Mass for the Dead so superficially for a few pennies or a dozen eggs that what I saw a Cardinal do in the Sistine Chapel here. Enough! On the other hand, with respect to the arts, my eyes and ears have found a much more wonderful market. Of course, Rome does not entirely subscribe to the grand notion that one can divide the former capital into three portions of the world. From the seven much-famed hills upon which it is built one can see little more, for a lack of tidiness and a plethora of bogs, perhaps the rubble of old buildings too, has for the most part filled the valleys. The *Pantheon,* a round temple of Jupiter by Agrippa, and the *Colisée* of Vespasian, in addition to a few triumphal arches and obelisks, are the only monuments surviving from ancient times that have been preserved to some extent. Truly, there is nothing more majestic that the tall columns of granite and vaulted cupola inside the first, and nothing thought larger and stronger than the inestimable decorated bulk of the amphitheater of Vespasian. Think of a round building that takes about a quarter of an hour to walk around – seven vaulted stories tall with a courtyard the size of the remaining portion – a place in which Vespasian baited wild animals and lions, and Domitian afterward allowed many thousands of Christians to be martyred. One gets real shivers when one wanders through the thing. In the two museums of the Vatican and the Capitol, one can finally see the world-famous statues of Apollo, Laocoön, Antinious, etc., before which every artist and connoisseur doffs their hats in homage, and rightly so. I have only known these things halfway previously, for I have only seen plaster replicas of them – Now I am able to while away half a day in front of them and cannot gape at them enough. Among the newer buildings, the Basilica of St. Peter truly deserves first place. A grand colonnade of 320 columns bound together at their capitals in a half-circle, in whose middle point across from the great gate is an obelisk, encloses with their vaults the side of the façade of the church. This corridor of columns contains the statues of 140 saints. To give you a small idea of the cost of the entire thing, I need only say that the cost of erecting the obelisk alone is reckoned to have been around 38,000 Roman scudi.[3] On both sides of this noble pyramid are magnificent fountains. One finally ascends a wonderful set of stairs to a portal of bronze that is worked out entirely in bas-relief. The great cupola is built in the manner of the Pantheon and is itself alone reckoned as one of the greatest masterpieces of modern times. I shall not say anything about the size of the church, for it is well-known enough that there is nothing else in the entire world that can be comparable. Only this little bit about the richness of the interior. The entire *ceiling* consists of several cupolas – all of the side walls have been plastered with *mosaics;* that is to say – the paintings are made from colored stones. All of the altarpieces are done likewise in order to defy time and decay. The columns, statues, and floor are made from the finest marble. If you realize that one must pay between 4,500 and 6,000 Ducats for a single well-made piece of *mosaic;* you will be able to have a good idea of the costliness of the interior of this temple, without making it necessary for me to give a running commentary on the length and breadth of gold, silver, and lapis lazuli. From the outside, the building does not seem as tall and from the inside as expansive as it is – in this the Italians find it the most artistic; but along with other people who believe in their feelings, I find fault in this view, for it makes less of a sublime impression than it should. The Vatican palace that abuts it on the right side of the colonnade does not reflect its neighbor. There are quite pretty rooms and paintings within, but the appointments of the whole are amateurish and constricted. Only two things got my entire attention, and those are first the so-called loges by Raphael and then the *Sistine* Chapel. I had already heard from those who know that one would need to have a much practiced sensitivity to recognize in *Raphael's* paintings the great living painter. My experience confirms this. When I saw my first painting by him in *San Giovanni in Monte,* when I saw St. Cecilia, I was not able to appreciate his simplicity completely, and I considered its creator as far lesser than *Guido Reni,* who from the moment I saw his masterpiece *Pietro e Paolo* in the *Sambierian* Palace[4] became my man. I went again on the second day and look – I felt something that I had felt by only a few works of art, and thus during the course of eight days I became all the more familiar with my man, and finally I was able to translate my soul from those superficially spoiled prejudgments of the craft completely into his own. Only now can I say from experience how difficult it is to feel and express nature simply. The aforementioned loges are now the main entrances to the second story of the Papal Palace. There are eight to ten paintings in *fresco* in the *vestibules* and on the sides by *Raphael,* and the rest by his pupils. The *subjects* have been reworked from the old and new Testaments and according to his great manner. The *Sistine Chapel,* finally, is known for *Michelangelo's* famous painting of the Last Judgment. He rises above *Raphael* in the strength of his active passion, and one cannot present anything more terrifying than this *fresco*. The anecdote is known that, in order to avenge himself on a certain Cardinal, *Michelangelo* had painted his face among the damned on this painting. The Cardinal complained to the Holy Father about this and demanded that he order the artist to alter his physiognomy; he was given the answer, however, that he [i.e., the Pope] certainly had the power to save a poor soul from Purgatory, but not the damned from hell. Thus, to this day the Cardinal stands with life and soul permanently depicted to the left side. In this chapel the Pope holds worship services on Sundays and holy days, and it is here where one gets to hear the famed Roman music. Tell my dear *Roman* that for the most part it creates a rather wide definition of the miracle. For a few times it is so good that one stands and marvels. But when one is more closely acquainted with the magnificence, one would wish it were better. The capella consists of sixteen to twenty singers, among whom hardly four castrati have bearable voices. Most everything is sung with divided chorus – but with the majority of the fugues, I thought of our German organists, who could have accomplished things better during Vespers. On my entire journey, I have not found a single good Italian organist. For this *Carnival* there are two *opera serias,* as well as three *opera buffas.* The one at the Liberti Theater is *by Sarti*[5] and will therefore be successful, for *Marchesini,*[6] who is now seemingly the greatest singer in Europe, will *debut.* At the [Teatro] Argentina the music is by *Mareschalchi,*[7] a wretched scribbler. *Fischer,*[8] who was formerly in Mannheim, debuts this winter on the stage. *Adieu.* Perhaps I shall write you again from *Naples.* In any case, you will have a letter from me as soon as I arrive in Paris.

Your

Most obedient son Joseph

P.S. I do not need to make assurances that I love all my friends and relatives. NB: Today the Emperor and our King attended High Mass at St. Peter's.

COMMENTARY

Original Buchen, Bezirskmuseum. The normal salutation appears to

be lacking in this letter, as if Kraus dashed it off rather quickly in a stream of consciousness. The detailed description of his Roman visit, particularly of St. Peter's, indicates that the composer was keenly observant of both the art and architecture of the Vatican. This interest implies that he found the music secondary.

1. Orig. *Hundsfut*.

2. The reference is to St. John the Lateran.

3. One must take Kraus's estimate of cost with a grain of salt, given that it was probably hearsay.

4. He means the Zampieri Palace; see Letter 61.

5. Giuseppe Sarti (1729–1802). The opera was his second setting of Metastasio's *L'Olimpiade*.

6. Castrato Luigi Marchesi (1755–1829).

7. Luigi Marescalchi (1745–1805). The opera was *Andromeda e Perseo*.

8. Ludwig Fischer (1745–1825), the bass who created the role of Osmin in Mozart's *Die Entführung asu dem Serail* and who was on tour to Italy.

63. Letter to his parents dated Rome, 3 January 1784

Dearest Parents!

I did not believe that I would be able to write once more from here, for I set my departure for today and hoped that I would have been able to finish off my small affairs by now. But because I was not able to have the honor of being presented to the Pope before yesterday, and because a small work[1] for our court had to be done in the meantime, I have to hang about here for a few days. I was pleased not least because I received your letter of the fourth of the p[revious] m[onth] through this delay. It would have had to follow me at least to Naples if I had departed this morning. You can imagine the joy I received with this missive, after which I had already longed for quite awhile and which was made all the more perfect by the assurance that you are all well. You will have probably received two letters already, one from Florence (which I posted only in Siena because I forgot to do it in Florence) and one from here. I enclosed one to H[err] Häussler in Würzburg and in it wished him good fortune on his nameday. I am happy that I did my obligation sooner in this case, rather than having you remind me about it. I shall certainly not least wish to participate in the happiness that is accorded to him by being able to empty a small glass of noncarbonated wine[2] in peace; for with schoolmasters it is something really quite unenviable to become disparaging as a professor, etc. It pleases me more than they that all my siblings were satisfied with the small gifts, and – [to remember][3] the countenance of my sisters at my farewell from them – for that I would give my last pair of pants, and

I am proud of the thought that I was worth such feelings to be a brother to such sisters. In my previous letter I have already described something of the magnificence of Rome. I still feel this with the new and the old, for I know that each small detail of importance to me interests you as well. Our King is now here, and for that reason no other special celebration was arranged than that in St. Peter's on the first day of Christmas, as I have already told you. Perhaps before his trip to Naples, which is now set for the 12th [of January], or only after his return this will also be performed with usual illumination of the Vatican and the fireworks on the Engelsburg[4] for the visit of crowned heads. The Emperor, who has already left before the New Year, it is said, will remain in Naples until the 23rd and thus will be able to pass through here with his sister. Moreover, today it is reported that the Archduke[5] arrived last night with his son. It's all the same to me – I wish to be able to present you with the entire platter of such state news, if only I had enough patience to yawn at such stupid matters. Now back to me. I believe that I have already reported to you in my Florentine letter how the King received me – the long and short of it. That means, he examined me about the first moments of my departure right up to the minute when I had the honor of giving him my obeisance. But I don't travel with the entourage, for this would be contrary to my goals; for during the time that the King awaited the Emperor,[6] I was already here, and even before the King arrived here, I had already seen the best and most important things. Now for a couple of Roman tidbits that are nonetheless not unimportant. I was remarkable at my presentation to the Pope[7] yesterday for at our entrance (there were four of us) he stood and immediately began the conversation; moreover, the Cardinal chamberlain said nothing about the kissing of hands and feet prior. Both were omitted because we were all presented by our agent here, *Chevalier de Piranesi*,[8] as Swedes; and even if I had been here alone a hundred times, I wouldn't have done the latter. The Pope was told everyone's name and profession. At mine, he said that he feared that music in his fatherland had not by any means progressed significantly in the last half of this century. If I were French, I would have most humbly begged pardon from his Holiness and assured him that *j'étois extrêmement enchanté des agréments divines de la Musique italienne*.[9] But I gave the Holy Father an answer drawn from a true German-Swedish forthrightness, that this comment simply proved that his H[oliness] was a connoisseur. The P[ope] looked down – laughed and probably thought: Now here's an amazing fellow. [I] don't have anything against that either. The other gentlemen in the *entourage* had already been presented on New Year's Day, but then I was with a few other of my expatriate countrymen at *Tivoli* looking at the magnificent ruins of ancient temples. It is true; if one is left so completely alone and views with amazement and an inner concentration the bulwarks of the towered buildings of a world power that once was, built to last forever – by my soul, one is ashamed to have been born 1,500 to 1,600 years later, for all of our little houses – not even excepting the Vatican Church, are just like a baby versus a grandmother. Next week I shall travel without fail to Naples and will write to you further from there. I do not need to tell my beloved siblings how much I love them. A return greeting to Herr Cousin Doctor and H[err] Pastor in Hettingbeuer.[10] My old Stålberg sends his compliments and thanks [you] for the remembrance.

> *Your most obedient son Joseph*

P.S. I have not yet been able to ask about P[ater] Remlert.[11]

COMMENTARY

Original Buchen, Bezirksmuseum. Much of the letter seems a personal response to his parents, but in between the lines one can read of Kraus's involvement with Gustav III's entourage. A painting, now in the Nationalmuseum in Stockholm, depicts the Mass attended by the Swedes and may include Kraus as one of the black-clad onlookers.

1. This is a reference to an unidentified piece of music, possibly meant for performance in Rome.

2. Kraus refers to the habit of mixing wine with naturally carbonated mineral water; he means drinking it without the water.

3. The original word, probably the infinitive suggested, was crossed out by Kraus and is illegible.

4. Kraus means the Castello San Angelo.

5. The Archduke is Joseph II's brother Ferdinand III, duke of Tuscany.

6. Gustav III met with Joseph II in Florence a few weeks earlier.

7. Pope Pius VI.

8. The Chevalier de Piranesi was the son of artist Giovanni Battista Piranesi (1720–1778).

9. "That I am extraordinarily enchanted with the divine nature of Italian music." Kraus's actual response seems equally as diplomatic, though with more pointed undertones.

10. The cousin in Hettingbeuer is unidentified.

11. Pater Remlert is unidentified, but may have been a Benedictine from Amorbach who was in Rome.

64. Letter to his parents dated Naples, 15 February 1784

You can trust me that I certainly wouldn't have let this letter wait for four whole weeks had I not believed myself that such a length [of time] was appropriate. I had to await first the permission of our King to depart Italy before I could write to you in order to be able to give you some indication of when I would be in Paris. Because my sojourn here in Rome already lasted longer than I had intended at the outset, I did not doubt that I would receive permission to continue my journey immediately after the King's arrival here. But they wanted me to investigate the conservatory in detail, and for that, it took so much time that one week after another went by without obtaining a point in time for my salvation. Today, I finally received from His Majesty oral orders to take myself off to France most promptly. Few orders in my life have been as pleasant as these. One doesn't require extra postage; but rather the way I have traveled hither and yon, I have tried out everything that had to be attempted if one must get to know Italy in order to comprehend why I so urgently desire to be rid of this country. It is truly no art to gape at Italy's lemon and orange trees on the main roads from a comfortable carriage – and to remain en route until one can find good accommodations and bearable food, and then with a calm head, good mood, and satisfied stomach stand astonished at the noble ruins of antiquity. Thus one learns only a portion of the surface but by no means knows the country and land itself. To tell you in confidence, in Naples I visited more of the old history and ruins than half of what I did for my profession. Naturally, here there are the most excellent conservatories and seminaries, but they certainly by far would not have occupied me fully. In order to give a child a legitimate name, I pretended to be interested in music, and in the company of a German painter by the name of Dähne from Leipzig and a Danish architect called Hansen,[1] I preceded our King fourteen days in advance to Naples. Along the way I had the advantage of my companions that no old cottage or little house of importance was left without investigation. In *Terracina, Molo di Gaetta,* and *Capua* I enriched my small antiquarian brain box by quite a bit. Naples, however, was beyond all my expectations. Consider a city on the most propitious edge of the Mediterranean Sea, spread out like the expanded wreckage of an amphitheater – expansive, comfortable. On one side of the ancient foothills the former location of the Roman navy under Pliny the Elder. To the left the terrible neighbor Vesuvius and the remains of the cities of Herculaneum and Pompeii[2] destroyed by it. Straight ahead the fruitful and most pleasant island of Capri, etc., which focuses the eye on the most interminable distance out to Sardinia and Corsica. Certainly, there is not a more beautiful and brilliant city that is to be found on God's green earth. And therefore, the Neapolitans are known to be the greatest villains in all of Italy. The city has up to 500,000 inhabitants, of which at least half do not know how they survive. There are 40,000 *Lazzaroni* alone who scrounge every day 10 Kreutzers through begging, as well as those who seek to earn their bread in another more honorable way. Because one cannot count on the police to guard their personal safety, it is therefore easy to understand that here too everybody from a state minister to the day laborer carries a dagger, and by night everything is illuminated by torches. Despite every precaution, not a day goes by that one does not hear of theft. You can draw a reliable conclusion if you know that in the city of Naples along, there are at any time over 8,000 people under arrest for the crime of robbery. The dialect of the Neapolitans and Sicilians is very *corrupt* and thus very difficult to understand, and their manners are like Jews. Everywhere one must arrange in advance if one wants anything, and one cannot be certain that when an innkeeper demands 8 Carolinas at the outset for a meal that he is certainly willing to let it go for two. The wine and almost all of the food is cheap, but lodging is expensive on account of the number of people. The richness of the churches is extraordinary. As tastelessly built as they are for the most part, they supersede all of the rest in Europe in precious adornment. The simply laid marble of certain altars certainly costs up to 50,000 Ducats. The devotion of the Neapolitans is like all of the rest of the Italians – hypocrisy. S[aint] January[3] is more the case than God Father, Son, and Holy Spirit. When Vesuvius begins to threaten, or some other misfortune dogs the Neapolitans; this is their usual prayer: Holy God the Father! Pray to Saint January to deal with us better. There is another idiotic custom that I have observed continuously. It is this, namely, that they don't stay at Mass any longer than the transubstantiation. As soon as this is over, they run from the church as if their behinds were on fire. The remaining character of the inhabitants is half Italian and half Spanish, and their taste is more ornamented than simple. According to my observations, this is the true reason why it has leaped ahead of all the other provinces in Italy in terms of painting, sculpture, and architecture. The city teems with huge palaces, and it is true at the same time that, with the exception of the *Corsini,* there is not a simple building done in the noble Roman style.

I am continuing this letter today on the 17th because I was prevented yesterday morning from doing so. I will certainly travel away from here at the end of this week. I have already related to you about the inner Naples; with the usual brevity I would like to tell you something about the region all around. To the west one goes through a monstrously large, manmade grotto on the road to *Pozzuoli.* On this street one meets on the left side the tombstone of the old Latin poet Virgil and on the right the well-known Cave of the Dogs, hot springs, and the *Solfatara.* The former got its name because one experiments with a poor dog, who has spent a few moments in this cave and sunk down dead, and it will remain dead if it is not thrown into the water, whereupon it revives. The hot springs pour with a horrible rushing from out of a high black cliff, upon which hang man-high pieces of *sal ammonaicum*[4] and other evaporated salts from nature. This warm water is used by the inhabitants as a cure against the French, who unlike anywhere else in the world, are as numerous and at the same time so innocuous as here. The Solfatara, however, is one of the most terrifying pictures of nature that one can see. This was for-merly a *volcano* or fire-spewing mountain like Vesuvius; it is now, how-ever, completely imploded. The mouth of the *crater* is about half a Ger-man mile in circumference and approximately a quarter-hour high, and consists of great pieces of cliffs of sulfur and other materials made by fire so that one must reckon it to be altogether about a mile. The floor is even and covered with light white brimstone. The most horrible thing about it is that with every step one takes the ground reverberates; a proof that everything beneath is hollow. Therefore, no one is allowed to ride or walk on it. I counted some thirty-odd great crevasses, out of which steam and small flames arose toward evening. In the center is a large opening, from out of which there issues a fearful noise and heat that almost causes one to faint in the proximity. Everything that is thrown down there is coated with *sal ammoniacum,* for which there is also a company in the vicinity.

Pozzuoli itself was a rather imposing city during Roman times; nowadays it is an unimportant place of *about* 4,000 inhabitants, however. The most remarkable thing around here are the columns of the old temple of *Jupiter Serapis* – undoubtedly the most beautiful temple still standing – which is built entirely of Carrara marble. One sees around here the remains of the amphitheater where S[aint] Januarius was thrown to the lions. One also sees his prison and the steps upon which he was led to the arena. From Pozzuoli one travels across the sea to *Bauli*. Here, the saddest scene meets the eyes. To the left is the ancient foothill *Misena;* beneath it the *Mare morto,* or the ancient *Styx;* in front the Elysian Fields; to the right the ancient city of *Baja* that was one of the largest in the world apart from Rome. There is barely a wall left of *Misena*. In *Baja* there are here and there the noble remains of the great palaces of [Julius] *Caesar* and Nero, the latter of which also contains hot baths. The only things somewhat left standing are three temples to Mercury, Diana, and Venus. Because the entrance is occupied by water, one cannot approach the Temple of Mercury in any other manner than on the back of a completely naked bearer, who wades through the last vault of a tri-vaulted dome; to the left is a walled passageway of about twelve steps, and through it one comes to a pile of rubble of a circular building modeled in the style of the Pantheon in Rome. In this particular manner one is brought back to dry ground. You should have seen me; what a peculiar figure I made hanging around the neck of a two-legged beast of burden with a tobacco pipe in my mouth. –It certainly ought to have been painted. From this point to the right is an ancient temple to Apollo and the ancient country house of Cicero, and thus one arrives at the Cave of the *Sybill* at *Cumæ*. By my soul, it was a worthy dwelling for such an old witch. It is so horribly long and so terrifying that one thinks at every moment that the ancient world would appear and cast a magic spell upon itself. This would now be a small description of the country to the west of Naples. Now on to the more important portion to the southwest. Certainly in this century more has been written about no other region in Europe than this one. In order to be clear, I first have to dredge up a bit of the history of this stretch of the world. Here formerly stood several Roman cities, among which *Herculaneum, Pompeii,* and *Stabia* are the best known. In the year 72 before the birth of Christ, Vesuvius, whose summit is at a distance of about a German mile from here, erupted and in a day, or rather in the space of a few hours toward evening as the people gathered at the theater, covered the entire city with ashes and lava material. *Pliny* the Elder, at that time *commander* of the fleet at *Misena,* immediately traveled over there, either to help the beleaguered people or perhaps out of simple curiosity, and was overcome by the fumes in the harbor. At least, this is what *Pliny* the Younger relates in a letter to *Tacitus.* Fifteen years later Vesuvius buried the remaining cities mentioned with its outburst of fire. And thus these unfortunate proofs of the destroying power of the volcano lay forgotten for 1,600 whole years underneath the foundations of newer smaller villages and country estates. Of course, their fate was known, but no one could pinpoint their location exactly. Herculaneum was first discovered due to a fountain that was being dug. From that time onward, one has always dug from time to time, and by and by found various buildings and ancient remains. Because the debris is very deep and up above the new spot of Portici with the royal estate has been built, the work has not proceeded so far; and, moreover, one desires to save the cost of taking the dug-out dirt to a new place opposite the ancient one. The only thing that one can wander through in this underground city only with the aid of torches is the theater. From here to Pompeii is about ten Italian or two German miles. Everywhere one sees signs of lava that Vesuvius has thrown out from time to time, until one finally arrives at the magnificent city. Because it was covered with only ash and not lava, and, moreover, it was not as deep as unfortunate Herculaneum, it was easier to dig here. Everything that has been discovered is open. A rather longer stretch of the main road up to a city gate and the buildings of that time on either side have been relieved of their covering in this manner. You can easily imagine how such a view must appear to foreign eyes. The foundations of the buildings back then were much simpler and thus much more beautiful than ours are now. There are no windows, but rather all light came through the doors, and because these had to serve such a purpose, of course, they were used much differently than ours. The rooms are mostly vaulted and the floors of the houses of the rich laid with mosaics. The walls are painted, although one is not able to perceive what their magnificent colors were made from, particularly the sky blue and sea green. Everything is rich with marble. In *Stabia* one has not yet begun to excavate. Therefore, I can only give you a brief report of those things that were excavated from *Herculaneum* and *Pompeii* and are preserved in the royal museum in Portici. From everything that has been found, one can conclude that the inhabitants had time to flee with their most treasured things when faced with misfortune. At the same time, there is a monstrously huge number of human bones that are most probably the remains of poor slaves, prisoners, etc. The museum consists of 24 rooms that are filled with dishes, idols, etc., that are ancient. Apart from a few of the better statues, sacrificial implements, and a collection of coins, one can find here the only collection in the world of household implements of the ancients. Knives, tongs, copper dishes, special iron machines to cook eggs, and even complete instruments for *surgery and birthing,* bath things, bands for the neck and head, teeth-pulling devices, etc., it all can be found here with the exception of no forks and no scissors. One wonders mightily when one sees the things that have been rediscovered and perhaps not even dreamed about after more than a thousand years, that our forefathers had it much better and far more perfect than we; for e[xample], glass of all sorts that one can find here that we still have in use, and gold braid that is worked with the finest of gold threads, and so forth. What makes the most piteous impression is that one sees that the unmerciful Vesuvius didn't even allow its victims to be fed first. A pie, a round piece of bread of about four or five pounds, a plate of boiled eggs, several small bottles of oil and wine have been unearthed; and it is certainly a strange phenomenon how the fire and heat have altered all of these things. The eggs still seem quite fresh, and from one that has been broken one can see that the heat simply dried them out. The *residue* in the flask of oil is half black and white and very heavy; on the other hand, in the bottle of wine it is an ash-gray *Tartarus.* More important is the proof of the softness and luxury of this decadent period. In a single wardrobe are some one hundred *phalluses* of all types, some with wings, some standing upright, some in the form of lamps, etc. But in order to see the main obscene event, one first has to obtain a permission slip from the ministry; which I could have done only with difficulty had our King not been here. This is a faun, who is lying with a she-goat. However filthy the concept is, it is done so magnificently and artistically. For whatever purpose such things served the Roman women certainly cannot be determined. On one house in *Pompeii,* the male member is carved into marble above the door. I am going to leave aside whether or not there existed bordellos then, or whether a merciful monk lived there, who helped out young men who played around too much from their distress. The paintings are no less of importance. They are all painted on dried plaster, thus they are not *frescos* as once believed. I convinced myself that the ancients exceeded the moderns in terms of the flowing *contours* and purity of line, but the more modern has left them far behind with respect to space and shadow and *perspective.* But I have also found two examples that they already knew about *perspective,* which is not otherwise believed. It is certain that their vases and lamps are inimitable in terms of form, taste, and detail.[5] It is remarkable that even in our day such vessels are made in the same form nearby, which one otherwise doesn't see in Europe. Enough of this now. It was now time to see over Vesuvius itself. Truly, when one looks upon this evil neighbor that continues to smoke and rumble, and considers all of the misfortune that it has already caused, one obtains a damned high regard for it. It consists of two mountains, the one toward the sunrise being Vesuvius itself and the other called Somma. One journeys from Naples to the aforementioned *Portici,* which lies a full half hour away, and from there a donkey is ridden up to the foot of the mountain that lies another half hour distant. Then one begins to wade through the eternal ashes with a guide [up the] mountain until one finally reaches the halfway part in an hour. Here one finds refreshment at a hermit's rest with wine and bread, in order to gather strength for the second half. Here the ash begins to get even hotter, and the most difficult thing is that there is no sure footing, but rather one often slides back a yard for every two forward. After the course of the second hour one finally reaches the hole at the top of the mountain. Of course, one waits first for a day when the wind blows toward the sea so that one is not choked by the fumes. I had good weather and thus was fortunately able to observe this terrible phenomenon. The crater or hole is certainly more than a German mile in circumference. You lie on your stomach at the rim in order to remain without dizziness, and thus you can look down about a hundred feet into the depths of the smaller hole. The thundering and boiling is terrifying. Picture a sulfurous caldron of around a half mile in circumference, from out of which flames of all colors pour forth, and with each gout of flame the entire mountain trembles and reverberates. One sees nothing but the eternal quaking and din of this smithy. Of course, one would have the impression that by sticking around one would put oneself in danger, but the greatness, the feeling of majesty so grips one that one lowers oneself a few yards more in order to be able to eavesdrop on nature in its most terrible and frightening work. Fumes always emanate from the abyss, but very seldom do the flames reach the upper rim. As soon as they should cease to smoke, it would be a sure sign that it would soon erupt. Because so many cities have already been buried by it, it is easy to notice how much the Neapolitans live in fear. In the 1770s the King and his entire court had to flee here from Portici at night in only their nightclothes in order to escape an eruption of this volcano. If it is also the most terrible probability that sooner or later Naples will undergo that horrible fate that has engulfed its neighbors, it is a poor substitute for living so carefree and pleasurably as the Neapolitans do. Now I have blathered on about the length and breadth of the magnificence of Naples. Now something about its music and then finished!

Naples is known advantageously above all other cities in Italy for its good music schools and great masters, that it partly has had and still has. It was the fatherland for *Vinci, Pergolesi, Porpora, Jommelli,* etc., and is still [the home of] a *Piccinni, Mano,* etc.[6] It is also known as the only *workshop for castratos,* and thus it is certain that here alone this sort of nursery survives. There are therefore three. In each, youths are trained in voice partly *free* and partly for money, and partly with a stipend. Of course, in earlier times they had better masters than now; but on the other hand they retain yet the good old-fashioned instruction of a *Durante,*[7] and they do well with it. Regarding the practical, there are four theaters. Because castratos are not allowed to appear on any but the royal main theater *San Carlo,* where only *opera seria* is performed, the capons have to earn their bread in the churches, at which considerable music is given each day. Among all of these immature creatures I have barely heard a single one who has had a good voice. *Aprile,*[8] who was a guest twenty years ago in Mannheim and in the manner of *castrati* has assembled for himself a bit of capital, is performing here now and pipes to our Dear God with his little old voice something each day. He told me that it was a shame that I had not heard him in Mannheim – in turn [I said] that I regretted that our Dear God therefore had not allowed me to be born ten or fifteen years earlier. The *opera seria* this year is called *Adone et Venere* by Pugnani,[9] who put into it a couple of violin solos and scratched them out nicely. But on the whole, the music is very mediocre, and the orchestra about which there has been so much noise is pitiful. The few women who are *debuting* in it are nothing but sinners who desire to desecrate *coloratura* in their autumn days. The single castrato *Roncaglia*[10] has a passable little voice, on the other hand. The primary comic theater is *Fiorentino*. The main actress there, *Sign[ora] Coletellini*,[11] is the best of her type that I have seen in Italy. The other two theaters, *del fondo di Separazione* and the *Nuovo* are not worth spit. Regarding the *compositions* for this year, the first opera at the *Fiorentino* was by *Cimarosa* and the second by *Tritto*.[12] Neither one was of particular value. Otherwise, *Cimarosa* is still Italy's best living composer when it comes to the realm of vocal music. He is a pupil of *Piccinni* and has cobbled together extraordinarily much for his young years already. The music for the *Nuovo* was by *Paisiello*,[13] really bad, and that for the *Fondo di Separazione* a true *pasticcio*. Concerning the metrical church style, I met one *Demagistri*, who I would place side by side with our *Homilius*[14] in Dresden. Fare well – if I am able to stop for a bit in *Livorno* or *Turin*, I will write you once more from Italy. Greet everyone who deserves my greetings.

Your most obedient Joseph

NB. Have you received my second letter from Rome with an answer to your letter?

COMMENTARY

Original Buchen, Bezirksmuseum, with a diplomatic copy in Uppsala, Universitetsbibliotek, Folio X270f in the hand of Hofrat Paul Lämmerhirt. This lengthy and detailed letter demonstrates Kraus's infatuation with Naples and its antiquarian and natural wonders, and as such can be considered one of the most realistic and descriptive correspondence travelogues of the period. The normal salutation is lacking, and the original letter has suffered damage due to the inferior paper upon which it was written.

1. The architect is Christian Fredrik Hansen (1756–1845); the painter is unidentified, though a miniaturist by the same last name was active in Germany around 1797.

2. The lost cities of Herculaneum and Pompeii were rediscovered only in

1709 and 1748 respectively, and thus their excavation was just beginning during Kraus's visit.

3. In other words, in Kraus's opinion the Neapolitans are two-faced rogues.

4. *Sal-ammoniacum* = ammonio-ferric sulfate, a common distillate of volcanic hot springs.

5. A corner of the letter is missing at this point; the text has been reconstructed by inference.

6. The composers are Leonardo Vinci (1690–1730), Giovanni Battista Pergolesi (1710–1736), Nicola Porpora (1686–1768), and Nicolò Jommelli (1714–1774). The two modern composers are Niccolò Piccinni (1728–1800) and probably Gennaro Manna (1715–1779). Piccinni's son Luigi (1764–1827) later moved to Stockholm in 1796, where he had some success as a composer of opera. There is a small gap in the letter at this point; it is unknown which other composers Kraus would have mentioned among the two contemporary ones already named, but likely there would have been two more.

7. Francesco Durante (1684–1755), one of the principal music teachers of the day.

8. Giuseppe Aprile (1731–1803).

9. Gaetano Pugnani (1731–1798).

10. Francesco Roncaglia (ca. 1750–ca. 1812).

11. Anna Coltellini, daughter of librettist and printer Marco Coltellini.

12. Cimarosa's opera was *L'apparenza inganna, o sia La Villeggiatura*, with the second work mentioned being *La scuffiara* by Giacomo Tritto (1733–1824).

13. Possible *Socrate immaginario* by Giovanni Paisiello (1740–1816), his last opera for the Teatro Nuovo from 1775 just prior to that composer's departure for Russia.

14. "Demagistri" (possibly de Magistris) is unidentified; the German organist is Gottfried August Homilius (1714–1785).

65. Letter to his parents dated Livorno, 16 March 1784

I have enough time to fulfill my promise, for I have spent several days here awaiting a comfortable opportunity to go to Marseilles by sea. Comfort and economy already brought me to the decision in Naples to travel from there by water. Then two circumstances intervened crossways, and I was forced to travel here overland. After my last thick letter that you will hopefully have received, I had of course been able to make my determinations about the place and therefore was quite finished, when I received orders from the King first to wait upon several letters and then a small package that he wanted me to take to Paris. This was delayed from one day to another until the week was over, and not before the evening of the sixth was the packet from *Caserta* sent along with the gracious permission to be able to depart. In the meantime, the few opportunities I had to travel by French ship had already sailed. On Sunday the seventh, therefore, I packed myself and my Stålberg up into a *Carozino*[1] and dragged off out of Naples at dawn, and after ten o'clock yesterday evening arrived here a bit bent but completely healthy. This is probably the last place in Italy that I will see, and no one could be more satisfied than I that my Italian pilgrimage will end here. As far as I can remember, I wrote to you six times from Italy. I should hope that all of the little scraps of paper have wandered to the Odenwald unopened, for then I hope you would have such a perfect lesson concerning my journey that it would be unnecessary for me to detail my last little route. Up to Siena the road had the same length that I measured up to Florence. The only noticeable place was *Pinibonzi,* where the roads to Livorno and Florence divide, and right before *Livorno* is *Pisa,* an old, large, and wonderfully built city famed for its excellent siting and healthy baths, and even more so for its early history, where along with the countryside and seacoast hereabouts it consisted of its own republic. In comparison, *Livorno* is an unremarkable place despite being the second largest city in Italy, but it is heavily populated as a center of the southern trade.

Still there, 28 April 1784

Who would have thought that I would still be sitting here! In the intervening time, the weather and wind made it thoroughly impossible to undertake my trip, but I can assure you that I have passed my time here with nothing less than uselessness. Because I could expect no occupation here, and I had no major acquaintance here either, I would certainly have found it difficult to imagine that I would have been able to sojourn for six whole weeks without boredom. But all the more so, each pleasure was as surprising as it was unanticipated. I have met through our consul here Swedes, Danes, and Englishmen, as well as my own countrymen. What is especially valuable to me is that I have obtained as a friend and therefore a fantastic and trustworthy *correspondent* in the part of Europe a local German preacher,[2] who is himself both a *composer* and author. This evening the ship will depart; the wind is, of course, not the best – and, moreover, [it] will offer a rather boring time at sea. For this I entrust myself to my French-speaking captain, for it will be much easier for me to talk to him, for he was part of the famed naval battle under *Grasse.*[3] Now another small piece of news of little weight. In *Pisa* I met a man from Heilbronn,[4] who has a muslin factory there and is doing well.

In conclusion, as soon as I arrive in Paris I will give you more news. Fare well and love me always with my

Beloved siblings

Your

Most obedient son Joseph

[P.S.] Give my greetings to my dear Hoffstetter. How did his keyboard pieces[5] get to Hamburg?

COMMENTARY

Original Buchen, Bezirksmuseum. The implication of his delaying his departure at the request of the King is that he may have been acting as a sort of diplomatic courier.

1. *Carozino* (recte *carosino*), or a wagon hauling freight.

2. This was Johann Paul Schulthesius (1748–1816).

3. The naval battle refers either to the Battle of the Cape off the coast of Vir-

ginia, where Admiral François Joseph Comte de Grasse defeated a British fleet in September of 1781 or the Battle of the Saintes, in which he defeated a Spanish fleet off of Martinique in April of 1782.

4. The linen merchant remains unidentified.

5. The precise identification of these lost works is not known, nor why Hoffstetter might have sent them to Hamburg, save perhaps to a publisher.

66. Letter to his parents dated Paris, 26 June 1784

I wanted to write immediately the day of my arrival on the 21st to make it known to you that the kid is finally here; [that is,] if I hadn't thought it better first to obtain a more secure lodging and at the very least be able to give you a trustworthy address. You have no doubt received my letter from Marseilles and are thus not the least amazed that I arrived here so late. The main reason was that my almost one week long sojourn in Aix was unpleasant for me – in order to spare you the necessary worry, I will remain silent completely about the small indisposition that overtook me.[1] Now I am again healthy and hope to remain so, and with all probability because the heat in the country around here is interminably weaker than it was in Provence – at the very least I blame the extraordinary warmth and the wine. Departing from Aix I made small day segments and finally came to Lyons on the 13th of this month, and afterward I stopped briefly here and there in *Vienne, Valence,* etc. I left Lyons on the 17th and came to Paris on the 21st toward evening. Until now I haven't yet made any huge leaps that I can relate to you. Paris is really quite large and here and there has magnificent town squares and palaces; but by a long shot it doesn't measure up to the notion that one receives from a distance about this wonder of the world. One can count almost a million inhabitants. Many of these hardly venture beyond the borders of the suburbs during their lifetimes and thus barely believe that people still exist outside of Paris. My maid asked me yesterday whether there were cats in my country, as well? – She made every effort to take me at my word; but she found it impossible to comprehend that these beloved little animals were as beautiful in Germany as they were in this country. The stage deserves to be praised, but somewhat less than usually happens. But another time about all of these things – it is still my intention to acquaint you with my arrival here.

Oh – how happy I am to receive your loving letters.

My address is:

a Monsieur

M. Kraus, Maître de Chapelle au Service de la Cour de Suede

À l'hotel de Marigni, Place du Vieux Louvre. Paris

Damned! – Yesterday I became twenty-eight years old and still don't have a wife![2]

Greet my beloved siblings and my dear Hoffstetter. I really don't need to ask you not to leave me too long without letters

Your Joseph

P.S. I've just received very unpleasant news:

M[on]s[ieur] *de Peyron,*[3] a member of the court and first page to our King, to whom he was a godfather, was stabbed yesterday afternoon in a duel.

COMMENTARY

Original Buchen, Bezirksmuseum. The salutation is missing from the letter. From the contents, at least one other letter from Marseilles to Kraus's parents was written; this has been lost.

1. Kraus was apparently ill in Aix-en-Provence.

2. It is inferred that Kraus's personal life was of concern to his parents, though it might seem that he had little time for pursuing the opposite sex.

3. The duel involved a French officer, Charles Adrien de Peyron, with August-Marie-Raymond Anglebert, comte de la Marck. It took place on 25 June 1784. The challenge was given ironically enough at a masked ball held in honor of Gustav III.

67. Letter to his parents dated Paris, 31 July 1784

Dearest Parents!

Had I not yet been on top of things, my poor letter of the 26th of June would not have gone better than the one from Marseilles. For I did not know that I had to have it stamped correctly, and therefore the poor devil had to remain in quarantine for almost three weeks until it was delivered along with the *Passe-avant*[1] for my bag. It was therefore also only natural that it was first able to arrive in Amorbach on the 22nd of this month. If the other poor soul from Marseilles is still among the living (for it would be too bad for my soul if such a heartfelt piece of work were to become lost), I would wish from the bottom of my heart that it would soon reach its place and address (NB, and not as round about as your poor dear little package). For, to be honest about it, I could barely read a quarter of your letter and only with extreme difficulty make out two others – and for the fourth, I shall reserve next week to study it – so badly did the letter carrier mishandle the letters. How this happened is really not so easy for me to comprehend. Your second letter with the address of Count *Creutz*[2] was probably able to arrive in good order at the proper place and address, that is – in Stockholm. The Count has been away from here already since October of last year and has assumed the post of prime minister of Sweden. Perhaps he will be so kind as to retain the little letter for me quite prettily and cleanly for my return. *Prosit*! The fact that I had to begin my scrap of paper with the story of the letters annoys me. But you will have to blame yourselves. As in all your letters, there is nothing more important than reading: "We are well" – and then I would have begun my answer of course in a similar vein and so on: "And that pleases me from the bottom of my heart." I have also made a habit a long time ago to read all of your letters backwards; for usually my dear mother gives me her assurance at the end that is the most interesting piece of news, above all else: "Kid! Your parents are healthy and have few complaints – ditto for your siblings – [and] ditto for your friends." I also want to comment on the side and thus appropriately report that if I were to have arrived home approximately several months ago – found your letters and read them through already three times without having to think about having paid the honorable concierge of the hotel 46 sous[3] for them. With that, I have just set down a solid recommendation to answer them in *courier* fashion – like – like: I would like to strike out the little words *courier fashion,* for it always bothers me a bit when I consider the travels of a *courier.* In confidence – the King really did send me with dispatches from Naples – and then the devil had to conjure up in *Livorno* such a good friend as *Schultesius* and such a magnificent English ale, so that the simpleton – *enough*! Now everything is fine again – a little bit of my household capital had to be put aside,[4] but it was, however, of so little *consequence* that he gave me his most gracious assurance on the same day that he would not want to exchange my handiwork for that of all my other colleagues here – and for which I immediately got back into His Majesty's good graces. And in order to make the compliment a little bit more real, he gave me his most gracious permission to determine the time of my sojourn myself, a circumstance that could not have pleased me more. And then, I would like to say, I sat down to answer your letter in all haste, stuffed my pipe, and then, as was required for it to go forward, began *ab ovo.*[5] Because I did not find on the first page anything other than "Letter, post office, *avertissement,* address, etc., etc.," I was of the opinion that I had to do it myself – something that should be entirely for-givable. *À propos,* because I still blather on about letters, I have taken the liberty of placing a formal *protest* in my dear mother's little brown trunk, into which to my knowledge all my letters have wandered, not to wish on her life for these grandchildren to be led into temptation thereby – which is well-meant advice for my dear mother. Little Joseph has his own little trap, which sometimes gives him pleasure to splash around when the puddles are not too deep and not worry whether he is getting his feet wet or a stuffy nose. Then all the little Josephs that will come after him in the future will try and imitate and find themselves in deep stir, which our good God should prevent with all grace. *Amen.*

Now to get into the little chapter from the back end, above which is written "regarding girls – wine, and other such things." Concerning the first, I have to confess penitentially that for this time the entire ser-mon about "much rather an honorable woman in the home than messing around with dirty things" should at least be started up to the point where the sacred love of the pious mother *Blanca* for her son Ludwig, etc., etc., for this year it has rather had little effect upon me. Why? That is a true secret – for only I and dear God know about it. To express myself more clearly, I would rather admit quite openly now that I have a much stronger *antidote* against such temptations than my dear mother gives me credit for. In short – for an entire year I have burned from head to toe, or rather unpoetically to say: I love the girl that I believe to have been created for me; and for me, any glance into the eyes of another would be a mortal sin. Who is the girl? *Hopsa*! I've already said that it is a true secret – and by my poor soul, so it is; the lovely thing herself doesn't have a clue that I think, see, and hear nothing but her – if here and there a little passage in my letters has not betrayed me – for of course one's mouth cannot be taken so seriously if one's heart is full. Calm yourselves; for if it is probably true that a man with a pretty, honorable wife at home would not *gallivant* about all over the place – it is certainly a thousand times more *evident* that a warm, real, fresh love in the breast of a lad perseveres in the face of all sorts of temptations better than all of the amulets on God's green earth.[6] Regarding the second, that is, wine, I have only a small word to say. And that is, because the water here is not potable, I drink wine when I am thirsty. My mother probably meant only white wine – and I've nothing against that; but I do not cut myself off from the honor of my red, for it is excellent, *probatum est* – I just drank a glass to your health. A bottle costs 15 sous. Thus it is not expensive – and at the same time has the most wonderful effect on the blood and really helps digestion. Please tell the Herr Cousin Doctor; if he wants my opinion this time, I would be well-disposed toward it and betray to him a little place in Frankfurt where one can get this same merchandise not watered down. One consideration deserves another.

Good night for today!

Sunday, 32 July [recte 1 August]

Good morning, dear mother! – it would be three times more pleasant to be able to surprise you in bed with this same greeting. But one has to do well with however it comes. Perhaps you are sleeping late this morning, and the large and small along with you (for it is just now four o'clock), unless perhaps the female barking has poked one of my sisters awake – that is: it is entirely possible, even though it is still quite early and there is enough time for one to go to Mass comfortably; it is entirely possible I say that one of my dear little sisters is rolling about restlessly in bed, with all sorts of important things passing through her head, such as, for example: what sort of bonnet she should wear – whether this one or that will have on this or that pair of shoes – whether Heja! – I dimwittedly might not have considered that my observations would have them trying to strangle me. Please excuse my impertinent assumptions and then enough of it! And in order that this not be *reciproce,* that is deserving advice of the same sort from my sisters, I have the honor of assuring them that I have left my nest more or less early this time for an honorable professional obligation. I have in hand a little work that is called "*Intermèdes pour l'Amphitryon,*"[7] a thing consisting of six quarto pages of cleanly written French verses and a whole list of pantomime dances, such as: *La lutte, la course, la ceste, Ballet des douze heures de la Nuit* and of course *ditto* one for *des Heures du matin, qui chassent les Étoiles* – and another similar one where Night lovingly *invites* her dear little stars to slip behind her dark cloak so that they do not illuminate Herr Jupiter on his secret path, who is [therefore] quite pleased with this rather pleasant activity. I have to put all this stuff into music, and the Monarch said that I would do him a favor if I could pull all this together pretty fast. And in order to accomplish this, I shall rather have to get up a few mornings somewhat earlier than usual. But – whoever came up with the proverb that the early bird gets the worm[8] was certainly no composer. For I always need over an hour to overcome the difficulty of having to trample chickens to death –

Blast and damnation![9] The 32nd of July! Wow! Now that was a howler! – of course, I am much too *comfortable*[10] to go over to my calendar that is lying behind in a corner, but I could easily have done the calculation in my head by reviewing my knuckles, and it becomes clear in the following manner: make a fist and then on the first knuckle of the thumb it is the 31st of March, the space between the finger next to it for the 30th of April, and then the next knuckle for the 31st of May, the next finger . . .

Regarding the good advice to promote myself through the *Musikalisches Magazin,* I would ask you most graciously to pardon me from doing it. I am by no means a lover of ceremonies that are made about me while I am still alive, and – to be honest, there is no desire to parade about in a journal in which friend Cramer has the exclusive privilege[11] of prostituting only his friends; – a nice example; the discussion of the psalmodies of his disciple Kunze.[12] And thus it could be called such and such, etc. –

COMMENTARY

Original Buchen, Bezirksmuseum. The final page of the letter containing the conclusion is missing; a portion of this was published by Silverstolpe as Letter 33.

1. *Passe-avant* = customs clearance.

2. Gustav Philip Creutz (1731–1785), author of the popular bucolic poem, "Atis och Camilla."

3. Orig. *pur in parenthesi,* or comment in parentheses. The sou was a French copper coin of little value; a Louis d'or was equal to 480 sous.

4. See Letter 65. The cryptic comments imply that Kraus was not able to fulfill his mission as a diplomatic courier and was fined for his indiscretion.

5. *ab ovo* = literally, "from the egg," or meaning from the start.

6. The entire tale about what seems to have been a love interest is highly lacunar, for Kraus does not mention details. Schreiber (Sch-JMK, 96), citing a reference by Silverstolpe, suggests that this unidentified woman was Maria von Born, the daughter of Ignaz von Born

(1742–1791) of Mozart opera and freemasonry fame. He was the head of Kraus's lodge in Vienna and the timing seems about right, for such to have occurred. No documentation of any such relationship exists, however, though Silverstolpe was in a position in Vienna to undertake further inquiries about it.

7. *Quatre Intermèdes pour Amphitryon* (VB 27), first performed at Drottningholm in 1787 as interludes to Molière's play put on by the French troupe led by Monvel.

8. Orig. *Morgonstund hat Gold im Mund,* the translation of which does not make sense in English; the idiomatic equivalent proverb has been used.

9. Orig. *Blitz und Hagel!* or Lightning and Hail.

10. Orig. *commod,* which can also mean being lazy.

11. Orig. *privilegium exclusivium.*

12. Carl Friedrich Cramer (1752–1817). Cramer's "privileged" friend is probably Friedrich Ludwig Æmelius Kunzen (1761–1817).

68. Letter to his parents dated Paris, 22 August 1784

Dearest Parents!

This is a day! It is true that one ought not to order our dear God about; but I'd like to bow and scrape, shaking my head if He wishes to give me another brusque shock of this sort during the few short years of my lifetime – how gladly I, like all of the other children of Adam, would like to have a small bit of life. For the past twenty-four hours it has rained nonstop and is so cold, that [I] want to have some warmth without further ado; if only I had an oven and some wood. And now it is the blasted fashion that only after the opera, that is about nine o'clock, one pays visits and around eleven sits down at the table – yesterday evening I had the opportunity to have *ported* a bit too much[1] (for on my honor our ambassador has the best *Porter* in all of Paris), and the devil would not be content without champagne, as well – and today I've got rheumatism throughout my entire body, and I can barely lift up my left hand high without the most exquisite pain. That is somewhat of a harsh penance for such a small sin. On the other hand, I've given myself the strictest counsel [that] the next time, rather, to have emptied a few more smaller glasses and keep to one type [of liquor].

If my last letter was too jovial, with the help of God this one will be much drier; for today everything has gone crossways for me. I have lit my little pipe six times already, and it doesn't catch fire, and the rain flows into my ears and has the same effect as women in such critical circumstances, when one chews blue paper or scratches on the wall. Today, by my soul, I could watch a hanging in cold blood – too bad that it is Sunday – God forgive me the sin! And if He forgives me this one, then it will be all right with the three that I write today in the same tone as my mother, but after a sideways beginning. At least half of my last missive must have been lost or forgotten; for otherwise I certainly would have learned whether my little package from Marseilles has arrived? And whether you probably examined a certain portion near the top – for my father is entirely correct that the little word "girl" in the first letter was half-joking;[2] the matter was not to be taken so seriously in the last; and I would, moreover, have bet that in the next letter my marriage counselor, Miss Anna Barbara, would have posed certain inquisitorial questions to me, and I had already decided to make a short tour around the porridge so that the curiosity of my dear sisters would be increased even more, if that were possible. I was so certain in my project that I read through your letter three or four times and am hardly able to convince myself that not even a little word of the affair appears. No matter – I'll save half a dozen answers and keep the little secret myself. And please do not greet me in the meantime, for my three Graces are riding about by coach as a warning that if they have the inclination a second time on a post day to make a pilgrimage to Weilbach and Miltenberg, they could leave a pretty little memento for their brother at home,[3] and that as a matter of course. Concerning the Jew in Göttingen, I would prefer if I made an end to it, and since it is in regard to only 4 L[ousi d'ors], then give it to him; I shall snag them back from him when we come together in Paradise. To the high and most honorable Herr *Patres fratres,*[4] etc., etc., Edmund, the H[err] Pastor of Hettingenbeuren, and Herr Wirth *salute plurimam.*

Your

Most obedient son Joseph

[P.S.] *à propos:* instead of the former address *à l'hotel de Marigni,* etc., put *à l'hotel de l'Ambassadeur de Suède, Rue du Bac.*[5]

COMMENTARY

Original Buchen, Bezirksmuseum. It would seem that Kraus was having a rather good time sampling everything that Paris had to offer a young gentleman. The dismal, cold, damp weather was the result of the eruption of the Laki volcano in Iceland.

1. Orig. *Ein wenig zu viel geportirt,* meaning that he had drunk too much porter, apparently Kraus's favorite ale. The resultant *Rheumatismus* is thus to be interpreted as a hangover.

2. From Kraus's glib comment, apparently his confession of a love interest provoked a strong reaction among his family members.

3. Meaning to write him a letter, with "home" referring here to Kraus in Paris.

4. *Patres fratres* = Father brethren, i.e., monks or pastors; *salute plurimam* = are all saluted together.

5. Kraus is now staying at the Swedish legation; the ambassador is Erik Magnus Staël von Holstein (1749–1802).

69. Letter to his parents dated Paris, 15 October 1784

Dearest Parents!

During the stay of our King, an intrigue arose here against our Director, who was here at the same time, that has now become so public that our ambassador has unabashedly come down on the side of the opposition and has spared, or rather, spares no effort to involve me. The a[sshole][1] knows that *Zibet* owes me the last two quarters of 3,300 Livres or 137½ Louis d'ors, and at the moment it is impossible to pay me, for he is staying at *Spa,*[2] and the a[sshole] wishes gladly to use this opportunity to advise me to participate in the complaints against Z[ibet] to the King. I will let it lie, for it is my Director that I have to thank for my entire fortune, and he is the only one who has heretofore defended me against all of the cabals – ingratitude such as this I would not forgive as long as I live.[3] Moreover, in order to force me against my will, the a[sshole] has denied me all aid and proclaimed quite flatly that he would be unable to advance me money. My honor and the honor of my Director are now hanging in the balance. Because the matter must occur as secretly as possible, I've no other recourse than to turn to you. I have therefore written my Director and in confidence said that, due to these circumstances, I would write to my parents. He and I would be eternally indebted therefore, if you would be able to help me at this time. In his last letter he promised that the entire sum will arrive here in a few months at the most. I can trust his word – and on that I promise you that as soon as I receive the money, I will immediately send it back to you. What I really need most immediately is 50 Louis d'ors or 550 Sk[illings], which translates to 1,200 Livres in the money here. Because the matter is so extraordinarily pressing, I have to ask you to take out a letter of credit for this sum as fast as possible in Frankfurt with *Bethman* or another *banker* and send it to me. If my dear mother would make the effort this time to travel to *F*[rank]*furt* herself to deal with the matter, I would be eternally grateful – my Director out of gratitude would already give me permission to travel to Germany a second time. NB, the letter of credit must have on it *a Vue*[4] and not at sight – that is to say – that it should be able to be paid out here as soon as I present it and not only after several weeks have passed. Dearest parents – if it is possible, please help, for I and my Director are truly devils roasting in the fire – the matter reminds me of a *Commission*.[5] Do your best and write me by the next post – I am walking around here and live on the mercy of God.

Your most obedient Joseph

COMMENTARY

Original Buchen, Bezirksmuseum. Kraus has clearly landed himself in the middle of a political mess. Although Cristoffer Zibet had long been involved in the various Swedish court intrigues, it seems that they probably boiled over during his absence from Stockholm, where the discredited clique surrounding the former intendant of the Royal Spectacles, Friherr von Barnekow, was fomenting unrest.

1. The identity of the *A:* (that is, *Arschloch*) is unclear, but it would seem from the following letter to be referring to the Swedish ambassador.

2. Spa (spelled "Spaa" by Kraus), a high-class resort town in Belgium today, where Zibet was apparently taking the cure.

3. Although Kraus's loyalty is touching, Zibet was not entirely honest in his dealing with Kraus, as it will turn out; he was quite liberal with the state funds that he was carrying.

4. *A Vue* of course means "at sight," but Kraus here is admonishing his parents to write it in French (hence the retention of his original).

5. The *Commission* was probably the matter of the diplomatic dispatches that Kraus was on the hook for when he arrived in France.

70. Letter to his parents dated Paris, 15 November 1784

Dearest Parents!

My dear mother, by my soul, your last letter has almost made me as anxious as you were with mine; and the bottom line on both sides is not half as dire. The true circumstance of the matter is this: because I have the right to take my quarterly salary always before the start of the quarter, I could have already asked for it on the 24th of June. At that time, the King was here, and our Director had to reach into his pockets all too often for certain matters in order not to have made it necessary to send to Sweden a second set of instructions regarding my requisition. During the last period of my Italian travels and those that I made through southern France, I restricted my small economy so much that I, God be praised, did not then need the disbursement so urgently – and now, in order to remove the usual thievery with the letters of credit in Stockholm and here from around his neck, I asked our Director upon his departure from here at the end of July to allow both quarters of my salary to be sent over from Spa, where he is now staying, along with the usual letters of credit, and to send it on from there. That I thought I could profit somewhat from this was the source of my uncomfortable position. My Director received the letters of credit, as I said, and forgot about me and lost the entire bunch of Swedish pennies gambling. Because prior to his departure and in my presence he expressly admonished and re-quested that our ambassador help me out in case of an emergency, he was unconcerned about me. In the meantime, the quarter came to an end and with it rent, etc., etc., had to be paid. The a[sshole], to whom I gave news of my predicament, did not refuse me completely, promising it as soon as the period was over. I trusted this – the time for payment came – and the a[sshole] became aware that Z[ibet] was in deep shit in Spa – and now he believed that this was the best opportunity to make a point. The first piece of advice from him to me was to write *directly* to the King – but I left that alone. And in order to force me to do it – he made excuses that he politely regretted that due to his own poor *economic* state he was not in a position of being able to help me out, etc. – Now the time had become too short to write first to Spa, where I already knew beforehand that it was impossible for the D[irector] to be able to send help from there, and because he was awaiting travel funds, to await an answer first from Sweden would have taken even longer. I thus had no option but to turn to you – if the entire matter were to remain secret; for in any other case, I would have been able to turn to a Swedish banker here, but at that point the entire dirty laundry would have been aired. The fault therefore was not mine, *quod erat demonstrandum,* and thus I am not such a miserable, awful spendthrift as my mother believes – although I also don't have reason to present myself as a virtuoso in this realm either. Regarding the other huge worry with its replacement – I ask you once more and assure you on my honor not to be worried. As soon as Z[ibet] returns home, I have my money and you yours, and my beloved siblings a *small percent* [as well]. In the meantime, I thank my good father a thousand times for his love for me, and for the past eight days I have been earnestly praying to our loving God to present me with a fortunate opportunity to be able to be of service to Him for this. Is that not so, dear mother? Your Joseph has not forgotten his prayers! The expression that my good mother quotes from me in her letter, and which she so caustically dismisses, is not half the paradox that it appears to be. The opinion was this, that the first and most important portion of true devotion in trade is the direction of one's strengths received toward the practices that please God – and this is the first Commandment of the Gospels, and with this enough!

20 November

In the intervening [time] I've had to move.[1] The last eight days have been fattened up simply with packing and unpacking, carrying things here and there, buying wood, making small talk and quarreling with the bearers, etc. No matter: you can still address your letters to the *residence* of our ambassador, for they will thus more or less be delivered more safely than to the *Hôtel Languedoc, Rue Grenelle S[ain]t Honoré,* where I now live. Now I am back on track and going about my work, and I hope that it will go well, otherwise, if things don't rain on it. There were still a few little items in my mother's letter of 25 Sept[ember] to answer. I will do it immediately so that I do not forget.[2] Regarding my affair of the heart, my dear mother has captured it in a little proverb: "Youth, it is said, appears to me to be so changeable that he himself doesn't know what is true about it or not." Correct! Second, it should be said that the news of my French story that depressed me for the past six weeks is meant only for our King alone and not at all for the merciful public here – at least, not as long as it is permitted for me to make my score known further. Third, I have the honor to assure you that Herr Vogler[3] has been boasting about quite horribly. He has supported his own high and mighty and expensive person here by giving lessons and instruction on the keyboard – as do his two pupils that he brought with him. Vogler had a single opportunity to perform before the Queen. For that he received, as usual, a gift and with this, things were finished. Thereupon he wrote two operas that won't be accepted, and if it concerns a journey, then he still has to borrow 80 Louis d'ors here. Would that not be fodder for a small printed anecdote in the newspapers? – Ah, well – if I weren't so lazy and comfortable, I would give you the pleasure of reading the entire marvelous thing by your Joseph in the Frankfurt rag,[4] and that will cost very little – it should only be what Vogler himself does – and thus I'll write my elegy myself. For, however, such a scurvy knave would be able to be considered higher than a head of cabbage, as has been done for him in Forkel's musical legends,[5] saying: Herr! *Ecce!* These are lies! – from which our dear God will in grace preserve me.

Your

own Joseph

COMMENTARY

Original Buchen, Bezirksmuseum. The quoted letter from Kraus's mother of 25 September has not survived, but it must have been quite stern, and the substance of Kraus's initial portion of his response was to placate his obviously worried parents by showing that his previous emotional outburst had somewhat diminished over the passing month. There is a certain sense of foreboding regarding Kraus's view of Abbé Vogler, who was to become part of the Stockholm saga in due course.

1. The new address is another sign that Kraus's relationship with the Swedish ambassador was not going well, although there appears to have been no real break, since he still believes that the legation could be used as a general delivery for mail.

2. The musical composition is unidentified.

3. Vogler was briefly in Paris on his tour of that year, probably hoping to revive the success he had back in 1782. Both the operas and pupils are unidentified. Shortly thereafter, however, the Swedish ambassador in Holland approached him with an offer to travel to Sweden, ostensibly as a replacement if Kraus did not return, as the rumors had it. It can be suggested that perhaps word of Vogler's availability came during the Paris stop from Staël von Holstein, possibly as a means of revenging himself upon Kraus's lack of compliance as part of the intrigues. There is no evidence that Kraus met Vogler in person in Paris.

4. Kraus finds Vogler's manner so abhorrent that he threatens to expose him in a German article; there is no evidence that he actually did so, however.

5. Johann Nikolaus Forkel (1749–1818), whom Kraus knew from Göttingen and with whom, according to Silverstolpe, he often debated the state of music.

71. Letter to his parents dated Paris, 3 February 1785

Dearest Parents!

It is only due to the fact that I am still awaiting the all-clear from Stockholm that I have delayed in answering your previous letter. My Z[ibet] is now back home – of that I've had news, but not everything is yet on a smooth track. It will play out how it will – I've made my decision in complete silence and it is resolute. I will not yet let out anything further, as long as it is not necessary, for I've been sent some money recently; but by far not that which I had a right to request, and then I've been asked quite politely in a little letter for forgiveness that everything transpired so irregularly, and the blame has been cast upon King Herod and his minions.[1] In the meantime, you should not worry – I will undoubtedly come myself and tell you the result of this entire nightmare, and then I hope to find you all together healthy and sound as you are now. My stomach and head are, God be praised, in good order for the moment. Sometimes there is such a gust of wind here that it blows a tile off the roof – but I am used to such things – and it is easy for one over the course of a decade to be buffeted about from all thirty-two wind directions and having one's hat blown off. By my soul, if there are times when I am in a fit of *spleen* – I take my pipe and sit down beside the stove – consider the story – as long as I am able to think – of how a child buys licorice and sugar paper for a Kreutzer at *Zubrodts*[2] – squashes the plums in the bag – plays at ninepins or three blind mice – learns the keyboard with the old Cantor, fiddle with the Rector, and how to bungle Latin – and like the day that my grandfather in the blue coat came to our main office in Buchen and looked me over from head to toe and told my father that he ought to buy me a pair of new black Lederhosen if I studied industriously – that day, when my father was in Miltenberg and closed the eyes of my good grandfather – how my mother cried when she learned of it – on that self-same morning that I served the old Deacon at Mass – who gave me a silver penny to comfort me . . . how the youth came to be in the hands of the Jesuits – and from time to time obtained his 30 Kreutzers from his good grandmother – that allowed him to be fed in Mainz with biscuits and cracked nuts – who went backward to Erfurt desiring to study to become a learned man – and then forced to return home to groom dogs, all the while the poor official had to put up with terrible anxiety – came to Göttingen – learned much, only not that which he was supposed to – set sail immediately thereafter to the north – and from there – going about hither and yon – and now is wading hat-in-hand with welted shoes through the Parisian mire – by my soul – that sometimes encourages me; for at least I am not following everyone in the adventure from the beginning to the Amen, and it is always such a comfort for a poor soul like mine.

Winter is quite impertinent here – but the price of wood is even more so. I already burnt up 4 Louis d'ors worth – now I am well into the fifth, and I am able only to warm my front side at one time – for me to include my backside, I have to turn about my stove as if I were on a spit – it's then that I often think of my Amorbach room!

My servant traveled to Germany a week ago – have a good trip! – now I am my Johann[3] myself and am quite happy with it. It was for me that I had a pair of boots on my legs from Kronenberg to Göttingen – and – what is most probable – they were still unpaid for – [I] would therefore like to ask you if you wouldn't mind paying him off in order to spare me a week of purgatory. I kiss my siblings with all my heart – as soon as I can send something, I will.

Please give my best regards to Herr Cavalry Captain Bingel[4] – it is a delight and pleasure in the eyes of God when one tobacco fancier thinks of another.

Always
Your most obedient Joseph

COMMENTARY

Original Buchen, Bezirksmuseum. Kraus gives no reason for this auto-biographical sentimental journey, save that one might imply a certain sense of homesickness.

1. "King Herod" probably refers to Barnekow, and his minions would be the anti-Kraus cabal.

2. Orig. *Zuckerpapier*, or a type of thin sweet candy wrapper; Zubrodt is obviously a bakery.

3. Orig. *Mein Johannes*, a reference to the quirk of celebrating his birthday on the nameday of St. John the Baptist.

4. Captain Bingel is unidentified, but probably a family friend.

72. Letter to Roman Hoffstetter dated Paris, 3 February 1785

It is not right that you deal so strictly with your friends. Must they first answer everything before you write back? Dear man! Do not do so again, for I love you too much to have to set you among the class of normal *correspondents*. For – that I would have forgotten about you, you should not really believe – that would be insulting to me, as a result, etc. You have *Piccinni's Didon* – that pleases me.[1] It is one of the most magnificent pieces that can be found on today's lyrical stage. The most excellent scenes are the third in the second act, the chorus in the sixth scene of the same act, the trio in the next scene; the first, third, and finally the fifth and last scene of the third act. Yesterday there was a *Concert spirituel*. The symphony by Haydn was the most popular and the execution quite good. M[ademoise]lle *Wendling* and an Italian tenor called *Giuliano* were whistled off stage. *Danner* and another Italian violinist named *Giuliani* were generally applauded. A sinfonia concertante by the brothers and sons *Thonberg* won approval. The concerto on the bassoon by *Devienne* was so-so.[2] The theater has been closed through the end of Lent, and the

Concert *spirituel* open daily – now there will be something to hear there. I will keep a special diary about this, and I promise you a copy of it. We recently received two new operas – by Piccinni, *Diane et Endymion,*[3] that didn't really please. The second by *Grétry* with the title *Panurge,* in the same taste as *Caravan,* a comic *piece* written in Grétry's usual taste,[4] has become half-jokingly a favorite piece of our public. Write to me soon about what is new there – why do you remain so quiet about yourself? Haven't you done anything new? – Answer me soon and – with more than I ask. Anything that I remain guilty in writing about I promise you I will bring to you orally.

Fare well and love always

Your

Kraus

COMMENTARY

Original Buchen, Bezirksmuseum. This letter, lacking a salutation, was probably included in the letter of the same date to his parents.

1. Kraus is probably referring to a score of the opera that Hoffstetter obtained for his collection of music.

2. The program of the Concert spirituel, the Parisian public concert series, is quite varied. Which Haydn symphony is not mentioned, though one of them was usually on the program. The people are Dorothea Wendling (1736–1811), composer Christian Franz Danner (1757–1813), violinist Giovanni Francesco Giuliani (ca. 1760–1828), and composer François Devienne (1759–1803); the tenor Giuliano remains unidentified, but the "Thonbergs" are a misspelling of the brothers Bernhard Anton (1742–1814) and Gerhard Heinrich (1745–1819) and cousins Andreas Jacob (1767–1821) and Bernhard Heinrich (1767–1841) Romberg, all of whom performed in 1784–1785 with considerable success at the Concerts spirituels. The sinfonia concertante was performed probably by all four, though it remains open who composed it.

3. Niccolò Piccinni's *Diane et Endymion* premiered 7 September 1784.

4. Grétry's operas are *Panurge,* which premiered on 25 January 1785 and *Le Caravane de Caire* from 1783; the former was later to create a scandal at the Royal Opera in Stockholm when it was produced at the beginning of the nineteenth century.

73. Letter to Anton Klein dated Paris, 7 February 1785

It would probably be yet another six months before you would receive a letter from me, if I had not just now decided to write whatever comes to my pen. Of course, there is no lack of trivialities here, and seldom does a day pass that something does not come to the attention of the attentive observer in some fashion that is worth seeing in a report; this would fill numerous diaries and many *letters to friends* if one cannot find it in the plethora of patronized journals, in which the learned merchant Jew picks up every little bit of sprouting grain in order to sell it again at the next opportunity to their domestic or foreign mercantile partners. For example, I had already intended to discourse with you on a bit of news on the theatrical-political history of Beaumarchais's *Figaro:*[1] but a journalist scooped me and demolished my joy, and thus I had to go on to other pretty things, and it will undoubtedly always be so, if I am not willing to get up out of bed before God's beloved sun and attend to writing (insofar as I would have the honor of being the first messenger) – but against which sin Heaven should protect me most mercifully. But from now on I will forgo the honor. Of course, I do not doubt that you have our journals and therefore are equally as acquainted with our scholarly and unscholarly events as we are, that is, up to a point – and it is no matter – but at least you will see my good opinion. Thus, for this time take note of single dissection of the opera *Didone* – an opera that has become one of our favorite pieces of our public and (what is more) has earned it so completely. The libretto is by Marmontel, the music by Piccinni.[2]

Madame de Saintonge and Desmarets[3] already arranged this story at the end of the previous century for the opera here, as did M[onsieur] le Franc de Pompignan[4] for the French stage. Marmontel is based upon both, and the noble simplicity of his outline and his great care not to diminish the eye of the observer with the filler material of eternal scene changes and superfluous ballets gives the music an opportunity to go directly to the heart. Both have so integrally worked with each other toward their goal that I cannot trust myself to compare it with another work, such as Alceste, which must half-lose during the completion of the plot what it otherwise would gain with regard to certain musical beauty. *Dido* was performed for the first time on the 16th of October 1783 at Fontainebleau, and on the following December brought to the great stage here. The drama has three acts, which the nature of the selection confirms. For the first, Dido loves Aeneas. But a sad presentiment tells her beforehand that she will be unlucky in love. She still hears the voice of Siché, her murdered husband, who threatens her with revenge. But – what are the presentiments to someone in love? Bright, like the sun between thunderheads, the picture of her beloved wells up in her soul, and all of the horrible phantoms vanish – "O toi, dont mon cœur est charmé, pardonne une erreur fugitive. Je ne serois si craintive, sit u n'étois pas tant aimé." – Piccinni has delivered with this transition already the most intimate and exact outline of his character in the piece.

Dido has arranged a hunt. The friendly intent is to be able to seek out with Aeneas the same sort of grotto where she formerly swore love on Juno's immortality. The brave people celebrate the upcoming union, when Aeneas appears, bringing with him the news to the court of the arrival of proud Jarbas. Of course, the moment the hero enters, one wishes to become acquainted with him. One does, but certainly not to his advantage, and the reason why is that the poet has done his best to portray the natural tendency of this weak and eternally indecisive man, who subsequently plays the hero throughout the entire piece. Of course, it would have been preferable to me if one had been able to remain faithful to the story without bringing on stage such an unlyrical bland soup; and as little as I had known of Aeneas other than in Virgil, I could have surmised that one could have done something better with the character in the case of necessity.

Jarbas arrives incognito under the name of his own ambassador. An arrogant boy, it is true, but (with the exception of Dido) probably every lady would have preferred him for all of his pride than that poor sinner like the hero of the piece. Jarbas allows Dido to remain in her present state as a widow, if she finds it appropriate; but if in case she, as rumor has it, proceeds so far as to desire to give her hand to an exiled Trojan Prince, he threatens to return as an enemy. Dido places her faith in the son of Cytherea, and assures the Herr Ambassador that it is one and the same whether his Numidian majesty wishes to love or be angry. "Ni l'amante, ni la reine, ne veut fléchir sur la loi. Je dispose en souveraine de mn empire et de moi. Le droit affreux del la guerre ne s'étend pas sur mon cœur; et le vainqueur de la terre ne seroit pas mon vainqueur." The music to these verses is so magnificent and powerful that one gladly forgets that it would perhaps have been more accurate if the strophe had been treated as a recitative rather than an aria. Dido distances herself; Aeneas will do the same, but Jarbas holds him back. "You would thus be the one who will make Dido happy?" The hero finds it appropriate to lie: "*J'ignore et mon destin & le choix de Didon*," as if he had forgotten the scene in the grotto, where he shortly before had spoken with Dido with tenderness. I take offense with the poet; for once he has taken the knights of the tournament as the model for his Aeneas, he must necessarily have known therefore that the greatest sin of all was to lie about courtly love. Jarbas too doesn't believe the story, even though it pleases him at the moment, and declares in his own inimitable courtly manner that he would wish that the knight would clear off. Aeneas doesn't want to, and of course a heated discussion breaks out, and Jarbas takes off his mask. "*Jarbas est devant toi.*" Aeneas answers: "*Je n'ai donc plus rien à t'apprendre, et Didon seule ici peut me donner la loi.*" Truly, this is an ignoble answer completely against the old custom, where, without further ado, one would have taken up the sword; here my two people settle down opposite one another and hurl the rudest insults at each other for a measured period. The nonsense stems from a misunderstood rule of Italian opera, in which the retreat of each of the most prominent stage actors must happen with pomp and circumstance. Should this not be able to occur without so unmercifully cramming the heart and ear with duets? – When I heard this for the first time in Gluck's first Iphigenia, it reminded me of Graun's "*Tal odio,*" etc., in [the opera] *Gli due fratelli nemici*[5] – a very cheerful little example! Aeneas leaves Jarbas alone, and then he [i.e., Jarbas] complains of his quandary to his father, Jupiter, and with this the first act ends. The principal requirement that in the first act one must get to know the characters was fulfilled enough by the poet and composer. But another question might be whether the predisposition of each character was done lyrically enough? Weak characters are already so foreign to musical epics that the contrast doesn't have any effect at all as in a [stage] tragedy. Experience tells me about this, however, that an indecisive character is even more unmusical than a weak one. I take Aeneas as an example, and whoever wants to have even more of them only has to look up Metastasio. Perhaps one can postulate why Italian singers work with their composers so diligently into a single club, singing Cato, Cyrus, Semiramis, and Titus as if they had all gone to the same school.

Act II. Aeneas leaves Elisa, the sister of Dido, to guess the origins of his anxiety; and she does it, which gives honor to the comprehension of this woman. The hero therefore has nothing left to keep secret from her. "He is in love; but at the recent sacrifice of his people the flames froze on the altar and a terrible sigh was heard from the sacrificial animal." The priest, with his eye directed toward Lazio,[6] explained the omen; it is there, he says, where we ought to make a sacrifice. People, tear apart the bonds that keep you here, and your obedience will placate the gods! – In this way, it is decided to leave Carthage. "*Plaignez un roi, plaignez un père, à qui son destin fait la loi. Suis-je, hélas, suis-je encore à moi? Didon me sera toujours chère; mais je fuis père & je suis roi.*" This aria has a magnificent vocal part; I would only have liked for the composer to have omitted the repetition of the last verse, because it is too wretched and of lesser worth than the original portion of the aria, and, what is the most annoying, it is impossible to declaim correctly.

Aeneas leaves it to Elisa to prepare Dido for his departure. But she thinks to make a completely different use of this confidence. "Jarbas (she argues, but note well, *à part en sortant*) has no further reason to rage, when he hears that his rival will withdraw." – Thus quickly [go] to the Numidian king with the news before he has a chance to begin his enmity. Aeneas is now alone. He feels his misfortune, is jealous that someone other than himself will come to possess so many perfections; but simultaneously he desires both his own best interests and those of Dido; but considers it probable that Dido will not easily change her old inclination: No – he gives her back her freedom and absolves her heart from all entanglements: Ah! – but not her pride – he must fear her love: he has too earnestly earned the forgetfulness of her breaking heart in order to be able to have the right to dare to complain about it: No – she shall be free! "My God, my God" – what rubbish! – the "thus the forgetfulness of her breaking heart" etc. is truly both unpoetic and unphilosophical. (Friend, parenthetically, I must extemporize on an old Italian tragedy called *Holofernes il buzzo*.[7] Before the general looks too deeply into his glass, takes himself off to bed, and his chamberlain stands around awaiting orders to clothe his lord, the poet has noted that at this point only beautiful and good things are to be brought to him, *monologice* or *diologice*[8] – for he says, when one has drunk a bit, it is easier on the lungs and thus many truths will be revealed that have remained bottled up forever – and it is also more comfortable for the actor, who in this instance is well-disposed to allow his lines to hang together, which would be quite unlikely here and would cause the interest to wane in general – Thus, after a little verse with a few times of *si-si;* after the next, *no-no,* and so forth – it lends strength to the lines.)

Dido arrives. Her people are inflamed by courage, desiring to skewer their common enemy. Aeneas, however, is of the opinion that things are not so dangerous. *"Jarbe demande à vous voir; déja son orgueil se modère."* How does Aeneas know that Jarbas wants to see Dido one more time? Does Aeneas know that Elisa[9] has betrayed his confidence? And this is simultaneously the only motivation for Jarbas to discover Aeneas's deception for the Queen! But, listen to Dido; the question is about Jarbas: *"Qui? Moi, le flatter! Moi soufrir qu'il pretend à ses vœux que mon amour répondre! Non, quand il auroit à m'offrir le trône et le scepter du monde. D'une guerre sanglante il nous a menace; je l'attends, vos dangers vont me remplir d'alarmes;a – mais, ces cruels moments passes, ah! Combine la victoire aura pour moi des charme! quel bonheur! Ces bien faits tant de fois retraces,par un seul aujournd'hui seront tous effaces. Je n'aurais plus sur vous ce pénable avantage; de vos mains, à mon tour, je vais tout reçevoir; ma gloire, mon repos, le salut de Carthage, c'est moi qui vais tout vous devoir."* Now the following aria: *"Ah! Que je fus bien inspire, quand je vous reçus dans mon cour! O digne fils de Cythére! Combine je rens grace à l'amour! J'ai beau le voir, je crois à peine ce que Venus a fait pour moi,"* etc. I don't know whether this aria would appear to you as flat as it did to me. Too, the great composer has apparently only used the situation, and one is hardly in a position to be annoyed at the vacuous compliments that the poet has put into the mouth of Dido. For such an aria from the lips of such a Dido as Saint Hubertus![10] – I would regard a steadfast man as human if he faltered – and I would gladly forgive my superstitious Aeneas if he forgot everything, everything about dreams, presentiments, predictions, etc. – but, by my soul, that would be a sin against nature to sigh a poor *"Hélas"* to her in answer to all this, and to allow himself to tell a lie in answer to the cry of Dido: *"Vous soupirez! Quell funeste image!"* [by saying] *"Les Dieux ma sont témoins que l'absence, le temps, rien ne peut de mon cœur effacer votre image; que je brûle pour vous des feux les plus constans.*" – "Why an explanation, [and] why this one?" Dido asks. ("For a heart such as mine a glance is sufficient.") Aside from the sinner Aeneas, this scene is a masterpiece of love. Anyone who has felt something similar in his breast would come, warm himself, and revere the resurrection of the happy moments enjoyed earlier. I thank the poet with all my heart for the opportunity that he has given the composer here to become immortal. Of course, it takes a St. Hubertus to be able to make such a thing comprehensible to one, and unfortunately – such fortune is offered to so few composers. Upon the command of the Queen, Aeneas calls his Trojans together for the ceremony of marriage. Jarbas uses this moment in his absence to discover the important secret concerning his beloved that Elisa had whispered into his ear. But because the news seems entirely improbable, Dido doesn't believe him how serious it is and assures him that, if King Jarbas will only forgive her a bit, he will have the pleasure of attending the nuptials. Jarbas answers: "*Tremblez donc, il est temps: mes coups vont éclater.*" Aria: "*je veux les voir réduire en cendre, ces murs où l'on m'ose insulter. Du trône où je devais monter, je vous forcerai de descendre. Je veux les voir réduire, etc. Je veux qu'erant fut ce ravage, et ne reconstrant sur les pas qu'un desert aride et sauvage, l'étranger demande Carthage, la cherche, et ne la trouve pas.*" – The last picture is certainly not new, but the music is life itself. One wanders among the ruins aimlessly with the searching eye of a pilgrim looking for traces of the former Carthage – searches in vain and is finally horrified by the remains. In the sixth scene, Dido reveals her decision to bind together her fate and that of Aeneas forever; her people and the Trojans should be united with her Prince at their head. The choral dialogue is a masterpiece and has such an effect that it is impossible to comprehend it without having heard it in person. The Carthaginians are filled with fire and courage to defeat their enemy under the leadership of the divine offspring. The Trojans surround their Aeneas, remind him of the fate of Troy and his son – of the command of the gods to lead them to Lazio. Aeneas becomes depressed – Dido notices it – demands an explanation – and Aeneas is finally forced to show his true colors. He does it, but in such a way that his manner is unclear – at the same time, it is clear enough for Dido to become angry. The chorus is silenced and at her command leaves Dido alone with Aeneas and her sister. I cannot remember seeing any other similar chorus with the same effect than in *Armide*: "Un seul guerrier!" There was a time when I was against any action in the chorus, and I had at that time aesthetical reasons for it; [but] this [and] the one in *Günther*: "*Sturm, machte mich wanken,*"[11] both finally made me whole, thank God. Now Dido confronts our hero more closely and finally learns what she feared to know. – "*Il est donc vrai!*" – if you hear these four words performed by St. Hubertus, you would bet your life and soul that you would feel completely the horrible situation. Now Aeneas recites the entire sermon that he presented to Elisa in the first scene of this act, only with the difference that he speaks of a completely different predicament than before – probably not only to say the same thing twice. He says now that his father has appeared to him in a dream, etc. Dido: "*Ah! Si l'erreur d'un songe effrayoit une amante, que ne m'ont point prédit les enfers et les cieux? – Vous parlez de sermens: crédule amante! Hélas! Il en est donc pour vous de plus saints que les notes?*" (Aeneas aside): "*O devoir! O tendresse, o pénibles combats!*" Does not the Queen speak here like a man and the man like a woman?

The trio that follows subsequently has a wonderful text. Dido is overwhelmed by the pain and sinks into the arms of her sister. How truly the composer has sensitively followed through with the most intimate gradations of the sorrowful situation of Dido right up to her complete faint, I am not able to describe to you at all. – Of course, the effect of this scene depends for the most part on the way it is performed, and this cannot admit even once the most superficial degree of mediocrity. But in order to be able for you to visualize the most comprehensive portrait of this tableau, I would wish for you to see Dido lying upon the breast of Elisa. Yet again she casts a tearful eye toward her beloved and says: "*Sans voir ton crime et mon outrage, laisse-moi mourir dans ses bras.*" Friend, I have seen the opera more than fifteen times and never were my eyes dry at this place.

Dido is awakened by the noise of the people, who call upon the hero to lead them against the Numidians, who are approaching, and with this the second act closes.

Act Three. The battle is not yet decided. Dido, who always perceives it as impossible that such a beautiful soul as Aeneas could really be a liar, frets now only about the danger in which her lover is now placed, and her first and last wish is "*Je ne veux del la victoire, que le retour du vanqueur.*" The aria "*Hélas! Pour nous il s'expose*" is excellent, inimitably and truthfully declaimed. – Her wish is fulfilled. Aeneas comes back victorious. Jarbas is killed and Carthage avenged. Now the face of the Queen is more hopeful, and the sweet thought that this due to all that her Aeneas has done is reward for her previous worry. But "*au comble de la gloire, au lilieu des plaisirs, quand rien ne manqué à nos desirs. Enée! Ah! De quells yeux tu revois ton amante!*"

Aeneas now has another story prepared. "Of course, Jupiter's son fell beneath my sword – but the father, in order that he be avenged, will part us from each other forever. The earth still reeks of the blood of Jarbas, even as the roar of the thunder announces the arrival of Mercury – the Messenger of the Gods brought to me the expressed command of the God of Gods – *Didon! C'est nes point un prestige.*" Dido: "*Non: c'est un indigne detour.*" This is the only answer that Aeneas can expect, and for once the poet has placed his hero in the ignoble position of having lost all faith and belief with the audience. Dido now feels the enormity of this insult, and because this scene is one of the most important in the actual preparation of the catastrophe; it is therefore necessary to follow its progress step by step up to the moment when the first thoughts of destruction arise in the soul of the unfortunate one. Dido: "*Quel prix de tant amour! Perfide! En me voyant si foible, si crédule, que ne m'annonçois-tu ton funeste dessein? Indigne du feu, qui me brûle, pour quoi l'avois-toi-même allumé dans mon sein? Aux manes d'un époux tu me rends infidelle; tu me fais de vingt rois blesser l'orgueil jaloux; pour toi seul . . . mais fautil que je les rappelled, ces bienfaits, dont l'oubli m'auroit été si doux?*" Aeneas casts the blame on the unmerciful gods. Dido: "*Qu'ai-je donc fait, cruel à tes Dieux, à toi-même, pour déchirer un cœur qui t'aime? Ai-je embrace les murs qui t'ont donné le jour?*" etc. . . . . "*Mon crime, hélas! C'est mon amour.*"

> Aria
> *Ah, prends pitié de ma foiblesse,*
> *Et du désespoir ou je suis,*
> *Qui consolera mes ennuis,*
> *Si ta cruauté me délaisse?*
> *J'en mourrai, tu n'en peux doubter,*

Et cette mort sera sanglante.
Daigne au moins, ah, daigne écouter
Les derniers soupirs d'une Amante,
Que pour jamais tuvas quitter.

Here is the first intimation of the terrible decision. But, friend, you should have been among the observers of this scene, seen her moved by the fine sensitivity of the composer, as he understood and maintained the impression of this important position. You would not have been able to hear without trembling the words: "Cette mort sera sanglante." The picture of the unfortunate already appears to be bloody before your eyes, and from this instant your soul would only be directed toward the fate of Dido.

Aeneas now cries out: "*Dans ce cœur malheureux que ne pouvez vous lire?*" – Dido: "*Non, je le vois, ton cœur n'a plus rien à me dire. Hé bien, je me soumets à mon sort regoureux.*" – It is only to go to meet death with more resignation that she asks Aeneas to remain behind for a few moments longer. "*Votre invincible cœur m'enseigne la constance, et je veux l'apprendre de lui.*" Aeneas: "*Didon, plus je diffère, et plus le mal augmente. N'attirons pas sur nous la colère d'un Dieu.*" Such a moral of little comfort for a heart like Dido's – and in her situation. – She answers: "*Va! Pour ta course vaga-bonde, hât-toi de te preparer. Remonte sur ces mers qui nous vont séparetr; va chercher l'Italie, errant au gré de l'onde. Il saura me benger, ce perfide element. Triste jouet des flots, des vents et de 'orage, environné d'écueils, menace du naufrage: tut e repentiras dans de fatal moment, d'avoir aban-donné le tranquille ravage, ou l'amour t'auroit fait un desting à ta pensée; tu gémiras,ingrate, de l'avoir offense tu l'appelleras vainement.*" Aeneas: "*Quelques dangers que me prepare, lesort qui m'accable aujourd'hui; un cœur qui de vous se separe, n'a plus rien à craindre de lui.*" – Dido: "*C'en est donc fait, Enée? . . . O funeste silence! . . . L'insensible! . . . Et Venus te donna naissance! Non, par les tigres allaité ton cœur en a la cruauté. Délevre-moi de ta presence, fuis. Mais tremble, cruel! Mon ombre te suivra. A toute heure, en tout lieu, fut-ce au bout de la terre, je te livre en mourant une éternelle guerre, et ma fureur me srvivra. Puissent remaitre de ma cendre des vengeurs attérés du sang de neveux. Qu'ils protent le fer et let feu aux rives où tu vas déscendre; c'est là le dernier de mes vœux.*" – She goes.

Absit everything that a commentator might state here is superfluous; but those that have seen and heard this scene in Paris, I tell you, these would certainly have forgotten the poet for the sake of the composer, and for the living and fiery action that no other than St. Hubertus exhibits, these would forget themselves, poet, composer, and everything else that we call art. One would see and hear only the Queen of Carthage, reserving for her alone all of his emotions.

Aeneas is on the verge of reversing himself, when the poet hurries to introduce a last resort, a deus ex machina that one can easily excuse. Anchises rises up out of the earth. You can judge for yourself how wisely the poet has used him. Aeneas: *"Que vois-je? L'ombre de mon père! Approchons: je frémis. Tous mes sens son glacés. Mon père, ai-je des Dieux mérité la colère?"* The Ghost: *"Le ciel commande. Obéissez!"* Aeneas: *"Hélas! Au désespoir je reduis une reine, de qui la bonté souveraine a souvé d'Ilium les debris disperses."* The Ghost: *"Le ciel commande. Obéissez!"* The shade vanishes and Aeneas continues: *"Cédons au pouvoir qui m'entraîne. Dieux terribles, vous m'y forcez!"* He goes – my thoughts are that this is a model for all ghost scenes that can be performed on the lyrical stage.

In the next that follows with thunder and lightning, one sees the hapless Carthaginians fleeing and the Trojan fleet sailing from the Phoenician harbor. Dido, wounded and distraught, enters, sees the furled sails, and falls into despair, raging: "Il m'échappe!" she cries, *"If fallit l'enchainer sur la rive, brûle sa flotte, avant qu'elle pût s'éloinger; dans le sang de son fils, dans son sang me baigner, enfin mourir vengée; ou du moins* (Women!) *en captive, le suivre où le destin le condamne à regner,"* ... Another look from on high at the sea that bears off her betrayer, – an overwhelming feeling that hope is folly – and then the decision to die. In order to pull off the completion of her decision, she has to disarm her courtiers and sister. She thus commands the priests of Pluto to prepare for a sacrifice to the shade of her husband. Left alone, she says: *"Je veux mourir. Je veu, pour déchirer son ame, la render téoin de ma mort. Je veux qu'en s'éloignant de ce funeste bord, le bûcher de Didon l'éclaire de sa flame – il sentira peut-être au moins quelque remord."* Then she gives her followers everything that Aeneas has left behind in terms of weapons and clothing, so that they can be burnt in the flames of the bier with her "pour détruir à jamais un souvenir funeste." Once more she embraces her sister. "*Ma sœur, embrassez-moi; je vais trouver enfin le repos après tant d'alarmes.*"

Usually, silence reigns at this juncture among the audience – to the solemn, grave music of the chorus of high priests, Dido ascends the pyre – lays the weapons of the Trojans around her, and says: "*Toi que j'ai tant aimé, qui m'as fait tant souffrir, hélas! Que n'avois-je à t'offrir cet empire éclatant où le destin t'appelle! Pardonne à ma douleur cruelle les vœus ensensés qu j'ai faits. Dieux! Oubliez-les à jamais.*" She sticks the dagger in her breast and falls – people run to her aid – in vain. – One more sigh for Aeneas and then her cares vanish forever. The priests light the pyre, and with swords held over the rising flames, the people swear revenge upon the Trojans and their descendants. The End!

The opera *Didone* is without doubt the most excellent opera by Piccinni and exceeds by far everything that we know in this genre by him; and what is more – he is perhaps the only one who has achieved the first rank among both comic and tragic composers. In general, the poet has used his entire repertory here as much as possible, and among the contemporaneous collaborators for the lyrical stage [he] is probably the best. And now another little word about him – You well know that he, the star of the anti-Gluckists, is the author of the brochure *Essai sur la revolution de la Musique en France.*[12] You have certainly also read the various small biting answers to this by the Gluckists, for example: *Le réponse d'un chanteur de l'opera – d'un hermite de la forêt de Senart – d'un gentilhomme allemande,* etc. But perhaps the bitter satire of a certain *Urlubrelu*[13] is lesser known, for the small pamphlet is now somewhat rare. The author possibly knew the weak side of the great academicians, for he loves money more than reputation, and thus for the year 1777 did a calculation of the income from the piece *Procris et Céphale* and one of the single pieces by Gluck. Here is an example of the comparison: "*Le mardi, 3. Juin, on donna à l'opera Céphale – la rente fut à 777 liv[res], Vendredi le 6, Iphigenie de Gluck, 3,265 liv[res] 10 s[ous]; dimanche le 8. Céphale donna 554 l[ivres], mardi le 10, 1,41 l[ivres] 10 s[ous], vendredi le 13., Alceste de Gluck donna 4,309 l[ivres] 10 s[ous], dimanche le 15, Céphale 625 l[ivres] 10 s[ous], vendredi 420, Iphigenie 4,400 l[ivres].*" Subsequently the income from Marmontel and Grétry's *Procris* 3,357 L[ivres] and that of Gluck's pieces 14,655 L[ivres], with the addition rather simple – but the conclusion of the artist is more or less none other than Pasquill[14] – and that is as it should be.

The latest operas for this year and the end of the previous are: 1) *Diane et Endymion* by M[onsieu]r le Ch[evalier] *de Liroux*[15] with music by Piccinni. After several performances, the author retracted the piece again, for it did not please the public in its first form. The opera was recently given again – the public seemed more satisfied with the collaboration of both authors than with the changes. Because the fault lay with the plot, it would be difficult to help it further. 2) *Dardanus* by Sacchini[16] – which had the misfortune to fail completely. It is really something very unpleasant for this famous composer always to choose mediocre librettos. You can read in last Saturday's *Mercure*[17] the last admonition that was given to him for this. 3) *Panurge* by Morel[18] and Grétry. Last year both authors brought an opera comique of the same sort as *Caravane* to the stage. It is well-known that the comedy is more Grétry's thing than high tragedy – but why does he only have to write for the main Opéra? The poet took the plot from Rabelais's *L'île des lanterns,* and it is treated comically enough for the most part. I do believe, however, that it is unworthy of the style and archetype of the lyrical stage. With respect to the first opera *Caravane,* a parody with the title *Le marchand d'esclaves*[19] was given at the Théâtre Italien. The development of the opera is truly a deus ex machina; that is to say, the arrival of the father therein is clearly the only device of the poet. In the parody, the unraveler of the knot arrives in a balloon resting upon a theatrical sky chariot. The slave merchant has a couplet on this occasion, which I desire to make better known for the edification of our lyrical poets. Here you have it – *sur l'air: J'ai perdu mon âne:*

> De lettres avenues
> Ne nous sont pas inconnues.
> Car l'on voit de tems en tems
> Des pères et des dénouements
> Qui tombent des nües.

The public here was so convinced that this couplet belonged among the best of his theater pieces, that they allowed it to be repeated three or four times. Moreover Grétry has been extraordinarily industrious this year. Apart from both the pieces for the Opéra, he has written two operettas for the Italian theater, *L'epreuve villageoise* by Desforges[20] and *Richard Cœur de Lion*. The material for the last one has been taken from the well-known ballad: the English King returns from the war in Palestine – and due to an old grudge is arrested on his journey on the orders of an Archduke and secretly kept in a remote castle in Germany. Blanchard, his composer and friend, discovers his whereabouts through a song, etc. I don't need to say anything more to you about what the French have made of this – a commander appears, with whom the daughter of an Englishman, who is sojourning nearby, is in love. Then a countess of Flanders appears, whom Richard loves – and the plot is so miserable that it annoys one. But for this one it is compensated for by the music, which is filled with original beauties.

M[onsieur] *le Comte de la Cépede, des Academies et Sociétés royales de Dijon, Lyons, Toulouse, Rome, Stockholm, Hesse-Hamburg, München, etc.,*[21] who is already well-known as an author of physics, has recently published a *poëtique de la musique* in two rather hefty octavo volumes. Of course, it is in the first book that the fundamentals of aesthetics are treated completely – but may our dear God protect with His grace all artists from completeness. I would rather send the book along to you myself than summarize the long sermon.

Perhaps you know that Blanchard[22] has made a hot air ascent above the crowd. – He frequently visits our theaters in the company of his American companions in order to be applauded. And yesterday it was said that Pilatre had sailed off to London in his globe. He must have something greater in mind, for he has provisioned himself for six months.

Good night, dear friend
Your Kraus

COMMENTARY

Original lost; the letter was printed by Anton Klein complete in the *Pfälzisches Museum* 2:964–993. Silverstolpe produced a Swedish translation for *Stockholms Posten,* which appeared in three installments in 1805. From the style of the writing, it seems clear that Kraus expected it to appear in print and not as a private letter, thus the rather more detailed contents. In this instance, the present author has chosen to leave the French quotations untranslated, as they give a better feeling for his choice of words and overall tone.

1. Pierre-Augustin Caron de Beaumarchais (1732–1799). The play is his *Le marriage de Figaro* from 1781, which initially passed the state censor but was banned by Louis XVI once he had actually read it.

2. The opera *Didone* had its premiere in Paris on 1 December 1783 following the usual court performance at Fontainebleau. The librettist was Jean-François Marmontel (1723–1799).

3. Louise Geneviéve Gillon de Saintonge (1650–1718) and Henry Desmarets (1661–1741). Kraus misspells the composer's name as "Desinarets," though this may also be a typo by the publisher.

4. Jean-Jacques de Franc, marquis de Pompignan (1709–1784).

5. Kraus is referring to the opera *Gli due fratelli nemici* by Carl Heinrich Graun (1704–1759), composed in 1756.

6. Lazio = Rome or the province in which Rome is situated.

7. *Holofernes il buzzo* = Holofernes Beer Belly, or a street theater parody Kraus may have seen in Italy.

8. *Monologice oder diologice* = monologues or dialogues.

9. Orig. *Elise,* meaning of course the sister of Dido, but here Kraus or the publisher uses the German spelling.

10. Antoinette Cécile de Saint-Huberty (1756–1812), the singer who played Dido.

11. This refers to Holzbauer's *Günther von Schwarzburg.*

12. Published in Paris in 1777.

13. *Urlubrelu* = a turbaned foreigner.

14. Pasquill = a person against whom satirical anecdotes are directed (also a surname, though it is difficult to determine whether Kraus means a specific person here).

15. Jean-François Espic, Chevalier de Liroux (1740–1806).

16. Antonio Sacchini, see Letter 82.

17. That is the *Mercure de France,* the leading Parisian newspaper.

18. Etienne Morel de Chédeville (1747–1818).

19. The author of the parody was Jean-Baptiste Radet (1752–1830).

20. Pierre Jean Baptiste Choudard (1746–1806); his pen name was Desforges.

21. Bernard Germain de Lacépede (1756–1825). The pamphlet was published in Paris in 1785.

22. Jean-Pierre Blanchard (1753–1809), who made the first ascent in a hydrogen-filled balloon on 2 March 1784. Pilatre is Jean-François Pilâtre de Roziers (1754–1785), who made the first manned hot air balloon flight on 21 November 1783 in a Montgolfier balloon. He was killed on 15 June 1785 when his attempt to fly across the English Channel failed and he crashed near Calais. The identity of the American friends is not known, but Blanchard was known to have associated with Thomas Jefferson. It is entirely possible that Kraus met Jefferson at one of the theatrical occasions.

74. Letter to Johann Samuel Liedemann
dated Paris, in March 1785

What I have to answer to the first little page of your *Etwas für mich*[1] goes together so completely that I have decided that I must be clearer. From my confession of faith take anything you will; I promise at least that you will hardly have found anything shorter of this sort.

Up to my twentieth year I thought little or not at all, but allow [me] to express wisely in all fairness that I truly was no small thinker. With restless spirit and a rather strong constitution, I read just about everything, argued with a rather terrible melancholy about pre-destiny, and read the *Robinson*[2] alongside. I stretched out my small hands toward every object, and seldom grasped short, but rather reached out a span and often a fathom ahead. This is called enthusiasm for a dreamer. Another situation would have made me into a fanatic. Those who love fire, love when it is stoked by bellows quite nicely; naturally – and thus so naturally that when I bound myself to my first friend Hahn,[3] I bound myself forever. Thus the two children read fairy tales, declaimed Klopstock, fulminated against those who scorn religion, and scorched the solemnities of Wieland's *Agathon*,[4] and wiped the sweat from our brows after such strenuous work. He whose body was weaker and with a less stormy spirit than I finally became its sacrifice – I remained behind and vegetated and had a thousand laughs fricasseeing together two such separate concepts as I and the human, such as they were. This sounds a bit apocalyptic, no? –but there is simultaneously nothing less terrible on God's green earth. The jackass considers his own ego, and if it ever occurs to him to think about the human, it is nothing less to him than a correlative concept. Against my will I had finally to have the experience of misfortune, and – forced, I bound myself utterly to my ego and gave over the human to whomever it pleased. Whether or not I did ill or good in doing so is not the question, for once it can be answered by whether I was able to think some other way? A human being with such a prejudiced and small heart, I grant you, is more righteous than our beloved God, – with one such paltry heart that one friend can fill it and fill it completely – this human being is forever lost to every cosmopolitan thought – and that is my lot. I am not a philosopher enough to satisfy myself. Always and forever my existence depends upon that of another. But even less can I govern myself than a Catholic with his beloved God, who every day has to be divided into a million pieces. – Now friend, do I need to tell you now what I think of an institute whose main purpose is cosmopolitan?

Fare well, my dear fellow, and may the assurance be a little comforting to you that Kraus has only one friend.

COMMENTARY

Original lost, published in Si-JMK as Letter 38. The original salutation and perhaps significant portions of the text have been excised. Although Silverstolpe published two other letters to Liedemann from Paris, he destroyed five others to which the merchant had given him access. These were dated 17 July, 24 August, 7 November, and 28–29 November 1785, as well as 7 February 1786. In a footnote, Silverstolpe noted: "Because the reader cannot obtain a clear understanding of its purpose in this letter, which in turn would probably not lead to a portrayal of reality, and while it leaves behind no trace, the letter is nonetheless completely anomalous, in that during this time it displays the author's degree of education and emotions, his sharp judgmental content, and his specific character. It can be read through without correctly discovering its intent, but not without clearly seeing the person that speaks. The same is true for the next letter which is based upon a riddle, completely without resolution, but within which the character of the one speaking equally lies open and does much to interest the reader." Åstrand notes (HÅ-JMK, 183–184) that these letters were "probably filled with the effusion of emotions that characterized the adherents of the Sturm und Drang and much of the new German literature of that time," which may be a polite way of saying that Silverstolpe censored what may have been considered normal for the male-bonding cult taking place during Kraus's time but which in the following century could be seen as betraying unacceptable moral relationships. In any case, it does appear that Kraus is answering a philosophical conundrum that Liedemann passed on to him, personalizing it to some extent.

1. "Something for me."

2. "Robinson" refers to Daniel Defoe's *Robinson Crusoe*.

3. See Letter 13.

4. Christoph Martin Wieland, *Geschichte des Agathon,* a play published in 1766–1767.

75. Letter to his parents dated Paris, in April 1785

Dearest Parents!

I have once again waited a dozen post days and that for nothing. Everywhere here my friends ask when I might depart, and how? To where? – and to this very hour I have to leave the question unanswered. The waiting, of course, sometimes piques my blood a bit, but of what use is it? I have never relieved my situation by pouting about for a week; and found to be the better for it whenever I've been able to glimpse such an immediate and uncomplicated vision in my little future. It must remain this way, and I'd like to see a preacher come around to convince me that my little head would be a little less better for being less worried about things it cannot relieve. Basta! Therefore, have patience with me. Perhaps the entire thing will be solved soon, and perhaps not soon! So let it be! Sometime I shall have to go away, and in each circumstance I hope that dear God will not allow me to lack decisiveness. At least I can assure you that I have made every effort to bring this little song to a close – written letters – set both friends and enemies in motion, if only to do so much as only to wave the flag; but all in vain, and with some twenty-odd epistles that I have bombarded everyone everywhere with I have achieved nothing other than obtaining a glimmer of light from afar. Postmaster *Lidiin*[1] in Stockholm wrote me that everyone there was convinced I had decided never to return, and this reason Hallardt in Wismar had been brought very much against me. I expended every possible effort to discover the source of this rumor. In vain! At least now I knew why Hallardt has not written me for so long. Our correspondence is now once again in order, but he still only trusts me halfway and is simultaneously gracious enough to tell me that the majority of the acquaintances left behind in Sweden are working on my behalf. May all of the dogs eat themselves to death for nothing and less than nothing, so that they are able to have the pleasure of living out the few days that one is granted in embitterment!

Regarding Alois, we are of the same opinion and surely it is better for the kid to be in Mannheim than in Miltenberg. My honest old director[2] will love him for my sake, and I will thus love the beloved mentor of my brother – the half of it and even threefold more. May he become an honorable fellow immediately! And then enough! The remaining stuff is all child's play.

Please greet my beloved siblings and our other few friends from the bottom of my heart. I wish Vogler a pleasant trip. His mission to Dresden and Berlin is a strict evangelical calling – just about like that of the Spanish dogs in America who served the humanitarian European missionaries by harassing the poor Mexicans into being baptized.[3] It's quite a nice thing to be a charlatan – their handiwork provides food, coaches, and horses, and then here and there they can do a little sightseeing – but my mouth doesn't water after it. Fare well and always love me.

Your

Joseph

[P.S.] *À propos,* in order to have my address correct, you must write it as follows:

À M[onsieur] Kraus, maître de Chapelle du Roi de Suéde

à l'hôtel de l'Ambassadeur de Suéde

à Paris

It is thus correct French

P.S. Hallardt has been made Swedish Counselor of the Exchequer.

COMMENTARY

Original Buchen, Bezirksmuseum. The political difficulties have now infiltrated Kraus's personal life, resulting in an unusual display of the invective.

1. Anders Lidin Jr., postmaster in Stockholm 1763–1812.

2. The reference is to Kraus's early teacher, Pater Anton Klein.

3. This scurrilous reference to the Spanish conquistadors means that Kraus has heard that Vogler has been hired ostensibly as his replacement.

76. Letter to his parents dated London, 15 May 1785

Bored by the eternal waiting and in order not to become even more scurvy than I already am, boredom has whipped me over here. Several days after the letter that I wrote to you recently from Paris, it occurred to me as I lay in bed that it would be a rather lovely thing for my spirit and stomach to see a couple of English tragedies in London and to empty a few mugs of good porter to the health of myself and the Holy Roman Empire. The next morning I set out in a diligence[1] and arrived here in good health on the fifth day thereafter. Now I run about from about five o'clock in the morning until the evening as long as it is safe on the streets, from one corner to the next satisfying my eyes and ears. Damn! London is almost a quarter larger than Paris, but by far less noisy, and although the streets are far larger and more capacious, and the population numbers about 150,000 more,[2] it is on the other hand less accessible than Paris. But the site and the Thames make the thing so picturesque that one cannot dismiss as impossible the desire to be able to live here for a longer period of time. But – by my poor soul, everything is determined by my much-put-upon wallet, for every three days 3 Carolinas are spent, including the operas of course. Just consider, there is a young fellow by the name of *Bedfort,*[3] a lord at the age of twenty, who has an income of 100,000 Guineas. – By damned – I'd like to have such a sum for only one year – but by my life I wouldn't like to be in his shoes; for he is one of the prime idiots in all of Great Britain. Because meat, bread, and beer is proportionally not so expensive, I'd therefore let well enough alone. But I nonetheless fear that the little fellow will become too fat; I think I'll make an end to it and in fourteen days or at the most three weeks be back in Paris. You can safely send your letters to my old address; for I have made arrangements on my departure that they will be retained there quite nicely. Please tell my dear Hoffstetter that everything is going quite well here with our handiwork.[4] The famed festival at Westminster Abbey begins at the end of this week and consists of the best Handelian things, about which he will learn in time through the newspapers. If not – I'll tell him myself. There are already various invited and uninvited guests from Germany, France, and Italy, and even Spaniards and Poles who have come here for this. Day after tomorrow is another concert benefiting Fischer, Kramer, *Ferrarese, Tenducci,* and others. *Lolli*[5] is now here and there is no end to the dabblers on the keyboard. It is amazing that the English, who are otherwise such great lovers of the organ, say the same thing that the French say about Vogler.[6]

Our greetings to the honorable and especially good friends, which are father, mother, siblings, servants, Hoffstetter, and Häussler.

Your

Most obedient

Joseph

[P.S.] As stated, in three weeks at the most I am back in Paris.

COMMENTARY

Original Buchen, Bezirksmuseum. The letter lacks the usual salutation. One should not take it seriously that Kraus comments that he has only made the trip "out of boredom." As Swedish Kapellmästare, his attendance at such a widely publicized European event would have been carefully planned so that he could witness and comment upon the music. See the following letter.

1. A diligence is a large stagecoach.

2. The population of London in the 1801 census was 1,096,734, but estimated at 650,00 in 1750; the statistical mean implies that the actual population was about 800,000 during Kraus's visit.

3. Francis Russel, fifth duke of Bedford (1765–1802)

4. Normally "handiwork" is used by Kraus to describe his own compositions, but here it seems to be used in a more generic sense to indicate those pieces he has heard.

5. The Handel Centenary Festival (also known as the Handel Commemoration Festival) began on 2 June; the musicians are oboist Johann Christian Fischer (1733–1800), violinist Wilhelm Cramer (1746–1799), soprano Adrianna Ferrarese (ca. 1755–1804), castrato Giusto Fernando Tenducci (1736–1790), and the composer is Antonio Lolli (ca. 1725–1805).

6. An obvious slam at Abbé Vogler, who was becoming known for inventing odd organ-like instruments called orchestrions.

77. Letter to Pater Roman Hoffstetter dated Paris, 11 June 1785

À Monsieur Hoffstetter

[Here is] something more from the Handel *Universarium*.[1] The best pieces by him were 1) his *Te Deum*,[2] 2) Pious Orgies from *Judas Maccab[beus]*: 3) How excellent is Thy name o Lord, chorus from *Saul,* 4) several choruses from *Samson*[3] and 5) from *Joshua,* and 6) the most excellent, his oratorio of the *Messiah.* The entire musical ensemble consists of domestic players – and for that reason you must later revisit my earlier news. Here is the list: 106 violins, 28 violas, 28 violoncellos, 18 contrabasses, 6 flutes, 26 oboes, 28 bassoons, 2 serpents, 1 contrabassoon, 12 horns, 12 trumpets, 6 trombones, 4 pairs of timpani, 68 sopranos, 60 altos, 100 tenors, and 102 basses; in total 607 persons. Dear God, you can imagine how well they endeavored to make music in Westminster church. What made me wonder the most among this musical hodgepodge was that all of the *Messiah* up through the final Amen was performed so clearly. –Did they all come out of a monastery?[4] – Listen, dear friend, would you do me a favor and make your Herr Simsson quite aware of where the little bottle is to be found, from whence once your little Kraus quaffed such delightful nectar – for I would like to announce myself in as friendly a manner as opportunity permits.[5] Don't forget it, and don't shove the note on top of the long little shelf, for I would like to surprise you with it earlier than you might foresee. I thank the great man Vogler breathlessly for how graciously he has treated both you and I. – At least, that is not how he normally does it.[6]

Your own Kraus

COMMENTARY

Original in the collection of organist Johann Christian Heinrich Rinck (1770–1846). Published in a diplomatic edition in the *Archiv für Musikwissenschaft*.[S] Currently, the collection of letters is in the Yale University Library. It is unknown how or under what circumstances a letter to Hoffstetter wound up in Rinck's possession, though one does gain the impression that it may have been one of those the monk gave away later in his life. See Appendix D.

1. *Universarium* = Handel Centenary or Commemoration Festival of 1785.

2. Presumably the Dettingen "Te Deum," not the Utrecht "Te Deum."

3. Kraus spells the name *Simson,* perhaps confusing the English title with the name of a local barkeep in Amorbach; see comment 5.

4. Kraus is expressing his amazement at the precision with which the performances were conducted, giving an insight into the abilities of the English ensemble.

5. Herr Simsson is unidentified, but presumably a local barkeep, given the context. The announcement would be the gift of some wine, possible that mentioned in Letter 78.

6. Kraus is being sarcastic here, but the inference seems to point to the intrigues in which Vogler was involved back in Stockholm. Hoffstetter also clearly had some correspondence with Vogler, which has not survived, but from this reference one might surmise that the Abbé was condescending or insulting.

78. Letter to his parents dated Paris, end of September 1785[T]

I would rather get to it immediately, I think, so that I don't once again find myself in the position of allowing your letters to go unanswered another quarter of a year. These are, of course, just those months when one

S. Friedrich Noack, "Eine Briefsammlung aus der ersten Hälfte des 19. Jh.," *Archiv für Musikwissenschaft* 10 (1953): 324.
T. That is, probably on or about 30 September.

roams around the countryside to sniff out rabbits, pheasants, and God knows what else . . . but I don't want this to be seen as some sort of excuse; I've had such hustle and bustle around me all the time that I can never catch my breath. Now that it is the turn of the wind and weather to play, I stuff my pipe and return to my nest, and thus at least have the advantage of being reminded of one's obligations more easily. In order to relieve myself of the former, I have the honor of reporting that I am vegetating, am in good shape, and await my salvation. The reason that I didn't explain everything further to you than about my obvious predicament was simply because nothing exceptionally decisive came of it. For, you cannot take me seriously enough that I would disclose a more intimate confidence to others than to you. Why can I not say anything more concrete about my situation yet? – Truly, it is nothing meant for a letter, unless it were something as dire as a lawsuit. Does my little Marianne therefore take me seriously? . . . Damn! If a little indiscretion had not occurred, surely everything would have been arranged and perhaps even now I would even [see] its trees, meadows, brooks, men, women, birds, etc.

Unfortunately, my letter to Bethman[1] came too late, and I've already received it sent back. The matter was that a Swedish engraver was traveling from here on through Switzerland to Frankfurt; but he arrived too early for me and from there left far too quickly to be able to take care of my little packet. Something so long hidden, however, should not be so swiftly given.

Please tell me what my dear *Hofstetter* is doing? Why does he not write me anymore? Does he believe that just because he wants nothing more to do with his monastery accounts that therefore he is to rid himself *totally* of all his friends? Or does he not wish to be so dear to me anymore as he was before? By my poor soul, if he does not write to me within the month, I shall sit down and write the most horrible epistle in Latin that has ever been fabricated since the Flood to his high and mighty and most worthy Grace to drive him to it *ex obedientia*.[2] It will make hell quite hot for him and affect his conscience.

A magnificent King of Sweden,[3] well-fabricated in Rome set in good gold in a ring awaits my mother, and a good, real topaz set in enamel blue and gold for my dear father. Thunder and lightning, I wish I only knew how I could deliver the things home practically. It is obvious that such small considerations are third hand.

Dearest parents,

Your

Joseph

[P.S.] You have written nothing to me about my other siblings? Hopefully, the branches are in blossom, no?

COMMENTARY

Original Buchen, Bezirksmuseum. Unusually, here the salutation comes at the end of the letter.

1. Bethman is a banker, no doubt forwarding a letter of credit to repay Kraus's parents.

2. *Ex obedientia* = in complete obedience.

3. The *König von Schweden* is a Riksdaler. The remaining gifts are expensive and just the sort one might expect an upper-class Kapellmeister to be able to afford, although his mention of them undermines his earlier statements of economic difficulties.

79. Letter to his parents dated Paris, 23 October 1785

Again, freshly answered in order not to be stuck in the glue again. Although I cannot answer every question so exactly or with special emphasis, I'll try at least to summarize things. Concerning the principal matter, I hope that dear God is the only one who will forgive my stupid pranks;[1] for it is He alone who knows that I never sin from an evil heart. I pray to Him from the bottom of my soul, but what is better and perhaps a thousand-fold more pleasant to Him is that I love Him with all my heart; and everything else that comes in between these two points is secondary but no less important to me. That is my confession of faith for all time. Concerning my household economy, it is of course not the best. I am partly to blame for this, but in part so are other people. Naturally, I excuse the latter far less than myself. What could finally be said about my vocation is that I have as little to say as in my previous letter. In order to give you an explanation concerning my sojourn, I have received permission from home to write something for the stage;

but with the condition that the libretto must first have the approbation of our King.[2] And our Gustav regarded the thing as too thin and too dependent upon spectacle, and thus graciously dismissed it. I still have another one but therefore don't know whether I'll be called back perhaps during this winter or given permission to await better fortune. Every day I await letters, and hopefully these will decide the matter more precisely. Therefore, my dearest parents, don't worry over much on my account; things will happen, and if they don't go as they should, at least I'll come through this patch. Please ask my little Marianne to write to me, and please remind my dear Roman of his promise, for the bottles are already loaded.[3]

Your
Most obedient Joseph

COMMENTARY

Original Buchen, Bezirksmuseum. The letter appears to have lost its salutation, but it is otherwise intact.

1. This is obviously some practical joke that Kraus has played, but there is no further information on the reference, save that his parents seem to have admonished him for it.

2. The identity of these works is unknown, though see Letter 81. It is clear that Kraus is still considered by the Swedish court to be their employee, whatever the intrigues and calumny against him. That both would require the permission of the king would suggest that they were intended for Stockholm and thus were in Swedish, or in a French that could be easily translated.

3. Probably a reference to a gift of French wine for Pater Roman Hoffstetter.

80. Letter to Marianne Kraus dated Paris, 26 December 1785

Dearest Marianna!

In order to prove to you how dear your letters are, I am answering one on the fly. Do likewise; our correspondence will thus remain quite healthy. I'm sorry that you don't have the music in hand already. The reason for this coincidental delay I've already told you about in my last letter. Soon I hope to snatch a more fortunate opportunity to satisfy you and in the best possible way to be able to recommend myself to your music club.[1] I am happy that you have done Kozeluch and Clementi.[2]

Kozeluch is a man of my heart. Clementi is more for the head and fingers. Abbé Sterkel for the lazy and short-sighted.[3] If you really want to get to know something good, then there is Mozart, Reichardt, Haydn, Hässler, Türk, Adam, Küfner, and my wonderful friend Albrechtsberger in Vienna.[4] What's happening with our theater in Frankfurt? What are the latest and best productions? Do you know Mozart's *Entführung aus dem Serail*? He is now working on his *Figaro*, an operetta in four acts, which I am quite looking forward to.[5] Piccinni recently gave us his *Penelope*, but it was not quite seen as successful.[6] For the most part, none of the operas that have been produced at Fontainebleau have been successful. On the other hand, the harvest in the field of instrumental music is thus more fruitful. The small and great write as if it was always their laudable normal practice, and perhaps it will remain thus, for there are always people who will read it. There is no lack of concerts, and consequently there is opportunity enough for musical attempts where one can prostitute oneself for good effect. As an example, yesterday a certain *Troni* presented at the Concert spirituel a motet that began with Gluck and ended with Jommelli.[7] The dear Parisians were not at all discomfited and clapped enthusiastically, which is not always the case. Truly, I sometimes believe I am dreaming when I discern a certain hand in motion in the works of Rameau, Gluck, Grétry, Philidor, Floquet, and Condaille,[8] which have absolutely nothing in common with God's green earth.

COMMENTARY

Original lost, published in Si-JMK as Letter 36. The comment on Wolfgang Amadeus Mozart's *Le nozze di Figaro* actually predates any previous documented mention of the opera and is prima facie evidence of his knowledge of Mozart and his music.[U] Contact may have been personal (through now-lost letters) or by means of Viennese acquaintances such as Haydn or Vanhal, or intermediaries such as Johann Traeg.

1. The *musikalische Klubbe* was probably one that his sister, who was studying art in Frankfurt, belonged to.

U. See Otto Erich Deutsch, *Mozart: Die Dokumente seines Lebens* (Kassel: Bärenreiter, 1961). The first public or private mention of the opera was an anonymous announcement in the *Pfeffer und Salz* on 5 April 1786, some four months later. See also Eisen, *New Mozart Documents*, 42.

2. Leopold Kozeluch (1747–1818) and Muzio Clementi (1752–1832).

3. See Letter 57.

4. The composers Mozart, Reichardt, Albrechtsberger, and Haydn are immediately identifiable. The others are Johann Wilhelm Hässler (1747–1794), Daniel Gottlob Türk (1750–1813), probably Johann Ludwig Adam (1758–1848), and Johann Jacob Küffner (1727–1786).

5. See the commentary.

6. *Penelope* was first performed on 2 November 1785 at Fontainbleau, but was later deemed unsuccessful when mounted at the Opéra.

7. Possibly Giuseppe Trani (1707–1797), a Viennese violinist, who was visiting Paris at the time.

8. Rameau, Gluck, and Grétry are all immediately identifiable. The others are Andre Danican Philidor (1726–1795), Etienne-Joseph Floquet (1748–1785), and Pierre-Joseph Candeille (1744–1827).

81. Letter to Pater Roman Hoffstetter
dated Paris, 6 January 1786

Best wishes for the New Year, dear revered man! But mostly, above all else, is the continuation of your friendship to me! How has it happened that it has been so long, so long since I have longed for a letter from you, that you allowed me to expect to read rather sooner? Is it because I have not written to you myself? Well, for that I've certainly enough excuses, such as, for example, that I always looked for your *next* letter that I thought would come from one post day to the next . . . that I promised myself to expiate my guilt with a *really long* missive, etc., etc. But, dear friend, I desire no discord; only that you do not find fault with an indifferent heart; for this would cut me to the quick.[1] Once again, if you love me as much as previously, don't let the man who is yours from the bottom of his heart await a letter from you in vain for much longer. In any case, I can bear witness for myself that I am unchanged

Your

Good friend Kraus

COMMENTARY

Original Buchen, Bezirksmuseum. The letter is apparently a goad to convince the reticent monk to pen a few lines.

1. There is no evidence that Kraus ever fulfilled his promise to write a lengthy letter, but the inference is that they may not have parted earlier without some disagreement. See Appendix D for the Hoffstetter correspondence regarding the two men.

82. Letter to Abraham Niklas Clewberg-Edelcrantz dated Paris, 16 January 1786

Most nobly-born Herr Royal Secretary

For the past few months I have awaited the departure of Herr Brussel (our decorations painter),[1] in order to present to Herr Royal S[ecretary] my gratitude for the letter and letter of credit he sent, and to give a tardy description of my own small affairs. I found it inexcusable that, in order to fit this circumstance, I would have taken the opportunity to make the packet larger; but because his illness was thought to be more serious than anticipated for him to begin his homeward journey soon, I hardly dared to excuse the negligent culpability of discharging my obligation: but I trust in the good will of Herr Royal S[ecretary] toward me, and the assurance that I can give in all good conscience that neither indifference nor a lesser distancing from deserving or retaining the friendship of H[err] Royal S[ecretary] has been the cause of such an unpleasant reticence on my part. I therefore ask that the H[err] R[oyal] S[ecretary] pardon me for this time and accept with alacrity my most sincerest feelings for all of the friendship that I have enjoyed this past year; my honest desire for the new one, and to allow me to count upon H[err] R[oyal] S[ecretary's] disposition from this point on.

Concerning what has happened with my musical element itself, I have cause to wish for more progress for myself for the New Year than previously. Among a dozen good possibilities for flutes, I have not met a single one who would have been perfectly suitable for us. I either met a virtuoso who thought only of Sweden as a place to be heard but without any desire to enter into an engagement with our orchestra, or someone else who, apart from the assured salary, still wanted to purchase hundreds of prescribed assurances about his future, return journey, etc. Because I neither considered that such gentlemen were created for us, nor had the least intention of proceeding beyond the orders given me, I have not allowed myself to be concerned with them further. The one, *Herman*[2] by name, that had been recommended, was forced to escape here for the sake of a bit of roguery, fortunately just before the negotiations had been concluded, and therefore we have less of a chance of an equally bad act at home. I am naming him so that just in case he should come to

Sweden, the H[err] R[oyal] S[ecretary] would be able to recognize his character in advance, which is not to be borne any place else. My recommendation would be to advertise immediately for the aforementioned instrument from Germany; all the more so, since the greatest portion of the flautists here are from the same country.

The situation of my own fabrication is frustrating: but not so strange in a country where everything depends upon *privilegium exclusivum*,[3] and in order for it to be purchased, it must be begged for with an eternal genuflection and bowing and scraping. I touched upon that I had come across a libretto by Marmontel.[4] *Didon* by him was the main impetus for it. His next works, *Penelope,* for example (etc.), were less successful. All of his pieces, moreover, are rather poor in terms of spectacle, and among the deadliest sins in his own eyes, the most deadly is not to invent the foremost and best piece he can in order to importune a poor composer to immortality. These circumstances required me to seek out another Apollo. I finally chose a libretto that, to judge from the outline, at least promised that which I sought. The subject was *Oedipe*.[5] After completing the first act, I learned that Sacchini[6] was working on the same subject under the protection of the Queen. Those that know authorship here would no doubt have given me the same advice I gave myself; to stop the work and do the same thing as the poet did with his unfortunate verses, to throw them into the fire. I fished about quite diligently for another libretto and was fortunate enough to come across quite a nice plan;[7] but the first necessary step here is to do it under a *powerful protection:* I have little prospect of completing such a work while traveling. It is thus completely obvious that, regardless of what I could have accomplished prospectively through this winter's work, I long to come home in order to be able to benefit from what little I know. The return journey, therefore, cannot happen until the roads are somewhat passable ... *id est* ... in the month of April.

Therefore, I take the liberty of requesting that the H[err] R[oyal] S[ecretary] send me at the first opportunity the letter of credit for the last quarter of the past year and the first of this. I am somewhat in debt from Italy and here for music and books that I purchased,[8] and I am obliged to repay it before I leave the neighborhood. Will the H[err] R[oyal] S[ecretary] have the friendship for me and advance me for this need, inclusive of the travel costs, 150 Dutch Ducats or 500 Rd [Riksdalers] Swedish?

For this, H[err] R[oyal] S[ecretary] will have obligated an artist who, to honor his future, wishes nothing other than to be able to benefit Sweden; and who longs for the happy moment to be able to assure the H[err] R[oyal] S[ecretary] in person with what honor he is due.

Your most nobly-born Herr Royal Secretary's
Most humble servant,
Kraus

COMMENTARY

Original Stockholm, Kungliga Biblioteket. This letter is one of the few to mention specific works, but it is unclear whether his opera was intended for Paris to make an international name for himself or for Stockholm. If the latter, the issue of protection or patronage would have been moot.

1. Johann Gottlob Brusell (1756–1829).

2. The identity of the flautist Herman[n] remains unclear.

3. *Privilegium exclusivum* = exclusive privilege, or right to do things.

4. Which text by Marmontel cannot be determined, but Piccinni set both of the works mentioned. See Letter 72 for an extensive criticism of *Didon*.

5. VB 21. It is not known if Kraus actually did destroy the first act of the opera he completed, but the work in any case has not survived.

6. Antonio Sacchini (1730–1786). The work referred to is *Oedipe à Colonne*, set to a text by Nicolas François Guillard (1752–1814). The patronage was Queen Marie Antoinette. Sacchini, however, passed away suddenly in October of 1786; had Kraus remained in Paris, he might have then received the necessary patronage for his own opera, since the Parisians were fond of such rivalries.

7. The *ganska artig plan* was probably the melodrama *Zélie* (VB 20), set to a text by Jammert d'Invilliers. The full text, which indicates that Kraus actually did complete the now-lost score, is in Stockholm, Kungliga Bibliotheket.

8. The books and scores were probably purchased for the Royal Academy of Music and not for Kraus's personal collection.

83. Letter to Abraham Niklas Clewberg-Edelcrantz dated Paris, 3 April 1786

Most nobly-born Herr Royal Secretary

Pardon me that I find it necessary to press the H[err] Royal S[ecretary] anew for an answer to my previous letter. I have now been living six months on credit and am completely without money, and therefore long to come home all the more, for I recognize that it is impossible to break through the cabals here without the protection that I lack. Allow me once more to repeat my request in my last letter that H[err] Royal S[ecretary] may honor his friendship for me and allow me to receive, apart from the two quarterly salaries due me, an advance of 500 Riksd[alers] in order to cover the costs of travel and to redeem the small musical debts in Italy and here with it. I long soonest for a favorable answer and thus have the honor to persist with obeisance

Your Herr Royal Secretary's
Most humble servant
Kraus

COMMENTARY

Original Stockholm, Kungliga Biblioteket. This letter is more of a memorandum than a reminder, though it does indicate that the composer was unable to make headway in Parisian musical society, not having obtained local support. It also notes that his salary has been in arrears for sometime.

84. Letter to his parents dated Paris, 7 April 1786

Of course, dear parents, I'm still sitting here like Herod in his little house, because I am awaiting the last letter from Stockholm every post day. I anticipate, however, that it cannot last for much longer, and then immediately to Amorbach. Hat, taffeta, etc., etc., everything will be quite nicely taken care of. Concerning the Mundauers,[1] I have not been able to question him yet, because due to an eternal catarrh I have not gone out myself. As soon as I can fly about, this will be my first step. The house number should be set out permanently so that [I] don't have to walk up and down a tight, sewage-filled street almost a quarter mile long in vain. No matter, I'll ferret him out in good order. But, why does the learned little Mazebil[2] in Frankfurt not answer me? The one who carried your little packet with the music has long since returned again and assured me that he gave it to Herr Schütz with his own hands . . . It is rather a bit unfriendly of my little Marianne not to let me know about it. Please carry the enclosed letter to Vienna to the post office and stamp it insofar as is possible. I wish my little Anna Barbara good luck in smoking tobacco, but with a pipe . . . go for it! Myself, I smoke one made out of clay; for already in December I've had a good morning done for me quite nicely with buckles, whistles, etc. The little story is quite pleasant to hear, [and I'll] tell it when I come home. My rags will also come along with me, so don't worry about it! I am pleased with my brother Alois; now there's a great fellow, if God wills it. If I didn't have the sniffles myself in such abundance, I would ask my dear father to let me have his; for a young buck can more easily endure the thing. The other unhappy news of death, etc., annoys me nonetheless. It would be fitting if for each good fellow that sails off in such a way, a few hundred scoundrels bite the dust.[3]

Another question of importance; how has last year's wine been rated? I ask this, of course, not for the present but rather as a wise man for the future. Extreme idleness, hunger, and cold have been as stupid a matter here as in Germany this winter. Of course, it is a bit more noticeable in a crowd of a million.[4]

A most honorable and very moral greeting to the titular Herr Rector chori[5] in Buchen, godfather and facilitator of feasts.

Your

Most obedient

Joseph

COMMENTARY

Original Buchen, Bezirksmuseum. This letter remains one of the most enigmatic of Kraus's missives to his parents, for it appears to refer to a now-lost one of theirs to him informing him of intimate and detailed local news. None of these seem to impact his own situation in Paris, and thus there is little of biographical importance to be gleaned here, save that one of his sisters has taken up smoking, a bold move for the age, and that he was anticipating imbibing the new wine upon his arrival home. He also refers to the cold, damp, and unhealthy miasmatic weather in Paris and Germany, which may have been a lingering result of the eruption in Iceland of the Laki volcano, which caused distress in continental Europe beginning in 1783.

1. The Mundauers are not doubt some of his relatives from Mundau who were visiting Paris.

2. Mazebil refers to his sister Marianne (a nickname?); the music is unidentified, but possibly keyboard works. See
Letter 79.

3. Orig. *ins Gras bissen.*

4. He is referring to the entire population of Paris.

5. This refers to Rector Pfister of Buchen, though Kraus is being sarcastic
here.

85. Letter to Johann Samuel Liedemann dated Paris, 10 June 1786

Dearly Beloved![1]

This news is the last that I will give you from Paris, for friend Kraus is clearing out and wandering up to the Gulf of Bothnia.[2] If you want to write once more to him before this, then you should address the letter to my father in Amorbach. – Now to your novel. My dear fellow! If only I could at this moment clasp you to me and embrace and kiss you completely for all of the pleasure that you've given me with it! . . . Good fortune! You have entrusted it to a man who is able to grasp it and to whom the language of the heart is neither unnatural nor foreign. Fortune and blessings upon the pious sufferers who anticipate another better life and through the travails of a severe fate rejoice in a distant – distant crown from the hand of their *Only One*! Of course, the thought has some unspeakable harshness, that evil is only evil to those who feel; that only *he* is damned to endure that which is simply the consequence of his crime. – But friend; without this expression of humanity I am certain that emotions would be only talked about forever, never treated. Take a fosterling of Mother Nature, who tenderly gives him daily cake[3] and almonds . . . to him everything is viewed through rose-colored glasses[4] . . . to him Philomela warbles joyously . . . and in the most terrible cases of humanity, with the unending pleasures of the most unhappy depression, raises his little body up high enough to babble about sensitivity with weak lips. Friend! Such a child remains a child *in sæcula sæculorum.*[5] And now enough with the moralizing. Just another small word: I love you without reservation, my dear fellow. Do the same, otherwise may the gracious heaven be merciful to you! May heaven ordain that we sometime will wander calmly hand in hand into another better world!

COMMENTARY

Original lost; copy published in Si-JMK as Letter 39. This letter exists only as an excerpt; it is possible that significant portions of the main body of the text, particularly at the beginning, and the colophon are missing. What was published by Silverstolpe gives a rather peculiar, and overtly emotional, view of Kraus's friendship with Liedemann, implying a degree of intimacy that may or may not reflect reality in a larger context, but that also certainly shows the sort of eighteenth-century intellectual male bonding cult that Kraus espoused. It can be suggested that the bulk of the excerpt, however, refers not to their relationship, but rather to the contents of whatever novel Liedemann had sent Kraus for his criticism. One can surmise that this was probably a mixture of sentimentality and moral overtones, possibly with some sort of quasi-religious content. It is also clear from the veiled criticism that Kraus gives that his previous declaration that he was happy to receive this artistic work from a close friend was tempered by his noticing inconsistencies in language and philosophical content. At least, the parable implied shows that Kraus was not convinced by Liedemann's main character. In that context, the final lines that seem to emphasize some personal intimacy can be translated as Kraus's diplomatic way of telling his friend not to take the criticism too harshly for the sake of their friendship and apparent sympathetic personalities. It is also telling that this appears to have been the final communication between the two, leading one to believe that Liedemann disagreed.

1. Orig. *Lieber Liebender!*, which is an unusual salutation under any circumstances.

2. That is, Stockholm.

3. Orig. *Zuckerbrod,* or pound cake.

4. Orig. *Alles glänzt in Rosenfarbe ihm,* or "everything glows to him in rose colors." The translation gives the modern English euphemism.

5. *Sæcula sæculorum* = forever and ever, as a quote from the Catholic doxology.

86. Letter to Abraham Niklas Clewberg-Edelcrantz dated Paris, 22 June 1786

Most nobly-born Herr Royal Secretary

For the letter of credit that has happily landed here I thank you most gratefully: it infuses new life into a body and soul, which, to tell the truth, has been damned shackled for quite awhile. Now I long for nothing more than to be home soon; but Satan's own circumstances have made it difficult to adapt to my pious wishes. My debt is around 300 Riksdalers. The delay in receiving the earlier and later funds rather often obliged me to borrow and maintain myself as best I could, so that therefore my economic affairs need to be resolved, something that I would like to achieve by and by. Thus I see that it would be difficult to find a way out with the 146 Riksdalers that the H[err] R[oyal] S[ecretary] has been so kind to supply me with, to make an honorable cleansing of my sins[1] and, moreover, to cover the journey therewith. My final request would therefore be that the H[err] R[oyal] S[ecretary] would be so kind as to raise the advance to 300 Riksdalers and forward a letter of credit for the rest of the 154 Riksdalers via a commercial firm in Hamburg to Frankfurt am Main: even better would be to send it directly to a banker in Frankfurt itself. In the hope that the H[err] R[oyal] S[ecretary] will most graciously support my request, I shall immediately depart on my journey after receiving the last quarterly salary payment and will await the H[err] R[oyal] S[ecretary's] favorable reply in Frankfurt. For it will be impossible for the purse to provide sustenance any longer. In the expectation of extending my thanks soon personally for the demonstrative friendship and goodwill shown to me during my sojourn abroad, I have the honor to remain with all respect

Your most nobly-born Herr Royal Secretary's
Most humble servant
Kraus

COMMENTARY

Original Stockholm, Kungliga Biblioteket. While the sums do add up, one might note that Kraus is conflating the absolution of his debts, his travel funds, and his usual salary, probably meaning that the sum itself is far too small to accomplish his return journey. See the next letter.

1. Orig. *aftvättning utaf mina synder,* meaning his indebtedness.

87. Letter to Abraham Niklas Clewberg-Edelcrantz dated Paris, 28 July 1786

Most nobly-born Herr Royal Secretary

Ready to travel already at the beginning of the month, I had little expectation that thereafter I would be bedridden for three long weeks with a respiratory illness that is now common here.[1] This guest was all the more annoying to me, for it would not let its host go without payment. Today was the first day I dared to go outside, and although the body appears still to be weak, I nonetheless hope to depart here next week. For the sake of my health and purse, I must journey via my home town in order to negotiate travel money, about which circumstances I informed the H[err] R[oyal] S[ecretary] in my last letter. It is thus all the more necessary, for I fear it will be difficult to expect the requested [amount] from Sweden in Frankfurt.[2] However, I thank you yet again for the last letter of credit and even more for m[y] g[ood] H[err] R[oyal] S[ecretary's] friendship for me and in the expectation that I will soon have the honor of showing the H[err] R[oyal] S[ecretary] my respect personally, I remain

The most nobly-born Herr Royal Secretary's
Most humble servant
Kraus

COMMENTARY

Original Stockholm, Kungliga Biblioteket. It is clear from the context of this short letter that he has finally informed his employer of his intent, already stated in his letters to his parents, of his returning to Sweden by way of his home in Amorbach. The excuse here, however, is that he doesn't expect the travel funds to arrive in a timely manner, implying that he might have to borrow money, probably from his parents, to complete the journey.

1. Most likely bronchitis or influenza.

2. Probably a second letter of credit drafted on one of the Frankfurt banks.

88. Letter to Abraham Niklas Clewberg-Edelcrantz dated Amorbach, 28 August 1786

Most nobly-born Herr Royal Secretary

There could hardly have been a greater annoyance for me than to be forced to give the H[err] R[oyal] S[ecretary] yet another written piece of information on my sojourn at a time when I clearly thought I would have had the honor or demonstrating my duty personally. A distressing relapse of the terrible and not-entirely-healed respiratory illness in Paris keeps me here steadfastly for a short time, to which the eternal rain and cold miserable weather have not contributed a little as well. But I anticipate a good recovery, and I count upon my good constitution soon to be myself again so that I am able to continue my journey. In the meantime, I beg my H[err] R[oyal] S[ecretary] to feel sorry for and graciously excuse his ill servant, and not to diminish his former friendship for him, who with the greatest respect continually remains

Your most nobly-born Herr Secretary's
Most humble servant
Kraus

COMMENTARY

Original Stockholm, Kungliga Biblioteket. If one reads between the lines of this and the two preceding letters, it becomes clear that, whatever the respiratory illness that Kraus caught in Paris, he has used it to prolong his journey for several months beyond the expected date of return, and in the intervening time to wangle a side trip to his parents' home in Amorbach. While one might take the letter at face value – that he in fact did have a relapse and was forced to recuperate in Amorbach – there is a certain perfunctory tone in the missive that this may have been more of an excuse than reality. In any case, it would appear the issue of travel funds is now moot.

89. Letter to his parents dated Wismar, 11 November 1786 at five o'clock in the morning

A heartfelt greeting from my Hallardt and his old, mortally ill wife. It really pains me to find her without hope of recovery. She has dropsy and there is no hope of a cure. Nonetheless, she treated me very well and lovingly, which is something that one can hope to expect from old, true friends. In return, I promised them something of my Marianne's work.[1] Please ask my dear sister to send something quite good here as soon as possible. I certainly know that it will come into good hands and be given a warm reception. At the moment I am traveling in company to Stralsund. Before I sail from there I shall write you once more. God grant my best parents and dearest siblings good health always

Your Joseph

COMMENTARY

Original Buchen, Bezirksmuseum. The
letter from Stralsund appears not to have
survived.

1. The work refers to a painting, as
Marianne Kraus was becoming an accomplished artist.

Interludium

Kraus arrived back in Stockholm shortly before Christmas of 1786 on
either 16 or 17 December.[V] His grand tour had taken four years and had its
ups and downs in terms of his relationship to both the Swedish cultural
establishment and his royal patron. On the other hand, it had brought
him into contact with the leading composers of Europe, all of whom regarded him and his work highly. As was noted in the aforementioned
contemporaneous notices,[W] he obtained a reputation among his peers –
indeed almost everyone he met – for his good character, excellent company, and innovative musical compositions. Despite whatever he may
have written about both intentional and unintentional delays in his itinerary, he was able to fulfill his obligations to the Swedish cultural establishment, both those given as the reasons for the tour at the outset and
those that were added during his travels. These included the observation
of the trends and styles in the arts, the collection of materials, mainly
books and music, and the evaluation and solicitation of potential hires
for the orchestra to increase its size and strength. While the letters often
present a rather less charitable picture of the quality of the latter, it is
clear from the documentary evidence that he was successful; for instance,
horn-players Wilhelm and Joseph Steinmüller were apparently recruited
from Esterháza, no doubt with Joseph Haydn's blessing. They arrived in
Stockholm in February of 1785 following a reputation-building and lucrative tour of Germany. On a personal level, he not only made close friends
virtually everywhere he went, he was able to reconnect with his family,
in particular his younger sister Marianne, who was beginning her own
career as an artist and was to become a confidant to her elder brother.

V. The exact date is not known, but his name appears in *Stockholms Posten* for
18 December as among those who have arrived back from journeys abroad.
W. See the Introduction, 13–14.

The only true difficulty apparently encountered by Kraus was the problematic relationship with the Swedish court, which has heretofore been blamed largely upon cabals instigated by the composer's enemies in an attempt to force him to abandon his official position in Sweden. That such indeed had occurred can be found in Kraus's mention in the letters (mostly without the names of the instigators revealed), as well as in biographical information that was no doubt based upon anecdotal evidence, as Silverstolpe related: "This cabal was quite public here at home and afterwards became all the more unmasked; but it was capable of nothing more than it somewhat delayed his return, and soon after became powerless, we ought to say, to which certainly Kraus's own clever and good behavior contributed."[X] That there were moments of concern can be seen by his own comments that the Swedish postmaster Lidin had warned him of the scurrilous rumor that he had decided to seek his fortune elsewhere, that is, not to return to Stockholm, which in turn even caused a momentary breach with one of his closest friends, Postmaster Hallardt. All of Kraus's biographers, from Silverstolpe to Leux-Henschen, have placed the blame on a group of people, who conspired to replace him with a well-known rival, Abbé Vogler. For this, all seem to have placed the final responsibility squarely on the shoulders of Gustav III, Kraus's patron. Leux-Henschen noted particularly: "If the offer to Vogler can hardly be traced back to his [i.e., Gustav's] own initiative, he still had to approve it. . . . From an historical standpoint Gustav III's fickleness and lack of fulfillment of promises has often been cited."[Y] Apart from the posthumous *lèse majesté* that this statement implies, the reality of the situation may have been rather more complex than biographers have heretofore noted.

X. See LH-JMK, 145–146 and HÅ-JMK, 137–138. *Denna cabale var här hemma ganska synbar och har efteråt allt mera blifvit afslöjad. Men den förmodde icke mer, än att den något fördröjde hans återkomst och den blef snart magtlös, hvartill Krauses eget kloka vi bore blott saga goda uppförandet säkerligen medverkade.*
Y. LH–JMK, 147. *Wenn die Berufung Voglers auch kaum auf seine Initiativenahme zurückzuführen sein dürfte, so muß er dieselbe doch gutgeheissen haben. . . . Von historische Seite ist oftmals auf Gustav III. Wankelmut und Nicht–Einlösen gegebener Versprechen hingewiesen worden.*

First, Vogler may or may not have been approached by Swedish agents intentionally to replace Kraus, but rather as another of the various foreign composers with international reputations who would be brought north on a specific commission for the Royal Opera. This had been the case with Dresden Kapellmeister Naumann, whose final Swedish opera, *Gustaf Wasa,* was premiered successfully in January of 1786. Since Vogler, whatever his controversial reputation, was certainly both available and well-known enough for this purpose, it seems only logical that negotiations were initiated with him. Apparently Kraus did not precisely warm to the idea, judging from the various offhand comments he wrote from Paris, but there doesn't seem to be any specific evidence that Vogler was being courted as his replacement, at least at first. Second, Gustav's own foreign political agenda began to supersede his cultural one, particularly since his return from his own travels to Italy and France, where he met with fellow monarchs such as Holy Roman Emperor Joseph II and received new assurances for increased state subsidies from France. Moreover, in August of 1786 Frederick the Great of Prussia died and Gustav sought to enlist his son, Friedrich Wilhelm, as well as their ally England, in a grand political scheme that would pit a European alliance against eastern powers such as Russia and Turkey. His plan was to wrest hegemony on the Baltic from his cousin, Empress Catherine the Great, while simultaneously fomenting a war with the Ottoman Empire in the name of Christianity. The great uncertainty in this scheme was the position of his neighbor to the south, Denmark; his militaristic intentions toward that country were clearly outlined in *Gustaf Wasa.* The emerging Realpolitik focused Gustav's attentions in a way that Kraus's own delicate situation was probably not even under royal consideration. The king most likely assumed that Kraus would eventually come back north to resume his duties in Stockholm at whatever time seemed appropriate or advantageous, trusting the administration of the Royal Spectacles and other cultural bodies to ensure that this happened. Indeed, proof of this can be seen a few days after Kraus's return when Baron Claes Horn noted in a protocol of the Royal Swedish Academy of Music: "If one wishes to find a master who is industrious enough to take on the public lectures in the musical sciences, i.e., someone like Herr Kapellmästare Kraus, it is my advice that he himself is to be immediately engaged."[Z] Since the recommendations were published only after many months of deliberations, it is clear by implication that Kraus's return was already anticipated some time earlier. Finally, the necessity of Kraus continually to petition his superiors may have been nothing more than trying to deal with a chaotic administrative situation from abroad. This would explain why the composer found it difficult to be paid his salary. His immediate supervisor, Cristoffer Zibet, had in fact run afoul of the Swedish court, most likely due to his profligate lifestyle and untrustworthiness. Kraus clearly refers to Zibet gambling away funds provided for his maintenance, and since diplomatic missions were expected to pay their own way apart from the state exchequer, additional funds from that source could not be equated with official resources to be used for the salaries of state employees, as they might today. It is important to note that Kraus not only managed to make a special journey to London as part of his official duties, he was also lodged for the bulk of his time with the Swedish ambassador, an appropriate situation for one of his stature, regardless of the state of his personal finances. The fact that it was difficult for Zibet's successor, royal librarian Abraham Niklas Clewberg-Edelcrantz, to solidify his position enough to undo the many problems caused by his predecessor can explain why Kraus was given permission to accept local commissions in Paris. Too, success there would not have been taken amiss at home in Sweden, either. Reading between the lines, the administration no doubt thought it would be most advantageous for their Kapellmästare to enhance his own international reputation as a composer, create new works that would then be available when he returned to Stockholm, and earn enough money to support himself until the administrative turmoil in Sweden had subsided. The gradual return to normalcy can be seen in Kraus's always respectful missives to Clewberg-Edelcrantz, beginning in January of 1786, no doubt a tithe of those he actually wrote to his new

Z. Protocols of the Royal Swedish Academy of Music 1770–1795, Stockholm, Kungliga Biblioteket; also quoted in German translation in LH-JMK (149). The same meeting found publisher and composer Olof Åhlström proposing that Kraus be named director of the Royal Theaters, i.e., to an administrative post within the Royal Spectacles.

superior. Clewberg's own situation, however, was made all the more complicated by the death of his superior and Kraus's mentor, Count Fersen, on 1 July 1786, as well as Fersen's replacement with Gustav Mauritz Armfelt. Leux-Henschen in particular blames the entire situation of the rivalry between Kraus and Vogler on him and another of Gustav's literati, Gudmund Göran Adlerbeth.[AA] This state of flux may have been the true reason for the rumor-mongering by a small group of people that ultimately amounted to little more than a tempest in a teapot.

With respect to Vogler, his contractual arrangements were equal to those of any other major figure brought to Sweden from the outside. When he arrived in June of 1786, he sought to establish himself in Stockholm more firmly during that period he was commissioned to compose his opera *Gustaf Adolph och Ebba Brahe*. He gave concerts, insinuated himself with some of the local poets, and wrote the usual series of compositions in honor of his employer and for the local public.[BB] The official title upon which he insisted and which was bestowed upon him, director of music, was an honorary one, although it may have been a means of ensuring that, in case the rumors concerning Kraus did actually turn out to be true, the cultural establishment would have a potential successor

AA. See LH-JMK, 146–147. She specifically accuses Adlerbeth of being behind the cabal due to his relationship with Kraus in Italy, which she derives from an earlier biographer, Birger Anrep–Nordin (AN–JMK, 57), who states that the author made no mention of Kraus among his often detailed musical descriptions of that journey, concluding that this was because the composer did not travel with the king's suite. She includes Armfelt for the same reason, although he followed Gustav III from Italy to Paris. It goes without saying, though, that lack of mention is not the same thing as enmity, and therefore there seems little actual substance to such conclusions.
BB. These included the Swedish Celebration for the Glorification of King Gustav III (*Svenskt festspel till Förhärligande af Konung Gustaf III*) and a cantata to a text by Bengt Lidnér, *Helig är Herran* (Holy is the Lord). The newspaper announcements of especially the latter show a great deal of egotistical presumption, for Vogler self-styled himself the "spiritual advisor of the Electorate of the Pfalz and Bavaria, First *Hofkapellmeister*, and Public Teacher of the Musical Sciences." See Georg-Helmut Fischer, "Abbé Georg Joseph Vogler: A 'Baroque' Musical Genius," in *Gustav III and the Swedish Stage*, ed. Bertil van Boer (Lewiston, N.Y.: Edwin Mellen, 1993), 87–88. By this time, Vogler had long since ceased his connections with the electoral court and, moreover, was never appointed *Hofkapellmeister* in either Mannheim or Munich.

waiting in the wings. Whatever the internal politics of the court, it seems that Vogler's expectations were considerably higher, and in October he founded his own School of Music in direct competition to the Royal Swedish Academy of Music. The reasoning behind this was that the official state school was too limited in its ability to educate native musicians, thereby forcing the country to rely upon foreigners. This was both invidious and ironic, considering his own lucrative contract as an alien to Sweden. Moreover, while it may have helped spur the Royal Academy of Music eventually to appoint Kraus as the director of curriculum, it was nonetheless seen as a direct slur against an establishment that had been created and nurtured by the king. This and his arrogant dismissal of his fellow composers in Stockholm no doubt made Vogler's position within Stockholm's musical life equivocal, as the letters from Kraus will demonstrate.[CC]

90. Letter to his parents dated Stockholm, 24 January 1787

I have written a month later than my arrival in order to give you something more concrete about my situation. You will note the approximate day of my departure from my last little scribble from Stralsund.[1] The journey took place on the ice up to the island of Rügen and then onward over the open sea. Hale and hearty, I finally reached Sweden. I was, of course, welcomed by my friends but less so by those who would have wished never to see me again. And this was the self-same respectable brotherhood that intrigued to bring *Vogler* to this court in order to honor our fatherland and with the intention of deposing me.[2] The little ditty took another turn to the great astonishment of these nice people. I took the rooster by the tail and made peace with *Vogler*. All joking aside, we're bosom buddies . . . right up to the matter of his boasting in foreign newspapers (which sometimes causes a bit of bickering between us); we have smoothed over all of the disunity between us and that

CC. See Fischer, "Vogler," 89–90. For example, Vogler wrote about the premiere of fellow German composer Johann Christian Friedrich Haeffner's *Electra* in 1787: "The music is atrocious!"

has discomfited our malicious patrons. Concerning our relationship, I have not found more easily a more pleasant man than he. He, of course, earns half again as much as I[3] – but what is it to me? For this he also has a greater household economy, his own coach and horses – all of those extra expenses that I don't need to have. In short, I am his guest every day since the little leaf has turned so wonderfully, so that even those people who made his fortune in order to cast me down have become his most virulent enemies, and Kraus, the only man whose arrival he feared, has proven that he is his own true friend.[4] But because of this, I am sorry for him. For without praising myself, I may say that I have been stingy compared with him. Without regard to his income of 1,500 Ducats per year, he is already in debt over his head. For the past six months [since his arrival] he has already exceeded his annual salary by 400 Ducats. I would be sorry if his enemies were to succeed in bringing him down again for this. But, it will go as it will go, but I shall be an honorable man dealing with him. *Punctum.*[5]

So much for the main event; about the other news and turns of my fate [more] next time. Write me as much as possible.

My beloved siblings I greet from the bottom of my heart. I ask my little Marianne to write to me especially. *Salutem* to all [my] friends.

Dearest parents
Your most obedient Joseph

P.S. Please be so good as to forward the enclosed letter to Mannheim.[6]

COMMENTARY

Original Buchen, Bezirksmuseum. Kraus apparently has forgotten the salutation, which he includes immediately above his signature. Here one can discern the congenial and forgiving nature of the composer, who confronted the potential rivalry head on and defused it. This appears to have been their first actual meeting in person, later intimations of Vogler as Kraus's early teacher notwithstanding.

1. See Letter 88; this note has apparently not survived.

2. These "enemies" were discussed in the Interludium, but this is evidence that at least some of the rumors were true.

3. Kraus's income at this stage was the equivalent of about 1,000 Ducats, though he may not have understood that, according to Vogler's contract (Stockholm, Royal Opera Archives, F 8A, F 8B–E, E A I C–D, D 6B 1786–1799), this may have been more of an advance on his opera commission than a true annual salary. The honorarium was initially set at 2,000

Riksdalers to be paid quarterly until the opera was completed. Only later in 1788 was Vogler put on a sort of salary; he negotiated to keep the same amount, as well as to receive in-kind emoluments of support for a coach and two horses, fodder, and a "pension" of 1,000 Riksdalers to be paid annually on the whim of the king following the end of his "service." In other words, it was not a permanent contract.[DD] From Kraus's letter, the coach and two may already have been purchased prior to the final contract and thus were placed therein ex post facto.

4. Musical evidence of this can be seen in the revisions of Christoph Willibald von Gluck's *Armide*, first performed and conducted by Kraus on 29 January 1787. There Kraus not only revised the orchestration somewhat, he also included two insertion ballet numbers (VB 39), one of which Vogler also reused in his prologue to the opera. The score is in Stockholm, Operansbibliotek, Operor A 8.

5. *Punctum* = period, though more in line with the Swedish benediction, *punkt slut*, or point closed.

6. The identity of the Mannheim correspondent is unknown, but his early teacher Anton Klein might be mentioned as a possibility.

91. Letter to his parents dated Stockholm, 15 March 1787

This time, my dearest parents, the fault is only half mine. For, if I had not today received your letter of the 10th of the previous month and if it had not come at an opportune time to for me to have written before you received news from me, I would then probably have waited yet another half an eternity for an answer. As soon as I know my own situation to some extent myself, I shall write you and enclose a letter for Hallardt along with it. It is incomprehensible to me that an otherwise so detail-oriented man would not have passed on the request.[1] Of course, the long-standing illness, death, and burial of his wife has plagued him quite a bit recently; it would therefore not be surprising if he forgot this in the middle of his confusion. But I shall immediately admonish him about it. A thousand thanks once again for your wonderful letter, and also as many pardons for the distress that I may have caused you, at least half-way innocently ... It won't happen again. Now to me! I have now begun once more to become insinuated into my old Swedish atmosphere,[2] and I hope to live in my same old way with all of my friends and remaining creatures, dead or alive. May God grant it! But I cannot say just yet that

DD. See Fischer, "Vogler," 83–84, 89.

on my part I am in the best of moods since my second sojourn here as I was during my first; several affairs, one that has been hanging around my neck for five years,[3] and the vexing intrigues which have unfortunately not been broken up by my handiwork, have slowly declined little by little in spirit after a somewhat difficult process.[4] If I must suffer through my remaining musical days, it will be thanks to a little superficiality that helps me bear much that is unpleasant. That I met *Vogler* when I arrived you know. My enemies concocted his engagement to supplant me, and to tell the truth, the whole thing was tied up in a packet. *Vogler* was warned to be careful of me as with someone who loved nothing more in the world than to intrigue, and who, because he was so beloved by the nation, had all the more opportunity to play out his little game.[5] In order to discredit me in advance, a hundred little stories were invented that, if they had been true, would of course not brought me honor, and *V[ogler]* believed it was necessary for his own interests to shove his oar in. Fortunately, I knew nothing about the entire situation; for, I probably would have done an about-face if I were to have learned about this stupid matter in Germany. I came and the entire thing all at once took a completely different course. My only trick was to look people directly in the face and with my usual forthrightness rub their noses in what I knew to be true. *Vogler* did an about-face and made every effort to praise me, and since the first moment we have lived together in friendship. But, unfortunately, this won't last long; for the court and country are already fed up with him and seek in a rather deliberate manner to make his sojourn so uncomfortable that I hardly believe that he will last a year here. The worst thing about this is that he is now already over his head in debt and made everyone enemies through his behavior.[6] At this point I am alone, for he has been on a pilgrimage for the past four weeks in the provinces to earn something though his organ playing. We'll see how this plays out. Concerning the court, I found upon my arrival a completely new administration that wasn't thinking of my benefit. Now the page has turned when they saw that I promised nothing I could not keep and did not make the slightest effort to use the momentary enthusiasm of a less-enlightened public for my own purposes.

I am sorry about cousin Schwarzmann and even more so for his poor survivors. I had a foreboding of it when I last saw him.

I wish my dear little Marianne good luck on her second scholarly journey.[7] Dearest girl! I thank you from the bottom of my heart that you have thought about my dear *Hallardt*. Perhaps you can do something to ease his sorrow that he bears for his dear old wife, who has sailed on before him and who I always called my second mother. He truly made me all choked up when I took my last leave of him in Wismar. Do me a favor and send him the lovely products[8] as soon as possible, and write me soon; for you know how good it makes me feel when I receive a letter from you.

To my dear brother *Studiosus,* I have the honor to thank him with all my soul for his well-styled letter for the New Year. I am deeply apologetic that I have not wished him *reciproce*[9] for four quarters the best wishes for all the beautiful things, for it has already passed by. At the same time, I ask that he be patient with a good will for a bit longer. My usual greetings to each and every one, and I am as usual

Your Joseph

COMMENTARY

Original Buchen, Bezirksmuseum. The letter elaborates a bit upon that of 24 January with respect to the cabals in general and Vogler in particular. It is apparently a response to a concerned letter from his parents regarding his situation and future in Sweden, knowing as they did that Kraus did not normally abide the tortuous and sometimes vicious court intrigues of the period with which his father in particular was probably well-acquainted.

1. Hallardt was apparently supposed to have facilitated the correspondence and flow of information but was unable to do so due to the death of his wife.

2. Orig. *schwedische Küchenluft,* or Swedish kitchen air, meaning something close to being back in harness to his position.

3. The "affair" (*Geschäfte,* but one of which is noted here) is unknown, but it may refer to the delayed performance of one of his operas, either *Proserpin* or *Æneas.*

4. See the Interludium and previous letter. Kraus may be exaggerating the severity of the cabal, for one can read clearly that it is dissipating.

5. Vogler was well-known for his ability to intrigue, and if he was involved, then the situation had the propensity to spin out of Kraus's control. It is clear from his description that it didn't. Moreover, if one believes the composer, he already had a sterling reputation in Stockholm, enough so that such were inconsequential, no matter how badly they made him feel. Vogler was allowed to concertize throughout Scandinavia to supplement his income, according to his initial contract.

6. Vogler's mannerisms were extremely egocentric and often a mixture

of arrogance and contempt for even those who supported him. For example, Mozart wrote to his father on 4 November 1777: "Herr Vice-Kapellmeister Vogler . . . is nothing but a joke; he is very conceited but has little ability. The whole orchestra dislikes him."

7. This journey was to Italy to study art. Schwarzmann is unidentified.

8. *Studiosus* = Kraus's youngest brother Alois.

9. *reciproce* = in return.

92. Letter to his parents dated Stockholm 20 May 1787

My little package will not be ready by this post day. Therefore, [here are] simply a few words until next Friday, when I shall send you a complete epic via Wismar.[1] In the meantime, I hope that both large and small are well. For this time [there is] another small matter that will not wait. Abbé Volger still has an aged father and a sister in Munich that he supports and for whom he is solely responsible, for which reason I am in the position to do him a service. He now wishes to send his family 40 Ducats in gold or 200 Florins, and that by means of the safest method and as quickly as possible, because the people there need it desperately; but he is not in the position of being able to obtain a letter of credit from here.[2] Would you be so kind and do a favor to both him and me of arranging for this 40 Ducats, and in the most expedient manner possible direct it to Munich to the following address: to *H*[err] *Staudinger living in Hofkistler's house,* by way of registered coach mail and at the appropriate post office obtain a receipt for it.[3] The Abbé requests that you let him know afterward where you would like it repaid? In Mainz? Or in Frankfurt? Or wherever he can arrange a letter of credit. But in the meantime, please have patience until the next post day, when you shall have a longer epistle from me.

A thousand greetings to my dear siblings from your Joseph

COMMENTARY

Original Buchen, Bezirksmuseum. Kraus is apparently preparing a package of gifts for his family. There is also a contradiction in his request, whereby Vogler cannot obtain a letter of credit, implied because of his indebtedness, but will do so later.

1. That is, via Postmaster Hallardt, who was Kraus's special conduit for correspondence now.

2. The implication is that Vogler is now borrowing money from Kraus, though little is known about this "aged father" or

sister. Vogler's own father, Jared Vogler, was a violin maker from Würzburg, so there is a possibility that he has misled Kraus.

3. It is interesting to note that here Kraus mentions the eighteenth-century equivalent of registered mail with return receipt.

93. Letter to his parents dated Stockholm, 11 June 1787

Dearest Parents

One post day has become several, because it has been impossible for me to find enough time to be able to devote myself seriously to correspondence, and I also wanted to finish off a couple of works at the same time.[1] Now to start afresh. How is everything at home? Hopefully, you are all well. Assure me of this as soon as possible. With me everything is *à l'ordinaire*[2] with respect to my health, but regarding the rest of my situation, I have not yet cleared everything up the way I would have wished. I don't believe that this will happen before the coming year, either; and then I hope that my good gentlemen will have both money and good will in their tills[3] . . . God be praised that the latter has never been lacking; with regard to the former, it has been damned difficult at this time. I therefore have to be patient about it and consider that the morsels will be all the more fat then.

4 July

Gaudium![4] Now I have my Hallardt here. The first thing he laid out on my table were the landscapes of my dear little Marianne. Of course, I'm really excited about it; for, by my soul, they are pretty. But – you should have seen the old fellow! He was quite beside himself and had three golden frames made for them; two for the paintings and – can you guess what was in the third? . . . Little Marianne's letter! Thank you – thank you, dearest sister for the joy that you have given both my friend and me. We'll cast about a bit to find something that can be a small consideration for it. You can see by the date, dearest ones, how obscenely it has gone with my correspondence. But please have a bit more patience! Next week the court goes to the country,[5] and I've permission to remain here for another month; I really want to and shall set myself to it. In the meantime, I didn't want to pass up the opportunity, for my Hallardt is writing. Up to now I've had my hands full. Fare well and love me. My siblings I embrace and am body and soul

Your most obedient Joseph

P.S. Abbé Vogler is not here at the moment.[6] I will speak to him in fourteen days, however. As soon as I receive the receipt, you will immediately receive the letter of credit through Bethmann.[7] In the meantime, I thank you from the bottom of my heart for the service to friendship that you have shown my friend.

COMMENTARY

Original Buchen, Bezirksmuseum. Kraus has clearly been busy in his obligations, which has resulted in a much-delayed missive and this one's brevity. It is clear from the context that his family has complied with the directive to transfer funds to Vogler's family.

1. The works are not further identified.

2. *À l'ordinaire* = as usual.

3. The good gentlemen are not identified, but it may refer to the final payment of his Göttingen debts.

4. *Gaudium* = "Heaven be praised" in this context.

5. The Swedish court usually went to Drottningholm during the summers; Kraus, like Vogler, probably had quarters in the artisans' village in nearby Canton. See the next letter.

6. Vogler's whereabouts are unknown, but probably in the Swedish provinces or in Norway.

7. Kraus means the well-known Bankhaus Bethmann in Frankfurt.

94. Letter to his parents dated Stockholm, 19 August 1787

Dearest Parents

Yesterday I returned from Drottningholm and was immediately received by my good Hallardt, who has been bedridden for the past four weeks and only now has made his first walk outside [to hand me] little Marianne's letter of 29 July. Truly, I am ashamed to have delayed answering her last letter for so long. . . . I would like it, however, if I no longer need to be embarrassed. My little sister has quite prettily read me the riot act;[1] for that, many thanks. I will, however, make every effort not to deserve it ever again. Of course, I always think about writing something more decisive, but I don't want to wait for it any longer. So much has been promised to me, that my matter will be resolved finally at the end of this month.[2] May God grant it! Then you will know everything.

It was certainly hot, for I demanded immediately and in *optima forma*[3] my dismissal if they were not to grant me what I was able to demand with good reason. Concerning Vogler, he will make good on the letter of credit as soon as he arrives back here in the city. He thanks you most sincerely for your kindness and desires to be able to serve you again in some fashion. I cannot speak of a subsidy for the letter of credit[4] – for Joseph needs (at least right now) something for himself continuously… but as poor as he is, he is still

   Your Joseph

COMMENTARY

Original Buchen, Bezirksmuseum. This letter was enclosed with the next one to his sister Marianne. Although it is clear that he is fully occupied with his official duties, the implication is that the question of hierarchy among the composers is still simmering and that Kraus has once more confronted the administration over this issues.

1. Orig. *Mein Schwesterchen hat mir's Kapitelchen waker herunter gelesen* = My little sister has read me soundly the little chapter from it.

2. The matter was no doubt who, Kraus or Vogler, was to be next in line for the position of Kapellmästare and who would retain musical authority within the establishment, though it is clear from earlier indications that Kraus had been promised the position.

3. *Optima forma* = in the best or most optimal form.

4. Orig. *Wechselüberständchen,* or small subsidy for the exchange (or letter of credit). Kraus's parents have no doubt written him to help foot the bill for Vogler, who has apparently not made good on his debt.

95. Letter to Marianne Kraus dated Stockholm, 19 August 1787

Dearest little Marianne of my heart

   A hundred and twenty thousand kisses for your most precious letter, divine girl! I'll survive, dearest, most beloved soul … even more and more bitter recriminations. … I really deserve them; but … as I truly live, I still love you, and I still hang inseparably onto your wonderfully good heart as in that moment that my weeping eyes followed after you for the last time in Geldersheim;[1] you are still daily in my most friendship-filled everyday thoughts; and yet I perceive that in the future there will never be a laughing face without yours being superimposed. Would that our dear God wills it that the thousand wishes of one individual would be fulfilled, and that we both would be certain of our happiness. Thank you for the little Mundau piece[2] – it is as if I were standing body and soul in front of the little nest. Hallardt's letter must undoubtedly have gone astray; each day that I am in the city I come and love and embrace you in your two little landscapes. I will pursue other commissions for you. Greet our other siblings a thousand fold. The letter to *Klein*[3] will follow shortly. The letter to French horn-player *Strasser*[4] has been delivered.

Ask our mother to greet my good *Häussler* very kindly – I would rather have the fever in his place.

Adieu, dearest beloved

Completely

your brother Joseph

COMMENTARY

Original Buchen, Bezirksmuseum. This note was appended to the previous letter, as promised. Evidently, Marianne Kraus has chastised her brother for his lack of attentiveness in no uncertain terms.

1. Kraus's mother and sister traveled to the town of Geldersheim near Schweinfurt to see him on his way north the previous year.

2. One of Marianne Kraus's landscapes from Mundau, where their relatives lived.

3. Anton Klein, his former teacher.

4. Franz Strasser, who was employed in Stockholm 1782–1788 and who was dismissed. The fact that Kraus has passed on a letter may have something to do with his leaving Stockholm.

96. Letter to his parents dated Stockholm, 21 February 1788

I would rather write just a few words this time, rather than let another post day to by completely. That I have loaded myself down with the sins of sloth is the real reason that I waited from the first days of the month to the last in order to be able to tell you something more certain about how my position has developed and what the situation has probably become over time. In short – I don't remember whether I spoke about it in my previous letter or not – *Vogler* intentionally or unintentionally played the fool with me through his crosswise *behavior*[1] ... God forgive him, for he's done double penance for it. I finally demanded my dismissal, which I of course couldn't expect, since they need me so desperately, and because the entire country was for me and against him, which naturally gave the matter a bit more weight. Three days ago the King finally named me his sole Kapellmästare and guaranteed me 600 Ducats for life[2] . . . Thus an agreement was reached. Whether I shall be satisfied with it for long, I do not know myself.

Next time I will write about it in much more detail. Greet all of my siblings and especially my dear little Marianne in Mannheim,[3] to whom I am threefold guilty in answering – I will assuredly write in the next weeks. Fare well, dearest parents, and forgive your little strophic songster[4]

Correspondent

Joseph

COMMENTARY

Original Buchen Bezirksmuseum. February is originally "Hornung." The entire brief missive seems focused on the rivalry that resulted in Kraus's being named as successor to Francesco Uttini, whose work he had been doing for over a year. Kraus's actual contract is dated 24 February 1788.[EE]

1. This refers to the contretemps of Letter 93. Apparently, Vogler, despite his protestations of friendship with Kraus, had become involved in some sort of duplicitous behavior once more, probably in conjunction with Kraus's enemies, who sought to establish him as Uttini's successor. How this played

EE. Stockholm, Riksarkiv. The contract reads: "Gustav Mauritz Armfelt, Friherr, one of His Royal Majesty's six principal chamberlains, Chief Intendant of His Hofkapell and Spectacles, Knight of the Order of the Elephant, Cavalier to His Royal Highness the Crown Prince, Adjutant General and Commander of the Nyland Infantry, and one of the Administrators of the Swedish Academy, hereby appoints Herr Joseph Kraus to be Kapellmästare Ordinarie with all of the privileges and rights pertaining to this position with reference to His Majesty's Court Orchestra which belongs to His Royal Majesty's Theaters; [he] is to follow no one else's suggestions other than those given by the Administration of the Hovkapell and Spectacles appointed by His Majesty, with all diligence to conduct the orchestra, build and maintain the same in good order, organize pedagogical works in singing and music, and to oversee and implement pertinent subjects in the curriculum where they are needed." Kraus signed it with the following statement: "I declare that I am perfectly in agreement with the conditions above and will do everything on my part to see them fulfilled. *Ut supra.*"

out in terms of paying back the debt to Kraus's parents is not known.

2. The salary represents an increase to 1,200 Riksdalers annually, or US$150,000–180,000 at current value rates (1 1788 Riksdaler = US$125–150, according to the Riksbank historical exchange rate conversion charts). This represents the salary of an important figure in Gustavian Stockholm, as his later inventory of his household effects will demonstrate.

3. His sister was apparently studying painting in Mannheim.

4. Orig. *liederlichen Briefschreiber,* or songlike letter writer.

97. Letter to his parents dated Stockholm, 31 March 1788

Dearest Parents

Last week I wrote to my dear little Marianne in Mannheim and promised her to become from this point forward a more industrious correspondent – I am beginning to keep my word. You will have received my last letter without doubt through Hallardt, along with both of his;[1] both of us long for an answer in order to be sure that you find yourselves well. With us the past few months have not gone so well. My old friend has more than half a dozen plagues, of course, of which each one hung on long enough to make a poor soul impatient; he bore every one of these bodily crucifixions with more Christian fortitude than I, who only had a real trial with my sour stomach,[2] which once the snow has gone and I can obtain vegetables, will be healed shortly and summarily enough. Of course, it will please the insane eating establishment most unhealthily always to be sitting about in the same place and making no other movement during the week than sometimes to be drawn by a pair of nags back and forth to the opera house – but there is no help for it.[3] Since Abbé Vogler has been terminated and my dear Italian[4] quite nicely retired, I am the sole plow horse. Apart from lunch and supper, where I can steal a bit of time to myself, to read for myself in one or another German or French newspaper what is proclaimed about the Turks, and to see what grain costs in Hamburg, the rest of my day is pure conscript labor – there is such a warbling and piping and time beating and organ diddle-dum-diddling from morning until evening and from evening until morning altogether so that even my sweat stinks of notes.[5] This would be all for the better, for I think that it would all be emitted at once from the ingredients of which a *corpus* consists[6] – whether it be musical, arithmetical, political, or anything else that ends in -al . . . if only the fine gentlemen would be more willing to open their wallets . . . but I have promised St. Cecilia a little light if she can move the fellows to *reason,* and by my soul, if she can do that, then I'll give her two.[7]

I've already told you in my previous letter that my main situation has already been decided and how; for the rest, I pray dear Heaven will strengthen me with patience. Now I have to come to a little matter that should long ago have been done – concerning the requested letter to St[adion] in Erfurt.[8] As true as my name is Joseph, I have sat down no less than a dozen times and tried to put pen to paper to draft noble congratulations . . . but by my honor – it didn't work. I really want to impart to my friends effusively how much I share in their happiness – but to a great nobleman I've nothing more to simper than in a sanitized expression that I'm most overjoyed that he has become greater by a yard and that one in deepest obeisance recommends his high and mighty Grace all the best. By my honor, I'd rather write him an entire opera for free and pay for the paper and copying fees myself. Greet my dear siblings and the few friends who are worthy.

With life and soul
Your Joseph
[P.S.] Old Hallardt sends his best greetings.

COMMENTARY

Original Buchen, Bezirksmuseum. Apparently, the language of the contract was not specific enough for Armfelt, so in addition to the formal offer and acceptance, Kraus wrote a codicil to his contract (Stockholm, Riksarkiv), which stated: "Since I have returned from this journey, I contact myself to remain in the service of His Royal Majesty for at least ten years, and during that time I will expend every effort to institute and set in the best order an educational curriculum at the Royal Musical Academy or the Opera, for which I shall recommend the most diligent and learned teachers and search out subjects that have a natural bent and ability, and remain under these conditions responsible that good singers are not lacking for subsequent roles. Moreover, I contract myself always to have a student in music theory, and for the rest to take special care and spare no effort to contribute to the function and appearance of the Royal Theater, and with such a statement complete everything that has been in my care and which my honor requires." This explains the rather hectic schedule contained in this letter.

1. The implication is that Hallardt has now become a regular correspondent with Kraus's parents as well, though only a letter or two actually survive. He apparently is to be the antidote to Kraus's sometimes evasive descriptions of his life in Stockholm.

2. Probably indigestion, though a stomach ulcer cannot be ruled out.

3. This is a satirical reference to Vogler's demand for a coach with two horses; apparently Kraus has asked for and received the same perquisite.

4. Vogler left in early February to travel to St. Petersburg after his contract was terminated. The *alter Italiener* refers to Uttini, with whom Kraus was on friendly terms.

5. It would seem from the cryptic remark that Kraus was somewhat of a news junkie.

6. Kraus means that other "emissions" of the body would be much more objectionable.

7. The remark is equally cryptic but may have something to do with his work load. The little light would probably be a new work of some sort.

8. Johann Philipp Carl Joseph, Graf von Stadion-Warthausen (1763–1824), who was appointed as ambassador to Stockholm in 1787.

98. Recommendation in support of the petition for a royal printing privilege by Olof Åhlström dated Stockholm, 5 April 1788

Herr Royal Accountant[1] Olof Åhlström has requested my recommendation concerning the petition he made for the engraving and printing of musical works. And because this undertaking, which as far as I know, is the first of its type in the kingdom, would give the lovers of music so much more pleasure than the already published compositions and works of the aforementioned Herr Accountant, which are testimony to his efforts to persist in aiding and bettering this venture and who has now achieved some success with those musical works lately engraved by him in terms of appearance and beautiful typesetting, [this venture] promises soon to be able to be compared with those that come from outside the country. Therefore, I have not hesitated in sending my recommendation, and desire that the Herr Accountant may be encouraged by being called to continue the distribution and progress of the science of music in the kingdom in this endeavor.

J. Kraus
Royal Kapellmästare

COMMENTARY

Original Stockholm, Kammerskolle-
gium (vol. 357–361 C II o a:131–133, now in
the Riksarkiv). This is a complete, long
sentence without punctuation written
in a formal and quite tortuous Swedish. Åhlström was granted the privilege
shortly afterward and began publishing
music as the Kongliga Not-Tryckeri.
Kraus was later to publish a number
of works with this firm.

1. Orig. *Kamereraren;* although it can
be translated (as here) as accountant,
it means more accurately either a type
of secretary (a largely honorific title)
or a state bureaucrat in the Gustavian
governmental hierarchy. Kraus is being
exquisitely formal and stiff in his official
recommendation.

99. Letter to Marianne Kraus dated Stockholm, 4 July 1788

Dearest Sister

Listen! However much I wish to avoid having you read me the riot act, it is not my intention to wiggle around it with a lie, and Your Sisterly Magnificence would not have been able to make the effort to go down to the Mannheim Post Office to inquire whether a letter to a certain *M[ademoise]lle Kraus* (without further title) has arrived there before and prior to declaring in such a dark, clear manner that the Herr Brother is going to be cut off. In any case, Your Strict Magnificence would find a receipt from the post office here at her service that at least will prove that such a letter to such an address on such and such a date was sent from here. Why the address has not been made more specific is only natural, since – shortly before, you wrote to me that you were moving; but to where? You didn't say – and so I thought, if it pleased other people consequently to ask around the *Comtoir,*[1] then now and again the trav-eling Miss Marianne could also do the same. I don't know if I thought incorrectly . . . what do you think? Quite a bit! Before I have to dither around corresponding or not corresponding further, I would rather take the blame. For I have not said that I have not entirely been innocent; I admit gladly that I would rather have been able to and should have writ-ten sooner, and more often. Forgive my sins as a *sister,* for as a *girl* you have nothing more to forgive me. For the psychological anatomy lesson that you've attempted to undertake in the matter of my heart, I thank you most cleanly. . . . Listen up, little doctor, you've bungled the job. – It may be that I cannot remain angry with anyone for long and am able to forget easily an insult, but that dependence and love depends solely upon my mood and is nothing more than acquaintanceship. Girl, this conclusion means a rather bloody awful honorific for your philosophy, and with this, enough! I've not received a letter from Dalberg;[2] the only one that I received through Count *Stadion* was yours. Here simultaneously is one to him (that is, the young Dalberg) for I do not know his address and therefore ask Papa to make an *envelope* for it and send on through his contacts. I would not like to write the Coadjutor[3] just yet until I have received an answer from his brother, i.e., Kobels (that is, the younger), whose title I also do not know. Be so kind as to write it on [the letter].

Greet our dear parents. They must excuse me that I do not write to them at this time, for today I really have too little time. A thousand greetings to our dear siblings.

And you, girl, may God forgive you if you are able to love your brother less even for a moment.

Yours,

Joseph

P.S. Hallardt is not here.

COMMENTARY

Original Buchen, Bezirksmuseum. The address on the bottom of a fold reads "To the well-intentioned little Marianne." Apparently this letter is a tongue in cheek answer to admonitions by his sister, perhaps due to his confiding in her another close relationship in Stockholm.

1. *Contoir* = post office, presumably in Mannheim.
2. See Letter 1.
3. The coadjutor in Mainz was Dalberg (see Letter 1), and Kobel refers to Ferdinand Kobell (1740–1799). Kraus has conflated two separate items here.

100. Letter to his parents dated Stockholm, 6 October 1788

I have waited the entire summer in vain for a good opportunity to be able to send you something more concrete. Unfortunately, now it seems more uncertain than ever before; the situation in the north* may never have been as critical as it is now, and God knows how this tragedy will end. You will doubtless have already read in the newspapers about the position in which we find ourselves; a position that one would not even have dreamed about even half a year ago. With this we hope soon for a better outlook; may Heaven grant it. What fate awaits our choir[1] is not known; but it must be revealed completely in short order. In the meantime, fare well, dearest parents, and write me soon. Everything kind and good to my dear siblings.

Your Joseph

[P.S.] If this letter gets through safely, you'll get a longer one next time.

COMMENTARY

Original Buchen, Bezirksmuseum. The asterisk was written by another hand (Kraus's father?) along with the comment: "Attack of the Danes and mutiny of the Swedish army." This refers to the invasion of Sweden from both Norway and Denmark in September of 1788; the "mutiny" was the not-so-secret Anjala League, a group of Finnish officers who sought a separate peace with Catherine the Great, who had been attacked by Gustav in August. By October, shortly after Kraus's letter, the conspiracy was crushed, its leaders jailed or exiled, and Denmark neutralized. The war with Russia, however, continued for almost two more years until the Peace of Värälä was signed on 14 August 1790. This treaty, ironically, was negotiated by Armfelt in his capacity as personal advisor and minister-at-large for Gustav III. Kraus's lacunar statements no doubt reflect the strict censorship and uncertain postal routes that were maintained during this war, thus the postscript.

1. Orig. *Kor*, which is clearly a code word for Sweden or its military forces.

101. Letter to his parents dated Stockholm, 3 March 1789

God be praised! That at least one of your letters went the right way, for I have been truly as anxious about you, dearest parents, as you have been about me. But it doesn't look like our correspondence will soon return to its old path, for neither this way nor that is secure. May Heaven soon grant us peace; of course, the state of affairs has to change drastically, and many heads will have to sacrifice their own private interests for the general good, so that they are more in accord with our good King than they have been heretofore.[1] We have before us a very tense and perhaps the most important parliament of this century. It has been suggested that by next week it will be concluded, and, one hopes, a little less stormy than at the beginning. But peace can hardly be considered this year. Even so, the entire history has still had little influence upon our opera and in all probability will have not the slightest from here on out. Russia and the Emperor have begun to economize by rescinding the pensions of their opera personnel, or giving them over to private *entrepreneurs*.[2] Our King has not even considered following their example. Just the opposite, our opera has never been more brilliant than throughout the duration of this very dangerous parliament. That the quarterly salary cannot be paid out as regularly as usual in peacetime is of course obvious, but that doesn't mean by far that one is to be graciously dismissed. To my coincidental friends who have made every effort of making their suffering on my behalf known in advance, I say this for their comfort; and, because they have participated so honestly in my fate, I hope that this news will bring them much joy.[3] The winter here was extraordinary, as you might well be able to imagine. I would have already had enough of the cold had the thermometer not danced up and down every moment. This sudden change in the weather has given me the sniffles and a cough, which has pursued me most stubbornly. We've still had minus 20°, and a month ago we had as low as minus 32°, whereas you on the Rhine have had from [minus] 16° to 18° at the most.[4]

Vogler is in Warsaw, and it is doubtful whether he will return, but in the meantime 200 Florins have already been deposited in the royal account;[5] as a result, his debt is erased.

Best and most heartfelt wishes to my dear siblings.

On the 19th I shall drink to my father's and my health.

Your Joseph

COMMENTARY

Original Buchen, Bezirksmuseum. Kraus is referring to the parliament (*Riksdag*) of 1789, during which Gustav forced the four estates (nobles, clergy, citizens, peasants) to adopt the Act of Union and Security, which granted him unprecedented powers as head of state. Kraus fails to mention that he himself had a part in the cowing of the members of parliament through a show of musical force consisting of a powerful introductory march rearranged from the first act of Mozart's *Idomeneo* (VB 154) and a large sinfonia da chiesa for the blessing at the opening (VB 146).

1. The parliament was hastily called amid fractures between the various estates, with Gustav receiving the support from the citizens and peasants against a coalition of the nobility and clergy, both of whom were wary of his usurping of power.[FF]

2. "Russia" is a code word for Catherine the Great, while the "Emperor" is Joseph II, who was involved in his own war with the Ottoman Empire.

3. Kraus is being sarcastic here; the "coincidental friends" (*ungebetnen Freunden*) were those members of the cabal,

but the inference here is that they were part of the nobility.

4. Kraus is using degrees Celsius; Swedish astronomer Anders Celsius (1701–1744) invented the scale, but it was Carl von Linné (1707–1778) who revised it and presented it in a thermometer that was in general use in Sweden by Kraus's time. It is unknown whether his parents would have recognized his temperature reference.

5. Vogler evidently repaid his debt from his concertizing; it is not known whether this included the funds that he had borrowed from the Kraus family, but since the composer makes no mention of it, it can be assumed that he made good on them.

102. Letter to Marianne Kraus dated Stockholm, 3 March 1789

Dear Marianne! Glory and honor to your painter's genius! May Heaven allow it to flourish, even if the vines have been so unmercifully frozen right before our eyes. D[alberg's] reply was pure summer rain[1] – look! That is a man, and your old court crone to whom you have delivered a work done by your own hands – [is] a goose; and from this we can draw an instructive conclusion never to spend much time with geese, either whiling away a few hours in their company or stuffing them full with the intent of being able to chow down on them with better appetite on St. Martin's Day. Because neither of these things can be your goal with the Goose of Mainz, you have subsequently done ill, extremely ill, to have courted the entire matter.[2]

FF. For further reading on the political divisions, see H. Arnold Barton, *Scandinavia in the Revolutionary Era* (Minneapolis: University of Minnesota Press, 1986), 165–170. The clerical estate was eventually wooed over to Gustav's side through a number of concessions, leaving the noble estate isolated and securing the funding to pay for the ongoing war with Russia.

Your thoughts *regarding continuing your education* are mine as well. Of course, it would be good if the patron understood the matter himself. But, dearest sister of my heart! even God Himself cannot be finished with it. Has He not certainly considered often to Himself: that one is to be a cobbler, tailor, tanner, and Behold! quicker than you can imagine yourself, one becomes a little president, the next is consecrated a bishop, and the third turns into a bureaucrat. So it goes! For that reason, we ought not to think ill of people who have longer arms and thicker heads, if you wish for their patronage . . . it would always be better if nothing happened at all. It annoys me that you have left off playing the keyboard[3] . . . but it is always good to exercise the fingers. You have pretty music, but I do not agree with your judgment. Mozart is, of course, often rich and witty with ideas, but a single *"Quand le bien animé"* in Dalayrac's *Nina* is dearer to me than *Die Entführung* and *Der Apotheker* put together . . . NB . . . if moving the heart is and ought to be the highest goal of music.[4] *Richard Coeur de Lion* is by Grétry.[5] There is much invention and variation therein, but it all runs about in such a superficial way, like a feather on the current of a stream. I would have wished that we lived closer together; then we would be able to communicate more easily with each other than now.

Nonetheless, always love me. . . . Listen, girl! As long as you don't lay down with a young man, I always have the hope that we can live an artist's life together.[6]

With life and soul
Your Joseph

COMMENTARY

Original Buchen, Bezirksmuseum. The musical preferences to his sister are done within the context of what she is to obtain within each piece, not on the quality of the works. She has, however, need of consolation, apparently due to a misadventure as an artist with one of her patrons.

1. Dalberg (see Letter 1) has apparently written to Kraus describing the incident with one of his sister's paintings, possibly a winter scene.

2. The "Goose" (*Gans*) is unidentified, though the characterization indicates probably someone from the Mainz court.

3. Apparently, this is in response to Marianne Kraus informing her brother that she has stopped practicing because she finds the musical material unsuitable to her interest.

4. The reference is to the opera by Nicolas Dalayrac (1753–1809) first premiered in 1786 in Paris. Kraus

clearly knows *Die Entführung aus dem Serail* (see Letter 79), but the other reference is to the popular Singspiel *Doktor und Apotheker* by Carl Ditters von Dittersdorf (1739–1799), which was being "revised" for Carl Stenborg's Swedish Comic Theater and which was later recomposed by Johan David Zander (1753–1796) as *Den Tokroliga Natten*.

5. *Richard* was first performed in Stockholm in 1791, becoming a signature piece of Carl Stenborg, but Kraus clearly refers to the original French published score from 1784.

6. Meaning "as long as you don't marry."

103. Letter to his parents dated Stockholm, 5 June 1789

I certainly owe my little Marianne an answer, and it is certainly not my usual laziness that is at fault that I am still in debt. For a long time, neither my head nor my heart has been on straight, but, dearest parents, please don't worry about this.[1] It is true that, partly due to my ill health, I have not been able to do my job since the beginning of February, but now I am beginning to drink seltzer,[2] and I hope through this means to be able to put myself back on my feet, for the entire rubbish consists simply of a stubborn hoarseness anyhow. I thank my dear little Marianne from the bottom of my heart for her little letter and the most cherished colophon, and for incessantly pining for my rabbit that is to come. There are now finally enough rabbits around here, and I would wish that I had been a bit less ambitious about the matter last fall and shot a few dozen less, so that I would not perhaps have been sick this winter. Who would have imagined that the music scribbler would become such a passionate hunter?[3] Despite all of the efforts, I have undertaken to ask around about the *Stripplin* family,[4] [but] I've found out nothing further than that I am certain that this name doesn't exist in Sweden. But so much I have learned is that it ought to be found in Mecklenburg. Your newspapers over there are a great deal more peaceable than ours, I notice. For here during the last month, everything has already been inflamed. God grant that we soon have peace. In the meantime, it is more unsafe on the sea than ever before, for thirty Russian warships crisscross the Baltic Sea, and twelve Danish ones will shortly join them. This year, therefore, I will hardly be able to arrange for my bundle of furs, unless I have the opportunity to bring it via London by an English ship.

Have you sent my letter to B. Dalberg via Kobel?[5] Would it not have been better to send it to his Herr brother in Mannheim? Vogler is now in Danzig; the poor devil has really had a time of it, for his traveling companion has conned him out of 2,000 Ducats or more. In the meantime, our opera and the remaining entertainment continue as actively as previously. Adie[u] I am with life and soul

> *Your most obedient Joseph*

[P.S.] A million kisses for my dear siblings.

À propos, next year Vogler will return to serve out his last fourteen months; I've been promised during this time to have permission to travel, and then I'll make the jump![6]

Husch! I'll be in Amorbach.

COMMENTARY

Original Buchen, Bezirksmuseum. Kraus's report that he has been ill and unable to work is clearly a ploy for sympathy, given that the previous letters show no sign of such incapacity, and his own work for the parliament indicates normal activity. He may have been deflecting a query about his household economy.

1. The "debt" is not known, though it could be he had not yet paid off the letter of credit obtained for Vogler, or that he still had outstanding debts from Göttingen.

2. Kraus probably means naturally carbonated mineral water, such as that found in the Swedish spa town of Ramlösa, a health beverage that had been known throughout Sweden since 1707.

3. Yet another indication of Kraus's passion for hunting; he has evidently promised rabbit skins to his sister.

4. This is a response to a newsworthy item involving the marriage of Maria-Josepha Stripplin (1735–1799) to Prince Karl Thomas von Löwenstein-Werthei-Rochefort (1714–1789), who died shortly after the wedding. The Kraus family interest comes because of the hereditary lands of Wertheim near their home of Amorbach.

5. See Letter 99.

6. Although Vogler was formally dismissed, he still had a residue of his contract to fulfill, apparently, and Kraus probably negotiated a sabbatical for himself because of it. Given their past sometimes close and sometimes awkward contact, it was probably deemed wise to ensure that the two were not together in the same city at the same time.

104. Letter to his parents dated Stockholm, 12 September 1789

The paintings have finally arrived, but unfortunately very damaged. The fault lay in the oil, which became liquid once more during the journey and ate through the paper in between. On the other hand, I and my Hallardt have my little Marianne to thank for a true day of celebration. Then you would have seen my old friend wander in and pace the stairs back and forth with the little packet under his arm, [crying] every half hour *"Eya, Eya!"* until I came down, which was the way it was. But, apart from this, something more detailed next. Up to now I've been grateful to my dear sister artist, to whom I am in debt, and am obligated to give the criticism that she has requested.

My health is not yet where I wish it to be. To follow the doctors, who have diagnosed my stubborn hoarseness as the result of too much sitting about and therefore importuned me to more and more vigorous movement, I have tramped about the entire summer up and down mountains, and after rabbits, foxes, and wolves, and have actually shot a few heavy pelts for winter. As soon as the evenings begin to become cool, my unpleasant guest arrives again.[1] Now, my swindler comforts me to have patience. This thing does not incommode me further anyhow, other than I cannot scream as loudly on this day or another than before; therefore, I can be pleased about it. I, poor devil, have thus eaten no meat or drunken wine for the past six months, but rather have been put on a strict Brother Abel's diet.[2] It would be too bad if nothing bore fruit. My stomach has won through it, because for the rest of it I am like a fish in water, with a good mood and pure in body and spirit. Next week I think I'll go out to my old [friend] to comfort him about his hemorrhoids. That will certainly be my plague in the final reckoning; for the most logical doctors that we have here were at least of the opinion that my entire illness stemmed from constipated bowels. I will therefore hope that it will once more allow them to run. Fare well . . . it will go as it will with respect to my hoarseness . . . it doesn't worry me too much when I know that my dear parents and siblings are well off. A thousand greetings to my dear little Marianne and my future brother Vice-bishop.[3] What are my little Anna-Barbara and Theresia doing? With body and soul

Your

Joseph

COMMENTARY

Original Buchen, Bezirksmuseum. Probably the most intimate of Kraus's letters describing his actual physical condition, but nonetheless contradictory in that he goes to great lengths to describe an invalid who nonetheless has spent a large amount of time outdoors.

    1. That is, the hoarseness, probably a form of vocal cord fatigue or laryngitis.

    2. Orig. *Bruder Abels Diät,* or a vegetarian diet.

    3. Orig. *Weihbischof,* or ordained bishop. Perhaps his brother Alois had aspirations of becoming a priest.

105. Letter to Marianne Kraus dated Stockholm, 28 January 1790

Forgive me, my dearest little Marianne, that I really do find myself in the position of having to ask for forgiveness. Water and a broad piece of earth divides us; I would thus often have so much and so many relevant things to say; today is post day, I think, so you should babble after the muse and your dearest sister ought to read something wonderful and warm by you; the morning comes and I lack time to write much, and I would like nothing whatsoever to do with less, for I have saved up too much. Thus I count one week to the next and stand and observe the end of the month and don't comprehend how it has been possible not to have written. Dearest soul! You know me. I am not forgotten; of that I am aware, and my head is far too close to my heart to be indifferent. If something happens that is insulting, unfortunate, or an attack, I really don't remember it all that seriously; therefore, as I have often so clearly demonstrated to myself, I am not cut out for philosophy at all. If there should come something that hits me crossways and shakes me to the core, of course there is a lot of terrible raging all about, but it doesn't amount to anything more than hot air, all blowing about quite powerfully in the moments that follow, and excuses me a bit and does no harm to others. But ask me sometime about a pleasure enjoyed; about a moment when my heart was completely into something; trust me! It would have been about twelve [or] fifteen years ago, [and] I believe that I could paint it for you as alive as if I were still enjoying it.[1] "Then we were waddling the little alley behind the office wall, arm in arm to the upper gate; the white dilapidated office house remained on the left; and when the eternal muck allowed, straight across the street to the city park, and then over the small, thick little stream to the road to Weilbach itself. There we looked straight ahead to the mountain; there must be something quite beautiful and interesting up there, I said; and after I said this, we were already on the narrow, cobbled, twisting path that unfortunately was not tight enough formerly for the evil Swedes when they came out to destroy the village of Zeisig. We walked ever upward, ever I in front of you or you in front of me, passing many fragrant little shrubs, many inviting resting places, and many noble rocky cliffs, until we were on top. As we were standing there, I directed my pair of eyes into God's world; you with the eye of an artist beneath your little hat were directed steadfastly above the Mutau mountains. There below, dearest, at the end to the left are our loved ones, who will rejoice to see us again in the evening; but of course the old office building will not ensnare the eye such as ours, because no one would dare peek through the walls like we would. Ah, the poor, poor little nuns who rolled the nasty Swedes down into the stream in barrels! Here was their chapel; to the north their cloister; and over there still the entrance to the cellar where the Swedes would probably have atoned for their sins, if they had not found it in Amorbach."[2] Well now, little sister, I'd like to chat around with you for an entire week, and it certainly would not become tiresome; if only I could sit nights there with you by the stream that winds its way from the Schneeberg down to the meadow. I almost stole it away from the old fellow; for what does Hallardt know of such things as the Gothardsberg? But the old fellow has let your little things grow on his soul, and I believe that he would immediately go to his grave if I would not have allowed him to notice it. In all four pieces the sky suffered the most, and the new varnish that I had an otherwise clever painter here cover them with has given them a very unattractive monotone tile color.[3] As interesting as our old place was, I would rather have wished that you would have done it from the perspective of the Gothardsberg. In the lower depths the old walls would have stood out more, and in the little town in the background I would have wished for you to outline our old house. About the rabbit, I can only say that I like him a lot, because he was done by your hand, for you know that I absolutely have no feeling at all for the still life, Dutch botanical physiognomies, and portraits of dead animals. Whether the artist has copied a duck or a goose that has been shot, as bass fiddle or a broom, a tulip or sauerkraut; it's all the same to me: but a dying stag – a wild boar, who even in the last moments of his life avenges himself on the dogs biting him, that is an entirely different matter for me; but that belongs to the painter of animals. Take God's beloved nature as it lives and is interwoven, and spy out the point where it stands as it moves up and all about one; then put yourself in the self-same point and create something of it! – I've seen *Tivoli* and *Ternate*[4] ten times over and never said anything more than "beautiful, beautiful" – the landscape painter Moore[5] led me there an eleventh time to another place barely thirty steps from my old vantage point from where I looked out upon the thing before; and I cried "magnificent, magnificent!"

Your present situations would please me if you would find sustenance for your artistic talent; you must be free to choose how you yourself feel, not how others feel. Not that which others say that "this or that place is paintable, very paintable; make me a little picture of it." No "we'd like to have a little collection, and the only thing missing is the backyard garden." Look dear! That is the plague from hell for the genius of an artist, and if he must, if he must keep on doing it for his daily bread, it is a deadly plague for him. But you have a soul about you that sees and observes with your eyes, and it is able to resonate within your feelings without flattery; for you are fortunate, and if it were not to be the way I wished, that you would have connoisseurs around you who were able to induce actual life into your power of imagination – then I do not know what you would be able to desire . . . not even independence.

Here everything goes on its old way. Nothing will possibly come of the peace. Everything is atrociously expensive, so that I can hardly make do (for, of course, I am no economizer). But the opera, concerts, spectacles, and masquerades go their usual daily course. Adieu, dearest girl, love your brother as much as you can, for he deserves it. Greet our old dear parents and dear siblings. Herr God! If I were there with you, I would crush you to my heart until you were half dead and yak into your ear until you were half deaf.

Your Joseph

COMMENTARY

Original Buchen, Bezirksmuseum. This relatively long missive to his sister begins with philosophy and ends with a critique of her art. The descriptive passage or reminiscence seems to have been clearly one taken from one of her Odenwald landscapes. Here, it is interesting to have an insight into Kraus's own artistic preferences. He does not like static still lifes, such as were common during the period, preferring more active paintings, the examples of which reflect his own enjoyment of the hunt.

1. Kraus is conflating the image of a landscape with an outing that probably occurred during his enforced stay in Buchen 1775–1776.

2. These references, ironically to the "evil" (*bösen*) or "nasty" (*garstigen*) Swedes, reflect an incident that occurred during the Thirty Years War of the seventeenth century.

3. The clever Swedish painter is unidentified, but could have been Per Krafft the Younger, who had painted Kraus's portrait about this time.

4. Both places in Italy described earlier in Kraus's letters from Italy.

5. Scottish painter Jacob More (1740–1793).

106. Letter to Abraham Niklas Clewberg-Edelcrantz dated Stockholm, 2 August 1790

To know that Herr Royal S[ecretary] has finally arrived safely [back] from Paris comforts us for the worries that we have had about everything up to now; and the 14th of July has no doubt been able to be healed of the ugly radical fever that was probably the consequence of the unpoetic beefsteak air of London.[1] My eternal illness[2] certainly doesn't have the same cause; but I believe that a month's vacation in Paris would have a more powerful effect on me than all of the foreign and domestic mineral water that I have of necessity poured through me. Our singing wares are doing well, even our poor Augusti,[3] who otherwise could rarely have delighted in an entire month of good health and who in the past three months was bedridden with 150 plagues; [she] now rests in peace. If only she would have left behind her gullet, [then] I would have less to yammer about. But Ah! – my poor aria with all of the brilliant coloratura.[4] By my soul, it would be a shame to leave a Swedish Kapellmästare, or all of the world's Kapellmästares, alone without singers. I hope, Herr Royal S[ecretary] will allow himself to be prodded into procuring for his wretched servant an appropriate plaything, so that he doesn't have to intone "by the river in Babylon."[5] Our remaining gaps are well-known in advance. We need 1) a good first violin (to be employed as concertmaster); 2) one or two good cellists; and 3) a good bassoonist. *Werner*,[6] whom your Herr Royal S[ecretary] has decided to engage, is awaiting orders to travel here; I wish with all my heart that this is to happen soon, for I need him desperately. Kexél[7] has assured me that he has graciously reported all of our other theatrical news; nothing remains but for me to state something old; *hoc est,* that no one longs more for a chief than I, and that I remain with eternal obeisance

Your most nobly-born Herr Royal Secretary's
most humble servant
Kraus

COMMENTARY

Original Stockholm, Kungliga Biblioteket. This letter serves as a brief reminder that Clewberg-Edelcrantz, in England and France on a diplomatic mission, was also charged with fulfilling the need for additional musicians for the Royal Spectacles. Especially difficult for the composer was the death of one of his favorite sopranos, Lovisa Sofia Augusti (1756–1790). Although she was no actress – contemporaneous accounts note that she had all of the dramatic ability of a statue – her vocal prowess was without compare in its flexibility and range. The opening sentences are a veiled comment on the political mission of the diplomat. On 9 July 1790 the Swedish navy crushed the Russian fleet at Svensksund, sinking 53 ships and capturing 9,000 prisoners. This, along with a threatened coalition between Sweden, Great Britain, Poland, and Prussia, dashed Catherine the Great's hopes of Baltic hegemony and provided the catalyst for the peace treaty signed at Värälä two weeks later on 14 August. This in turn allowed Gustav to turn his attention to the situation in France. Kraus's mention of the "ugly fever of the radicals" and the date, 14 July, the one-year anniversary of the beginning of the French Revolution, are telling, although he is cautious enough to turn it into a comment on the weather and his own health.

1. The date of the fall of the Bastille in 1789; the mention of "beefsteak weather" may refer to the well-known economic hardships imposed upon France as a primary cause of the Revolution.

2. Orig. *kranklande,* meaning illness or debilitation, but really a pun on *kränklande,* meaning outrage. With this in mind, the next lines can be interpreted that the mineral waters Kraus ingested were known for their emetic effects, which symbolizes something similar for the situation in Paris.

3. Lovisa Augusti, née Salomoni, had actually long since given up major roles at the Royal Opera, instead turning more toward a concert career. See the commentary.

4. The aria is the cantata *La Primavera* (VB 47)

5. The reference is to Psalm 137, specifically the conclusion of the first line: "Yea, we wept."

6. Dominicus Franz Werner (1760–1807), who was also proficient on the trumpet and horn.

7. Olof Kexél (1748–1796), the general amanuensis of the Royal Spectacles and publisher of a theater almanac.

107. **Letter to his parents dated Stockholm,**
21 November 1790

Since the peace I've become the eternal *Juden Vicarius.*[1] Counting from
the first of September right up to this evening at six o'clock, I have had
time enough only once to sleep through an entire night; that is, in my
own bed. Now, finally when everyone goes about skating on the ice, I
hope that I can do some good for my poor legs. Please forgive me, dearest
parents, that for this reason our correspondence has thus been limited.
At least it was good for my body with all of this rushing about; for I now
find myself really a bit lighter than I was during the summer months,
which were quite unpleasant for me this year. You ask me again about
Vogler and how his relationship with the administration is here? I had
believed that I had already answered the question long ago. But if I've
forgotten, which is easily possible, I'll do it now. Vogler still has fourteen
months left to serve in order to fulfill his contract. He has no warrant
or diploma from the King,[2] but rather only a written agreement with
our administration. These fourteen months I shall be free to travel. But
because our administration is quite weary of him, he has received not a
single answer to any letters that he has sent our administration since his
departure. I have been the most ill-served, therefore, for according to his
contract, he would have had to have been here last year already; he asked
for me to serve yet another year due to his economic obligations, with
the promise that he wished to serve in my stead the next. I finally gave
in to the poor devil: and now he writes me and the last post day to the
King himself from Darmstadt that he wishes to come, that he so magnificently portrayed the victory that we won at *Svensksund* in Frankfurt,
that now all of Germany has come over to the Swedish side, and even
more such nonsense: and he requests simultaneously to set a new opera
that will be a marvel for the entire world, etc., etc. And what happened?
Instead of an answer, yesterday the King allowed a short comedy to be
performed and portrayed by dear Abbé Vogler true-to-life and with all
of his mannerisms, walk, speech, conducting, wigs, and Cleric's collar:
in short, completely the way he stands, walks, talks, and behaves, played
so naturally upon the stage by an actor that the *public* almost laughed
themselves sick.[3] By my poor soul, I call that unmercifully answered. As

sorry as I am about him, I truly still wish that I would soon have him here in order to be able soon to set sail once more for Amorbach.

No word about your last serious epistle. As long as I have breath, I would know of no more horrible thought to think than be forced to live in God's green earth without *parents*.[4] I thank God that He has allowed me to enjoy this blessedness for so long, and even if it is thought a hundred times prudent to anticipate such misfortune, it is as it is, for in that I shall remain as long imprudent as I am able. Moreover, there needs be no inheritance on my account. My siblings need it: oh well, it is good that they have it. If I need something, then I shall tell my siblings. Adieu! Please greet all those blessed beings whose welfare is as close to my heart, as well. Especially, a thousand kisses to my dear Marianne. As soon as I am able to write, you can count on an answer.

Your Joseph

COMMENTARY

Original Buchen, Bezirksmuseum. The tone of the letter implies that Kraus has been all too busy with his official duties, and perhaps he wishes to deflect anticipation of the aforementioned sabbatical. His description of the satire that Gustav III wrote, in which Vogler was portrayed in such a scathing manner, *Födelsedagen* [The Birthday], represents Kraus's final ascendancy over Vogler in the eyes of the Swedish cultural establishment. Indeed, the subtext is that Gustav (and perhaps Kraus) was offended by the obnoxious petition that somehow seems to have been sent to both of them. The apparent boastful tone probably did nothing to mitigate Vogler's international reputation as a charlatan. What Kraus does not mention is that he composed music for the comedy, and therefore must have been party to its creation.[GG] The tone turns more serious toward the end of the letter when it becomes clear that his parents have informed him of their intention to disinherit him. While his casual dismissal of this fact seems to indicate a sense of generosity, it may well be that he was beginning to receive commissions that would compensate. An entry in the diary of Constatin Beyer (*Tagebüchern 1784–1829*, now in Erfurt, Stadtarchiv) reads for 23 March 1790: "Tuesday – [spent the] afternoon at the cathedral, where I observed the preparations for the solemn funeral obsequies for Emperor Joseph II that will be done tomorrow morning. The

GG. The work is discussed in the present author's article, "Gustav III's 'Divertissement med sång' *Födelsedagen*: A Gustavian Political Satire," *Scandinavian Studies* 61 (1989): 28–40.

funeral trappings were almost finished. The music, a Requiem by Kraus from Stockholm, was rehearsed." This work (vb 3) appears to be lost; it was most certainly not the surviving Requiem in D minor (vb 1), which had been written back in 1775 and heretofore attributed to his university years in Erfurt, however. The setting of this work clearly indicates the limited resources of Buchen and is relatively primitive in style.

1. The reference is to the afore-mentioned Peace of Värälä; *Juden Vicarius* = substitute for a Jew.

2. Kraus means a royal contract or privilege.

3. The actor was Gabriel Schylander (1751–1811), renowned for his comic timing and mimicry.

4. This is a response to the sensitive issue of legacy that his parents have obviously broached.

108. Letter to his parents dated Stockholm, 22 February 1791

Now it is certainly *post festum*[1] to wish my little Marianne a good journey – hopefully, she is already across the mountains. Wishes and music – that have already been a quarter of a year in transit and therefore will come too late in any case. Well and good! It would have been better if I'd have brought them myself. Already at the end of October one of our German doctors, who had served as a medic in Finland, took on the commission of taking a small packet with him to our fatherland. – He brought it to *Gottland*[2] in good order – where the poor devil fell ill with military fever and died. – Now I have my poor orphaned package back in my hands and now have to manage how to send it on in another way. That is the reason that you have not received an answer to your last letter.

Abbé Vogler is here again, and we interact with each other as wonderfully Christian a manner as before. Now it only depends upon whether my opera[3] will be given this year or not? – in the case of the latter, my vacation is assured. In a flash! – I'll then be there in Amorbach. Of course, I can't expect a certain answer before early next year. But then again I don't need to make any grand travel plans either. Adieu – write me soon. All my love and best wishes to my dear siblings. Fare well, dearest parents, and do not forget

Your Joseph

COMMENTARY

Original Buchen, Bezirksmuseum. The package no doubt contained music

and other trifles, gifts for his family, but the difficult delivery indicates the uncertain state of the post during this time.

1. *Post festum* = after the celebration, or here after the fact of her departure to Italy on a study tour.

2. Gottland is the island of Gotland. The identity of the German doctor is unknown, but the entire explanation demonstrates once again that Kraus often used acquaintances as couriers instead of relying upon the postal services for large packages, no doubt due to the need to evade the various and anonymous customs inspections. The inference is that this lost package also contained a letter (now lost).

3. The reference is to *Æneas*, which was apparently scheduled for rehearsal during the fall for a premiere on the king's birthday in January of 1792.

109. Letter to his parents dated Stockholm, 15 July 1791

Now I *am able,* moreover I *must* write now. My situation is finally decided: *Vogler* has his dismissal, and I have been graciously refused to be allowed to travel this year. I'd like to burst with anger. I've been looking forward to it for years – and served gratis for my colleague for one and a half whole years – and even at the beginning of this year I received completely valid assurances for a sabbatical of eighteen months – I made all the preparations for the pilgrimage – writing no more letters, for I thought to myself: all of this and even more you can quite nicely tell in person – and what a *surprise* it would be if the Swede were suddenly to show up unexpectedly in the Odenwald – all, all of the beautiful speculations – gone straight to hell. In short, my Abbé received in May the chance to take a little trip to Norway without permission in order to strum into the honest citizens of *Christiania* the last judgment, and with his strumming to breathe life into his asthmatic pocketbook:[1] the court got behind it and believed that they had the best opportunity to rid themselves of this guest – and feared that such a good circumstance would perhaps not come again soon, and – hardly had my miracle worker returned than, in a flash – he also received the clearest dismissal in *optima forma* at home. Good-bye to the journey – the hangman may thank the moron that through his idiocy another poor devil is forced to do penance, however. But enough of this – for the past several weeks I've certainly added a few more gallstones[2] to my body – I'll have to see how I can get them out again. In the meantime, they've tried to console me by saying that my permission will not vanish – I'll have the pleasure another time – God grant that these gentlemen keep their word. How are things with little Marianne? – Damn! One cannot trifle with a girl who is in the position of fulfilling her threats against her brother. But she would be more serious if she learned of the reason for my extended lack of correspondence, and then she could sulk a bit longer. To my remaining dear siblings, all my love and best wishes. Greet my good, honest dear friend Hoffstetter[3] from the bottom of my heart. He will forgive me that I do not answer him this time: it will, however, not be forgotten.

Therefore, fare well, dearest parents, and be loving
Your Joseph

COMMENTARY

Original Buchen, Bezirksmuseum. It is clear that Vogler was hoisted on his own petard, but that Kraus, who had expected to have him share his duties during his sabbatical, was forced to forgo all expected rewards for his service and remain in harness. Vogler, on the other hand, seems to have annoyed the administration enough to get himself fired, remaining contract or not.

1. Christiania is today's Oslo; the concert tour for his own benefit most likely featured his Orchestrion, an instrument that included sound and light display and upon which Vogler often improvised scenes drawn from numerous sources; here Kraus seems sarcastically to mention the Book of Revelation.

2. Kraus means here what today would be called venting one's spleen or tasting bitter bile.

3. This is the first mention of Roman Hoffstetter since Kraus's return to Sweden; it would seem that the monk had finally written him a note on some musical matter.

110. Letter to Marianne Kraus dated Drottningholm, 12 November 1791

Many thanks, dearest little Marianne, for the mild rebuke. I would have earned something sharper; for that, most heartfelt thanks that you were so forgiving. It makes me happy that you have made the leap from Vesuvius back into the heart of the Odenwald without a single incident; that proves to me once again that which I always consider an article of faith in our artist's bible, that is, with the exception of idylls or moonlight poets, painters of flowers or miniatures, no one wants to write *fecit* beneath something that has been kneaded out of marzipan.[1] Is it not something magnificent to wander about with a healthy head and warm soul among the majestic ruins? I don't regard it as the apex of achievement that you have not shared this rapture with me. I would like to while away the many small hours chatting with you; you would thus remind me presently of this, presently of that small bit of stone that has given us pleasure; and then when it would come to the larger stuff, and we completely [and] unintentionally mocked the Devil, *per dio,* how much good that would do me.[2] Ah well – [I] have to be patient until our dear God once more drives us together. In the meantime, I am not annoyed that you are happier than I. You weave with creatures whose empathy enfolds you in warmth: on the opposite side I sit and hold my breath not to have come to complete maturity in my own noble country. A true Patagonia for a lover of moralistic desserts.[3] If you give them something pathetic, they chew and chew on it, making like they would choke biting it; Bah! I go for the small nibble and stuff it into the little toothless mouth; you should see how happy they are and how lovingly the children smile with wide grins at it. It is of course rather difficult to deal with such a flock, who don't even have the graciousness to allow themselves to be sheared, even if they have the wool pulled over their eyes by someone like, for example, *Vogler.*[4]

God's grace, my dear little Marianne. I've not seen anything of your Roman letters.[5]

Your Joseph

COMMENTARY

Original Buchen, Bezirksmuseum. This brief reply follows news that she has returned from her trip to Italy.

1. *Fecit* = done or made, but the reference is to soft bread made from marzipan as a candy.

2. The majestic ruins are those of Pompeii; the orig. *ein Sapperlot herauspluften* means "to force out the devil," and *per dio* = by God.

3. Orig. *Naschmäuler,* or snacks after dinner. Kraus's reference to Patagonia really means "wasteland at the end of the earth."

4. Orig. *Wollendieb drüber herkömt* = when a wool thief comes upon them.

5. The "Roman letters" were clearly ones sent by Marianne to her brother, similar to those he sent to his family almost a decade earlier. These have been lost.

111. Letter to his parents dated Stockholm, 9 December 1791

God be praised that He has finally taken our poor little Franz to Himself! *He* alone could make an end to the eternal suffering [and] help my poor brother, for whom we were unable to do anything more than fruitlessly empathize. He is surely among his transfigured siblings who have preceded him. And *he* will await us when the hour of our calling has come.

COMMENTARY

Original lost; this excerpt published in Si-JMK as Letter 49. It lacks salutation and colophon, and it may be assumed that it was considerably longer than the few short lines that Silverstolpe included. The fragment is a response to the news of the death of his brother Franz. Silverstolpe penned a brief comment: "This brother of Kraus was feeble-minded, the result of a long-term nervous illness, during which he had to be confined."[HH]

112. Letter to his parents dated Stockholm, 13 March 1792

I would have answered earlier if I had not been awaiting my old Hallardt, who also wanted to give his little bit to the post office along with it. He went out into the country for fourteen days due to his poor eyes to obtain the advice of the doctors here, but in the end after consulting hither and yon, he had to sail off as half-blind as he had arrived. Even with all of the promises [he received] all at once, this is the first bright day that his glasses were made usable, and he has used them to write to you. Thank you for the second letter – so I am once more back in the accounting![1] Hmm, you'll see that nothing will come of it; for now I have determined most strongly always to have a day in advance of the post day. If it were not for this, I would certainly have waited until next Friday in order to be able to chat somewhat longer than today, when I've gotten my hands full. Because of this, dear parents, only so much for today; that I am well and have dealt better with my paper money than

HH. *Denne Broder till Kraus var svagsinnt, såsom följd af en mångårig nerf-sjuka, hvarefter han måste hållas instängd.*

I would have believed.[2] Good work – at least a bit of thanks is due, and the breadbasket is now raised so high in the air that one has to jump up so vigorously with health in order to be able to snatch a few crumbs from it – quite naturally, this makes for quite a good mood, even if the purse is to be emptied for it. Ah well! It was not always so previously, and probably won't remain so forever, and at the same time I probably won't get a single grey hair for the joking around.

Adieu! Greet my little Anna Barbara and little Theresia a thousand times – I am obliged to answer little Marianne and Alois, and this obligation I shall surely bear until the next post day.

Your

Joseph

COMMENTARY

Original Buchen, Bezirksmuseum. The light tone and inference of the letter demonstrates Kraus's secure and well-paid position, with a clear surplus of funds.

1. Orig. *zurük in der Rechnung,* probably meaning that Kraus has been reinstated in his parents' will, no doubt in the aftermath of no longer needing to provide care for their late son Franz.

2. A sign that Kraus has successfully invested some of his income?

113. Letter to Abraham Niklas Clewberg-Edelcrantz in Stockholm, undated but before 14 May 1792[II]

I have received the note concerning the division of the music that Herr Royal Secretary has been pleased to send me: but I am obliged therefore to make the necessary reminder that, because the music was unfortunately completed before the note, the former does not correspond well at all with the recommendations of the latter. Because time is short to make comprehensive modifications, I take the freedom of proposing the

II. See HÅ–JMK, 232. The date is a terminus ante quem for the funeral ceremonies for Gustav III, which took place on 14 May. As this concerns the Funeral Cantata (VB 42) and given that the king died only on 29 March, the commission would have been forthcoming only thereafter – and this letter implies that the work is finished and under rehearsal, which means that it must date from sometime during the first two weeks of May.

only possible way of making it doable, if the note – as well as the music I have done – is to be able to be followed.

The music consists first of an *Entrata,*[1] which lasts until the king and Court have taken their places.

Thereafter the first section of the Funeral Cantata itself is to begin and must be executed *without pause.*

The Psalm before the sermon – and thereafter the listing of the dignitaries.

Following the burial, and the Psalm that is to be sung while this occurs, comes the second section, which, like the first, must go *en suite* until the end.

After that, the prayers, blessings, Psalms, and finally the music for the recessional.[2]

It is absolutely impossible for me to divide each of the sections into two, and Herr Royal S[ecretary] would no doubt find it harsh that on such a sorrowful day only the poet and composer alone would be required to mourn once more for their slaughtered work, when they have already so obviously taken part in the general bereavement.

Another unpleasant bit of news for me was that our chorus will teach those who are listening to sing into their wigs.[3] Herr Royal S[ecretary] will allow that I find this undoable if even a note or syllable is to be heard down below in the church; apart from this, it is impossible to place a chorus of 48 people if we are not allowed to disperse them over the entire outer lectern.

At the burial of Carl XI, the music in the church[4] had a single small platform for 8 violins, 3 chalumeaux, 2 basses, and 4 singers. The number of vocal and instrumental performers this time rises to 104 people

Your H[err] R[oyal] S[ecretary's]

Most humble servant

Kraus

COMMENTARY

Original Stockholm, Kungliga Biblioteket. Shortly after Kraus's last letter to his parents, on 16 March 1792 his patron Gustav III was shot at a masked ball by Jakob Anckarström, who was part of a conspiracy to assassinate the monarch. Kraus was in attendance at this event and no doubt witnessed the deed firsthand.[JJ] Initially, the wound was not thought fatal, but as efforts to retrieve the bullet were unsuccessful, Gustav succumbed to sepsis and died on 29 March. The obsequies were hastily arranged, with court poet Carl Gustav Leopold (1756–1829) and Kraus commissioned to write the funeral music. The procession of the king's casket to the Riddarholm Church took place on 13 April, for which ceremony Kraus composed a *Symphonie funèbre* (VB 148). Thus the Funeral Cantata (VB 42) was composed and rehearsed in the month that the body lay in state for the burial, which took place on 14 May. Kraus felt the loss of his king deeply, indicating perhaps a closer relationship than might have appeared in the letters home. As he was rehearsing the cantata, he became so emotional that he fainted on the podium and was able to collect himself only after being comforted by the regent, later Carl XIII, and giving free rein to his tears. On the other hand, not all were as entranced by the work. Gjörwell, otherwise known to have been a friend of both poet and composer, noted stiffly: "A verse on command and a noise sounded according to Herr Kraus's ears."[KK] Nonetheless, these works were and still are considered some of Kraus's most heartfelt and finest compositions. All of the biographers, beginning with Silverstolpe, have wondered why the composer did not impart this momentous news to his parents. Their conclusions vary from now-lost letters that did so to, as Åstrand notes, "discretion, or concern for the oversight of the police."[LL] Whatever the reason for his historical silence, it is clear that his parents would have read about the assassination in their local newspapers, since it was a singular event.

1. The *Entrata* was probably a different work than the Introduzzione to the Funeral Cantata, the first part of which, as Kraus subsequently states, had to go *en suite*; that is, at one go. The identity of this work is therefore open to question, although it can be suggested that it was a Funeral March by his colleague Johann Christian Friedrich Haeffner, which was published in the *Musikaliskt tidsfördrif* for that year in piano reduction.

2. The recessional is likewise unidentified; perhaps a repeat of the Haeffner march?

3. Orig. *hårpungerna*, or hair bags.

4. The music on this occasion was composed by Anders Düben Jr. (1673–1738).

114. Letter to his parents dated Stockholm, 25 June 1792

It is now going a bit slowly with the correspondence of my dear old Hallardt; otherwise, our dispatches would have been delivered a few post days earlier to the post office. I have spent a few days with him in the

JJ. The court uniform he wore on this occasion is now on display in Buchen at the Bezirksmuseum.

KK. *En vers på befalning och et ljud stämdt efter Hr Krauses öra.* See Olle Holmberg, *Leopold och Gustaf III* (Stockholm: Bonniers, 1954), 299.

LL. See HÅ–JMK, 232: *discretion, eller bekymmer med polisövervakningen.*

country and certainly more pleasurably than the circumstances of his ill health and the extremely irritating shaking[1] might have expected. He can barely differentiate the flower bulbs with the help of his glasses, and then he is momentarily forced to allow his eyes to rest after the least exertion. If it is bad weather outside so that we can't consider going for a walk, my old fellow is immediately once more at his desk to try and finish his reply to Amorbach, and after a few minutes, as the white paper becomes painful, he takes the glasses from off his nose and wanders over to my corner, where I was lying lengthwise on the sofa.[2] "No, friend," he called, "the letter won't be finished today; as soon as I try and look at the paper, everything immediately becomes a massive blur before my eyes." Ah well, I said, we'll wait until another time. My poor friend! I fear that he will not be able to write for much longer. In a few weeks I'll visit him again in order to convince him to accompany me into the city; then I shall understand a bit better how to get him into a good mood, as I would as if I were his house guest.

My situation is the same with respect to my income; and therefore I don't worry about it for a moment; for as long as it sits correctly on his neck, the head of a dismissed Kapellmeister is always worth as much as six dozen heads of bureaucrats among his colleagues, whether or not they are allowed to sit on top of whatever office or bureaucratic rump they always wish. I therefore have had no special worries about it, nor do I need to have. The opera goes along its old path, and the Regent has already found a fund for the operetta and comedy to build a new theater[3] that ought to be ready by the fall – thus, from this side of things, as long as it remains calm, one can fear no changes.

À propos – yesterday I was 36 years old – damn! And still no wife?[4] Ah well – it's probably for the best. There is already not enough for the Kapellmeister, so how would I be able to feed a Kapellmeister's wife on top of it? Moreover, this thought also occurred to me some two years ago, as well. That which I desire for my next 37th is a *good mood,* which God be praised I always have, and a few *less debts* than I had once upon a time, and subsequently, a few dozen Ducats in my pocketbook at the end of the year, which I do *not* now have.[5]

Adieu – for this time I've begun to write too late in order to be able to write an epistle that I wanted [to write] and should have done. Greet all my siblings; with the next post day, dearest parents, promise my little Marianne a letter from me. This time I'll keep my promise as I am named Joseph.

COMMENTARY

Original Buchen, Bezirksmuseum. Kraus's correct birthday, as noted earlier, was 20 June, not the 24th as he writes in this letter, due to his penchant for celebrating on the feast of St. John. While the tone of the letter is relaxed and conversational, he is clearly answering some cautious inquiries about what the death of his patron means for his position in Sweden.

1. The "shaking" could be a symptom of Parkinson's Disease, while the blurred vision was no doubt caused by glaucoma, both old-age onset.

2. Originally, Kraus mixes present and past tense in his narrative; the present author has chosen to regularize it up to the point where he relates his conversation in the interests of preserving the composer's story with some consistency.

3. The new theater was housed in the renovated Stockholm palace of the de la Gardie family, which had been used as an arsenal. This was finally dedicated on 1 November 1793, with the Royal Dramatic Theater and comic operas being performed there. Kraus saw the demolition of the old Bollhus Theater and most likely the beginning of the construction of the new house, now called the Arsenal Theater, in the early fall of 1792.

4. Kraus's parents have clearly asked about his marital status, but he has answered with a typically deflecting reply.

5. Of course, given his rather substantial salary, this plea of poverty is nonsense.

115. Letter to Marianne Kraus dated Stockholm, 28 June 1792

To my sister Marianne

Do you notice that I've kept my word and of course appropriately so; for my own name is now at stake. Thank you, dearest little Marianne, that you don't do the same thing to me; for that reason I still love you. May Heaven grant that we are able to while away a little piece of our lives quite nicely with each other: in truth, many hairs would first become gray before this happens. That would be my wish, but probably not yours; for you and your artistic gate curtseys right and left so much that you perhaps would feel right at home with your Egyptian meat stew,[1] and would easily resist the attempt to be transported to your Joseph in the desert. But, who knows whether or not art itself will finally drive you to me at some point? We have both seen Naples: Stockholm is certainly richer in painting than there and has more prominent views than perhaps any of the other famous cities in Europe. I thank you for the sympathy you take for my position, but where the hell did you fork up that pithy saying *"everything happens for the best of everyone?"*[2] Have they hung you in Mainz or some other place? – Hmm! You would have been conned there in your business. Ah well, in general, it's all just as well as *"Why? Because!"* But this gives one awful comfort, by my soul, or rather none at all. Adieu, dear sister; if I get the opportunity, I'll send you some music by the end of the fall.[3] Send me some of your seven items;[4] but of course it would be incomparably better if you came yourself. Fare well and love me always

    Your Joseph

COMMENTARY

Original Buchen, Bezirksmuseum. It is difficult to ascertain the allusions and private jokes that Kraus includes in this jesting letter, though it is clear that a visit to Sweden has been under discussion.

1. The reference is a biblical one, referring to the Patriarch Joseph and his sojourn in Egypt.

2. Orig. *daß alles zum Besten des Ganzen geschehe.*

3. This is an indication that Kraus was still composing music during the summer of 1792, implying that his Funeral Cantata was not considered by him to have been his own swan song, as has often been portrayed in the scholarly literature (see Si-JMK, AN-JMK, Sch-JMK, LH-JMK).

4. The seven items refer to her paintings she promised to send her brother.

116. Letter to his parents dated Stockholm, 30 November 1792

Since last summer my hemorrhoids have plagued me so damnably and gotten the upper hand, [so] that this winter I shall find it difficult to stick my nose out in God's free air. If only I could give this devil's tool to the emigrants on the road. They would not have wanted to keep it. Ah well, they would willingly have thrown it into the *channel* between *Calais* and *Dover*,[1] as previously the fat man threw out the red chamber pot into the canal outside the door to the office in Buchen: first mumbling in his beard, then turning each coat pocket (of which he had four on each side) in and out, and heaving every bit of garbage into the water so that he would be as free as possible from every large and small sin at once.[2] But, unfortunately, I shall not be rid of my household plague so easily. Let's see how it goes. Outside there is noise and tumult. Ah well, due to the exchanges, it is not so expected that one will see humanity turning somersaults over it. Among them it must still be rather despairingly troubled to sit right in the middle of such active people. And yet, dearest parents, I would rather desire more to be with you than here – truly it is a sort of homesickness – also, if I get my health back again in the new year; then may the red and green caps fight with each other right and left, and the Rhine and Main be shelled on this side and that, as it will – I shall be in Amorbach immediately.[3]

Unending thanks, my dear little Marianne, for your couple of friendly lines. If it was always the first desire of your *healthy* brother to live out the little life he has left beside his little Marianne – what do you think it means to *one who is ill*? I must remain obligated to my dear Alois not only for the requested philosophical and non-philosophical *Commentarium* on the great Frankfurt ox, but also even an answer. I've seen nothing of the letter with the Ducats.[4]

All my siblings are most lovingly greeted and kissed by me
Joseph

COMMENTARY

Original Buchen, Bezirksmuseum. Here is a serious indication that his health has been failing, but the self-diagnosis of hemorrhoids seems more of a deflection.

1. Orig. *Emigranten,* but Kraus probably means the French refugees fleeing the Reign of Terror in France.

2. This is obviously a reference to a local incident in Buchen that may have occurred early on in his life. The identity of this uncouth individual is not known.

3. This may be an indication of the spread of the French Revolution beyond the borders of France.

4. His parents have clearly sent him some funds, though for what reason cannot be determined, since there is no indication that Kraus required them. Perhaps it was an advance for travel, meaning that they may not have been entirely convinced of the security of his position. They would not have known about the political success of his opera *Marknaden* (The Market Place) earlier in the fall, which solidified his connection with the regent, Prince Carl of Södermannland (later Carl XIII).

Epilogue

This is apparently the final letter that Kraus wrote; on 15 December, only two weeks later, Kraus died in Stockholm. At his bedside was a trusted friend, the notary Henrik Engmark, whom he entrusted with the disposition of his will (Appendix A). On 24 December Hallardt wrote to his mother that "the illness was tuberculosis, which he himself would not believe." He continued: "He is already buried, which occurred in the most silent manner possible at his own request and at the estate of Count [Niels] Barck, who was also one of his friends, which lies some eight miles outside the city. . . . The connoisseurs of music intend to perform a funeral music of his own composition to the memory of their late friend and give the proceeds to the poor." On 22 February 1793, Engmark himself wrote a letter to Kraus's father, stating:

> Herr Kapellmästare, ignoring all of the pain that is the result of a strong tuberculosis, went toward death with a courage and a fearlessness that religion prepares its adherents, and that is only a characteristic of strong spirits and such men as God has endowed with extraordinary talent. Continually bedridden during the last days of his life, I saw him take his last breath and closed his eyes as my tears flooded down.[MM]

MM. The letter is found in Buchen, Bezirksmuseum. On August 29, 1794 Engmark penned a second letter to Kraus's mother in response apparently to repeated inquiries regarding her son's will, and the effects such as his gold watch which were to have been sent back to his family in Germany. Engmark excused his lapse in communication, noting that a number of factors had prevented him from fulfilling his commission. He also provided a synopsis of Kraus's final illness: "Now your most gracious Madame wishes information from me on your beloved son's illness and death, which I must report to you with a sorrowful heart, namely, at the beginning of the year 1791 he got a cough and hoarseness through a cold, which got somewhat better during the succeeding spring. But during the entire summer he had to live at court in the country palace of Drottningholm that lies about a mile outside the city; it is situated in a damp place surrounded by water, where he was weakened to such a degree partly by the air and partly by the night watch that the hoarseness returned. The following year or 1792 he added the plague of hemorrhoids, and because at the same time he had to return to Drottningholm, the last deterioration certainly ceased; instead, however, a pernicious wasting disease came upon him with such extraordinary force, especially since it was followed by a fever. I was with him as often as my duties

Kraus was buried at Brunnsvik on a promontory called Tivoli after a procession drawn over the ice. The intended memorial concert did not occur before 1798, and a monument was designed by Carl Sundvall in 1800, although it was never erected. Not until 20 June 1846 was a tombstone placed over the grave. It contains an epitaph created by Fredrik Silverstolpe: "Here are the mortal remains of Kraus; the immortal lives in his music" (*Här det jordiska af Kraus. Det himmelska lefver i hans toner*). One need not accept the final diagnosis of consumption; during this period, many respiratory diseases were lumped together under this rubric, and it would appear that Kraus's health was continually compromised, especially when it came to his lungs. One notes, however, that the final hemorrhaging that occurs in the final stages of tuberculosis seems not to have been present. The fact that he had such a short final illness may well mean that the disease was really a virulent form of pneumonia. In any case, his final letter, containing a more cheerful tone than was probably warranted, seems to imply that he looked forward to the continuation of his career in the future, something that this relatively sudden death tragically prevented.

(MM cont.) allowed, often at night, and the last eight days of his life I was at his bedside inseparably. I must also say with considerable comforting that religion and his philosophy gave him patience in all of his pain and peace in his soul, which in turn had the effect that he went to meet death nobly, blessed by his mother and sisters, and so weakened died in my arms. God! What a moment! I will draw a curtain over the tragic picture that I painted for myself over the loss of such a friend. What would a tender mother's heart not recognize? Lucky is he who has lived so that he dies missed and at peace!" From Engmark's somewhat synoptic description, it would seem that the composer suffered mainly from exhaustion, which along with other ailments contributed to a compromised immune system. The attack of the "wasting disease" appears to have come about without warning, but remains otherwise difficult to diagnose precisely.

The Last Will and Testament of Joseph Martin Kraus

RECEIVED AND READ BY THE PRINCIPAL NOTARY IN HIS ROYAL Majesty's and Kingdom's Consistory the Most Noble and Capable Herr Henrik Engmark, the undersigned, who under the terms of Chapter 18:1 of the Laws of Inheritance has been designated under the Royal Rights of Citizenry by the Royal Kapellmästare Herr Joseph Kraus during his lifetime on the 13th of December 1792 to execute to his heirs the following will and testament word for word as follows: Suffering from a severe and pernicious illness I have been made aware that my life will soon end, and therefore I have chosen to arrange and give recognition to in the first instance in consequence of Herr Royal Chamberlain and Most Nobly Born Count Nils Barck's promise made to me, that my last wishes are to be buried out at Bergshammar at a place that the Herr Count will himself designate; in the second instance that the Notary in the Royal Swedish Consistory, Herr Henrik Engmark, who has always shown the most firm friendship toward me and in whom I place complete trust, I do hereby appoint the so-designated Herr Notary not only to arrange for my immediate burial, but to take under his charge all of the effects that are in my name and domicile to distribute; To clarify my final wishes further, Herr Notary Engmark shall pay my housekeeper and servants the remainder of their annual salary that is due them, as well as pay their debts and bonds, and allow them to retain whatever possessions that they are legally entitled to that remain. In testimony of this I have signed this by my own hand in the presence of these good men, in Stockholm on 13 December 1792. J: Kraus.

That Herr Royal Kapellmästare Kraus of sound mind and of his own free will has made the aforementioned will and disposition, as well as having witnessed his signature by his own hand *at supra* [we are] H. Ölmenström and Sven Thorßander.

Be it resolved that due to the Herr Royal Kapellmästare having died, thus and hereafter Chapter 18 Article 1 of the Laws of Inheritance have been arranged with and communicated to the closest heirs of the deceased, and an official transcript has been given to them; if they within a night and hour thereafter do not find reason to object that this should be lawfully instituted. The hour and day prescribed is hereby established according to command by Gustav Biörk.

COMMENTARY

Original, Stockholm, Riksarkiv. This tortuously written testament is followed by a thirty-page inventory, made by Engmark "in the presence of the deceased's housekeeper Miss Sara Engmark, his servant Peter Sandbom, and his maid Anna Stina Björkman, all of whom were [also] present at his death." The sum total of his effects was valued at 295. 32. 9 Riksdalers (worth approximately £105,000 or US$166,950 at current economic currency exchange value), and the inventory reveals an extensive household of an upper-middle-class, highly respected, and well-paid court official. Engmark had hoped that Kraus's friend sculptor Johan Tobias Sergell would craft a monument, and while a plaster model was prepared, and nothing came of it until 1846 when architect Carl Gustav Blom-Carlsson erected the tombstone that still stands in the suburb of Bergshamra (alternatively spelled "Bergshammar" in the document) outside of Stockholm. While the household goods were distributed according to his will, certain personal belongings were returned to his family in Amorbach, including the often-pawned watch and his formal court costume. The remainder of his music library, especially his autographs, was given over to the Royal Spectacles, though some dispersal of this probably began shortly after his death since Silverstolpe was able to procure a number of autographs from the local antiquarian market. No inventory of the musical works was made. His extensive collection of books has disappeared without a trace.

Letters from Kraus's Family
to Fredrik Silverstolpe

A.) Letters from Kraus's sister Marianne Lämmerhirt and her husband Georg to Fredrik Samuel Silverstolpe (hereinafter FSS) 1800–1802.

1. Letter to FSS from Marianne Lämmerhirt
dated Erbach, 24 September 1800

With great pleasure I take over the message of my dear father to announce the timely receipt of Your Worship's letter, along with our most sincere gratitude for all of your friendly efforts on behalf of our unforgettably beloved late brother. My dear old parents are truly working on answering your biographical questions and will seek to fulfill with all their strength the wishes of Your Worship; the few interesting letters that we still possess by our brother you will also receive in copy along with other small works from his youth. My feelings at reading your wonderful letter, which my good parents immediately shared with me, are impossible for me to describe. I was glad and wept, for truly there is no better or permanent monument that you could erect to my dear brother than to give the details of his life to the world. How gladly I would also

These letters are bound into a volume in the Silverstolpe Collection, Universitetsbiblioteket, Uppsala, Sweden (X270f); they were published in a diplomatic edition in Helmut Brosch, "Quellen zur Biographie von Joseph Martin Kraus," *Mitteilungen der Internationalen Joseph Martin Kraus Gesellschaft* 5/6 (1986): 1–35. The letters written by Silverstolpe containing the questions he wished the family to answer have been omitted, although they can be found in sequence both in this published version and in the original source volume.

like to contribute to it, but I only lived with the deceased a short time. In that, you were far more fortunate than I. It was only during his return journey to Sweden in the year 1786 when he visited us for the last time that we got to know and to dearly love each other. Before then, when the good brother spent more time in the house of his parents, I was still too young a child, and he seemed much more a man than a youth of sixteen years when he lived with us almost an entire year. His early death wiped out so many of the beautiful plans that we had considered for our future. We had thought we would lead such a wonderful life together, and it was my firm decision to accompany him back to Sweden if he had been able to undertake his planned journey to Germany during the last year of his life. Fate determined otherwise. In him we lost much, for our good, worthy parents he was the only son they cared about at the time, who they correctly put forward as a model for the rest of his siblings, and still none of us can think of him without being moved. Forgive me that I've babbled on so extensively about this, but I speak of course with the friend of my brother, who already has shown that he is capable of sisterly affection. Now I have a request. I am convinced by your goodness that you will not think ill of me for it. For a long time it has been my most ardent desire to be shown the area surrounding my brother's resting place, even if it were only a cursory sketch within which the place of the burial is indicated. If this does not show a gravestone, I would like to erect a monument for myself and my family, since I dabble a bit in this art. Your Highness would be bound to me eternally if he could facilitate this for me. Please let me know your answer at your leisure, for already the hope that I might bring this wish to fulfillment has given me great joy. My address is Madame Lämmerhirt, born Kraus in Erbach im Odenwald, and you can also include a letter to my father, for we live only five hours distant. Not to strain your patience, I must close. Please accept the most esteemed assurance of our admiration and believe that I shall remain grateful for my entire life,

Your Worship's
most obedient servant
Marianne Lämmerhirt,
born Kraus.[1]

COMMENTARY

As a general rule, all of the letters henceforth from Marianne Lämmerhirt, Pater Roman Hoffstetter, and others call Silverstolpe *Euer Wohlgeboren* or *Euer Hochwohlgeboren,* which translates more or less literally to "your well-born" or "your most nobly born," though in this time (and afterward) it was used more in the generic fashion: "Sir" or "Gentleman." Given the recognition of all of the authors of Silverstolpe's important social position as chargé d'affaires to the imperial court in Vienna, translating this as a commonplace colophon and within the body of the letter seems too impersonal and distant for the tone and context, although it is appropriate for the salutation. Therefore, the archaic form "Your Worship" has been employed in those

circumstances. The other salutation, *Höchstgeehrter Herr,* has been translated as "Most Honorable Sir," though the translation does not evoke the same tone of high respect as the original.

1. On 24 December 1800, Silverstolpe wrote to Kraus's father, expressing his appreciation for this letter from Marianne Lämmerhirt. He notes that the requested sketch of the tombstone for her brother cannot be sent due to the insecurity of the post and the fact that the rendering has not been completed in Sweden. He asks for further biographical information to be sent via the chargé d'affaires to the Saxon court, Herr von Héland. He also notes that he included a letter to Roman Hoffstetter, to which he has not yet received an answer.

2. Letter to FSS from Marianne Lämmerhirt, dated Erbach, 19 January 1801

Most Honorable Sir!

Only the nearby rumors of war and the restless refugees that it causes, as well as the uncertainty of receiving letters from the post, have prevented me from answering your lovely friendly letter. I would that I were able to tell you all of my emotions upon receiving it. They are, however, feelings that do not lend themselves well to words. It was as if I had finally found my dear unforgettable brother half-mirrored in such a close friend! It also seemed to be upon cold reflection so improbable that perhaps I would still once have the privilege of making your treasured acquaintance personally. This thought has given me many quite a few happy hours in considering everything I wanted to ask you, for everything, even the most trivial thing about my dearly departed would be important for me to hear, thanks to the fate that we were sundered by a rather large bit of land in between. You would have become quite annoyed with me, but I want to tell you only in confidence and to have heaven preserve you from an hour of tedious women's prattle. And yet you will receive from me quite a few missives to read. I have to set them down immediately, for I am only a woman. Reading into your letters, please accept my most heartfelt thanks for your generous support of my request regarding the aforementioned sketches. I am really extremely glad, and of course to have those created by your hand would be of double worth to me, and still you give me hope of a reminiscence when you return to your fatherland, for it would give me eternal pleasure to create it for you. I will also send you something of my own work, as soon as they can be done following my household chores. Don't expect anything good, for I have never aspired to art, and since the time I was bound to marriage there have been so many other distractions, especially with the smaller creatures, that there has remained little time left for the fine arts.

There exists of my brother as far as we know only a single well-done portrait, made in Bologna for the famed Padre Martini, which the deceased had painted in the year 1783 on his journey through there. The sonata, of which you had the kindness to send me the themes, I received from Sweden. I am enclosing a letter from Pater Roman Hoffstetter. The arias noted therein I will no longer want returned until the mail is more secure again. Your Worship will receive a complete listing of everything that I still have of my brother's music. I only received fragments from Pater Roman of the operas *Proserpin* and *Aeneas,* along with a *Stella coeli* that the deceased composed during his visit to Amorbach for the monastery there. I know nothing about an opera *Azire,* for such a small thing my good brother knew was not to my taste. My musical knowledge encompasses only light sonatas and small songs. Come to think of it, I have another request. I possess the collection of songs that were published in Stockholm by Silverstolpe and in commission by Breitkopf und Härtel in Leipzig, but I don't understand No. 20 in Swedish. Would you be so kind as to send me this text in German. Because of its many diversions, I desire especially to know the meaning. This collection of songs has already given me so much pleasure whenever I want to make my husband happy. He always regales me with No. 7, *Der Abschied, Skuda winkt,* etc., etc.

Due to the housing of troops, partly, his age, and mainly the still painful memories of his most beloved son, my father has had no desire to work through the biographical questions. He passed on to me during my last visit everything that can be useful for your purposes, and my husband is now truly occupied with copying the letters. Because our parents have little awareness of music, our brother was only perfunctory in expressing himself on this in all of his letters. But it will be interesting to read the correspondence about this that the departed undertook during the tour with those who understood the art. I remember a certain Kapellmeister Reichardt from Berlin to whom he wrote diligently and esteemed highly, as well as a Lutheran pastor Schulthesius in Livorno. I am certain that if your most noble sir turns to these two men, that they will also contribute something to your cause. Finally, I assure you that quite soon you will have everything that we have around here that will aid your most gracious undertaking. At the moment, we hope for a real peace soon. Did you receive the three little works by my brother that my parents gave to the Herr Agent Dieffenbach[1] for Your Worship as he passed through Miltenberg? My husband has just now given me the task of sending you his friendliest regards. I therefore close and am eternally flattered to dare to name myself with all due respect

Your Worship's
most humble servant and
friend: Marianne Lämmerhirt
[P.S.] My good parents and siblings greet you sincerely.[2]

1. At this point is a caret with a postscript at the end of the letter that reads: "At the place of Herr Imperial Agent Haintz in Vienna [can be found] 1:) Schäfersgedichte; 2) the tragedy *Tolon*; 3) *Etwas [von und] über Musik."*

2. Note written by FSS: "Arrived 7 February 1801."

3. Letter to FSS from Georg Lämmerhirt dated Erbach, February 1801

Most Gracious
And Esteemed Herr Legation Secretary!

The approaching confinement of my wife has currently occupied her so much that I must ask Your Worship to allow me the liberty of continuing the correspondence in her stead this time, in so far as I am able to touch upon the answers to the biographical questions. First though, here is something regarding the copies of the letters that the late Kapellmeister sent his parents, which are included herewith. There are still a few more extant that I have not seen in copy because they deal either with simple family matters or, as is the case with the majority, concern his financial matters, which of course made necessary no small support on the part of his parents. Everything concerning his character or life I have carefully set out and I hope that Your Worship will find some material for your purposes. It is regretted very much that this is almost the only thing we can contribute to the beautiful monument that you wish to erect to the deceased, for he lived too short a time under the eyes of his parents, who might have been able to comment on his successive development. Only one year, namely the year before he went to Göttingen, was he with them; and throughout that time then they had to fight against a shameful cabal that was designed to destroy entirely the honor of his worthy father and thus the latter had of necessity to direct his entire attention to this matter. Even though later on, even before he went to Sweden, these shameful cabals had been mitigated, these were the main reason for him to deny his fatherland and seek his fortune in a distant land, as this is indicated in the first two letters from Göttingen. The 20th question – "Which music did he treasure as a beginner the most?" – would have been very interesting. No one here can give specific information about this. He had to learn and perform music with his first teacher, Rector Pfister, those of which he had were mostly without authorship. Moreover, with Cantor Wendler and Pater Keck in Mannheim he composed his music mainly himself without bothering anyone else.

What he then found himself liking cannot be determined. His staged development can best be judged from his own works that he continually produced from his early years onward. Because I myself dabble a bit in music, I dare not give my humble opinion about them, if scores still exist, especially of the sacred music. These are individual parts and thus it is difficult to follow the progression of the harmony. They have to be heard in order to be able to judge them, for which we of course have no opportunity here. I can perhaps say something in the future about the symphonies. Perhaps it is not inconsequential a remark that almost all of the siblings of the late Kapellmeister had a prodigious talent for music, and that they might have been led further down that path had they had better teachers in their youth. The Holy One who died in a cloister in Mainz played keyboard quite proficiently, and his brother Franz played violin so well that he was able to perform a concerto in Mannheim. I may not say too much about my wife, for she probably will read this letter, but I am quite proud of her. The successor in Fürth[1] plays his violin quite proficiently as well and thus takes a special pleasure in composing pieces himself in his free time. He would have especially benefited much from a good education, for even though he understands nothing about theory and thus naturally runs along with many errors, he often brings thoughts to the forefront that require nothing more than a editing to be called quite good. Especially fugal movements give him joy.

Please accept now my most effusive regards along with the greetings of my wife, with which I have the honor to remain

Your Worship's
most humble servant
Lämmerhirt

1. That is, Kraus's brother Alois.

4. Letter to FSS from Georg Lämmerhirt
dated Erbach, 15 March 1801

Most Gracious
And Esteemed Herr Legation Secretary!

Hopefully Your Worship has received the packet that I sent off to you last month. I would not have bothered you so soon again with a letter, for I still am not able to tell you anything special about the older works of the late Kapellmeister that I wish to rehearse here; I have been delegated by my dear in-laws to ask Your Worship with reference to the correspondence shared with you, within which the deceased spoke and was able to speak freely with his parents, particularly when his dear parents had to endure considerable hardship, but was cautious regarding the musical works and rarely if at all mentioned them in any fashion, so that his relatives were spared from [knowing about] them. As superfluous as I consider this reservation, I am still guilty of calming my most worthy in-laws who would not wish to see a matter raised that later on was once again resolved through the intervention of their sovereign.[1]

Moreover, I dare [to ask] if Your Worship is aware that a not-unique selection of the correspondence has been published in No. 18 of the third year of the *Musikalische Zeitung*?[2] To my great joy I found therein the appendix of the Swedish song, whose excellent translation into German I and my wife requested, and thus it is doubly precious to us. If my assumption is well-founded, I thank you with the warmest of hearts for the pleasure that you have created for us by this.

My wife, who fourteen days ago presented to me joyously with a young daughter, sends her most effusive greetings, and I have the honor of remaining with the assurance of my most perfect esteem

Your Worship's
most humble servant,
Lämmerhirt[3]

1. It is clear that Lämmerhirt fears that the correspondence contains subjects that would indicate Kraus's antagonism against the elector of Mainz for his father's indictment, and therefore might raise an issue that would seem ungrateful to officialdom.

2. Lämmerhirt refers to the review of the *Airs et Chansons* in the *Allgemeine musikalische Zeitung* for 1801, in which the song "Ynglingarne" is translated into German as "Meersturm, offner Schlund."

3. Silverstolpe answered Lämmerhirt on 15 April 1801 with letters to him and his wife, wherein he asks further about a thematic catalogue in their possession. He also notes that he has sent Haydn's *Creation* to Pater Roman Hoffstetter, and he offers to send further pieces in return for her help. Moreover, he notes: "from Herr Rector Pfister's letters I understand that he possessed a few quartets and symphonies that Kraus had set in Mannheim freely and without score." He urges her to contact Pfister for the two oratorios, *Die Geburt Jesu* and *Der Tod Jesu,* among other sacred works in order that they not be lost. He also wonders if she would not mind asking Hoffstetter about the missing final scenes from the opera *Æneas.*

5. Letter to FSS from Marianne Lämmerhirt, dated Miltenberg, 17 April 1801

Most gracious Sir! Most worthy friend!
The uncertainty regarding the package that we sent already on the 28th of February to the address of Herr von Heland in Dresden should

excuse my urgent request that Your Worship should inform us of the posting, since with such long delays and in case the package has not taken a certain route the postage label we put on here might become invalid.

Too, several weeks ago I posted a letter to you in Vienna, and I hope you have received it. Please have the kindness to address your reply to me here in Miltenberg, for I have undertaken a short excursion with my children for a few months to my dear parents after my recovery from my successful confinement. The quartering of the French is still quite onerous for us, and the care of my littlest girl robs me of the pleasure of being able to correspond with Your Grace with more length. I repeat only that with my prayer that your much treasured friendship along with the best greetings of my parents I can assure you of my most unbounded esteem,

Your most obedient friend
Marianne Lämmerhirt, born Kraus

COMMENTARY

It is clear that her letter and Silverstolpe's of 15 April crossed in transit and that she is answering in lieu of her husband once her confinement at her parent's home in Miltenberg was ended.

6. Letter to FSS from Marianne Lämmerhirt, dated Miltenberg, 28 May 1801

Dear Sir! Most treasured friend!

Among friends cannot be found empty excuses, even when I assure you of the impossibility of being able to be in the position of answering your kind letter earlier. You can speak openly about my procrastination, but I also want to assure you that our correspondence belongs among the most pleasurable of my occupations, and it must resume since you once more have given me hope of your personal assurances, which pleases my family.

I thank you very much for your well-wishes for my little girl, for such are rewarded through her continual health and growth for which a mother cares and worries constantly.

Above all, dear friend, please accept my most heartfelt gratitude for the gift I received. Would that I were able to enjoy the symphony like my husband!¹ Because I understand nothing of musical composition, I have to be patient until the time that I have the opportunity to hear it performed. Would that I were able to be a few magnificent hours at your Royal Kapelle.

The cantata by Mozart is very pretty, for we have already found it in the volume of songs that this great master published. I am however ever so much grateful for it, as if I had first known about it.

Herein you will receive answers to the nine points, as much anyway as I can remember with the help of my dear parents, and you ought to receive even more, and thus I put my patience to the test in earnest! Moreover, I do not require either thanks or excuses from you for the efforts I have already contributed and are able to provide toward your most worthy undertaking, and it has already been rewarded by reawakening reminiscences of such a beloved brother, in the hope of being able to support the memorial that you are establishing through that which I still possess, and – if I were to be completely frank? – that such a small conceit (that one ought to allow a woman to indulge, insofar as I still am deserving in a small way thereby if one could participate in your biography by presenting Kraus to humanity body and soul in the right view) to be known and treasured. A sister too finds such manifold rewards in this work that therefore requires no further thanks from my friend.

You are considering publishing this biography only after a few years. This has been one of my desires that has been close to my heart for half an eternity, but your reasons for doing this are too important and well-founded to be able to oppose it for any reason.

To conform to your instructions, today I am sending another package to you through the customs officer Grossmann, in care of the address of Herr Diefenbach, whose contents will fulfill your wishes; this is the list of everything that I have of the operas *Æneas* and *Proserpina;* the aria of Dido, which you wished to obtain from Pater Roman is also among them. How much it would please me if the lost scenes were to be truly found in Sweden; I almost hope for it because I wish it.

To prove to you that we do not mistrust you, you are receiving now all of the original letters that you don't possess yet to peruse at your leisure and to copy. That you will make discreet use of these, you do not need to be reminded.

If I should find something among the few letters lying about the house that would interest you, you will receive them, along with copies of the pieces for which you have sent me themes. I have requested from Rector Pfister all of Kraus's music, but I received the unpleasant answer that these have all been lost. The few that Pfister did send along you will receive among other items. These are two arias, a small symphony, and the oratorio *Der Tod Jesu.* The one on the birth of Jesus is lost, though not the themes, for soon after its inception, still in the year 1777, Herr Rector Pfister cobbled together a Mass from it, which I now have. Among the letters from Göttingen that the deceased wrote about to his brother Franz, you will find a new recipe due to this bowdlerization. If possible, I shall obtain a copy of the portrait once painted in Erfurt, and since I understand something about this profession, I would have copied it out myself, but I never received instructions regarding it. If you cannot learn anything about Schulthesius, to whom the portrait collection of Padre Martini came following his death, or perhaps if this friend cannot give us information when you write to him, I shall put aside my recommendation. I got to know him during my two-day sojourn in Livorno, where he showed me and my companions much friendship. He was a friend of my brother, and this was reason enough to seek him out.

It has made me quite happy to hear that the text to my favorite song, *Skulda winkt,* is by our dear Joseph, and now I enjoy it with double pleasure.

Is it not possible to also obtain some additional letter material from his friend Liedemann that would be useful to you? You should write to him. He must not have put too much store by his friendship with the deceased, if he doesn't want to contribute considerably to your noble enterprise.

In the letter of 28 October there exists a list of many musical works that he wanted to tell our brother Franz, who was still living at the time, about, but of which nothing remains with us. He must have taken these to Sweden with him. My brother Alois has the quartets that were published by Hummel. For a long time I could not fathom any real reason why no continuation of the first volume by Kraus had appeared, but after your explanation it is now clear. I hope that with a general and lasting peace everything can be once more brought into order. Consequently it is a pity that our late friend's works were botched so badly. These must have been set far too seriously for the Herr Virtuosi, who unfortunately now desire to promote manners and little trills just to show off the dexterity of their fingers, and therefore most of the things are so altered and disfigured that often the composer himself cannot recognize the production of his own spirit. On one such occasion I remember that I and my brother the last time he was in Amorbach visited the monastery there. At the gates we were surrounded by a large work of music. Stop, little sister, my dear Joseph said, let us listen a little to what is being served up here. After five minutes my brother laughed from the bottom of his heart. "I almost wasn't able to recognize my own work. Truly, to be left like that is more than anticipated; it is true castration."

Would you be able to develop something similar to the published songs in Sweden if the opportunity presents itself some time. That would please me greatly, for I would be able with the aid of my husband to enjoy them without difficulty. Certainly I can promise you that I will not make any copy to distribute, in the case that some of them should appear in print in due time.

It was certainly not equivocal for myself and my family to receive your pleasant news on the close relationship you have with Baron von Leijonhufvud, to whose consideration we are all indebted for having had this most worthy man hold back Kraus in Stockholm, as an original letter dated 3 August 1779 will prove. The deceased had as his greatest wish to thank this most worthy confidant for his continual care of everything, for it was through this most honorable man that he first learned of the cabals, and my brother never ceased to express the name of Leijonhufvud without gratitude. I have passed on your greetings to Herr von Klein.

Now in conclusion I have a request; I hope you will not take it amiss by your friend. It is that it takes far too much time to make my way through your German, no doubt due to your lack of practice. This is the main reason for your own lack of self-confidence and since you are determined to continue our correspondence by your own hand, I would ask for you not to humble me through such lack of confidence too much, for as a native-born German I too write my mother tongue in a very error-filled way, but I expect with friends that they pay more attention to the sense than to beautiful and correct grammar. But I have allowed myself to have learned how to read well and competently, and thus my dear friend, please write to me in whatever manner bears the least amount of effort. I hope I shall understand you.

Also, please accept my indebted gratitude for the German text you sent about the *Jünglinge*. That you through your kind intervention in the [*Allgemeine*] *Musikalische Zeitung* have made this piece enjoyable for us Germans for the first time you ought to certainly receive a silent, heartfelt thanks from each and every connoisseur. And now an entire stack of the friendliest greetings from the entire Kraus family to you, especially from my husband, and the assurance that I remain with unbridled sincerity

Your Worship's
most obedient servant
and true friend Lämmerhirt
born Kraus[2]

[P.S.] May I ask you kindly to take charge of this enclosure?[3]

1. Probably the *Symphonie funèbre.*
2. Note by Silverstolpe: "Arrived 7 June 1801."

3. The small enclosure (*Beischluß*) no doubt refers to the packet of music.

7. Letter to FSS from Marianne Lämmerhirt dated Erbach, 18 October 1801

How can I thank you, most treasured friend, for the receipt of the drawing of our unforgettable friend's tombstone? How can I describe for you the feeling inside that this evoked? You knew the boundless brotherly love that the deceased and I had for each other. You have moved me to tears to see the tombstone that he chose himself. Dearest empathetic friend! You understand the mute gratitude of his mourning sister.

I take the liberty of sending to you a remembrance for the most precious gift. I have chosen an object that I believe will conform to your taste. It is a piece on the ruins of the famous Colosseum in Rome. I count on your perceptiveness to seek not the artist within, but rather the sister of your friend. I would have preferred a picture of the area around here, but domestic affairs prevent me now from dealing with such matters, and you would not have seen the fulfillment of my promise any time soon.

Regarding your kind and very correct comments on the two drawings, I will make the best use of them, and certainly take to heart the beautiful light from out of which the monument so beautifully emerges. It has pleased me exceptionally that you have chosen to give me such an interesting return present as a remembrance. This will always have the greatest worth for me and be in a place of honor next to the silhouette of my brother.

I am most glad to have the songs that you have promised me again. The two arias that you requested, as well as the two symphonies and the oratorio, you will receive along with this letter. Anything else that we have of Kraus's music, you will receive immediately, as you desire. The packet that you have been continually kept abreast of was not from me, but rather was the score of Haydn's Creation. What you may yet wish to know is that Herr Pater Hoffstetter did not share such music so willingly with my husband, who wished to peruse it, and perhaps out of worry that the return would be delayed for too long. I am enclosing the original of the very modest and [unimposing] Mass that you requested.[1]

May I without great difficulty obtain a drawing of the sketch for the sarcophagus of Herr architect Sündwall?

Of the printed sonatas, I received two from Herr Engmark, one in E major and the other in E-flat major. If others exist apart from these, they would give me great pleasure to have. I have thus for that reason not answered your kind inquiry, for I assumed that my husband had noted them among his catalogue of themes.

Now finally, please accept most honored friend the assurances that in each language, as soon as I understand it or can make it comprehendible, your letters are so very pleasant and that I am proud to dare to call myself

Your Worship's
proper friend
Lämmerhirt, born Kraus

[P.S.] You will marvel [at the news] when I tell you that my husband sends his best greetings and has made an occasion to perform the Funeral Music. Even further, you will be astounded at the short time that was set aside to rehearse the music, for Count Fürstenau of Erbach, a great lover of music, whom we have to thank for his public support of the very small musical society we have here, was suddenly taken by a fatal heart attack during a symphony. My husband stood nearby, and I was also close. It was all the more moving that two days later the first rehearsal took place in the same room, and as imperfect as this was, it nonetheless made a great impression upon me, for I still see the dying Count in his place, and coincidentally my brother playing the instruments lying there. The thought was that this was the last work of our departed friend, and everything affected my emotions so greatly. My husband also made considerable effort, for he had only 48 hours after it was decided to perform a funeral music for the burial of this music-loving friend, including the copying out and holding rehearsals. And NB, because Herr Pater Hoffstetter had a score at the time, it had to be obtained from there [e.g., Amorbach]. But the pleasure of being able to hear the music at this time overcame all of the difficulties, and because we lack a few of the instruments, these were hurriedly obtained from the area, and all of these people were serious, for they did not do 10 repetitions, but rather it went as well as possible after three rehearsals. My husband was quite richly rewarded for his efforts, and was not a little proud of the fact that he was certainly the first to have performed this music in Germany. I did not need to have this pleasure rewarded with much money, and this, dear friend, we have to thank you for your kind gift of the score!

1. This is the Mass in E minor/D major, which is mentioned in the previous letter as the bowdlerization of the oratorio *Die Geburt Jesu* by Rector Pfister. The word "unimposing" is a reconstruction of a missing word in the original.

8. Letter to FSS from Georg Lämmerhirt dated Erbach, 4 April 1802

Most Gracious
And Esteemed Sir!

A small indisposition of my wife, for which she has principally to protect her eyes, gives me the liberty of writing instead to Your Worship and informing you of the timely receipt of the music and letters of my late brother-in-law. We are obligated with special gratitude for the songs that were enclosed therein, for they were completely unknown to us and most of them were exceptional. The requested music will certainly without fail be mailed from here on a post day in the future. Only a few are lacking, which most likely Herr Rector Pfister still possesses, but which my wife will obtain shortly. As well I am enclosing some others that were formerly to be found in the rubble of Herr Pfister. Also, a bravura aria that was only recently made known to us by Herr von Dalberg in Mannheim, about which we did not know, although you are already acquainted with it.

Hopefully my wife will feel better before the packet is sent, and then she herself will be able to write a few lines. In the meantime, please receive her most heartfelt greetings and from me the assurance of my greatest esteem with which I remain

Your Worship's
most humble servant,
Lämmerhirt

9. Letter to FSS from Marianne Lämmerhirt dated Erbach, 27 May 1802

I am almost embarrassed, most honored friend, to write such a bagatelle in a letter after so long a silence. I have left you to wait in vain for the requested music, but this was not my fault. A small misunderstanding delayed for several weeks the posting of the Mass that I wanted to send you, and in the meantime two of the agents died. I was thus forced to wait until a new one was elected in order to be certain that this matter would be forwarded to the address of Herr Diefenbach. Now nothing has changed, for the son of the first agent has taken over the business for the court here.

Now I have to speak freely of my knowledge before the seat of judgment of friendship, acknowledging my sins with an open heart, for all of these were the true reasons for delaying the posting of the music, but in no way a little letter wherein I could have reported. That was handled badly by me although I could have offered a dozen of the usual excuses, and in order therefore to wash myself clean, I would rather recognize my guilt, in order that I may hope to receive your forgiveness.

Please accept at once my most sincere gratitude for the little songs you sent. I have often been afflicted in my voice, which has never progressed in step with my desire. Of course, I cannot give any special praise for this to my rough teacher Rector Pfister, who sought only his own purpose not to have his pupils learn to sing but to crow. I would not want to say too much about this honorable elder, for it would make him die 10 years early, for he still considers me today as one of his best students, and that unfortunately may indeed be true.

Through your undertaking to translate my dear brother's opera into German you have in the very attempt allowed me to have the fulfillment of a highly improbable desire. To hear such a work! But we poor creatures are still chained to the obligations of our destiny. I pray daily to my Creator not to allow me never to live as a woman that I once desired to be, and thus I shall not have to do penance gladly for this existence for all eternity. It is not true that you have come to know me as a foolish woman, and now you always laugh. I don't take offense, for as a friend you don't mean any harm.

Ah, my children are now beginning to crawl, and I have to pay attention to them, otherwise I would be tempted to fill yet a few pages with foolish things. Accept my most gracious and heartfelt assurances of my most sincere friendship and esteem; remain my friend!

Lämmerhirt, born Kraus

10. Letter to FSS from Marianne Lämmerhirt dated Miltenberg, 12 August 1802

My most honored friend, I would have answered your letter of 19 June much earlier, had not a long-desired joy intervened, about which I want to inform you. I had hoped at the funeral of our lately deceased Prince-Elector of Mainz to hear the magnificent funeral music once again, and that in a better performance than the first time, for on such occasions many good musicians come together. Naturally, my husband carefully observed that the score did not fall into the hands of strangers, of which I already was quite glad. For such music has to make an impression on each human being who possesses a modicum of healthy emotion! Thus so many of these would wish to express out loud that it is a shame that Kraus no longer lives. This, dear friend, went directly to my heart, but the main pleasure was that I now wanted to experience this music in its totality, and thus I had despite all my efforts learn to forebear. I could get it performed, partly because too many old customs ruled in which one Prince-Elector after the other had to be confirmed on the ground, and this now-lengthy period of mourning has caused our new Elector much care, otherwise I would have immediately turned to him, because our friend was known and treasured during his visit in Erfurt, where Herr von Dahlberg was governor, by this man. I, however, have no hope of hearing this wonderful music of my dearest more than once, and should it be even on my deathbed, I would certainly go peacefully to sleep with high thoughts of God and immortality and with the joyous hope to find my dearest brother once again on the other side, which would make me feel less bitter about death.

I gladly grant you the wish that you would still like to retain the music you have had from me for a longer time and leave it entirely up to your discretion as to the return.

That you have traveled away from the city, I simply hope for your own pleasure and continuation of your well-being, but not that it had to be for health reasons. According to my wishes, dear friend, you ought to have to enjoy a long span of unbroken good health, for the world is not rich in men with great spirits and good hearts. There are two men who deserve to achieve an age of great ability. Of Herr von Dahlberg I hope with time he will publish even more pretty little things that I would have shared with you once upon a time. I believe that I have made you aware in my earlier letters, that I do not doubt that if otherwise Herr Engmark is amicable and still lives, that he would also have much interesting to say about my late brother, if Your Worship would approach him. I especially remember a travel diary that Kraus kept on his journey to Italy. This must surely have been found among his effects after his death and would be able to offer much material for your biography. I know of no words that can express my thanks for your so inclusive and heartfelt statements within your wonderful letter. You have shown yourself to be such an upright friend to an entire family that you don't even know personally, and how fortunate you must have been at first instance for our brother? I cannot set anything equal to that other than the honest acknowledgment that we feel the entire value of you friendship entirely and know how to treasure it.

It must be proven to you that I have only now at the end of this letter passed on the most ardent best wishes from us and all those who have participated in your higher promotion as Royal Chamberlain and how much I appreciate your many considerations as well. I have all of the necessary admiration for such a high position, but even more inwardly in my soul do I write my admiration for men of inner worth, I'm going to break off this sentence, for otherwise I would fall into a tone of flattery and I already know all too well your great modesty. I add only the wish that you are convinced of it and may you feel the most grateful friendship that our entire family has for Your Worship without exception, especially

Your

friend Lämmerhirt

[P.S.] In four weeks I shall leave here. I have spent already six weeks with greatest pleasure with my children at the home of my good parents, both of whom send their best greetings to you. My husband also gave me the task during his last visit to write quite a few niceties from him.[1]

---

1. At the end of this letter FSS penned a brief note: "Between this letter of 12 August 1802 and the next that follows from 23 February 1815 I received yet another letter from Frau Lämmerhirt, which was delayed during my sojourn in St. Petersburg. Within this one I found two notes: one, that she invited me in November 1803 to be the godfather of a son named Joseph Carl; the second that her mother, Frau Kraus, died in Miltenberg on 21 August 1804, after a 50-year marriage with her surviving 80-year-old husband. She was 71 years old." This letter has not survived.

11. Letter to FSS from Marianne Lämmerhirt dated Erbach, 23 February 1815.

Most esteemed friend!

You will be amazed finally to receive a letter from me after so many years. It was not forgetfulness, for I should no longer honor the memory of my dearest brother if I were able to cease treasuring you. So much has happened in the intervening time of our correspondence that I would love to describe to you on many sheets of paper. But I shall only write this letter with the intent of bidding me to enter into your friendly thoughts and await with longing to hear you how you are living. God grant you are guarded against such terrible trials as mine. I still don't know where

I gained the strength to survive, but I would have been ungrateful not to have recognized the goodness of God in my misfortune. I heard the most terrible thing that a wife who loves and honors her husband can hear, but with the relief of the faith of my friends and the shield of God, as well as the love of my children surging in my consciousness I was able to muster my inner strength and thus my fatherless five children obtained a mother! O how much I am grateful for the consideration that my dearest parents and my sensitive brother Joseph are no longer alive, for I would perhaps have been less able to bear my sorrows so steadfastly. Before I give you, my intimate friend, a description of the death of my unforgettable husband, I would first calm you with the assurance that I have never lacked courage, have always been aware of a mother's duties, have always considered how to strengthen everything to guard my health, and now have already won so much through this that I can prove to myself that *a human being can do anything he wishes,* but that he must only do it in all seriousness.

The 7th of November 1813 was the unlucky day that made me a widow. Ah, God, how shall I describe it. In short, Lämmerhirt became the victim of an overextended act of honesty. The Russian army had to be given a large amount of supplies. Eight days before his end my husband sought to arrange to send these the most expedient way. A very considerable amount had to be contributed by our Herr Count, and Lämmerhirt took care of this, for he had been in charge of the entire household of the court already for many years. Unfortunately, our merciful lord was absent. Even though my husband looked unusually fearful and I myself had lived through the terror of housing the Russians, I could not predict things at all. The evening before his death he was far more serious than usual and was extremely agitated. This did not worry me since I knew he was much occupied the entire day. He also had much color to his face and looked quite healthy and fresh. About noon on the 7th he said good-bye to me as usual, but he grasped my hand and pressed it more than normal. As I recalled later, he went to his official desk as always, prepared a few documents for his lord, read a letter to the Countess who had been called before the courts, worked a bit in his usual office at the palace, and left there as it became dark. He did not arrive for supper, but since this often occurred during these uneasy days, given that he worked nights until ten,

I waited for him until eleven, then midnight, but I did not believe any other thing than he had ridden off on some immediate necessary business and had forgotten to tell me about it beforehand. Early in the morning I went to the Countess, but the only question asked was: Where was Lämmerhirt? Several inquiries and riders were sent out to those places where he would have had business to attend, and I became quite uneasy that I had no presentiment of what had happened. I looked into the window of his study, for it occurred to me that he had suddenly become ill, and I searched the office thoroughly. Finally, and most unwillingly, the door to his room was broken open, and I went in with them. Luckily, the young Count found a small slip of paper lying on the desk next to his watch that my husband had written to me. He immediately sought out the Countess to inform her and assured me that every effort would be made to find where Lämmerhirt might be and that he would immediately dispatch a bevy of servants. But this lord knew after his departure what my husband had said to me, that the terrible truth always seeks a way to find the unfortunate. A quarter of an hour from here they found him dead in the water, and all efforts to save him were in vain. I heard about my misfortune from friends, and I and my four children were brought immediately to the palace, where I have lived for four weeks altogether.

I can never have earned the love and friendship that the gracious Countess has shown me. I pass over the first terrible days, and I suffered the second quarter even more than the first, which I lived as if in a dream. It was a great comfort to me to see how everyone loved and treasured my husband, but I felt even more what I had lost in him. And my poor children, especially the youngest who have reached the age where they need their father the most, when I regard them I am moved, but the hope and the strong faith in God has given me courage again. I sought to fulfill my motherly duties with strength and hope to raise my children to be good, useful people. That is much, but it is everything that I can give them. My economic circumstances are such that I must be frugal. But I am satisfied if I remain healthy and live long enough for my children to be able to understand and be as upright as their unfortunate father was.

Forgive this long letter with its sad contents, but one suffers the less through telling of things to friends. My heart still says that you are my friend. I now feel joy in music more than ever, though for many bitter hours I have not felt it. The portrait of my brother hangs above my keyboard, and I feel doubly blessed when I play through some of his compositions. This too leads to a more emotional feeling of the beautiful and noble. I now know this through experience, and now I and my children send our regards in hopes of your magnanimous friendship and await with longing a nice reply. I also wish to learn whether or not I still ought to hope that the biography of my brother may appear in print thanks to your friendly efforts. My dear, late father still longed for it in the last years of his life. He died in his 86th year in 1810, and my eldest sister also passed away two years ago. I loved her above all of my siblings, save for my brother Joseph. In this time I am to be allowed only the assurance of your most noble friendship.

Your servant, Lämmerhirt, widow.

B). Answers to Questions Posed by FSS *to the Kraus Family*

1. Written Questions and Answers Posed to Kraus's Parents

Q: Was he born in Amorbach?

A: No, he was not born in Amorbach but rather in Miltenberg am Main, a city in the Mainz Electorate, where his grandparents on his mother's side lived.

Q: Was he born in 1757, in which month, and on which day?

A: He was born not in 1757 but rather in 1756 on 20 June.

Q: Did he have another baptismal name other than Joseph?

A: Yes, he received the name Joseph Martin.

Q: What was the baptismal name of his father? His mother? His Siblings? How many of these are still alive? What is their occupation? What can you tell me about his ancestors?

A: His still-living father's baptismal name is Joseph Bernard, his still-living mother Anna Dorothea, and he had thirteen total siblings, among which nine have died, as brothers and sisters, and moreover in their youth, with the exception of a brother named Franz Bernard who was thirty and who died a year and a half before his elder brother, the Kapellmeister, after a fifteen-year-long nervous illness; also a sister named Katharina Josepha, who he loved very much and was the first born following him, but who went to sleep with the Lord due to the same lung condition as the deceased as a nun in Mainz at the Franciscan cloister at the age of twenty-three.

The will of the Lord be done. And yet both the parents and the still living siblings, all of whom loved the aforementioned deceased as good brothers and sisters from their most inner being, continually renew their grief and shed tears over their deceased.

Of the remaining siblings still alive are four, with three sisters, of which the eldest by name Anna Barbara is still unmarried, and the second by name Theresia is employed at the city office König in Amorbach in the service of the Mainz Electorate, where her father was the assessor and town governmental representative until his retirement. The third sister named Maria Anna is married to the court counselor of Erbach, Lämmerhirt.

The youngest brother named Johann Alois Ignatz has accompanied the official of the Electorate of Mainz, Vogtey, from Frankfurt to the main official in Starkenburg in the Odenwald.

Of the late Kapellmeister's forefathers one should note that his grandfather on his father's side was Rupertus Kraus, an innkeeper in Markflecken Weilbach near Amorbach in Odenwald, and on his mother's side, his grandfather Martin Schmitt was an architect living in the city of Miltenberg am Main.

Q: What had his late father initially decided he should do?

A: According to his wishes, he was trained in jurisprudence so that he consequently could be of aid to his father in his profession.

Q: Where did he do his first studies, or what education did he have?

A: In Buchen in the Electorate of Mainz, a small city in the Odenwald where his father was the city official for 14 years, there he received instruction and education until his eleventh year.

Q: Where were his studies continued?

A: Next in Mannheim.

Q: Who were his teachers?

A: In Buchen, the still living Rector Pfister and the late cantor Wendler. In Mannheim, among other professors, the two Kleins of the Jesuit School and among these one was the then Electoral Confidential Advisor Herr Klein.

Q: Which academies and universities did he attend?

A: After the Mannheim Academy, he attended university in Mainz, Erfurt, and Göttingen.

Q: Did he receive an academic degree and where?

A: He never received an academic degree.

Q: Which science interested him the most?

A: Poetry, and above all every philosophical work in law and *ius publicum.*

Q: What did he lean toward in the course of his academic studies?

A: An insatiable curiosity about all subjects.

Q: What profession did he decide upon?

A: In the beginning the liberal arts and jurisprudence, and then music and foreign languages.

Q: In which did he make the greatest progress?

A: In the beginning, in the law profession, but afterward in music and foreign languages.

Q: Did music appear to be a draw for him already in his youth?

A: Yes, already as a child he was drawn toward music.

Q: When did he begin to immerse himself in music and study it?

A: As soon as he reached his eleventh year in 1767, when he arrived in Mannheim at the Seminarium where there were daily exercises in music, and throughout the entire five years he immersed himself in music; likewise in Mainz and Erfurt.

Q: Who were his very first teachers in music and where?

A: He received his first lessons in music in Buchen, and his first teacher was Rector Georg Joseph Pfister, as well as Cantor Wendler.

Q: Who did he have later on?

A: In Mannheim he had various teachers on the violin, as well as Herr Abbé Vogler in composition and in [*blank space here*]. In Erfurt too he sought out several professional artists and traveled to Hamburg and Magdeburg to listen to them and learn something from them.

q: When did he begin to take seriously making this art his profession?

a: Principally in 1777 and 1778 in Göttingen.

q: Which masters did he admire the most as a beginner?

a: In the beginning various ones, which one can glean from his expressions in the musical treatise *Etwas über Musik* of 1777.

q: What is the chronology of his education up to the year of his travel to Sweden in 1778?

a: In 1768 he arrived in Mannheim, and there he remained five years up through the end of the year [e.g., December], and there he matriculated in the five grades there. Thereafter in 177[3] he went to Mainz, where he read Latin and philosophy. From there he went to Erfurt to study jurisprudence, and remained there the next two years when he was called home and stayed there an entire year. Afterward he requested to go to Göttingen, and upon permission from his parents traveled there in the month [*blank space*] in the year 177[8],[1] remaining there until the month of [*blank space*] 1778, when he undertook his trip to Sweden.

q: Are there anecdotes that bear testimony to the particulars of his intelligence, spirit, and genius both in his younger and in later years?

a: 2

q: Do a few samples of the undertakings during his childhood and youth still exist, both in the liberal arts as well as in music? Are these attempts to be found in written subjects or in essays on the arts? Does something exist that one might call the first attempt at music composition?

a: In the academic and fine arts there exist essays by him:

1) *Die Schäfersgedicht* from the year 1773, in print.
2) A small work, *Von dem Menschen Handeln,* that he began writing and did not complete.
3) The tragedy *Tolon,* published in the year 1777.
4) A musical treatise, *Etwas über Musik,* published in 1777.

Concerning anything that can be called his first attempts at musical composition, in hindsight several of these are described by

Rector Pfister from Buchen in his given testimony, especially the two composed oratorios for Christmas and Good Friday.

Q: What was his mood during childhood? How was it as the years progressed? Did he portray the philosophical attitude that seemed to permeate his manner of thinking and his whole character during later years?

A: His mood during childhood was happy and alive. [He was] full of fire, and it was in his nature always to accomplish in his studies anything that would make everyone happy. But early on he also betrayed much awareness of philosophical concepts, which seemed to be at the core of his entire manner of thinking and character in later years.

Q: Is one able to obtain all of the still extant letters to read that he wrote during his university years, during his travels abroad, during his sojourn in Sweden, in short, from his earliest youth until his death?

A: Herewith we are providing in copy all of his letters for you to read, including the original letters to Pater Roman Hoffstetter in Amorbach.

Q: Letters to him would be interesting?

A: His parents have none of these letters. These must have been found in his effects after his death and need to be searched out there.

Q: Is it not possible to receive a list of his musical works that he left with his relatives?

A: 3

Q: Has his portrait been painted, sketched, engraved, or printed in any fashion?

A: The portrait of him during his youth when he was studying in Erfurt can be found at his parents', but as a grown man and Kapellmeister he allowed himself to be painted during his Italian journey for Padre Martini, which he thought quite true to life as proven in his letter from Florence of 4 October 1783.

Q: Did he, as some have said, set the Odes of Horace to music, and which ones?

A: His parents know nothing about this. He must have done this in
    Sweden.

Q: May one request to read the poems that still exist by him?

A: The poems that we have here in our possession have already been
    gathered and sent, and to these you should refer.

Q: Did he really write a tragedy, and what is it called?

A: Yes, and it is called *Tolon,* published in 1777.

Q: Did he write anything else?

A: Apart from that which we have already noted, nothing is known
    about anything else.

Q: Was he of the Catholic faith?

A: Yes, and in his letter from Göttingen of [*blank space*] he points it
    out expressly.

1. The last number of this year, 1778, and a previous one (1773) are
    missing, indicating that his relatives were uncertain about the
    precise dates.
2. This question remained unanswered. The most likely reason is
    that it was overlooked in the rather substantive answer for the
    previous one.
3. This question too remains unanswered, perhaps overlooked by
    his relatives.

2. Additional Written Questions and Answers Posed to Kraus's Parents

Q: Was Kraus really born on 20 June?

A: Yes, but he had the caprice to celebrate his birthday on the
    twenty-fourth because he said that Johannes had become a
    great man.

Q: How many siblings are still alive and how many have died?

A: Including the Kapellmeister, there were fourteen, of which four
    are still alive and therefore ten have died.

Q: When did his father move from Buchen to Amorbach?

A: On 21 August 1778, when we were correctly forced to when
     our father was once more given a position that was equivalent
     in nature to the one he had held after a three-year suspension.
     He moved from Buchen to take up the position as treasurer in
     Königstein. He remained there until 18 January 1783, when he
     moved to Amorbach. His first years of service he remained town
     scribe in Amorbach, three years as a bachelor from 1750 until
     1754, where he married and remained another five years 1754 until
     1759. Afterward he was state official in Burken until 1761 when he
     subsequently obtained the entire Kellerei to govern.[1]

Q: Which year did the young Kraus spend at home and when did he
     go to Göttingen?

A: He was called home from Erfurt due to the trials of his father from
     the end of November 1775 and remained until November 1776,
     when he went to Göttingen, and from there directly to Sweden.

Q: Is the family name of his mother Schmitt?

A: Yes.

Q: Did Kraus write the text to both oratorios?

A: Yes.

Q: Was it in Erfurt that he learned fundamental composition or was
     it on his journey through Magdeburg and Hamburg, where he
     sought out famous composers?

A: Already in Mannheim Kraus learned the fundamentals with
     Vogler, who was at the Seminar at the same time, but Kraus
     assured [us] upon his return from Erfurt that he first learned what
     true composition meant. He had a special admiration for both
     Bachs in Hamburg and Magdeburg.

Q: How about on his journey abroad?

A: We are only able to give an incomplete answer, for in the majority
     of his letters we can see that he made his journey to Sweden by
     way of Wismar, which is also shown by his acquaintance with the
     Royal Counselor and Postmaster Hallardt there, who was his dear
     friend. He also visited Berlin, as far as I remember, and mainly
     those courts that did not lie too far from his path and where music

could be expected. In October 1782 he came to us in Königheim [i.e., Königstein], where he stayed a few weeks, because our father had to move to Amorbach already. Our brother then went to Mainz and Mannheim, from which he returned to Amorbach in January 1783 once more and stayed with his parents. He remained there until May when he went via Regensburg to Vienna, and from there to Italy, France, and England. From Paris he returned via Frankfurt, where I was at the time taking a course in painting, and together we visited our dear parents. This occurred in August to September 1786, when my mother and I accompanied this dear friend by way of Würzburg, where we spent several very nice days in Geldersheim with a good friend. But then the parting was all the more painful, perhaps due to the precognition that this would be the last time we would see him. He traveled on his route through Saxony to Stralsund and then immediately to Stockholm.

COMMENTARY

These two lists of questions and answers exist only as draft fragments in the Deutsche Staatsbibliothek in Berlin (Mus. Ms. Theor. 500, Varia 103). It is not known how they got to Berlin. In the preceding letter, it is clear that Silverstolpe wished to obtain as much information as possible and thought that his enlisting Kraus's family would be the best way to go about it. The second set of questions is complete, but it is not known whether the first set is or not. From the various missing answers, and several patently wrong statements contradicted by other evidence, it is clear that the familial memories were not entirely trustworthy after over a decade. Moreover, some of the information was passed on not from familial memories, but rather second-hand from letters solicited from Kraus's former teachers (see Appendix C).

1. His position was (originally) Amtskeller, or administrative officer, and the Kellerei was the official residence of the governmental representative in small central German towns. Burken is today Osterburken, about 15 miles south of Buchen.

Letters from Kraus's Teachers to Fredrik Silverstolpe, 1800–1802

1. Letter dated 20 September 1800 from Georg Joseph Pfister to Joseph Bernhard Kraus.

Oh, how pleased I was to have been yet able in my waning days of my life to have the honor, fortune, and pleasure of adding something to the biography of your late son and Kapellmeister.

The undersigned was the first school rector who had the fortune back then to have your five-year-old son in class, instructing him in Latin and music. His ebullient humor and exceptional talent were the same in both subjects, and from it one could discern what would become of him over time.

Barely seven or eight years of age, he was already so established in Latin essays that he could be recommended to a higher class. His disposition to music was equally so exceptional and miraculous, so that he was able to overtake in the range and ability of his descant voice that of his female soprano colleagues within the first quarter of the year, and also on his small violin, which was so large he could not quite encompass it, he performed in a trio the first part and I his teacher the second on the church organ to the wonderment of all; this he continued on into his tenth year of age, when he was accepted as highly capable in Mannheim at the Music Seminar there.

No wonder that during the five [years] he spent in school in Mannheim he was able to take first prize each term in the subjects taught there, and returned home with many gifts and awards. He also made such progress in music under the brilliant court virtuosos there that he was able to play the most difficult concertos by the various authors such as Fränzel, Kamawich, Kramer, etc., and became as the proverb says a *Discipulus ultra Magistrum.*[1]

In Mannheim he also began to compose small quatros and symphonies freely without score,[2] which I still have in hand today. From Mannheim he went to Mainz *ad Philosophiam,*[3] and thereafter in jurisprudence to Erfurt. There he told me upon his return that he had learned completely how to compose music. Here in Buchen he remained an entire year due to the indictment of his Herr Father and composed for my pleasure and that of all friends of music all sorts of sacred music, among which two oratorios on the birth and death of Jesus[4] were especially excellent and due to their beautiful poetry as well as harmony were heard and admired by both clerical and secular men annually in church.

All of this music I still have in hand and these will be noted and respected by each connoisseur as the best and most tasteful pieces of perfection above all others.

From Buchen he traveled to Göttingen, and for his farewell the entire music ensemble here gathered in the Kellerei and performed one of the symphonies with trumpet and timpani calls he had made himself to wish him a good journey with a thousand blessings.[5] Anything further beyond Göttingen I leave to his dear parents.

I still feel the joy that he caused me when he first arrived in Buchen from Sweden and visited me first, and with these words hugged me: I must thank you most of all for my fortune, for you laid the first and best foundations for music and Latin!

Oh, what I might yet have gratefully experienced. You grim Death! Why did you rob me of him? The blessed Herr Prelate in Amorbach[6] once told me over the table: Herr Rector, you and all of Germany have the honor of having raised a Kapellmeister of the King of Sweden.

Georg Pfister, Rector in Buchen

COMMENTARY

The letter, of which only an old copy has survived in the Bezirksmuseum in Buchen, was written at the request of Silverstolpe, who solicited Kraus's family to provide information about the composer's youth and training from former teachers. Pfister, despite his self-aggrandizement as Kraus's first and most thorough teacher, was not noted particularly for more than local competence, and thus his claims to have provided grounding for his pupil must be taken with caution.

1. The composers, mangled badly by Pfister, can be identified as Iganz Fränzl (1735–1811), Christian Cannabich (1731–1798), and Wilhelm Cramer (1745–1799), all three of whom wrote challenging violin concertos. The other "various court virtuosos" are not named, but it can be assumed that they were members of the Mannheim Kapelle. The Latin term *discipulus ultra magistrum* means a student who has excelled beyond his teachers.

2. Orig. *aus freier Hand ohne Sparta,* meaning Kraus wrote the compositions out directly into parts without needing a score. The term "quatro" probably means in context orchestral quartets rather than string quartets (*quadro*), given that the former were common in Mannheim. This is, however, open to interpretation.

3. *Ad philosophiam* = in philosophy, meaning a liberal arts curriculum.

4. The oratorios are *Die Geburt Jesu* (VB 16) and *Der Tod Jesu* (VB 17).

5. Orig. *Musik-Chor,* meaning the ordinary musicians resident in Buchen, mainly as an orchestra. The symphony (VB 131) has not survived.

6. Herr Prelate in Amorbach presumably refers to the abbot, Hyazinth Breuer (1753–1794).

2. Letter and Appendix dated 6 November 1800 from Pater Anton Klein to Marianne Lämmerhirt

The reason for this long delay in answering your gracious letter of 29 September is an absence for an extended time and the hope of finding something about my dear late friend, your Herr brother, by a thorough search of my letters. My papers have become disorganized due to much fleeing and the tremendous bombardment and destruction of our city, and many have disappeared. Truly, I cannot find any letter from my good friend Kraus. I thus send to you here that which I have not been able to dismiss from my thoughts for thirty years and which will not be forgotten over any length of time. It is my great joy to have the opportunity to deliver this small addendum to the memorial of my friend.

Please greet Herr Silverstolpe and keep his friend and keeper of the soul of your Herr Brother in your good thoughts. I remain with the most perfect sincerity,

Your most humble servant
Klein

The late Royal Swedish Kapellmeister Herr Joseph Kraus from Miltenberg in the Mainz [Electorate] was under my care for three years, from September 1768 to September 1771, and under my instruction a credit to all youth who study. He excelled by means of talent and industry far above his fellow students. He had a happy demeanor, natural intuition, and expressed quite early on a healthy sense of judgment and aesthetical feeling. Moreover, he truly had in this the appearance of an angel, and I cannot describe how much pleasure he gave me in the three years of my teaching.

At that time I was involved in a hard struggle against prejudice and pedantry that permeated the study of German language and literature in the Latin school of the Gymnasium here. The young Kraus repaid my efforts with the progress he made in this curriculum. He was right behind me, as well as a supporter of disseminating a taste for the literature of the fatherland. He not only encouraged his fellow students, but also other youths whose teachers did not want to give up their old prejudices against German authors. I shared with him our contemporary poets and the best translations of the French essayists, all of which he read. He created excerpts that were testimony to the most fortunate usage of the teachings that were passed on to him. No beauty escaped him, and I read to him from the most famous poetic and prosaic works quoted passages in order to ascertain his core diligence at the beginning of the public lectures, but I soon realized that I was able to allow him access to this or that work in a very short span of time. When he finished reading one, he then turned to the next.

One can recognize a milestone in the spread of German literature in the Pfalz, when he and three other fellow students publically read a German poem. The numerous and receptive gathering of people were so taken by the correct diction, by the emotions and fire of this youth, that from this time forward none of the enemies of German literature dared to mount public attacks, but rather the patrons of the Gymnasium took him under their protection and even the court, at which only French was spoken, became aware of it.

The annual prize was always given only for Latin prose and poetic essays. Nonetheless, the young Kraus obtained first place. He had a great competence in Latin verse and composed several poems of considerable length. My profession tore me from this dear young friend. Our parting was that of a son from his father.

I shall search all of my letters and perhaps will be able to find something by him, for he wrote to me often for many years. One year after our farewell he sent me Idylls[1] that he had composed and published in Mainz; perhaps these are already in the hands of Herr Biographer.

The perceptive letter by him I received in 1785 from Paris and which I published in the *Pfälzische Museum* Vol. 2, p. 964 I include herewith.

Receptivity for the most noble and beautiful, generosity and graciousness, forthrightness and a desire to express friendship and emotion, leadership, a grateful heart, and morals that were without guile or superficiality comprised the gregarious character of the noble youth.

COMMENTARY

The letter from Pater Klein exists only in a copy in the Bezirksmuseum in Buchen. The situation, where the occupation of the Pfalz by Napoleon's troops was an ongoing process, no doubt contributed to the loss of what must have been a voluminous correspondence between Kraus and Klein, if the published letter (no. 73) is any indication. It is clear from the tone of the addenda that the Jesuit treasured their friendship greatly, and moreover it demonstrates that the composer was well-versed in the literary trends of the time.

1. Meant here is the *Versuch von Schäfersgedichte,* of which unfortunately no copy has come to light.

3. Letter of 5 October 1800 from Pater Alexander Keck to Alois Kraus

Dearest Herr Alois,

As surprising and pleasant as your missive was, the memories of one of my best and most talented students that I ever had were equally depressing. He came to me at the Seminar as a beginner in music. I presented him as a soprano, in which range he sang with heart and without fear solos and recitatives, but soon I put him on violin, on which he made laudable progress. He began shortly thereafter to compose by ear, and when the world-famous Herr Vogler[1] came to him, he studied diligently with him in secret, [and] composed after his departure a concerto for two violins, which he and another pupil by the name of Fuchs performed in the church to much approbation. In the fifth year of his residence I gave over to him half of a musical play, for I did not have enough time, and which he succeeded doing with great applause. Even with this, he did not shirk from seriously applying himself to the Latin sciences and carried off the best prize in that in all five years. And at that time German literature became noticed, and he began during the night hours to compose a pastoral poem that he published the following year in Mainz, where he had gone to study philosophy, and he sent it on to me. Subsequently he went from Göttingen to Stockholm and, when he had the fortune of being allowed by the king to travel, he returned to me in Mannheim, spent a few days at the Seminar. But there he had other business to attend to, visiting the Electoral library, obtaining material for his Swedish profession, and moreover demonstrating his knowledge. At home he also composed a symphony that he took in score with him, and instead of this he left an edition of his engraved quartets at the Seminar. He promised me to compose a new Mass[2] for the jubilee of my ordination, which was to occur the following year, and to invite all of the Seminar students he still knew, and if it were possible, to travel from Stockholm to Mannheim himself to produce it. Could any greater sign of his love for me be expected or conceived?

My God, the Lord has torn him from me. He was great, and as long as he was with me he demonstrated to me that he feared God and had the Eternal as his goal. It is this that I wish to answer to your question, dear Herr Alois, or rather I should have said formerly, Little Alois. Yesterday in Wertheim I received your most worthy letter, having arriving there Monday last. Perhaps I shall have the honor during this sojourn to speak with you personally and to greet you as my dear cousin. Who would have thought this a year ago? Please give my regards to my dearest Frau Baas, who showed me so much kindness formerly in Heppenheim. Lord God grant you peace. With regards

Your most humble servant
A. Keck

COMMENTARY

Letter preserved at the Bezirksmuseum, Buchen. The tone of the letter is more conversational, with hints that Alois Kraus probably also studied under Pater

Keck for a time; it is unknown how close a familial relationship the Jesuit had with the Kraus family, although the familiarity of the final lines seems to indicate some. The cities Wertheim and Heppenheim indicate that Keck had already left Mannheim by 1800, probably to avoid the French occupation. Keck too takes more responsibility for Kraus's education in music than was the practice at the Music Seminar, but the remarks on the composer's progress and achievements are similar to that found in Klein's letter.

1. Vogler was neither *welt-berühmte* nor even known as a teacher of music during Kraus's time there. Here Pater Keck has muddled his memory with Vogler's later reputation. "His departure" refers to Vogler's departure to learn musical composition in Italy in 1768; it is not known even if he stayed in Mannheim prior to that date, and in any case, his "teaching" was not available to the young Kraus for more than a month or two at the most. This statement, however, may have been the source for the answers given above by Kraus's family to Silverstolpe's questions about Kraus's early teachers.

2. The Mass (v b 2) has been lost, and it is even unclear whether Kraus actually fulfilled his promise.

Letters from Pater Roman Hoffstetter to Fredrik Silverstolpe, 1800–1802

1. Letter dated 4 September 1800

Most nobly born and especially highly honored Sir!

As pleasant and flattering as the receipt of the most treasured missive, with which your Grace so honored me on the 23rd of August, was, it is consequently now most unpleasant for me not to be in the position of being able to comply with the best intentioned and expressed request about the sending of contributions toward the spirit, possessions, works, etc., of our late Kapellmeister Kraus, was well as [I] might wish. Nonetheless, [I] had the pleasure of having been honored with his always precious friendship, as well as having often enjoyed a very pleasant and extensive exchange – when he was here in Amorbach – both in the Kellerei here with his parents, as well as in my living quarters in our monastery. But due to my unfortunate hearing *defect,* which at that time had already begun to become much the worse, I lost unfortunately all of the advantages, all of the pleasure almost entirely. In addition, of all of his letters, of which he wrote to me a huge number especially during his travels from Italy, Paris, etc., and within which many interesting incidents, *anecdotes,* and commentary was contained, I can only find four and these only the shortest of them, even though I've searched long and hard throughout my papers carefully. Perhaps they were mistakenly

The original autographs of these letters is in Uppsala, Universitetsbibliotek, Folio X27of. They have been reproduced in a diplomatic edition in Hubert Unverricht, *Die beiden Hoffstetter* (Mainz: Schott, 1965).

gathered among other letters, which were destroyed two years ago after my rooms were emptied, the greatest number of which were burdensome and of no use to me anymore. This occurrence now angers me all the more, since I would have been in the position now to have delivered much good and useful material to the proposed work. However, I shall send old Herr *Kraus* this consequentially very small remainder, which contained news of the *Concerts spirituels* in Paris and something similarly important from London honoring the late *Handel,* so that he, if he thinks it worth the effort, can forward them on to Vienna.

Regarding the musical works of the late Herr Kapellmeister, [I] once possessed a substantial number. His opera *Proserpina,* which, if [I] am not in error was his first, [I] copied out for myself almost in its entirety, so, as well as the greater part of another – *Æneas* – which was still in progress during his last visit here and not quite completed. He also promised me to send the remainder from Stockholm of the *score* of a *Miserere* that I had cobbled together at that time, and that he demanded of me to take with him, which did me great honor. I happily also possessed quite a lot of individual *arias and motets,* with Italian and Swedish texts, as well as his 6 printed *quartets,* of which he himself gave me a copy. All of these I gave away to one of his sisters a few years ago, because she urgently asked for them, and I had just come to a decision at the time due to my increasing *handicap* to adjure music altogether. Since then, I have not been able to withstand my musical association for long, and began again as well as I was able to go to the keyboard to compose, and now [I] regret my former generosity. – only a few arias that [I] can't seem to find right now and for which only a single melody remains, and a *Duet for Soprano and Tenor* in G, still remain with me. Mainly, however, a *Stella coeli* that he was commissioned by me to set for our musical ensemble when he was here in Amorbach in 1783. In truth, it was a brilliant, masterfully-set work! [It] is in C major, begins in three-quarter time. After a brief *ritornello* and short introduction for *solo tenor,* a pleasant, majestic chorus begins that finally transitions into a beautiful, deeply conceived fugue in C minor. The conclusion is done by a very accessible, highly pleasant *solo* organ, and in this as well the *soprano* has a short *solo* at the beginning, after which a full tutti follows, replete with obbligato organ throughout. He gave me the *original* of it, his own *autograph* consisting of 22 concisely written pages in oblong format; and to set this he didn't require two whole days! Throughout the entire work there is not a single note crossed out, even though the fugue is especially deeply developed. Truly! He was a great man! And he would certainly have been even greater had death not removed him from the world so early.

Of his remaining works, [I] have partly seen and partly also heard:

a) A large bunch of various individual *motets,* with Swedish as well as Italian text.

b) 6 keyboard *trios,* that he once played himself in my chamber, and that I accompanied on the *violin.* They were magnificent! Filled with the most beautiful thoughts and turns, [they] perhaps appeared afterward in print, or at least he seemed at the time to have the desire to do so.

c) Several, very full-voiced, very beautiful and brilliant symphonies, that he set in Paris, creating them with all possible art. We played them at his parent's home only *à quatro* because we didn't have the necessary people, and they still gave a marvelous effect!

d) Also, [I] have heard a *Te Deum laudamus* by him that he composed back in his early years before he went to Hamburg and Sweden, which even then portrayed the secure skill of a future first class *composer.* His Herr father retired with honor from his official duties a few years ago due to his advanced age and now lives in Miltenberg, some two hours from here, by his own means.

One of his sisters, who was in a cloister in Mainz, died already many years ago.

Another, as far as I know the eldest, lives in Miltenberg with her parents, is nonetheless unmusical, and more or less very diligent; [she] substituted for her father in the last years of his office in virtually all of the business of the Kellerei.

The third, married [and living] four hours from here, plays keyboard, sings, and possesses a great talent still in painting. The fourth and youngest is engaged with the successor of her father at the same Kellerei.

The younger brother, who is rather competent on the *violin* and *cello,* has a clerk's position about seven hours from here, in Fürth if [I] am not mistaken.

The late Herr *Kraus* had for the most part nothing good to say about Italian *composers,* and only a few of them appealed to him, among these mainly *Piccinni,* whose opera *Dido* he praised to me for much but not all of it. It was given then in Paris during his sojourn. *Jommelli* had his higher approbation and more completely. A *Miserere* with Italian text that [I] had by him, pleased him [e.g., Kraus] greatly, and he gladly took it with him when I gave it to him. *Gluck* was his man, the model, that he diligently studied in theatrical matters, and I believe he would have become a second *Gluck,* perhaps even more, had he lived longer! Often, when he raised his dear *Gluck* higher than the stars, and I to the contrary my dear *Haydn,* for whom [I] have always been an enthusiast on my part, [I] came crossways with him, [and] we entered into a musical debate, which he finally decided to my satisfaction that *Gluck* once and for all was the greatest master in all things for the theater, but *Haydn* was the same for all of the remaining musical disciplines. He had memorized almost all of *Gluck's* works, played these often to me without seeing a single entire page of the *overtures,* long *recitatives,* choruses, *etc.,* and to such a degree that he never forgot any of the parts, expressing everything in order.

Regarding the aforementioned *Stella coeli,* [I] once upon a time sent off a copy to Vienna, but I don't know any more to which address, upon the request of the dearly departed, who wrote me on his journey to Stockholm from Vienna. If nonetheless Your Highness doesn't know about it and in any case would love to look over it yourself, then [I] am ready to serve you with the original and only await your command.

That you have made the very interesting and highly welcomed decision on behalf of the entire musical *public* to author the biography of *Kraus* yourself pleases me no end, and moreover because I am entirely convinced that this work could not have come from a more talented pen than yours. If only I could deliver a significant contribution in good, usable material to it, or at least [I] hope with confidence that the old Herr *Kraus* is able to deliver completely everything he knows best regarding the entire life story of his late son from beginning to end, his musical studies, his progress, achieved greatness, etc. Only an exact, complete catalogue of all of his musical works might be difficult for him, perhaps even impossible, because he mainly wrote the majority of his greatest and most important works in Sweden, which, as far as I know, were never published. But Your Grace would himself be able to fill this in with the information from there. Kraus would have, as has been told to me, counted only thirty some odd years before he died! In so few years, so great! What would he have become had he lived on a number of years more!

Here in this country we are at present in a terrible, utmost critical situation. A barbaric, inconceivable horde of Egyptian scythes have invaded the length and breadth of everything, wallowing in the fat of the land, and will continue to wallow until everything is nothing but stumps and sticks. It is all the more terrible for us if, as the French themselves maintain a few days ago, the sorrowful war begins again with new ferocity. They have already become so powerful and arrogant that it is difficult – [I] would almost say, impossible – to avert it, and so it would be that one seeks finally with united strength to mitigate the overbearing evil, although there has been no likelihood of this happening up to this point.

Forgive this digression, as well as my hasty, disorganized correspondence! For I cannot take the necessary time out of fear to postpone an earlier dispatching of letters to the old Herr *Kraus*. [I] wish to enclose nothing more than – the most personal heartfelt wish to see the hoped-for fulfillment of this most cherished decision; and then finally in the certainly non-obeisance assurance of every exceptional and most perfect sincerity and esteem, with which [I] have the honor and pleasure of being

Your Worship's
Most attentive servant,
Roman Hoffstetter.

2. Letter dated Amorbach, 3 November 1800.

Your Grace is herewith finally receiving the requested arias by Kraus, and I have to ask your gracious forgiveness immediately that the posting was so long delayed. The duet was in the beginning so hurriedly and illegibly written that it was without doubt necessary to copy it out anew in order to be able to send it; moreover, I lacked the required score paper, my supply of which has long since run out completely, since we can never acquire this in the nearby countryside, and the postman, who always brings it with him from Frankfurt, has not been able to come here for a long time, probably because now everything is occupied by the French. In order not to delay the posting even longer, [I] was finally forced to gather together all of the empty leaves that [I] could still find. Thus there was the binding, nebulous matter of *copies,* for which [I] once again have to beg your indulgence. Along with that, I feared simultaneously that the *duet* would be of no or little use to your Worship for it lacks text; because it was in Swedish, for those who are unknowledgeable about this language it is most difficult to write, [and therefore] it was left out of the copying in order not to stop [me] from a work for which I would moreover have had little use. At that time, [I] truly did not think that the aria could in time be sent somewhere else, where one might be better able to use the text and it would be unfortunately missed; otherwise, [I] would have placed it within as far as I had been able.

I would gladly have included the 3rd aria in A-flat in $\frac{3}{4}$ time, but to my shame it was impossible for me to find, although I already searched all of my music and correspondence with the utmost diligence; and yet [I] must still find it, for I am certain that [I] have never let it out of my hands. In this case [I] come across it, [I] shall write it out quickly and have the honor of sending it to you.

That Kraus had written an earlier opera besides *Proserpin,* namely *Azire,* was unknown to me entirely; if this still exists, which [I] do not doubt, you will find it with his sister, for he truly treasured her among all of his other siblings and would not have kept it from her. As well, [you] no doubt will also find the two missing scenes from *Æneas* [there], failing which it would be truly a pity, for this opera is extraordinarily pretty [and] written out by the deceased with special diligence. I only know of these two operas, *Proserpina* and *Æneas,* by him. The funeral music on the death of the late King is also, as it has been told me, beautiful and magnificent throughout, but [I] have not yet seen it. How much else flowed from his wonderful pen about which [I] have no knowledge, for didn't he write the most and best [works] in Sweden?

I've been told so many beautiful things about Haydn's magnificent *Creation,* that a thousand times the innermost desire of mine has arisen at least to be able to look through the score of it, and since this will now never happen, [I] would like to obtain at the very minimum the piano score that has been announced in the papers, if only the accompanying high price of 11 f. that is beyond my funds were not an unresolvable obstacle. The work must truly be very thick, for the piano score alone to be set so high! Without doubt, the new work, the Four Seasons, of which Your Highness has graciously told me, will be equally so magnificently received, for from this pen nothing but good can come! This great master, musical Creator, may I say, has already written so much that is unbelievably beautiful that one would hardly believe that he was uncreative.

Really, Herr *Vogler* is no longer in Stockholm? Since *Kraus's* death I heard nothing more from him, apart from the news that was recently reported in the Frankfurt newspaper that he was in Berlin and in process of realizing his new invention of an organ with fewer pipes than usual. This person seems to me truly to be very adroit with regard to music theory and in keyboard performance, but in composition he is, in my view, universally beneath *Kraus* and can thus never equal him.

In order not to trouble Your Highness any longer, for now [I] give you only my most ardent assurances of my unlimited esteem that I have and continue with the most treasured honor to have,
Your Worship's
most humble servant,
R. Hoffstetter

3. Letter of 8 May 1801

Dear Sir,

[You] have shown such generosity and goodness with the posting of the *Haydn* masterpiece in return for my trifle, and thus have so completely astounded me, so eliciting my gratitude, that [I] feel obliged to express myself as happily as possible. I could hardly believe my own eyes when I saw this magnificent, in its own way singular work in my hands, and moreover was completely surprised that Your Grace himself took on the cost of *shipping* as well. Truly, that is too much! and much more than I had dared or was able to hope for! Accept my most fervent, much-obliged thanks! May I be in the position of being able to show some similar sense of reciprocity. In hindsight, I now wished more than ever before that I had not been in such a hurry to sell my music collection several years ago, for this was quite substantial, containing well above 100 operas in addition to a large number of various printed and manuscript works, and therein I would have been able to find perhaps something with which I might have had the pleasure of being able now to absolve at least a portion of my considerable debt and obligation. The small remainder consists of only the following: *Le Tableau parlant, Le Huron,* and *Le Magnifique,* all three well-known by Grétry and printed, the first two in a single volume and the third by itself; *Les Pecheurs* by Gossec, as well as *Toinon et Toinette* also printed and bound together; a manuscript large opera by Scarlatti, *Isÿpile;* a cantata by Reichardt with English text, which I left out of the copy. I obtained it from Herr Kapellmeister Kraus, who seemed to set some value on it; it is quite pretty with a fugue at the end. Further, a recitative by Haydn, *Ah, come il Core mi palpita,* as well as his beautiful *Stabat mater, L'amore in compagna,* an intermezzo by Borghi, two volumes within which a scene is missing, however; the opera *Catone in Utica* by Graun; *Acis und Galathea* by Hasse, and from the same person various oratorios; *Ciro riconosciuto* by Sarti; *Il gioco di Pecchetto* by Jommelli. *Die Auferstehung von Lazarus,* an oratorio by Rolle, is completely written out but not put in the required sequence, because in the beginning I only wanted to make an excerpt from it, and by and by I wrote out all of it. Finally, Graun's *Der Tod Jesu,* printed; *Esther* by Ditters[dorf], and various arias by various authors. May there be something appropriate to be found among these, and with pleasure [I] would post all of it without the necessity of sending it back again. My own recent works of lesser or no worth [I] dare not bring into the equation; they are only Masses, that nonetheless have honored [me] in this area with some approbation. Perhaps the people aren't used to better. But to be performed there in Vienna, where there is a confluence of masters and masterpieces, would be presumptuous.

I have still not begun to study *Haydn's* magnificent *Creation* with diligence. First, I would like to complete to the end a Mass that is in progress, for fear that an earlier study would rob me of all desire to continue to work; then when [I] am finished I would fall upon it hungrily, for already with the first cursory glance that was impossible for me to withstand I discovered a thousand beautiful things. The storm itself is wonderful, and contains everything that one can think appropriate to something wild and ferocious (and at the same time pleasant) to the highest degree. Both works [I] shall preserve without spoiling them with the smallest annotation, and will return them most gratefully, though I would ask your most kind permission for which I flatter myself in being able to obtain the opportunity to copying them out first. It would be a shame to let them out of my hands uncopied!

The third aria by *Kraus* [I] have not yet found and I am certain however that I never gave it away; perhaps it was negligently included in the packet when I sent the operas to the young *Madame Kraus*; [I've] therefore written to Miltenberg and because I am almost certain in my supposition, she will have the honor to send it on immediately when she receives it.

In the aforementioned copying of the *Duet in G* I garbled the last bit of the conclusion and am not able to decipher the thing, for probably in the press of time [I] was not able to write out the ending, and it is likely moreover that [I] wrote this out in such a hurry and poorly, which is not the case with the rest of the others.

Finally, we have been relieved of the long-term destructive *visitation* of the French and thus are able to breathe freely again. Don't the French do a lively dance and hop about! Often when the officers amused themselves with bowling in our monastery garden, I looked down from my window with amusement, for the jumping and hopping about had no end as long as the bowling ball rolled. Regardless of whether it was hit or miss, there were always caprices all over the place. Our region and principally the monastery suffered much. We usually had about 30 officers in the building in addition to one or two generals, and them not withstanding, in the last days an entire *company* arrived to lodge with us; it was only with effort that they were finally convinced that there was no room, but they must have thought probably that there was better fodder in the monastery than in the *private* homes of our poor city here. It seems that the French are not great practitioners of music; among the many that we saw here during this terrible war, there was not a single one of them that showed himself to be either a connoisseur or amateur.

In the hope and expectation at your command of whatever I have the pleasure in any case to send you, [I] am moved moreover once more to repeat my aforementioned thanks, for as it is certainly so personal and forthright as any unbounded display of sincerity, it is thus that I have the most precious honor of not having it end.

Your Worship's
Most obedient servant
Roman Hoffstetter

4. Letter of 25 July 1801

Dear Sir,

[You] herewith are receiving back the magnificent *Creation* by Haydn, for which I can express [only] the most obligated gratitude possible for your most generous sharing. Notwithstanding, [I] copied all of it from beginning to end, and [I] would thus have sent it back to you much sooner if I didn't have to obtain the necessary paper from Frankfurt and then had to await its receipt another five or six weeks. Only with this copying did [I] first have the opportunity to observe more perfectly all of the many beautiful things that the great *Haydn* gathered together in this masterpiece from everywhere. It is truly beautiful to the highest degree! But only in the largest courts, where the largest, most complete orchestras are, can a performance take place, because so many instruments are necessary for it. The *trombone* that often appears in the operas of *Gluck* and in many other places [I] don't recognize, and [I] don't know what sort of instrument it is. The contrabassoon is also unknown to me, unless it is the same as the *Sarabant* [e.g., serpent], or whatever the thing is called, as it seems to me. The introduction of the *Creation* is very deep and dark; [I] had to study it long and hard before being able to understand the musical sense, but it was easier with the arias, choruses, accompanied recitatives. Everything is magnificent, unique in its own way. It is astounding how this great man has written so much already and moreover in all of the musical genres, and now the newspaper announces a new work, the Four Seasons, which is as beautiful and magnificent, though not to a higher level as the *Creation*. How can that be possibly organized with this new text? [I] cannot comprehend.

Time and time again I have been urged at least once to write to Herr Kapellmeister *Haydn,* sending him one or another of my Masses for his study, review, and most welcome commentary. But [I] don't have the courage, for it seems to me unfeasible, not least because the famous man certainly has more to do than being able or willing to take the time to bother with a common dilettante. And further, the distance is so great that the cost of freight would be more valuable than the entire clump of Masses is worth.

The aforementioned Kraus aria your grace will no doubt have received, for *Madame Lämmerhirt* wrote to me about my inquiry that it actually exists among the musical collection that she obtained from me and that the entire thing would go off to Vienna shortly.

The engraving of the *Creation* is very pretty, nice, and correct; in the entirety there is hardly a little note missing, but rather it will be praised highly; certainly a decisive advantage for the publisher! The list included would go far beyond 400 exemplars!

Your Grace will accept once more my most obedient thanks for all your exceptional kindness, and have the goodwill to believe that the greatest part of my well-being consists of being certain of your most treasured goodwill, and forever [I] shall hold you in the most perfect and incontrovertible esteem and with *devotion* I dare to remain

You Grace's
most obedient and obliging
servant,
Roman Hoffstetter

5. Letter of 27 November 1801

Dear Sir, forgive my presumption; it was impossible to hide my importunity and caution.

Haydn's Creation was immediately copied and sent back to Your Grace on the 20th of July with the most humble and obedient thanks, in order not to take advantage of the exceptional kindness of Your Grace for too long. [I] gave the packet of the most generously given material to Herr *Grossman* in Miltenberg to post. He in turn certainly believed that it had long since already been received correctly and in good condition in Vienna. Therefore it was so unexpected and enlightening to me to learn just recently from a letter of *Madame Lämmerhirt* that this did not happen, although Herr *Grossman* maintained at my inquiry that it was done promptly.

Now I am obligated eternally to make everything right and not allow myself to be guilty of being unworthy of the kindness of Your Grace and the goodwill that will always mean so much, or of being able to be found wanting in some fashion. It is and remains impossible to be calm until I receive a good and soothing explanation for these things within my responsibility and care, which I take the liberty of being able to pass on most obediently to Your Grace.

Moreover, I flatter myself to maintain continually the honor of offering my unbounded and highest possible regard, and with which I dare to call myself for all time

Your Worship's
most humble and obedient
servant
Roman Hoffstetter

6. Letter of 11 January 1802

Dear Sir,

Your most honored [letter] of the 14th of last month gave me endless pleasure and thus my cares then were completely relieved, and for that I am obliged with most forthright and obligated thanks.

With pleasure [I] seized the opportunity to grant your most honorable expressed wish to see something from my very inconsequential musical factory in the Odenwald, most obligingly but at the same time with fear and trembling; knowing perfectly well my great weakness, [I] cannot do anything without fearful expectation of a judgment that will come from over there, where one sees the musical profession more clearly than elsewhere – not excepting Berlin. I am not only afraid of the great *Haydn,* whose knowledgeable eye nothing escapes, but of the deep insights of Your Grace as well, of which I have been completely convinced ever since the first letter you honored me with. [I] must therefore ask for your good consideration, simultaneously with a reminder that he who wrote it never had the advantage of receiving only the most rudimentary instruction in theory, and moreover has had to do without a keyboard, as well as the advantage of being able to hear all of the music that my *handicap* now prevents me from hearing each and every voice, here and afar, and moreover the complete full harmony.

The Mass would have been sent earlier, but first [I] wanted to make a new copy of a score that was no longer readable. Would that my copying skills had been better undertaken! With the light of the short days back then during which [I] wrote most of it, I didn't make much progress, even with four eyes.

Due to oversight and haste it happened that the strange transition from C to B♭ in the *Credo* and *Incarnatus* crept in, for I wrote the *Credo* in F in this, the seventh of ten [Masses] three years ago, which appeared to me to be too presumptuous and *profane,* and therefore I inserted another from No. 10 into the copy, although it too is of lesser quality. Now I ought to have inserted the *Incarnatus* in F, but I continued to write out No. 7 and did not notice the erroneous transition before half the movement was finished. Thus I must plead *mea culpa* and ask pardon; may this be the only mistake within. I now also have to admit that in a few *passages* I have probably deserved to have my dear *Haydn* wagging his finger at me; to me, everything that flows from *Haydn's* pen is so beautiful and has made such a deep impression upon me that I cannot help, no matter how hard I try, but imitate it. Moreover, when [I] wrote the Mass, I was completely convinced that it would molder here in the Odenwald, and I never thought that it would in time be viewed by the great man himself!

I have gone through and studied with great pleasure *Kraus's* Funeral Music. A magnificent work! In my opinion, perhaps one of the most progressive masterpieces that *Kraus* ever wrote! It is unique in its genre and must have a wonderful effect – when completely staffed. It was performed last fall on the occasion of the funeral of the Count of Erbach, but it failed to have the same effect due to the lack of the necessary players. Thus it will be performed here at the monastery once more at the command of Herr Count, but [I] cannot fathom the reason. We too cannot staff it completely, for we have no bassoon.

Herr Kapellmeister Haydn will probably remain the entire winter in Vienna. I would dare to ask Your Grace to give him my best and most humble regards and assure him of my boundless, highest possible admiration and honor. Now that *Die Jahreszeiten* has long since been completed, what will this great master of composition, the inestimable musical cornucopia, write? He should write and it would be a pity for the entire musical world if he did not!

Finally, I hope and wish for a timely and humble receipt of the poor thing on its way, and have the eternally precious pleasure of offering my most complete and boundless regards, and daring to call myself

Your Worship's

most humble and obedient

servant

Roman Hoffstetter

7. Letter [Postscript] of 23 January 1802

Postscript

No sooner had the packet with the Mass been sent off to Miltenberg that [I] first realized that in my missive then I allowed to slip in an error by mistake – regarding Kraus's Funeral Music. I hasten to correct it now. Because the Herr Count had commissioned one more performance of the music at his request, here it was decided erroneously that the first *production* in Erbach had misfired, that it failed to achieve its full effect, and thus I was told. As I have now heard, the situation was, however, completely different. Because it had made such a terrific impression, we came to the conclusion to perform it here once more, so that we would be able to participate in the enjoyment.

Now in time [I] have been instructed about another grievous error concerning the return of *Haydn's Creation,* which [I] myself allowed to go back without having shown it first to *Madame Lämmerhirt.* Convinced that the determined time of six or more months graciously granted by Your Grace ought not to be taken literally on my part, [as well as] not to trespass upon your graciousness, and moreover that I must exercise all possible care that the volume is not damaged in the slightest, [I] have hastened quite a lot with the copying and return, and thereby urged *Madame,* who had requested it of me when [I] had barely received it, even in the first days, to have patience until my copy was completed, after which I would gladly share it immediately.

I am very sorry to have failed to comply with the carrying out of the intentions of Your Grace, and thus [I] ask most obediently for your indulgence and forgiveness, for which [I] flatter myself that I might dare to believe, for on one hand it came about due to my view simply of a mistaken, insupportable opinion and on the other that is was to my disadvantage that my *copy* became thus too crabbed, unreadable, and almost unusable as the result of my great hastiness.

A short while ago I was given an essay to read from the *Zeitung für die elegante Welt* containing a bitter critique of *Haydn's Creation,* which angered me to the depths of my soul. The author in complete seriousness fears that *Haydn* intended to set back music composition 30 or 40 years back into the dark ages! He, who has read everything from the past, observes more deeply than one sees and perhaps even will see.

[The ending is missing.]

8. Letter of 25 May 1802

Dear Sir,

Regarding the shipment of one of my Masses that had been requested most graciously on the 14th of December of last year, which was a duty for me to fulfill. I truly copied it immediately and already on 12 January gave the packet to Herr *Grossman* in Miltenberg to post. And thus it is all the more unexpected, as I have recently learned from *Madame Lämmerhirt,* that up to 18 March and perhaps until now nothing has been received in Vienna. At the same time I was reminded of the new order regarding the sending of packets that appeared in the Frankfurt newspaper some six weeks ago, in which I read that in the future nothing more would be allowed to pass into Austria without an exact listing of the contents attached. Perhaps this was the fate of my poor packet, which now subsequently lies under arrest in a post *office.*

Had the Herr Postmaster known that the thing contained simply music and not Brabant lace, they certainly would have let it pass easily. But, the words, old music, should have been placed visibly on the packet, and this, unfortunately, [I] forgot to do. My first thought when it was too late was that nothing else remained but that I ask Herr *Grossman* to post a label after it. Whether or not this happened and with what success I have not yet heard the least news.

This situation cannot be anything other than being most unpleasant and forces me immediately to take the liberty of asking Your Grace whether the packet has perhaps during the intervening time – as would be very much desired – arrived or, what would be the opposite case, to track it down!

I must now ask your indulgence for my importunity and ask that Your Grace at once accept the most honest assurances of my boundless admiration and homage, with which [I] have the honor to be and to proclaim myself

Your Worship's
Most obedient and humble
Servant
Roman Hoffstetter

9. Letter of 22 June 1802

Dear Sir,

Your most honored [letter] of the 9th was highly welcome and pleasant to me in double hindsight, for it relieved me on one hand of a burdensome worry, and on the other also testified to the good disposition that Your Grace generously expressed in the most flattering terms regarding the Mass that [I] sent, as well as my humility, for it would be all the more pleasant and precious, the greater the value I set on your insightful judgment and generous approbation, and for this I must give you my unbounded gratitude. Once [I] had completed the *copy* now in your hands to the end, [I] would thus have asked to have the presumption to keep it as a small tithe of my ceaseless gratitude and my earnest effort. And because from the beginning it was and is my most ardent desire to be able to demonstrate my sentiment in some sort of manner, [I] would be pleased if you would further take a copy of my other Mass in progress, as soon as I am relieved again of the stress on my eyes. I dare to flatter myself in the hope that this one might please someone to some extent! In this case, would it be possible to send the packet in the same format as the first? Or, to make it smaller, rolled or folded?

Although I don't understand French myself, there are several here among us who are quite proficient and to whom it gives pleasure to translate such beautiful letters as yours are. Your Grace can be assured that they will serve at your pleasure.

Saint *Vogler* was recently in Bohemia, were, as the newspaper said, he allowed his newly invented *instrument* to be marveled at; the world seems to be too narrow for this man! He has already been to every place and the ends [of the earth], but I don't remember having read that he was once in Vienna. This puzzles me and there really ought to be a reason for it, although I cannot fathom what?

May the pleasant summer sojourn contribute a lot to your pleasure and great prosperity, for there is always in such places a pure air that is better for the health than in the thick, restricted confines of a large inhabited city!

From the depths of my soul and with all my heart [I] wish to have the honor and pleasure of being with lifelong and boundless honor and esteem

Your Worship's
Most humble and obedient servant
Roman Hoffstetter

Bibliography

Albrecht, Theodore, ed. *Letters to Beethoven and Other Correspondence.* Lincoln: University of Nebraska Press, 1996.

Anderson, Emily, trans. *The Letters of Ludwig van Beethoven.* 3 vols. London: Macmillan, 1961.

———, trans. *Letters of Mozart and His Family.* London: Macmillan, 1938, and later editions.

Anrep-Nordin, Birger. *Studier over Joseph Martin Kraus.* Stockholm: Isaac Markus' Boktryckeriet, 1924. (AN-JMK)

Åstrand, Hans. *Joseph Martin Kraus Brev 1776–1792.* Stockholm: Gidlunds förlag, 2006. (HÅ-Brev)

———. *Joseph Martin Kraus: Den mest betydande gustavianska musikpersonligheten.* Stockholm: Gidlunds förlag, 2011. (HÅ-JMK)

Barton, H. Arnold. *Scandinavia in the Revolutionary Age.* Minneapolis: University of Minnesota Press, 1986.

Bauer, Wilhelm, Otto Erich Deutsch, and Joseph Eibl, eds. *Mozart: Briefe und Aufzeichnungen.* 7 vols. Kassel: Bärenreiter, 1962–1975.

Brosch, Helmut, "Quellen zur Biographie von Joseph Martin Kraus." *Mitteilungen der Internationalen Joseph Martin Kraus Gesellschaft* 5/6 (1986): 1–35.

———. "Quellen zur Biographie von Joseph Martin Kraus: d) Fragment des Reisetagebuchs von Joseph Martin Kraus 1783/1783." *Mitteilungen der Internationalen Joseph Martin Kraus Gesellschaft* 9/10 (1989): 8–20.

Clark, Stephen. *Carl Philipp Emanuel Bach Letters.* Oxford: Oxford University Press, 1997.

Cramer, Carl Friedrich. *Magazin der Musik,* Hamburg, July 26, 1787, 1378.

Deutsch, Erich Otto. *Mozart: Die Dokumente seines Lebens.* Kassel: Bärenreiter, 1961.

Eibl, Joseph, and Walter Senn. *Mozarts Bäsle Briefe.* 4th ed. Munich: DTV, 1991.

Eisen, Cliff. *New Mozart Documents: A Supplement to O. E. Deutsch's Documentary Biography.* Stanford, Calif.: Stanford University Press, 1991.

Fischer, Georg-Helmut. "Abbé Georg Joseph Vogler: A 'Baroque' Musical Genius." In *Gustav III and the Swedish Stage,* ed. Bertil van Boer. Lewiston, N.Y.: Edwin Mellen, 1993.

Geffray, Geneviève. *W. A. Mozart: Correspondence.* 7 vols. Paris: Harmoniques Flammarion, 1986–1999.

Heartz, Daniel. *Music in European Capitals: The Galant Style, 1720–1780.* New York: W. W. Norton, 2003.

Holmberg, Olle. *Leopold och Gustaf III.* Stockholm: Bonniers, 1954.

Kraus, Joseph Martin. *Etwas von und über Musik furs Jahr 1777.* Frankfurt am Main: Eichenbergischen Erben, 1778; fac. ed., ed. Friedrich W. Reidel, Munich and Salzburg: Emil Katzbichler, 1977.

———. *Joseph Martin Kraus: Kammermusik I.* Stuttgart: Carus Verlang, 2006.

———. *Tolon.* Frankfurt am Main: Kessler, 1776.

———. *Versuch von Schäfersgedichte.* Mainz: n. p., 1773.

Leux-Henschen, Irmgard. *Joseph Martin Kraus in seinen Briefen.* Stockholm: Edition Reimers, 1978. (LH-JMK)

Matsson, Inger, ed. *Gustavian Opera: Opera, Theatre and Dance 1771–1809.* Stockholm: Kungliga Musikaliska Akademien, 1991.

Mörner, C. G. Stellan. *Johan Wikmanson und die Brüder Silverstolpe.* Stockholm: Ivar Hæggströms boktryckeriet, 1952.

Müller von Asow, Hedwig, and E. H. Müller von Asow. *The Collected Correspondence and Papers of Christoph Willibald Gluck,* trans. Stewart Thomson. London: Barrie and Rockliff, 1962.

Noack, Friedrich. "Eine Briefsammlung aus der ersten Hälfte des 19. Jh." *Archiv für Musikwissenschaft* 10 (1953).

Palmqvist, Arne. *Die Römisch-Katholische Kirche in Schweden nach 1781.* 2 vols. Uppsala: Almqvist och Wiksell, 1954.

Reichardt, Johann Friedrich. *Autobiographische Schriften.* Halle: MDV Verlag, 2002.

———. *Musikalische Monatsschrift.* Berlin, 1792.

Riedel, Freidrich W. *Das Himmlische lebt in seinen Tönen.* Mannheim: J und J Verlag, 1992. (FR-JMK)

———, ed. *Joseph Martin Kraus in seiner Zeit.* Munich and Salzburg: Emil Katzbichler, 1982. (K II)

Robbins Landon, H. C. *The Collected Correspondence and London Notebooks of Joseph Haydn.* New York: Essential Books, 1959.

———. *Joseph Haydn: Chronicle and Works.* 5 vols. Bloomington: Indiana University Press, 1976–1980.

Sawodny, Wolfgang. "Einige Bemerkungen zur musikalischen Vorbilduing von Joseph Martin Kraus" In *Joseph Martin Kraus in seiner Zeit,* ed. Friedrich Riedel. Munich and Salzburg: Emil Katzbichler, 1982.

Schreiber, Karl Friedrich. *Biographie über den Odenwälder Komponisten Joseph Martin Kraus.* Buchen: Bezirksmuseum, 1928; rev. and expanded ed., ed. Helmut Brosch, Gerhardt Darmstadt, and Rainer Trunk, Buchen: Bezirksmuseum, 2006.

Silverstolpe, Fredrik. *Biografi af Kraus.* Stockholm: J. Hörberg, 1833. (Si-JMK)

Spaethling, Robert. *Mozart's Letters, Mozart's Life.* New York: W. W. Norton, 2000.

Stahelin, Martin. "Joseph Martin Kraus in Göttingen." *Göttinger Jahrbuch* (1992): 199–230. (St-Göttingen)

Suchalla, Ernst, ed. *Carl Philipp Emanuel Bach Briefe und Dokumente: Kritische Gesamtausgabe.* 2 vols. Göttingen: Vandenhoeck und Reuprecht, 1994.

Unverricht, Hubert. *Carl Ditters von Dittersdorf: Briefe, ausgewählte Urkunden und Akten.* Studien zur Musikwissenschaft 54. Tutzing: Hans Schneider, 2008.

———. *Die beiden Hoffstetter.* Mainz: Schott, 1968.

Van Boer, Bertil. "The Case of the Circumstantial Meeting: Wolfgang

Amadeus Mozart and Joseph Martin Kraus." *Eighteenth Century Music* 1 (2004): 85–90.

———, ed. *Gustav III and the Swedish Stage.* Lewiston, N.Y.: Edwin Mellen, 1993.

———. "Gustav III's 'Divertissement med sång' *Födelsedagen:* A Gustavian Political Satire." *Scandinavian Studies* 61 (1989): 28–40.

———. "Gustavian Opera: An Overview." In *Gustavian Opera: Opera, Theatre and Dance 1771–1809,* ed. Inger Mattson. Stockholm: Kungliga Musikaliska Akademien, 1991.

———. *Joseph Martin Kraus: A Systematic-Thematic Catalogue of His Musical Works and Source Study.* Stuyvesant, N.Y.: Pendragon Press, 1998.

———. "The Travel Diary of Joseph Martin Kraus: Translation and Commentary." *Journal of Musicology* 8 (1990): 266–290.

Wolff, Christoph. *Mozart at the Gateway to His Fortune.* New York: Norton, 2012.

Index

BERTIL H. VAN BOER received his baccalaureate degree from the University of California in Berkeley and masters in music history from the University of Oregon following additional studies in composition at the Mozarteum in Salzburg, Austria, and in German literature at the University of British Columbia. His doctoral work was done at Cornell University and Uppsala University in Sweden, from which he received his PhD in musicology in 1983. An active professional violist and conductor, he has performed with orchestras in Austria, Canada, Germany, Sweden, the United States, and Nicaragua. As a musicologist, he has written extensively on music of the eighteenth century, with emphasis on opera and music in Scandinavia, with articles appearing in *Journal of Musicology, Svensk tidskrift för musikforskning, Ars Lyrica, Journal of Musicological Research, Historic Brass Society Journal,* and *Scandinavian Studies,* as well as numerous international symposium and conference reports. He is the author of several books on Scandinavian music and Swedish-German composer Joseph Martin Kraus, including the thematic catalogue of his works, and has edited volumes for A-R Editions, the Carl Philipp Emanuel Bach Complete Works, and the Symphony 1720–1840 series. He is currently professor of musicology-theory at Western Washington University as well as past president of the Society for Eighteenth Century Music.